ORIENTAL STUDIES

edited by

S. M. Stern and R. Walzer

vol. III

DOCUMENTS
from
ISLAMIC CHANCERIES
First Series

FLORENCE, Palazzo Vecchio

VASARI

Lorenzo The Magnificent receiving gifts presented by the Mamlūk Sultan's Ambassador

(*p.* 39)

ORIENTAL STUDIES III

DOCUMENTS

from

ISLAMIC CHANCERIES

First Series

Essays by
J. Aubin, B. G. Martin, V. L. Menage, S. A. Skilliter
S. M. Stern, J. Wansbrough

Editor
S. M. Stern

University of South Carolina Press
Columbia, South Carolina

Published in Great Britain by Bruno Cassirer (Publishers) Ltd., 1965
First published in the United States of America
by Harvard University Press, 1965
Published by The University of South Carolina Press, Columbia, S.C., 1970
Standard Book Number: 87249-178-1
Library of Congress Catalog Card Number: 74-93306
Printed in Great Britain

Table of Contents

TWO AYYŪBID DECREES FROM SINAI

by

S. M. Stern

It is an unexpected piece of good fortune for the student of Islamic history to recover documents bearing the signatures of Ayyūbid rulers such as al-ʿĀdil, al-Afḍal, and al-Kāmil. Such documents are preserved in the archives of the Monastery of St. Catherine in Mount Sinai and form, together with documents of the Fāṭimid, Mamlūk, and Ottoman periods, a unique and truly splendid series.[1] The form of the signature is, of course, only one of the many details of chancery practice about which these original documents provide important information. Two of them from the reign of al-Kāmil, petitions by the monks of Sinai and bearing the sultan's decree on their verso, have been published by me in another place [2]; here I publish the remaining two documents, decrees by al-ʿĀdil and al-Afḍal.

In introducing these documents I can be brief, since the procedure which brought about their issue, and most of the features which appear in them, have already been clarified in my previous studies referred to in the footnotes to this page.

Decrees were issued by the rulers in response to petitions from their subjects in which they told of their grievances. Thus the two decrees published here were also presumably granted after the monks had presented petitions asking for the ruler's protection. That in neither of them is there mention of the petition, as there often is in decrees of the Fāṭimid and Mamlūk periods, is presumably due to mere chance. The other two Ayyūbid documents from Sinai are in fact petitions endorsed with the sultan's—i.e. in both cases al-Kāmil's—decree. (The second of these documents refers also to a petition which had been presented by the monks to al-ʿĀdil some years after the date of the decree published

---

[1] For information about the medieval documents of the Sinai archive see ch. 1 of my book *Fāṭimid Decrees*, London 1964 (pp. 5 ff.).

[2] "Petitions of the Ayyūbid Period", *Bulletin of the School of Oriental and African Studies*, 1964, pp. 1 ff.

here.) It is seen, then, that the decrees were sometimes unceremoniously written on the back of the petitions, whereas at other times they were issued in a much more formal way, written on a long scroll, with large spaces between the lines. It seems natural to suppose that the choice between the two forms depended on the importance of the matter in hand; and in the case of the Ayyūbid documents such an explanation seems to fit. The decrees endorsed upon the petitions deal with rather trivial subjects, whereas the two decrees written out as independent documents contain general orders concerning the monks' welfare. Against this it may be remarked that some of the formal decrees of the Fāṭimid and Mamlūk periods deal with what to us at least seem unimportant matters, so that we may perhaps conclude that the choice of the form was to some degree arbitrary.

I

Let us then take the first document. From 591/1194–5 al-ʿĀdil was the effective ruler of Egypt. After the death of his brother Saladin he was at first the sovereign of the eastern part of the Ayyūbid territories, while his nephews al-Afḍal and al-ʿAzīz reigned in Damascus and Cairo, respectively. Al-ʿĀdil, however, skillfully managed to intervene in the quarrels between his nephews in such a manner as to emerge the real gainer. In 591 he accompanied al-Afḍal on his invasion of Egypt, but then brought about a reconciliation between him and al-ʿAzīz and remained with al-ʿAzīz as his mentor and the de facto ruler of the country.[3] So it was to al-ʿĀdil that the Sinai monks presented their petition. After he had pronounced his decision—either orally, or in the form of a short endorsement of the petition—the present decree was drawn up in the Chancery, on 16 Muḥarram 592/21 December 1195. Comments on some of its features are best given after the reproduction of the text and its translation.

---

[3] Ibn Wāṣil, *Mufarrij al-Kurūb*, ii, 50 ff., and more especially p. 54; Ibn al-Athīr, xii, 77–8; Ibn al-ʿAdīm, transl. Blochet, *Revue de l'Orient Latin*, iv (1896), pp. 208–10; Abū Shāma, *Kitāb al-Rawḍatayn*, ii, 230; idem, *Dhayl al-Rawḍatayn*, p. 7; Sibṭ b. al-Jawzī, *Mir'āt al-Zamān*, ed. Jewett, pp. 282–3; al-Maqrīzī, *al-Sulūk*, i, 125 ff., especially p. 129; Ibn Taghrībirdī, vi, 123–5.

Monastery of St. Catherine, Sinai, scroll no. 11. Dimensions: 507(?) × 19·5 cm.[4] Plates I–XII.

Al-'Ādil orders to treat the monks of Sinai according to the old customs and to protect them and their visitors.

بسم الله الرحمن الرحيم
منشور تقدّم بكتبه المولى الملك العادل
[الحمد لله وبه توفيقى]
السيّد الأجلّ الكبير العالم المؤيّد المظفّر
المنصور المرابط الهمام سيف الدين ناصر الإسلام
معين الإمام غياث الأنام جلال الدولة
تاج الملّة مجير الأمّة سيّد الملوك والسلاطين
سلطان جيوش المسلمين، قامع الكفرة
والمشركين، ابو بكو بن أيّوب خليل أمير المؤمنين
قرن الله النفاذ بنهيه وأمره، وأنطق
ألسن العباد بحمده وشكره، ونوّر بالحسنات
مواقيت ليله وساعات فجره، وأحيا الآمال
بما يمطره سحاب سيبه ويمتدّ به أيّام برّه،
وتضمينه انّا لم نزل ولله الحمد نذبّ عن الرعايا
الذين فوّض الله تعالى أمرهم الينا، وأحالت
الشريعة الطاهرة فى حياطتهم علينا،
فنكفّ كفّ الأذى عنهم، ونجازى على
الإحسان من سلك طريقه منهم،
ونقيل عثرتهم، ونكشف كربتهم وغمّتهم،
ونضاعف ذلك لبطاركتهم ورهبانهم،
وقسّيسيهم وكهّانهم، وساكنى
الصوامع من زهّادهم، والمنقطعين بالديرة

[4] See A. S. Atiya, *The Arabic manuscripts of Mount Sinai: a handlist of the Arabic manuscripts and scrolls microfilmed at the library of the Monastery of St. Catherine, Mount Sinai*, Baltimore 1955, scroll no. 11. Atiya gives the length of the scroll as 57 cm. which is obviously a mistake. A calculation based on the photographs, which shows that the scroll is about 25 times as long as it is wide, gives ca. 5 metres, so that it is possible that 57 is an error for 507.

من عبّادهم، ونقدّم عليهم من ارتضو تقديمه
وتقدّمنا بان يجروا رهبان هذا
الدير المذكور على عادتهم المستمرّة،
ويقرّوا على القاعدة المستتبّة المستقرّة،
وان يتوخّوا بالرعاية والحماية، والحياطة
والكلاية، ويمنع من يتعرّض لأذيّتهم، او
يطمع فى مضرّتهم، او يتعدّى بقطع
رسومهم الجارى بها ماضى عادتهم، او
يتطرّق لإخافة سبيلهم المسلوك لزيارتهم،
وان لا يفسح للعربان ولا لغيرهم من الموافقين
والمخالفين لهم فى الأديان فى اهتضامهم،
ولا فى تكليفهم نقض ما أقرّوا عليه من
أحكامهم، ولا يعارض زوّارهم من البلاد الشاميّة، بوجه من وجوه إضرار او أذيّة،
وسبيل كل واقف على هذا المثال
من الأمراء والولاة أجمعين أيّدهم الله والنوّاب
وكافّة المستخدمين حمل الأمر على حكمه،
والانتهاء الى واجب رسمه، والإنكار على
من خالفه بعد علمه، عاملين
بفحواه، معتمدين على العلامة
الشريفة فى أعلاه، ان شاء الله تعالى
كتب سادس عشر المحرّم من سنة اثنتين وتسعين وخمس مائة
الحمد لله وحده وصلّى الله على سيّدنا محمد وآله الطاهرين
وسلّم تسليما كثيرا
وحسبنا الله ونعم الوكيل

TRANSLATION

[The signature :]
Praise be to God, who is the cause of my success.
In the name of God, the Merciful, the Compassionate.

This is an open decree, the order for the writing of which was given by the Master, the Victorious King [al-Malik al-ʿĀdil], the Most Excellent, Great, Learned, Divinely Assisted, Triumphant, Victorious, Combating, Heroic Lord, Sword of Religion, Helper of Islam, Assistant of the Imam, Succour of Mankind, Majesty of Empire, Crown of the Muslim Denomination, Protector of the Community, Lord of Kings and Sultans, Sultan of the Armies of the Muslims, Subduer of Unbelievers and Polytheists, Abū Bakr, son of Ayyūb, Friend of the Commander of the Faithful, may God make valid his orders and prohibitions, make the tongues of men speak his praise and thanks, illuminate by good deeds the times of his nights and the hours of his dawns, revive hopes through the bounties which his clouds rain and in which his beneficent days are spent; and [he ordered] to include in it as follows: We never cease, thank God, to protect the subjects whose affairs were entrusted by God to us, and whose welfare was put by the pure [religious] Law into our hands; we remove harmful hands from them, and reward those of them who follow the path of benevolence; we forgive their stumbling, and avert their sorrow and misfortune. We double this for their patriarchs and monks, priests and clergymen, their ascetics who inhabit cells, and religious who retreat into monasteries; and we appoint as their superiors those whom they prefer.

We have ordered to treat the monks of the aforementioned monastery according to their old-established custom and to leave them to follow their long-settled and agreed rules, and to accord to them protection, guarding, safe-keeping and defence; to prevent people from doing them harm or from intending damage against them, or from transgressing by changing their current customs, or from proceeding to render unsafe the road which is used for visits to them; and that the Bedouins, or for that matter anyone else, whether of the same religion as they or not, be kept from oppressing them or forcing them to relinquish the rules according to which they have been treated; and that visitors to them from Syria be not interfered with in any manner of harm or damage.

Let all amīrs and governors (may God assist them), lieutenants, and officials in general, who become aware of this ordinance, be sure to act according to its order and follow its instruction and to disapprove of those who knowingly contravene it—acting in conformity with it and relying upon the noble signature above it, if God (may He be exalted) wills.

Written this fifteenth of Muḥarram, the year Five-hundred Ninety Two.

Praise be to God alone, and may God bless our lord Muḥammad and his pure family and give them much peace.

God is sufficient for us; how good a Keeper is He!

We may begin with pointing out a curious blunder: in lines 23–4 the monastery of Sinai is referred to as " the aforementioned monastery "—though it had not been mentioned at all. The clerk in drawing up the decree was obviously following an earlier document and copied an inappropriate formula.

The document is a *manshūr*, i.e.—since the word has obviously to be taken in the same meaning which it had in the Fāṭimid period [5]—an " open decree " having no address and delivered to the beneficiaries, instead of being sealed and posted to the authorities whom it concerned. Its external form corresponds to that of the Fāṭimid decrees [6]: it is written on a long scroll made up of a number of sheets glued together at their shorter side. A long scroll was needed, since, though the text is quite short, the chancery practice demanded that large spaces be left between the lines; such " conspicuous waste " of paper was a royal prerogative.[7] The long upper margin (*ṭurra*) is another sign of elegant waste of paper: " The upper margin is long in letters written by great men to subordinates, whereas it is medium in letters written by subordi-

---

[5] See *Fāṭimid Decrees*, diplomatic commentary part 1 (pp. 85 ff.). Ibn Shīth in his treatise for secretaries, which will be often quoted in this study since he wrote in the Ayyūbid period (cf. for him my article on the Ayyūbid petitions [above, note 2], p. 8) writes (*Ma'ālim al-Kitāba*, ed. Q. al-Bāshā, Beirut 1913, p. 46; summarized by al-Qalqashandī, vii, 21): " It was never known to leave letters open in the hands of those delivering them, except in cases concerning grants of money—since the nobility of a letter is its seal, and there are no letters more noble than those of the sultan." These words can hardly be pressed so as to make them include all kinds of documents; Ibn Shīth probably means to say that letters bearing addresses had to be sealed—excluding, however, *manshūrs* which had no addresses. Under the Ayyūbids we find some diplomas of appointment described in their own text as *manshūr*; see al-Qalqashandī, xi, 51 ff., 53 ff., 59 ff. (these passages are also quoted in the article " manshūr " in the *Encyclopaedia of Islam*, by W. Björkman). These diplomas turn to the beneficiaries in the second person, so that one should assume that they were not open letters, but were sealed and addressed. If so, one would have to conclude that the term *manshūr* here lost its original significance, and was transferred (presumably from diplomas in the third person and turning to the officials and subjects in general—cf. below, note 97) to all kind of diplomas of appointment. As I have said in the passage referred to above (in *Fāṭimid Decrees*) the history of the word *manshūr* is still rather obscure.

[6] Cf. *Fāṭimid Decrees*, diplomatic commentary part 3 (pp. 103 ff.).

[7] Cf. Ibn Shīth, p. 40 (the first sentence quoted by al-Qalqashandī, viii, 20–1): " In letters emanating from the sultan one leaves space between the lines, so that there are about three or four fingers between two lines. This is not done in letters addressed to the sultan, in which there are no more than two fingers between two lines [read *al-saṭrayn* instead of *al-sulṭān*] ".

nates ", says Ibn Shīth.[8] The slight upward slant of the lines is another peculiarity of chancery practice; this is further accentuated by the frequent writing of the last words above the lines (see lines 4, 6, 7–10, 21–2, 25, 30–2, 34—three tiers—36, 42). As I have explained in connection with the Fāṭimid documents, it is not advisable—at least not yet advisable—to attempt to identify the name of the script used in the decrees. At any rate the writing of this decree is a splendid example of chancery script, superior not only to the next piece, but possibly also to all the Fāṭimid documents from Sinai.

In its structure our decree closely follows the documents from the last years of the Fāṭimid period which have been preserved in Sinai and are published as nos. 8–10 in my *Fāṭimid Decrees.*[9] The framework of the opening part is identical with the corresponding formula of the Fāṭimid documents: " This is an open decree, the order for the writing of which was given by so-and-so; and [he ordered] to include in it as follows ". The last words introduce, in the Fāṭimid decrees and in ours, the expression of the general principles which motivate the ruler's decision—what is called in the medieval diplomatic of Europe the *arenga.*[10] There is no reference to any particular grievance on the part of the monks; the text directly continues with the sultan's order to protect them from all annoyance in general and to ensure the safety of the pilgrims visiting the monastery in particular. There follow, as in the Fāṭimid decrees,[11] final injunctions to the local authorities to obey the sultan's order; the formula used here is discussed below, pp. 34–5.

A feature unknown in the Fāṭimid decrees is the reference to the ruler's *'alāma* authenticating the decree (*mu'tamidīn 'ala'l-'alāma al-sharīfa fī a'lāh* (" relying upon the noble signature above it ").[12] A similar formula of *corroboratio* also occurs in al-Kāmil's decree on the back of a petition,[13] and there is ample evidence in the documents preserved in literature to show that the formula was indeed a customary element in

---

[8] P. 46 (cf. al-Qalqashandī, vii, 20). *Ṭurra* means here " upper margin ", and not *ṭughrā*, as explained by C. Cahen, *Bulletin of the School of Oriental and African Studies*, 1952, p. 72.

[9] See *Fāṭimid Decrees*, (pp. 70 ff.). As I have pointed out there, p. 73 note 1, a document reproduced by al-Qalqashandī, *Subḥ al-A'shā*, x, 466, opens in the same manner.

[10] Ibid., part 4 of the diplomatic commentary (pp. 107-8).

[11] Cf. *Fāṭimid Decrees*, diplomatic commentary, part 7 (pp. 113 ff.).

[12] For the *'alāma*, i.e. the ruler's signature, see below, pp. 24–5.

[13] Published as no. 2 of the " Petitions of the Ayyūbid Period " [above, note 2].

Ayyūbid documents.[14] Its lack in al-Afḍal's decree published below is perhaps due to no more than a vagary of the clerk. The absence of the formula in the Fāṭimid period immediately prompted the hypothesis that it was the legacy of Seljūq chancery practice, from which the Ayyūbid derived it through the intermediary of the Zengids, and indeed a cursory examination shows that it was used in the Seljūq period. At the end of a letter in a formulary of the Seljūq period we find *wa-i'timād bar tawqī' kunand*, " and let them rely upon the signature ".[15] I assume—until I am proved wrong by earlier occurrences of the formula—that it was introduced by the Seljūqs who were also the authors of that new method of signature, the *ṭughrā*. The formula was then adopted by the Seljūqs of Rūm, in whose documents we find *i'timād ba-tawqī'-i humāyūn sāzand*, " let them rely upon the majestic signature ", or words to this effect.[16] In the Mamlūk decrees the formula is somewhat different : " the noble handwriting (*al-khaṭṭ al-sharīf*) is evidence for its contents ", or similar phrases [17]—though we also find a phrase which comes nearer to the Seljūq and Ayyūbid pattern : " Let one rely in this matter (*wa'l-i'timād fī dhālika*) upon the noble handwriting at the top, which serves as evidence ".[18] From the Rūm Seljūqs the formula passed to the Ottomans, in whose fermans we find it in forms such as *'alāmet-i sherif üzre* (later *'alāmet-i sherife*) *i'timād qïlsïz* (*or qïlalar*), " Rely " (or : Let them rely ") " upon the noble signature ".[19] Similar formulae of *corroboratio* are found in certain

[14] The formula recurs at the end of some of the diplomas of appointment reproduced by al-Qalqashandī, xi, 33 ff.: *wa'l-i'timād 'ala'l-'alāma al-sharīfa* (p. 34 ; the same on p. 48 with the additional words *fī a'lāh*) ; *wa'l-i'timād 'ala'l-tawqī' al-ashraf bihi* (pp. 37, 48) : *wa'l-i'timād fī dhālika ajma' 'ala'l-tawqī' al-ashraf al-'ālī a'lāhu'llāh wa'l-'alā'im al-dīwāniyya fīhi* (p. 51). *Tawqī'* is, as is well known (cf. *Fāṭimid Decrees*, p. 127), synonymous with *'alāma*. The addition of " and the signatures of the *dīwāns* " in the last example obviously refers to the marks of registration which are accompanied by the officials' mottoes ; as we shall see (below, pp. 36–7) by these signatures responsibility was assumed for the contents, so that it is understandable that here it is said that reliance should be made on the ruler's signature and the signatures of the *dīwāns*. The passage quoted below, note 103, also refers to the formula *wa'l-i'timād 'ala'l-'alāma*.

[15] Al-Mayhanī, *Dastūr-i Dabīrī*, ed. A. S. Erzi, Ankara 1962, p. 111.

[16] See O. Turan, *Türkiye Selçuklulari hakkında resmî vesikalar*, Ankara 1958, nos. 1–3, 24, 30, 32–3, 36, 38, 63, In nos. 34, 49, 50, the plural of *'alāma* : *'alā'im* is used instead of *tawqī'*; this may include the signatures of the officials of the *dīwāns*, cf. above, note 14.

[17] The different forms occurring in the documents from Sinai are tabulated in H. Ernst. *Die mamlukischen Sultansurkunden des Sinai-Klosters*, Wiesbaden 1960, pp. xxxi-xxxii.

[18] No. 50 in Ernst's edition ; similarly nos. 30–1, 45.

[19] See F. Kraelitz, *Osmanische Urkunden in türkischer Sprache aus der zweiten Hälfte des* 15. *Jahrhunderts* (Akademie der Wissenschaften in Wien, Phil.-hist. Klasse, Sitzungsberichte, vol. 197), Vienna 1921, pp. 18, 29–30. For the chronological sequence : first

types of documents of the Ṣafawid chancery, e.g. *wa-chun ba-tawqī'-i ashraf-i a'lā muwashshaḥ wa-muwaḍḍaḥ gardad i'timād numāyand,* " when it is adorned by the most noble and most excellent signature, let them rely upon it ".[20] The preceding rapid sketch ought to suffice here, since my aim was not to pursue the formula through the whole of its course in space and time, or to track down all its minute changes, but to trace back the Ayyūbid formula to its Seljūq origin, and incidentally to draw attention, by a brief excursus, of the radiation of yet another Seljūq chancery convention.[21]

The final formulae resemble those of the Fāṭimid documents and consist of the date and of conventional religious phrases natural at the end of documents : praise of God (*ḥamdala*), blessings upon the Prophet, and the *ḥasbala,* i.e. the sentence " God is sufficient for us ; how good a Keeper is He ! "[22] The following is the translation of the paragraph by Ibn Shīth referring to these final formulae [23] : " The *ḥamdala* is not put at the end in the cases of documents containing decisions [read *tawāqī'*] about grievances, though it is sometimes put in the case of decisions about grants, written at the verso of the petitions ". We may interrupt here and note that the decree on the verso of petition no. ii,[24] being a " decision about a grievance ", does not have the *ḥamdala* at the end ; the decree at the verso of no. iii, however, also a " decision about a grievance " has the *ḥamdala* as well as the *ḥasbala.* Here, as in other cases too, the chancery practice has achieved no perfect consistency. " At the end of the document one stops at that part of the line where the *in shā'a'llāh ta'āla* happens to end, and does not go on in that line, but writes the *ḥamdala* in a

---

'alāmet-i sherīf üzre, then since the end of the fifteenth century the gradual prevalence of *'alāmet-i sherīfe,* see P. Wittek, in *Wiener Zeitschrift für die Kunde des Morgenlandes,* 1961, p. 112. The connection between the Rūm Seljūq and the Ottoman formulae was noted by Wittek, ibid., 1960, p. 275.

[20] See H. Busse, *Untersuchungen zum islamischen Kanzleiwesen an Hand turkmenischer und safawidischer Urkunden,* Cairo 1959, p. 41.

[21] The most celebrated instance is of course the *ṭughrā,* for which see C. Cahen, " La tuğra seljukide ", *Journal asiatique,* 1943–5, pp. 167–72 ; P. Wittek, " Notes sur la tughra ottomane " (second article), *Byzantion,* 1950, pp. 286–8 ; and my *Fāṭimid Decrees,* pp. 143 ff. For another instance, the indication of the " message " (*risāla*) delivered to the chancery, see my article " Petitions from the Ayyūbid Period ", [above, note 2], pp. 15 ff. Cf. also below, p. 35, for another detail of Ayyūbid chancery usage possibly derived from the Seljūqs.

[22] Cf. *Fāṭimid Documents,* part 8 of the diplomatic commentary (pp. 119 ff.).

[23] P. 50, quoted by al-Qalqashandī, vi, 266.

[24] Published in the article " Petitions of the Ayyūbid Period " (see above, note 2).

separate line.[25] There should be no difference in the width of the lines, or in their height—it being preferable that they are rather high. One should not overstep the first line, though one can sometimes indent as against it.[26] It is, however, permissible to overstep in the case of the *ḥamdala*.[27] After the *ḥamdala* one writes ' God is sufficient for us ; how good a Keeper is He ', without ' and '—just as it is found in the Koran . . . The right place for this formula to begin is a third of the way from the right along the line, and it is ended wherever its text comes to an end ".[28]

AL-'ĀDIL'S TITLES

Having described the structure of the decree and discussed the main features of its text, a few words may be said about al-'Ādil's titles which figure at the beginning. Since it would lead us too far to write a systematic study, which, to be of full utility, would involve the investigation of the titles of the Ayyūbids in general, I confine myself to quoting al-'Ādil's titles as they appear in other archival documents, in order to illustrate our document and provide material for future studies. I then compare these titles with the titles which appear in al-'Ādil's inscriptions and comment on their main points, without in the least aiming at completeness.

In a letter by al-'Ādil to the Pisans, of which the heading only is known,[29] this ruler bears the following titles : *al-mawlā al-sulṭān al-Malik*

---

[25] In our decree this prescription is complied with ; in al-Afḍal's decree the *in shā'a'llāh* is indented at the beginning and is written in a line of its own, with the end of the line left blank. Ibn Shīth seems to have in mind documents where there is no date at the end, but the *ḥamdala* follows immediately after the last line of the text ending with *in shā'a'llāh*. Al-Qalqashandī (vi, 234) quotes this passage from Ibn Shīth, but in a different form : " . . . it [the formula *in shā'a'llāh*, not the *ḥamdala*] is, however, written separately in one line." Indeed, al-Qalqashandī himself prescribes (p. 233) " blank space to its [scil. the *in shā'a'llāh* formula's] right and left."

[26] These two sentences refer to the arrangement of the document as a whole. " There should be no difference in the width of the lines "—this seems to mean that the spacing between the lines (see above, p. 14 and note 7) should be uniform. The " height " may refer to the height of the lines themselves, i.e. of the letters. The second sentence prescribes that the beginning of the lines (on the right side) should be in a straight line, though an occasional indenting is permissible—such indenting as can be observed in our document in lines 23, 44, and 45 (the line of the *ḥasbala*), and in al-Afḍal's decree in lines 41 (*in shā'a'llāh*), 43, 45, and 46 (the *ḥasbala*).

[27] Our documents make no use of this feature.

[28] In fact, all the extant documents have *wa-ḥasbunā*, against Ibn Shīth's rule. The Koranic verse whence the *ḥasbala* is derived is iii, 173. The indenting prescribed by Ibn Shīth for the *ḥasbala* is observed in our documents.

[29] Amari, *Diplomi*, no. 22.

al-'Ādil al-sayyid al-ajall al-kabīr al-'ālim[30] *al-mujāhid al-muẓaffar al-humām ghiyāth al-anām sayf al-dunyā wa'l-dīn sulṭān al-islām wa'l-muslimīn sayyid al-mulūk wa'l-salāṭīn khalīl amīr al-mu'minīn.* In a letter from 1215 addressed to him by the Pisans[31] the sultan is called *al-sayyid al-ajall al-sulṭān al-kabīr al-Malik al-'Ādil al-'ālim al-'āmil al-mujāhid al-murābiṭ al-mu'ayyad al-muẓaffar al-manṣūr mu'īn* [read so for *sayf*] *al-imām ghiyāth* [read so] *al-anām sayf al-dunyā wa'l-dīn sayyid al-mulūk wa'l-salāṭīn nāṣir al-islām wa'l-muslimīn Abū Bakr b. Ayyūb khalīl amīr al-mu'minīn.* It will be noticed that though the titles correspond in general, the order is not quite the same in the different documents, and that each document shows various additions and omissions as against the others.

It is also instructive to compare the titles which figured in documents sent to Pisa and Venice, the originals of which are lost, but of which there are extant Latin or Italian translations. The dragomans did on the whole good work and rendered the titles in a recognizible form. In a letter of 574/1179 (Amari, 2nd series, no. 11): Dallo re giusto et victorioso,[32] victorioso dell cittadini fedeli,[33] spada della fede del mondo,[34] soldano di tutti gli exerciti delli saraini[35]; in another from 575/1180 (Amari, 2nd series, no. 12): Rex iustus et victoriosus, conservator et spada legis Saracenorum,[36] princeps militie Saracenorum,[37] Bubeccher Maccumata, filius Iob, fidelis elmire Elmomin. These documents (like the inscription of A.H. 579 mentioned below) belong to the period of Saladin, when al-'Ādil acted as his brother's lieutenant in Egypt; the following documents were issued during his reign. At the beginning of no. 22 in Amari's second series (perhaps from 1208), we have a considerably abbreviated titulature, since the passage in question evidently renders the text of the

---

[30] Amari has queried this word, but it can be seen in the original and is confirmed by the parallel texts.

[31] See Amari's notes to *Diplomi*, no. 27 (p. 412). Incidentally, in line 3 of no. 27 read *a'azza'llāh anṣārah* (instead of *amṣārah*).

[32] The first *victorioso* may render *al-muẓaffar* or *al-manṣūr*. It seems that the translators did not meticulously render all the different titles which are in fact not easily differentiated.

[33] This probably translates (though in a rather queer fashion) *nāṣir al-islām*; I cannot tell why the translator chose the word *cittadini*.

[34] *Sayf al-dunyā wa'l-dīn*; perhaps we have to read *della fede* <*et*> *del mondo*.

[35] *Sulṭān juyūsh al-muslimīn.* The name and the title *khalīl amīr al-mu'minīn* are missing.

[36] This seems to be a contracted rendering of *nāṣir al-islām wa'l-muslimīn sayf al dunyā wa'l-dīn.*

[37] *Sulṭān juyūsh al-muslimīn.*

sultan's *ṭughrā*, in which only the main titles of the ruler were included : Elmelec Adel, ensis totius mundi,[38] rex super omnes reges,[39] Abubecre filius Iob, consanguineus chalif obediens.[40] In the body of the document an even more drastically abbreviated title is given, in accordance with the conventions of the particular type to which the document belongs.[41] In the safe-conduct dated 612/1215 (Amari, 2nd series, no. 26) we find one new title : Lo re giustissimo, spada della fede et del mondo, soldano delli Turchi et delli Persi, e[42] Bubacchara filio di Aiup, Kalil Emir Elmominim. The title " soldano delli Turchi et delli Persi ", which probably stands for *sulṭān al-'Arab wa'l-'Ajam*, is discussed below (p. 24).

In addition to the documents, we have a number of inscriptions which provide information about al-'Ādil's titles. There is no need for detailed references, since these inscriptions are conveniently put together in vols. 9 and 10 of the *Répertoire chronologique d'épigraphie arabe*. In the following sketch the evidence of the inscriptions is taken into consideration.[43]

As I have said, I do not propose to include a thorough study of al-'Ādil's titles, but shall confine myself in the following paragraphs to summarizing the information provided by the texts which we have just discussed. This task is made easier by the existence of studies devoted to the titles of rulers whose usage actually constitutes the background of, or runs parallel with, al-'Ādil's own : Elisséeff's systematic study of Nūr al-Dīn's titles,[44] and Wiet's remarks about those of Saladin and Ghāzī, Saladin's son and ruler of Aleppo.[45] These authors have built on foundations laid by the studies of M. van Berchem ; since, however, they use much richer materials, I shall rather refer to their articles, where the interested reader can find the references to van Berchem's relevant studies.

---

[38] *Sayf al-dunyā wa'l-dīn.*

[39] *Sayyid al-mulūk wa'l-salāṭīn.*

[40] *Khalīl amīr al-mu'minīn.*

[41] See below, pp. 30–1.

[42] This *e*, which makes no sense, is either to be deleted, or else must be taken as the remainder of a phrase lost by the copyist's error : *e<t delli Arabi* (?)>.

[43] The *Répertoire* is abbreviated as *Rép.*; *CIA* stands for *Matériaux pour un Corpus Inscriptionum Arabicarum.*

[44] N. Elisséeff, " La titulature de Nūr al-Dīn d'après ses inscriptions," *Bulletin d'Études Orientales*, Damascus, xiv (1952–4), pp. 155 ff.

[45] G. Wiet, " Les inscriptions de Saladin," *Syria*, 1922, pp. 307 ff.; idem, " Une inscription de Malik Ẓāhir Gāzī à Latakieh," *Bulletin de l'Institut Français d'Archéologie Orientale*, 1931, pp. 273 ff.

In our decree and in the letter to the Pisans the titles begin with *al-mawlā al-Malik al-'Ādil al-sayyid al-ajall. Al-mawlā* in the chancery documents corresponds to *mawlānā* used in epigraphy [46] and the difference of usage in the two kinds of documents seems to be consistent. There is nothing to say about the " personal " title al-Malik al-'Ādil. *Al-sayyid al-ajall,* " the most excellent lord ", is, as he has been pointed out by van Berchem,[47] a legacy of the Fāṭimid period when it was borne by the viziers. In inscriptions it appears, curiously enough, very rarely : there is one known example for Saladin, and one for al-'Ādil.[48]

A significant feature is the presence of the title *sulṭān* before the name *al-Malik al-'Ādil* in the letters to and from the Pisans : in the first it is inserted between *al-mawlā* and *al-Malik al-'Ādil* in a formula which is otherwise identical with that of the decree, whereas in the second the formula is differently arranged.[49] It has been shown that Saladin has never officially assumed the title of sultan, and al-'Ādil himself only adopted it late in his career.[50] The lack of the word sultan in our decree is therefore in order ; it first occurs in an inscription of 605/1208–9.[51] The composite title " Sultan of the Armies of the Muslims " which occurs among the other composite title is a different matter, since in that position and in such a compound it does not have the full force of a sovereign title which it bears if standing at the beginning of the series.[52]

---

[46] For *mawlānā al-sulṭān* see *Rép.* nos. 3639, 3650–1, 3660 (*al-s. al-a'ẓam*), 3679, 3682, cf. 3685–6), 3727, 3807, 3815, 3947, 3967.

[47] In *CIA*, ii, 107.

[48] See Saladin's inscription of 583 (*Rép.* no. 3420 ; no. xii in Wiet, " Inscr. Saladin ") and al-'Ādil's inscription no. 3800/A (*Rép.* x, 276), undated.

[49] *Al-mawlā* is missing and the titles begin with *al-sayyid al-ajall al-sulṭān al-kabīr al-Malik al-'Ādil.* Cf. the inscriptions of Saladin and al-'Ādil quoted in the preceding note, which also begin with *al-sayyid al-ajall* and are lacking *mawlānā.*

[50] Cf. van Berchem. *CIA*, i, 299 ; Wiet, " Inscr. Saladin," pp. 313–4, and more especially " Inscr. Gāzī ", p. 281.

[51] See Wiet, " Inscr. Gāzī ", loc. cit., where the assumption of the title by the various Ayyūbid princes is described. Van Berchem (see preceding note) states that " in his later inscriptions al-'Ādil does not bear the title of sultan." It is true that this title is omitted before his name in some inscriptions : some inscriptions from Buṣrā (*Rép.* nos. 3724, 3818) and Damascus (nos. 3728–9, 3806), and some others in which he is named as the father of the ruler who is the author of the inscription (nos. 3629, 3661, 3717, 3721–2, 3752–3, 3779, 3780, 3801–2). In most of the inscriptions the title of sultan is inserted ; see nos. 3638–9, 3650–1, 3660, 3679–80, 3682, 3727, 3807, 3815.

[52] Cf. Elisséeff, p. 180 : " Or le sens de ce terme est différant selon la place qu'il occupe dans le protocole. Il n'est souverain que lorsqu'il vient en tête des titres."

The title in *malik* is followed, as usual, by a number of adjectives :[5

al-kabīr, " the great " (decree, Pisan letters)

al-'ālim, " the learned " (idem)

al-'āmil, " the worker of deeds " (only in letter from Pisans)

al-mu'ayyad al-muẓaffar al-manṣūr, " divinely assisted, triumphant victorious " (decree, letter from Pisans ; *al-muẓaffar* alone i letter to Pisans)

al-murābiṭ, " campaigning " (decree)

al-mujāhid, " fighting the holy war " (letter to Pisans ; both *al-murābiṭ al-mujāhid* in letter from Pisans.

al-humām, " heroic " (decree, letter to Pisans)

Of the compound titles, which, as usual, follow upon the simple ones the first place is taken, according to the general rule,[54] by those wit *dīn* and *islām,* in our case *sayf al-dīn* and *nāṣir al-islām,* which appea regularly in the documents, diplomatic and epigraphical. There is however, one detail which deserves to be noted. In the decree we hav the shorter form, whereas in other documents there is found the fulle form *sayf al-dunyā wa'l-dīn.* As is well known, this latter is the properl " sovereign " form [55] ; yet in this case it is not sure whether we ought t attribute any significance to the difference, since already in his inscriptio of 589/1193 (*Rép.* no. 3463) al-'Ādil bears the full title *sayf al-dunyā wa'l dīn* ; it is possible, however, that he denied himself the " sovereign " title in chancery documents during his regency.[56]

The titles composed with *imām* (" Helper of the Imam ") and *anām* (" Succour of Mankind ") are a legacy of the Fāṭimid period in which the were attributed to the viziers.[57] They do not occur in the extant inscrip tions of Saladin, though they were no doubt used by the chancery. Ho capricious epigraphical usage was and how cautious we must be i drawing conclusions from our lacunary evidence, is shown by the fact tha

---

[53] For *'ālim* cf. Elisséeff, p. 170 ; for *al-mujāhid* and *al-murābiṭ,* pp. 171–3 ; and fo *al-mu'ayyad* etc., pp. 173–4. Al-Ādil's inscription *Rép.* no. 3629 has *al-'ālim al-'ābid,* n 3660 *al-mujāhid,* nos. 3651, 3679, 3755, 3918 *al-mujāhid al-murābiṭ* ; nos. 3651, 372 *al-muẓaffar al-mu'ayyad al-manṣūr,* no. 3679 the same three adjectives in a different order *al-muẓaffar* alone no. 3800/A ; there also *al-humām.* In 3660 we find *al-manṣūr* alone.

[54] See van Berchem, *CIA,* i, 445 ff.; Elisséeff, p. 156. For *sayf al-islām* cf. Elisséef p. 179.

[55] See Elisséeff, pp. 176–7.

[56] *Sayf al-dunyā wa'l-dīn* occurs in *Rép.* nos 3639, 3650–1, 3660, 3679, 3724, 3727–9 3753, 3755, 3800/A, 3802, 3806–7, 3815, 3818 ; *sayf al-dīn* in nos. 3629, 3686, 3717, 375 3925, 3965, 3967.

[57] Cf. *Fāṭimid Decrees,* pp. 57, 64, 74–5 ; Wiet, *CIA,* ii, 152, 175 (for *anām*) ; 84–5 150 (for *imām*).

whereas the title compounded with *imām* does not appear in al-'Ādil's inscriptions at all, *ghiyāth al-anām*, " succour of mankind " appears in one inscription only published from the notes of van Berchem in the appendix of vol. x of the *Répertoire* (no. 3800/A). The series in *dawla, milla, umma,* which have a long tradition behind them, appear in Nūr al-Dīn's inscriptions,[58] but not in those of Saladin or al-'Ādil. The proud titles " Lord of Kings and Sultans " and " Sultan of the Armies of the Muslims " or " Sultan of Islam and the Muslims " call for no special remarks.[59]

The Ayyūbids, for obvious reasons, used a great variety of titles which recall the defence of Islam.

In our decree al-'Ādil uses *qāmi' al-kafara wa'l-mushrikīn*. Several titles composed with *al-kafara wa'l-mushrikīn*: *qātil*, " killer ", or *qāhir*, " conqueror ", or *qāmi'*, " subduer ", " of the unbelievers and poytheists ", occur in the sixth/twelfth century.[60] The same title occurs in the solemn inscription dated from 605/1208–9 (*Rép.* no. 3639)—the same in which al-'Ādil is given the title of sultan in the first time ; but here further phrases of similar character are added : *qāmi' al-kafara wa'l-mushrikīn, jāmi' kalimat al-īmān, qāmi' 'abadati'l-awthān*, " subduer of the unbelievers and polytheists ", the unifier of the word of belief, the subduer of the adorers of the idols." [61] In *Rép.* no. 3651 we have *qātil al-kafara wa'l-mushrikīn qāhir al-khawārij wa'l-mutamarridīn*, " killer of the unbelievers and polytheists, conqueror of the rebels and the insubordinate." [62] A new combination of familiar titles occurs in *Rép.* no. 3679 : *qāmi' al-khawārij wa'l-mutamarridīn qāhir al-kafara wa'l-mushrikīn*.

---

[58] Elisséeff, pp. 182–5.

[59] For titles composed with *al-mulūk wa'l-salāṭīn* cf. Elisséeff, pp. 186–7 ; *sayyid al-mulūk wa'l-salāṭīn* is attributed to al-'Ādil also in the inscription no. 3679. *Sulṭān juyūsh al-muslimīn* occurs in *Rép.* nos. 3639, 3650 ; in nos. 3629, 3651, 3660, 3679, 3727, 3800/A, 3802, 3828, we find *sulṭān al-islām wa'l-muslimīn* (*sulṭān al-islām* in no. 3806, *sulṭān al-muslimīn* in no. 3818). For *sulṭān al-islām wa'l-muslimīn* cf. Wiet, " Inscr. Saladin," p. 314.

[60] See Elisséeff, loc. cit.

[61] For the phrase *jāmi' kalimat al-īmān*, which occurs among the titles of Saladin and is frequent at later times, see Wiet, " Inscr. Saladin ", p. 314. For *qāmi' 'abadat al-awthān*, cf. the similar *qāmi' 'abadat al-ṣulbān*, " the subduer of the adorers of the crosses ", borne by Saladin (ibid., p. 315).

[62] For *al-mutamarridīn* cf. Elisséeff, p. 188 ; the combination *al-khawārij wa'l-mutamarridīn* is usual in the Mamlūk period, Elisséeff, ibid. *Qāmi' al-kafara wa'l-mushrikīn, qāhir al-khawārij wa'l-mutamarridīn* is attributed to Saladin in a letter of the caliph to him, quoted by Al-Qalqashandī, x, 145 ff. (cf. Wiet, " Inscr. Saladin ", p. 316).

Qāmi' al-kafara wa'l-mushrikīn is the formula in *Rép.* nos. 3724, 3727, and 3800/A.

We have seen that in the Italian translation of a document by al-'Ādil he bears the title " soldano delli Turchi et delli Persi ", which does not recur elsewhere but cannot be condemned for this reason alone. The restoration of the original text is somewhat problematic. In the first instance one would take the original to be *sulṭān al-Turk wa'l-'Ajam*, and since the title is unique, there is no decisive argument against such a re-translation. On the other hand we find that such later Ayyūbid rulers as al-Ashraf, al-'Ādil II and al-Ṣāliḥ did bear the title of *malik*, or *sulṭān*, *al-'Arab wa'l-'Ajam*,[63] so that it is possible that al-'Ādil's title was also *sulṭān al-'Arab wa'l-'Ajam* and the translator, by a double substitution, used the word " Turk " in a vague meaning of " Saracene, Muslim ", and rendered by it *al-'Arab*, which he also took to mean the same.

There are a few further titles which occur sporadically, but require no further comments in the present context.[64]

Finally, the title *khalīl amīr al-mu'minin*, " friend of the Commander of the Faithfull ", figures, in its ordinary position at the very end, in almost all documents and inscriptions. It occurs already in the inscription of 579/1183.[65]

After the decree had been drawn up by the Chancery it was presented to the ruler for signature ; he signed with his motto : *al-ḥamdu li'llāhi wa-bihi tawfīqī*, " Praise be to God, who is the cause of my success." The signature was appended between the second and third lines, i.e. the first and second lines of the text, excluding the very first line occupied by the *basmala*, the opening formula " In the name of God, the Merciful, the

---

[63] For al-Ashraf see his inscription *Rép.* no. 3989 ; for al-'Ādil II no. 4164 ; for al-Ṣāliḥ no. 4308. Baybars bears the title *s. al-'Arab wa'l-'Ajam wa'l-Turk*, *Rép.* no. 4554.

[64] *Nāshir al-'adl wa'l-iḥsān*, " Propagator of justice and bounty," *Rép.* no. 3639 ; *ḥāmī* (in no. 3724 *mālik*) *al-ḥaramayn al-sharīfayn*, " Protector (or : Possessor) of the two noble sanctuaries [of Jerusalem and Hebron]", nos. 3639, 3650, 3727 ; in no. 3651 he is described as possessor of Egypt, Syria and Akhlāṭ, in 3724 there is even a longer list of his possessions.

[65] Cf. van Berchem, *CIA*, i, 83 ; Wiet, " Inscr. Saladin ", p. 319. For the significance of the title cf. also Wiet, " Inscr. Gāzī ", pp. 288–9.

Compassionate." [66] This was obviously done because it was convenient not to leave any space between the ritual phrase and the beginning of the text ; in contrast an extra large space was left between the next two lines in order to accomodate the signature. The signature itself consisted, in accordance with classical Islamic usage, of a motto, which was the same in the case of all the Ayyūbid rulers. There is no need to give here the evidence, since the subject has been fully treated in the book on the Fāṭimid decrees.[67]

When finished, the decrees were usually circulated among the relevant offices of the central government in order to be registered ; our document, however, bears no registration marks like many of those of the Fāṭimid and Mamlūk periods and also the second Ayyūbid document published here.

When all this was done, the decree was delivered to the monks, who had to submit it themselves to the provincial authorities concerned with their affairs [68] ; finally it was deposited in their archive,[69] where it is preserved to this day.

II

The second decree was issued by al-Afḍal " outside Damascus " on 5 Dhu'l-Qa'da 595/29 August 1199. In Muḥarram 595/November–December 1198, al-'Azīz, ruler of Egypt, died. After a long dispute the amīrs agreed to seat his infant son al-Manṣūr on the throne, but invited his uncle, al-Afḍal, to act for him as regent. Al-Afḍal willingly undertook this task and came to Egypt. On 3 Rajab/1 May, however, he left for Syria in order to take possession of Damascus, but al-'Ādil, who had

---

[66] This is the position of the *'alāma* in the Fāṭimid period, as attested by the two decrees (nos. 6 and 8) the beginning of which has survived. For the Ayyūbid period we also have the express statement by Ibn Shīth (p. 32) who says (speaking of letters, not decrees) : " The *'alāma* of the sultan is in the third line, counting the *basmala*, in a space between the lines." Also Ṣāliḥ b. Yaḥyā, in his Histroy of Beirut, in describing a document by Saladin, mentions that the Sultan's motto is in the third line (" under the first line after the *basmala* ", ed. L. Cheikho, p. 51). Similarly the signature of al-Ṣāliḥ, apparently consisting of his *ṭughrā* (p. 54 ; read *ba'd al-basmala al-sharīfa wa-saṭr.*).

[67] See *Fāṭimid Decrees*, pp. 152–4 .

[68] Cf. ibid., p. 90.

[69] Some Fāṭimid decrees contain a phrase ordering that after the perusal by the authorities the document should be kept by the beneficiaries ; see *Fāṭimid Decrees*, pp. 116–7. Our document has no such phrase, but al-Afḍal's, published below, has (lines 39–40) : " let this be deposited in their hands after it had been read, as a proof in the future ".

previously retired to the eastern provinces of the Ayyūbid realm, antici-
pated him and occupied the city. Al-Afḍal encamped at the pass of
al-Kiswa, south of Damascus, but when he was joined by his brother and
ally al-Ẓāhir, king of Aleppo, they advanced as far as the Mosque of the
Foot, between al-Kiswa and Damascus.[70] For the rest of the year they
remained in camp there, and, as Ibn Wāṣil (p. 101) puts it, " the year
came to an end while the city [of Damascus] was being closely besieged."
It was obviously in the camp near the Mosque of the Foot " outside
Damascus " that the decree discussed by us was issued.

Monastery of St. Catherine, Sinai, scroll no. 12. Dimensions : 287 × 13·2 cm. (according to Atiya). Plates XIII–XIX.

Al-Afḍal orders to treat the monks of Mt. Sinai according to their old customs and
protect their property. The amīr Shams al-Dīn Abū Saʿīd Aslam is instructed to observe
the order.

بسم الله الرحمن الرحيم

خرج الأمر العالى المولوىّ

[الحمد لله وبه توفيق]

السلطانىّ الملكىّ الأفضلىّ لا زال

عالى المنار ، نامى المبارّ ، منصور الأنصار ،

5 مسعود الإيراد والإصدار ، نافذا فى

الأطراف والأقطار ، بإجراء جماعة

الرهبان بطور سينا المبارك سلّمهم الله

على عادتهم فى حفظهم ورعايتهم ، وصيانة

أحوالهم وحمايتهم ، وتيسير مطالبهم ، وتسهيل

10 مآربهم ، وان لا يعترضوا بأذيّة ظاهرة

ولا باطنة ، وان ترفه خواطرهم لتكون

المرفهة الساكنة ، وان لا يعرضوا فى

كرومهم ونخيلهم وزروعهم بإضرار ، ولا

مقاسمة ولا احتجار ولا اقتطاع

---

[70] The sources are the same as those enumerated above, note 3 : Ibn Wāṣil, iii, 87 ff.,
95 ff., 98 ff. ; Ibn al-Athīr, xii, 91 ff. ; Ibn al-ʿAdīm, pp. 216–9 ; Abū Shāma *Kitāb al-
Rawḍatayn*, ii, 234 ff. ; Sibṭ b. al-Jawzī, pp. 296 ff. ; al-Maqrīzī, i, 145 ff. ; Ibn Taghrībirdī,
vi, 146 ff. For al-Kiswa see R. Dussaud, *Topographie historique de la Syrie*, p. 321 ; for the
Mosque of the Foot, Dussaud, pp. 308–9 and J. Sourdel-Thomine, in *Bulletin d'Etudes
Orientales*, Damascus, xiv (1952–4), p. 73.

شيء من ذلك بوجه من وجوه الإجبار، وان لا يكرهوا بمساكنة غيرهم، ولا يخزن غلّة ولا غيرها فى ديرهم، ولتكفّ أسباب المسآءة العايدة بضيرهم، والأمير الإسفهسلار الكبير الأخصّ الموفّق الأمين، شمس الدين عدّة المجاهدين، عمدة الملوك والسلاطين، خاصّة أمير المؤمنين، ابو سعيد أسلم أدام الله تأييده ونعمته، وتسديده ورفعته، وأجزل من كل خير موهبته، يقف عند هذا الأمر ولا يتعدّيه وليحذر من تجاوزه الى ما سواه، ويشملهم بكل إرعآء فانهم رعايانا ورعاياه، وليخفّف الوطأة عنهم لمكان انقطاعهم فى ذلك المكان الشريف، ولا يمكّن احدا من أذيّتهم فما منهم الا من هو المسكين الضعيف، وليجرهم على عوائدهم وأحكام تواقيعهم التى بأيديهم وأمرنا هذا لذلك مؤكّد، ولأثواب الإحسان اليهم مجدّد، وسبيل كل واقف على هذا المثال من مقطع ووال ومتولّ لقلعة أيلة حرسها الله الامتثال لمراسمه، والوقوف عند معالمه، والتجنّب لمظانّ الحيف ومآثمه، وليكن العمل بحسبه فى اليوم والغد، وليقرّ بأيديهم بعد قرآءته حجّة لهم فيما بعد

ان شاء الله تعالى

وكتب فى خامس ذى القعدة سنة خمس وتسعين وخمسمائة

بظاهر دمشق

الحمد لله وحده وصلواته على سيّدنا محمد نبه وآله
وصحبه وسلامه
وحسبنا الله ونعم الوكيل

[Between lines 5 and 6 a signature in cipher :]

الملك لله

[Registration marks :]

[Between lines 6 and 7, right side :]

[1a] لينسخ فى ديوان النظر الخاصّ المصرىّ المعمور|| ان شاء الله تعالى

[1b] نسخ والحمد لله عليه توكّلى

[On the left side :]

[2a] لينسخ فى الديوان ان شاء الله

[2b] نسخ والحمد لله الواحد العدل

[Between lines 7 and 8 :]

[3] نسخ الحمد لله على نعمائه

TRANSLATION

[The signature :]

Praise be to God, who is the cause of my success.

In the name of God, the Merciful, the Compassionate.

The exalted order of the master, the sultan al-Malik al-Afḍal—may its light continue to be exalted, its charities to increase, its victories to prevail, whatever it begins and end to be fortunate, and to be executed in all lands and regions—was issued to treat the community of monks in the blessed Mount Sinai (may God give them peace) according to their custom, by guarding and protecting them, defending their affairs, facilitating their business and making easy their occupations. They should not be interfered with through open or concealed harm, their minds be reassured so as to make them confident and quiet. Their vineyards, palm-trees, and fields should not be interfered with by damage, sharing, enclosing, enfeoffment, or in any way of constraint ; they should not be forced to live together with people not belonging to them, and no grain, or other goods, should be stored in their monastery, and all evil actions causing them harm should be prevented.

Let the amīr, the great general, our intimate courtier, the one assisted by God, the trustworthy one, Sun of Religion [Shams al-Dīn], Armament of the Fighters for the Faith, Support of Kings and Sultans, the Intimate Friend of the Commander of the Faithful, Abū Sa'īd Aslam (may God prolong his help, welfare, support, and greatness, and may He give him ample share of all benefits) obey this order and not transgress it, and beware from passing it by in order to do something else. Let him encompass them by all protection, since they are our and his subjects, and let him deal with them with a light touch on account of their having retired to that noble place, and let him allow no one to harm them, since all of them are poor and weak. Let him treat them according to their customs and the rulings contained in the decrees which are in their hands. This order of ours confirms this and renews the garments of benefaction towards them.

Let fief-holders, governors, and the governor of the fortress of Ayla (may God guard it), who have cognizance of this order, obey its commands and follow its instructions, and avoid actions smacking of oppression; and let it be acted upon to-day and to-morrow, and let this be deposited in their hands after it had been read, as a proof in the future, if God (may He be exalted) wills.

Written this fifth day of Dhu'l-Qa'da, the year Five-hundred Ninety Five, outside Damascus.

Praise be to God alone, and His blessings and peace upon our lord Muḥammad His prophet, his family and his companions.

God is sufficient for us; how excellent a Keeper is He!

[Between lines 5 and 6 a signature in cipher:]

Kingdom belongs to God.

[Registration marks:]

[between lines 6 and 7, right side:]

[1a] Let it be copied in the Office of the Private Superintendance for Egypt (may it flourish), if God wills.

[1b] It has been copied; praise be to God, in Him I trust.

[on the left side:]

[2a] Let it be copied in the Office, if God wills.

[2b] It has been copied; praise be to God, the one, the just.

[between lines 7 and 8:]

[3] It has been copied; praise be to God for His bounty.

This decree follows a different pattern from the preceding. Its exordium: "The exalted order . . . was issued" is a formula which is often used to introduce the main part of a decree containing the *dispositio* and coming after preliminary matter such as the *arenga* (if there is one) and the *expositio*.[71] Here, however, this formula is used to open the decree and the *dispositio* is preceded by no preliminaries. As we shall see presently, ours is not an isolated example of this form. It may also be pointed out that the titles of the ruler are given in an extremely abbreviated form. All this seems to suggest that the pattern adopted here is lower in the hierarchy of forms than the fuller pattern represented by al-'Ādil's decree. It is, however, wiser to reserve judgement, especially as there is hardly a difference to be discovered in the subject matter which should have brought about the use of a more formal pattern in the one, a less formal pattern in the other document.

I am unable to identify the amīr Abū Sa'īd Aslam to whom the sultan's order is more especially addressed. Since the provincial governors are separately referred to, he must have been a high official of the central government, or perhaps the governor of the Sharqiyya province, in which case the word " governors " may refer to the governor of al-Ṭūr, possibly subordinate to him.[72] The governor of Ayla is separately mentioned. This exhortation to obey the sultan's order addressed to the officials particularly concerned is customary (the phraseology is studied below),[73] as is also the instruction that after use the document be kept by the beneficiaries as evidence for the sultan's order.[74]

THE EXORDIUM

We have seen that the exordium of the present document is different from that of al-'Ādil. We shall discuss some parallels to the type used in our document and then identify a third type.

The exordium used in our document recurs in some documents of the Ayyūbid period the originals of which are not known, but which are preserved in translations. A safe-conduct by al-'Ādil, perhaps from the year 1208,[75] begins : [Hec est] securitas omnium mercatorum pisanorum.[76]

---

[71] Cf. for instance *Fāṭimid Decrees*, nos. 3–6, 8, 10, and pp. 111–2, and for the Ayyūbid period the diplomas of appointment quoted by al-Qalqashandī, xi, 53 and 60.

[72] According to Ibn Shīth, p. 42, the title *khāṣṣat amīr al-mu'minīn*, borne by Aslam, belonged to the highest class of civil officials. Aslam was obviously a member of the military; but the statement that the title was indicative of high rank probably is valid also for them.

[73] See below, pp. 34 ff.

[74] See above, note 69.

[75] Amari, *Diplomi*, 2nd series, no. 22 (p. 283).

[76] This does not seem to form part of the document, but is a heading added by the translator.

Elmelec Adel, ensis totius mundi, rex super omnes reges, Abubecre filius Iob, consanguineus chalif obediens.[77] In nomine Domini. Exiit magnum preceptum altissimi regis Melec Adel sultani, Deus custodiat eum et augeat ei honores, et sit firmum preceptum etc. The Arabic original of the formula no doubt read : *Kharaja'l-amru'l-'āli'l-mawlawiyyu'l-sulṭāniyyu'l-Malakiyyu'l-'Ādiliyyu* (then some eulogies). Another safe-conduct of which we posses a fifteenth century Italian translation [78] began obviously with the same words, which were rendered rather awkwardly by the translator. Here too we first find the sultan's titles, obviously representing the *ṭughrā* : Lo re giustissimo, spada della fede et del mondo, soldan delli Turchi et delli Persi, e Bubacchara filio di Aiup, Kalil Emir Elmominin. Then follows the translation of the exordium : Avemo facto lo comandamento grande colla victoria, comandatore soldano Elmechi giustissimo, Dio gli dia gratia, et gratia, che scrive questo scripto de salvocondocto. A decree ordering the restoration of the *funduq* of the Pisans in Alexandria begins [79] : In nomine Dei, qui est pius et pietas.[80] Exiit equitatis preceptum,[81] cuius Deus augeat honorem [gratias agimus solo Deo [82]] in designatione restaurationis fundaci, domus scilicet, in qua Pisani stare consuevere, in terra Alexandrie [83] etc.

We have translations of similar documents concerning the Venetians. A letter addressed to the provincial governors and granting privileges to

---

[77] This is the translation of the sultan's *ṭughrā*. The *ṭughrā* consists, as is well known, of the ruler's name and some of his titles, written in the form of a cipher. The Ayyūbids used the *ṭughrā* alongside the motto (see *Fāṭimid Decrees*, pp. 154–6), though it is impossible to recognize the principle which regulated this or the other form of signature. The translation shows that the *ṭughrā* was placed above the *basmala*, in contrast to the motto, cf. above, pp. 24–5. For the titles contained in this and the following documents see pp. 19–20.

[78] Amari, *Diplomi*, no. 26 (p. 285), dated 612/1215–6. *Grande* is probably *al-'ālī*, though the addition of *colla victoria* is puzzling. *Comandatore* could be for *al-mawlawiyyu*.

[79] Amari, no. 26 (p. 290). If our explanation in note 81 is correct, this document can also be attributed to al-'Ādil.

[80] " Pius et pietas " is the awkward attempt to translate the synonymous *al-raḥmān al-raḥīm*.

[81] It seems to me obvious that this is a mistranslation of *kharaja'l-amru'l-*[*'āli'l-mawlawiyyu'l-sulṭāniyyu'l-Malakiyyu'l-*]*'Ādiliyyu*, where *al-'Ādiliyyu*, " of al-'Ādil ", was wrongly rendered as " equitatis ". It is more difficult to account for the absence of equivalents for the other titles (put above in square brackets).

[82] This seems to be a somewhat inaccurate translation of the signature *al-ḥamd li'llāh wa-bihi tawfīqī*, which occurred, as usual, between the first and second lines of the text, and was therefore incorporated by the translators into the context.

[83] The words *domus scilicet* are probably added by the translator in order to gloss the term *fundaci*.

the Venetian merchants begins [84]: Exivit altum mandatum maioris domini, Imperatoris fidelis—cui Deus det victoriam et altitudinem et magnitudinem etc. At the same date there was issued to the Venetians a document permitting them to have a *funduq* in Alexandria [85]: Exivit altum preceptum domini et senioris Soldani, fidelis Imperatoris—quem Deus honoravit et manifeste magnificavit [86] etc.

Finally, we have a similar document from a somewhat later date, a safe-conduct granted by al-ʿĀdil II to the Venetians in 636/1238.[87] It begins as follows: In nomine Domini. Exivit altum preceptum [Hic [88] est signum soldani quod interpretatur: 'Gratia Deo de mea fortuna] Dominus soldanus Melech Aladel, spata legis, Dominus det ei vitam! fecit preceptum ut scriberetur cartulam fidantiae etc. The words in brackets refer to the sultan's signature, and " Gratia Deo de mea fortuna " is, not a bad translation of the Arabic formula *al-ḥamd li'llāh wa-bihi tawfīqī*. Altogether, the translator was a painstaking and fairly competent man,[89] and the exordium is also very well rendered.[90] We shall not deal with the body of the document, but take the opportunity to show that the final formulae as they appear in Latin garb are those known from original documents. The end of the translation reads: Scripta fuit per legationem de mirum Gemelodin faciam Soldanis. Et necesse est ut cognoscatis istas causas et sciatis; et erit lo ben cum gratia Dei. Et ista fidantia scripta fuit

---

[84] G. L. Fr. Tafel and G. M. Thomas, *Urkunden zur älteren Handels-und Staatsgeschichte der Republik Venedig*, Vienna, 1856–7 (Fontes Rerum Austriacarum, Diplomataria et Acta, xii-xiv); see no. 245 (ii, 188). Here the translation is perfect: Exivit altum mandatum= *kharaja'l-amru'l-ʿālī*; maioris domini=*al-mawlawiyyu'l-sulṭāniyyu*; Imperatoris fidelis = *al-Malakiyyu'l-ʿĀdiliyyu*.

[85] Ibid, no. 246 (ii, 189). Also here the titles are well translated.

[86] The Arabic perfects—standing for the optative—are translated literally.

[87] Tafel—Thomas, no. 294 (ii, 336 ff.); J.M.J.L. de Mas Latrie, *Traités de paix et de commerce concernant les relations des chrétiens avec les Arabes de l'Afrique septentrionale au moyen-âge*, Paris, 1864–72, appendix, p. 72. I have dealt briefly with this text in *Fāṭimid Decrees*, pp. 153–4.

[88] The text is preserved in two copies, one of which reads *hic* " here ", the other *hoc*, " this [is the signature of the sultan] ". Further variants are *domine soldane, Melecheladen, ista cartula*.

[89] It is a sign of the conscientious work of these interpreters, both Florentine and Venetian, that mostly they do not fail to indicate such diplomatic details as the signatures.

[90] The original read: *Kharaja'l-amru'l-ʿāli'l-mawlawiyyu'l-sulṭāniyyu'l-Malakiyyu'l-ʿĀdiliyyu sayfi'l-dīni adāma'llāhu baqā'ahu bi-katbi hādha'l-amān*. Since this phrase was interrupted by the motto, there is a slight confusion in the syntax of the translation (*kharaja'l-amr* is rendered doubly by " exivit altum preceptum " and " . . . fecit preceptum ").

a die decima tertia intrante mense Novembris anno Machometi sexcentesimo trigesimo sexto. Gratia Deo soli, et adoratus Domini supra Machumeto. Deus predicat nos et justus est. I have explained in another place what it means that the document was written "through the message" of the amīr Jamāl al-Dīn : i.e. the sultan's order was transmitted through him to the Chancery.[91] Unfortunately the meaning of *faciam Soldanis,* presumably the title of the amīr, still eludes us. The next phrase obviously corresponds to the conventional phrase: *wa'lamū hādhā mina'l-amri wa'malū bihi in shā'a'llāh,* "Take cognizance of this order and act accordingly, if God wills." The translator misread, however, the word *wa'malū,* "and act", and thought it was a repetition of *wa'lamū,* "take cognizance"; thus he mistranslated it as "et sciatis." The whole passage can be restored as follows: *Kutiba bi-risālati'l-amīri Jamāli'l-Dīn . . . Wa'lamu hādhā mina'lamri wa'malū bihi in shā'a'llāh. Kutiba thālitha 'ashara . . . sanata sittin wa-thalāthīna wa-sitta mi'a. Al-ḥamdu li'llāhi waḥdahu wa-ṣalawātuhu 'alā sayyidinā Muḥammadin wa-ālihi wa-ṣaḥbihi wa-salāmuh. Ḥasbuna'llāhu wa-ni'ma'l-wakīl.*

A third type of exordium is used on the decrees written on the back of petitions. Al-'Ādil's decree of 598/1202, which is not extant, but is quoted in al-Kāmil's decree on the back of petition iii published by me,[92] begins: *Rusima a'lā'llāh al-marāsim al-sharīfa . . . bi-an* etc., "It has been decreed (may God exalt the noble decrees) . . . that etc.". Al-Kāmil's two decrees (on the back of petitions nos. ii and iii) begin: *Rusima bi'l-amr al-'ālī . . . an* (or infinitive) etc., "It has been decreed by the exalted order . . . that etc.". In the Mamlūk period this exordium was obviously used for documents of minor importance. From al-Qalqashandī (xi, 47 ff.) we see that the diplomas of minor appointments were introduced by it, and were called *marsūms* from the verb in question. Administrative decrees in minor affairs follow closely the pattern of this type of diplomas,[93] so that most of Mamlūk decrees from Sinai also show this kind of exordium. It is hardly a coincidence that in the Ayyūbid period we find the formula in decrees written on the back of petitions: the exordium was evidently reserved in that period too for documents of small importance.

---

[91] "Petitions of the Ayyūbid Period", p. 17. There I have also suggested that Jamāl al-Dīn may be identical with the amir Jamāl al-Dīn Mūsā b. Yaghmūr.

[92] In the article referred to in the preceding note.

[93] I deal with this subject in the article "Petitions from the Mamlūk Period", to be published in the *Bulletin of the School of Oriental and African Studies.*

I still owe some remarks about the final injunctions to " take cognizance " of the sultans' order, " and act accordingly ". This simple form, as it is found in the decree by al-'Ādil of 598/1202 quoted on the back of petition iii (*fal-yu'lam hādhā wal-yu'mal bih,* " Let cognizance be taken of this and be acted accordingly "), and in the Latin translation of al-'Ādil II's document, has a long history, since it is attested for the 'Abbāsid chancery of the tenth century and occurs frequently in the Fāṭimid period.[94] That it was common in the Ayyūbid period can be seen from a passage by Ibn Shīth, who, in his paragraph on final formulae, writes as follows [95]: " The sultan writes to officials of his kingdoms: ' Take cognizance of this and act accordingly (*fa'lam hādhā*—read so for *bi-hādhā*—*wa'mal bih*), if God (may He be exalted) wills.' ' It will be well, if God (may He be exalted) wills ' is written by the highest dignitaries of the bureaucracy to their subordinates ; the words ' Take cognizance of this and act accordingly ' at the end of a letter can only be used by the sultan." Yet already in the Fāṭimid period we have various enlarged forms : a frequent one says that all officials concerned, when they read the decree, or it is read out to them, should obey it—or words to this effect. The extant original Ayyūbid decrees follow this type, but show the particular feature of expressing the injunction by the phrase *wa-sabīl kulli wāqif 'alā hādha'l-mithāl,*[96] " Let all who become aware of this order " (thus both decrees) obey it " acting in conformity with it " (thus al-'Ādil's decree), or—" and let it be acted upon (al-Afḍal's decree). Al-Kāmil's decree on the back of petition no. ii has in a similar manner *wa-sabīl kulli wāqif 'alayh,* " let all who become aware of it . . . act according to its contents." Some of the numerous Ayyūbid diplomas of appointments quoted by al-Qalqashandī also have similar formulas and al-Qalqashandī expressly states that this is the regular way of ending such diplomas : " Then it is said : ' Let all lieutenants who become aware of it act accordingly', or words to this effect." [97] There are many examples for this usage of the phrase *wa-sabīl* from various chanceries of

---

[94] See *Fāṭimid Decrees*, pp. 113–4.

[95] *Ma'ālim al-Kitāba*, p. 50.

[96] Under *sabīl* Dozy in his *Supplément* quotes from the late dictionary *Muḥīṭ* the phrase *sabīluna an naf'ala kadhā,* " il nous sied d'agir ainsi " ; we have now for this usage the early examples provided by the documents. I translated " let . . . obey it " rather than " it befits them to obey it ", since the phrase *sabīl* corresponds to the jussive prefix *wal-* in the phrase *wal-yu'lam* etc.; in reality it all comes to the same.

[97] The rule is found in al-Qalqashandī, xi, 32. The documents in which the formula appears are reproduced on pp. 33–7, 47–51. These diplomas speak of the dignitary whom they concern in the third person, so that they are, I think, open letters. Those addressed

the sixth/twelfth century. Among the documents written for the Seljūq chancery in the first half of the century by Mu'ayyad al-Dawla al-Juwaynī the injunction is often introduced by the *sabīl* formula : e.g. no. 1 *sabīl-i mashāhīr wa-a'imma wa-akābir etc. īn ast kih* etc., " Let the notables, imams, great men etc., do so-and-so." [98] Similarly in many of the documents composed by Bahā' al-Dīn al-Baghdādī for the chancery of the Khwārizmshāhs in the second half of the century.[99] I also happen to have at hand an example from the 'Abbāsid chancery from the early years of the century.[100] It looks therefore as if this formula were also derived from the Seljūq chancery.[101]

Al-Afḍal's signature calls for no comment : his motto is the same as that of al-'Ādil, since, as we have explained, all the Ayyūbid sultans shared the same motto for their *'alāma.* There is, however, an additional signature nothing like which appears in al-'Ādil's decree : the curious cipher between lines 5 and 6 reading *al-mulk li'llāh,* " Kingdom belongs

---

(in the second person) to the dignitary, have not this formula but the injunctions customary in the Fāṭimid period, such as *wa'lam hādhā wa'mal bih* (" take cognizance of this and act accordingly "), pp. 43 ff., 51 ff. [the documents on pp. 56 ff., 61 ff., 63 ff., are from the Fāṭimid period, and are put here erroneously by al-Qalqashandī, who did not seem to have recognized their correct origin] or *fa-taqallad mā qullidta,* " take up the dignity to which you have been appointed " (pp. 54 f.).

[98] *'Atabat al-Kataba,* ed. Muḥammad Qazwīnī and 'Abbās Iqbāl ; see in addition to no. 1 also nos. 6, 13, 19, 21, 24, 34. The other documents have different formulas of injunction, such as *farmān chunān ast kih . . .* ," the order is that . . . " (nos. 2, 4, 7, 15, 17–18, 20, 22–3, 26, 29, (read so p. 73, l. 7, for *wa-ān*) 30–2, 33 ; *īn mithāl farmūdīm tā . . .* (or *ṣādir gasht*), " we have issued this ordinance in order that . . ." (nos. 3, 11, 16, 33) ; or still other formulas. All the preceding numbers refer to the first part of the book, containing documents of a public nature ; the second part contains private letters which are no concern of ours here.

[99] Bahā' al-Dīn al-Baghdādī, *al-Tawassul ila'l-Tarassul,* ed. Aḥmad Bahmanyār ; see pp. 29, 37, 42, 45, 55, 73, 77, 89, 99, 109, 117, 121, 124, This list comprises almost all the diplomas of appointment. One (see p. 94) has *mithāl chunān ast kih . . .* " The order is that . . . ", another (see p. 114) *farmān-i a'lā a'lāhu'llāh bar an jumlat ast kih . . .,* " the highest order (may God exalt it) is to the effect that . . . ". The remaining three documents have no such formulas. It is clear that the practice of the Khwārizmian chancery follows in this particular, as in many others, the Seljūq example.

[100] See H. F. Amedroz, " Tales of Official Life from the ' Tadhkira ' of Ibn Ḥamdūn, etc.," *Journal of the Royal Asiatic Society,* 1908, p. 470.

[101] The probability of Seljūq influence is confirmed by this consideration : we have a great number of documents belonging to the same genre : diplomas of appointments ; and whereas those of the Fāṭimid period follow a different pattern, those of the Ayyūbid period introduce a formula which is found in exactly the same position in documents of the Seljūq chancery and a chancery such as the Khwārizmian which demonstrably depends on the Seljūq one.

to God." It is no doubt a countersign of some high dignitary, to whose identity I have, however, no clue.

Our decree has a few registration marks. The procedure of registration has also been explained in connection with the Fāṭimid decrees,[102] but there are some points which require discussion. Al-ʿĀdil's decree has, as has been pointed out above, no registration marks. Our decree, which has some, is lacking a feature which appears in many Fāṭimid documents: the order in the body of the decree prescribing registration in the appropriate offices. This does not mean, however, that the formula was in abeyance in the Ayyūbid period: al-Kāmil's decree on the back of petition no iii has it (*wa-thubūtih bi-ḥaythu yuthbat mithluh,* " and after registration where its like are registered ") and there is a reference to the formula in a literary source.[103] In the registration marks the verb *nasakha,* " to copy ", is used. In the Fāṭimid documents the ordinary verb is *athbata,* " to register ", but occasionally we also have *nasakha* ; the two verbs seems to stand for the same thing. A third verb, *nazzala,* which can be translated as " to register " also occurs, without our being able to discern any difference in the meaning.[104]

Just as in the Fāṭimid period, the registration marks consist of two parts. First there is the order to register the decree in a given office, then the remark that the order of registration has been carried out. Passages in literary texts indicate that the orders of registration were given by

---

[102] See *Fāṭimid Decrees,* pp. 167 ff.

[103] I think at least that this formula is meant in a passage by Ibn Shīth (p. 23), which it will be convenient—on account of the obscurity of part of it—to reproduce in the original :
ولا يلزم هذا الكاتب اذا انصرف من الخدمة عمل حساب ولا يؤاخذ بما صدر منه فى الأموال بتوقيع او كتاب لانه اذا وقّع عدو موقعه بان يثبت [read so instead of يثبّت] فى الديوان بحيث يثبت مثله فيخرج من الدرك فيه ويرجع الأمر الى من يكتب التوقيع فان اخلّ بهذا لزمه بعض الدرك اذا نوقش. وقد اعتمد بعض الكتّاب فى هذا الزمان ان يقولوا فى آخر المكتوب: والاعتماد على العلامة وليس هذا مخلصا من المؤاخذة لان السلطان او صاحب الأمر ليس من وظائفه ان يتأمّل المكتوب
This surely means that the clerk drawing up a document concerning finance avoided responsibility by including the phrase " after registration where its like are registered " ; since by this entry he, so to speak, made the validity of the document dependent of the orders of registration added subsequently by the high officials responsible for this (as we shall presently see). I cannot explain the words عدو موقعه ; the purport of the sentence seems to be : " since, when he draws up the document, he adds in it that it should be registered etc., so that he cannot be held responsible." The second half of the passage is also very interesting : the ruler does not assume responsibility for the contents by his signature, since he often has to sign documents without reading them. Thus it is rather the officials of the *dīwān* who assume responsibility for the documents, by entering their order of registration.

[104] See *Fāṭimid Decrees,* p. 168.

certain high officials. Ibn Shīth attests that in some cases it was the head of the Office of the Army who wrote in the orders of payment : " Let it be registered (*li-yuthbat*) in the Office of Supervision for the Armies (may they be victorious), if God (may He be exalted) wills ".[105] Certain kinds of document drawn up in the Finance Office were endorsed by the head of the Office of Supervision with the order : " Let it be registered (*li-yunazzal*), if God wills." [106] In another context Ibn Shīth writes : " And he (the head of the Office of Supervision) writes on decisions (*al-tawāqī'*) and grants : ' Let it be registered in the Office of Supervision of such-and-such sultan, if God (may He be exalted) wills ' ".[107] The Office of Supervision was the central financial organ of the Ayyūbid administration,[108] so that its working was of special importance. This is brought out well by a passage in another treatise on Ayyūbid bureaucracy, al-Nābulusī's *al-Luma' al-Muḍī'a*, one of the aims of which was to influence the sultan against parvenu officials. He speaks[109] of a certain al-Ẓahīr al-Ṭunbudhāwī, who from humble origins rose to high office : " He allows his son to write on documents entries only appropriate for the vizier, namely : ' Let it be registered (*li-yuthbat*) in the Office of the Supervision of the Offices (may they prosper). By God, only those ought to make such an entry who have risen to a rank which is not reached by the scholars and excellent men of the country. This empire is too noble for such rabble to write entries which only noble lords used to write." It is seen what importance was attached to the note ordering registration in the Office of Supervision (even if al-Nābulusī, pursuing his own bias, may be guilty of some exaggeration)—the reason being that the office, the *dīwān al-naẓar*, was the supreme financial authority of the administration, and in matters involving finance responsibility was assumed by this signature for the transaction in question.

The first entry in our document refers to the *dīwān al-naẓar*, and the order for registration was probably made by the head of the office. The name of the office is followed by two adjectives : *al-khāṣṣ*, " private ", and another, the reading of which is doubtful—the suggestion to read *al-miṣrī*, " the Egyptian ", is offered with due reserve. I have no other evidence for the use of these adjectives in respect of the *dīwān al-naẓar*.

---

[105] *Ma'ālim al-Kitāba*, p. 26 (read *wa-ṣāḥib* <*dīwān*> *al-jaysh yaktub*).

[106] Ibid., p. 27.

[107] Ibid., p. 28 : *fī dīwān al-naẓar al-fulānī*—the offices often bear in their name the name of the ruler, added in the form of a *nisba* : *al-'Ādilī, al-Afḍalī, etc.*

[108] Cf. Cahen's note in his edition of al-Nābulusī's *Luma'*, p. 30, note 28.

[109] P. 62.

The first seems to suggest that the office concerned was not the Office of Supervision of the state finances, but that of the private purse of the sultan. The addition of "Egyptian" may be explained by al-Afḍal uniting (or pretending to unite) the sovereignty of Egypt and Syria, so that a separate administration would have been needed for each of the two countries. The clerk who carried out the registration added to his mark his motto, in the manner well known from the Fāṭimid period. In mark no. 2 the name of the office seems to have been omitted by an error, since *al-dīwān*, "the office," can hardly mean a particular office. No. 3 is a registration mark which is preceded by no order, so that it does not reveal the identity of the office. Registration brought to an end the process of the issue of the decree, which was then, as we have explained in connection with al-ʿĀdil's decree, delivered to the beneficiaries, the monks of Sinai, for presentation to the provincial authorities and safe keeping in their archive.

The commentary provided in the preceding pages for the two Ayyūbid decrees does not aim at the exhaustive treatment of any one of the problems of Ayyūbid diplomatic, but mainly attempts to illustrate the documents themselves by discussing various points in them needing comment. If any generalization is to be deduced from the particulars which had been touched upon, it is this: the practice of the Ayyūbid chancery was in many respects a continuation of that of the Fāṭimid period, which underwent, however, important changes, many of them due to the impact of Seljūq practice.

A MAMLŪK COMMERCIAL TREATY CONCLUDED WITH THE REPUBLIC OF FLORENCE 894/1489

by

John Wansbrough

The commercial treaties concluded between the Mamlūk Sultans and the maritime republics of southern Europe often involved long and complex negotiations. The purpose of this study is to describe the steps in the conclusion of one such treaty between Sultan Qā'itbāy and the Republic of Florence in 894/1489. The first part will be a relation of the embassies which led to the formulation of the treaty, and the second part an analysis of the documents upon which negotiations were based.

I

In one of the most elegant chambers of the Palazzo Vecchio Giorgio Vasari painted the ceiling with a scene of Lorenzo the Magnificent surrounded by the gifts of a foreign ambassador (see Frontispiece). The picture is somewhat idealized and perhaps only a symbol of the many times in which the Medici prince was so honoured. In his memoirs, however, the painter recalls having begun the work in February 1559 and declares that it was meant to represent a particular embassy from the Sultan of Egypt ("Ricordo come questo anno [1559] al principio del febraio si cominciò a dipigniere a olio la camera di Lorenzo vechio nella quale vi si fè drento a olio nel muro una storia grande quanto gliè presentato dal Soldano molte sorte d'animali . . . ").[1] It is not difficult to

[1] G. Vasari, *Il libro delle ricordanze*, ed. Aless. del Vita, Arezzo 1927, p. 81. See also N.N., *Le pitture del quartiere di Papa Leone in Palazzo Vecchio*, Florence 1861, pp. 12–13; and A. Lensi, *Palazzo Vecchio*, Milan-Rome 1929, pp. 161–5 and plates, pp. 181, 182, 183, which show the interior of the chamber but not this painting. The picture is in the ceiling of the Sala di Lorenzo Magnifico in the Quartiere di Leone X, at present occupied by the

determine which of several Egyptian embassies to Florence Vasari wished to depict; so impressed were Florentine chroniclers by the event that no fewer than five have left record of it. Their attention appears to have been attracted less by the ambassador himself than by the gifts which he brought from Qā'itbāy for Lorenzo. Surely it was the bizarre note struck by the arrival of these gifts in Florence and the impression that they made on the chroniclers which induced Vasari to select this event as an appropriate expression of the grandeur of Lorenzo's rule.

A list of the gifts is to be found in a letter to Lorenzo's wife Clarice Orsini de' Medici, then in Rome, from his secretary Pietro in November 1487 who noted a bay horse, long-eared goats and fat-tailed sheep, balsam, musk, benzoin, wood of aloes, vases of china, coloured stuffs including cottons and muslins, sweetmeats, myrobalans, and ginger (" Un bel cavallo bajo; animali strani, montoni e pecore di vari colori con orecchi lunghi fino alle spalle, e code in terra grosse quasi quanto el corpo; una grande ampolla di balsamo; undici corni di zibetto; bongivi, e legno aloe quanto può portare una persona; vasi grandi di porcellana mai più veduti simili, nè meglio lavorati; drappi di più colori per pezza; tele bambagine assai, che loro chiamano turbanti finissimi; tele assai colla salda, che lor chiamano sexe; vasi grandi di confectione, mirabolani e giengituo ").[2] Except for the animals the gifts were those customarily sent with envoys from the Mamlūk Sultans.[3] Although Pietro da Bibbiena did not describe all of the " animali strani " other chroniclers of the event did. In his " Diary ", in an entry dated 11 to 25 November 1487, Luca Landucci mentions a giraffe and a lion in addition to the goats and sheep,[4]

---

office of the Sindaco and Vice-Sindaco and therefore not open to the public. Lensi, loc. cit. has adduced from Vasari's correspondence evidence that the chamber was decorated during the period between April 1556 and May 1558 despite Vasari's own assertion in his memoirs. Since the painter had not been an eye-witness to the embassy he may have got his description from an oral tradition or from one of the written sources listed below, very likely Landucci. Neither of the two works on the Palazzo Vecchio cited above states that the painting is of an Egyptian embassy, which is however clear from Vasari's memoirs, probably the source of the correct description attached to a photographic reproduction in the museum of the Palazzo Medici-Riccardi.

[2] The letter is reproduced in the appendix to A. Fabroni, *Laurentii Medicis Magnifici Vita*, Pisa 1784, II, 337.

[3] See my article " A Mamluk letter of 877/1473 ", in *BSOAS*, 1961, p. 209, and the references p. 202 n. 3.

[4] L. Landucci, *Diario Fiorentino* 1450–1516, Florence 1883, pp. 52–3. The author writes sceptically of the animals' provenance and includes the tale of a Florentine youth whose curiosity about the lion cost him his life.

an account confirmed or repeated by Landini,[5] Rinuccini,[6] and Fabroni.[7] In all these relations the name of the Egyptian envoy appears but once, and that where it might least be expected : in Landini's commentary to the Aenead. There he is called " Malphoth ", which appears as " Malfott ", " Malfota ", " Malphet ", and " Mazamet Elmalfet " in the documentary sources to be examined below. Renderings of Muslim names in European languages are often deceptive but it seems likely that the Mamlūk envoy to Florence was Muḥammad ibn Maḥfūz al-Maghribī, for whose embassies to Catalonia (Naples ?) and to Florence on two other occasions there is evidence.[8] It may even be that Malfota (the form of the name which occurs most frequently in the Florentine sources) was a familiar figure in Florence and therefore did not attract as much attention as did his gifts in 1487.

The Egyptian chronicler Ibn Iyās, who mentions the embassy of Ibn Maḥfūẓ to Catalonia in 883/1479, has unfortunately no record of the three Florentine embassies. A certain amount of information can be pieced together from Florentine sources.[9] In a letter from the Signoria to its consul in Pera, B. Salvuccio, dated 20 December 1487, a month after Malfota's arrival in Florence, the Egyptian envoy is described as having been sent to resume negotiations for a commercial treaty, interrupted by

---

[5] C. Landini, *Commentar. Virgili*, Florence 1492, Lib. XII, fol. 303v.

[6] F. Rinuccini, *Ricordi Storici*, Florence 1840, II, 143.

[7] A. Fabroni, *Laur. Med. Mag. Vita*, I, 182–3. The briefest account is that of S. Ammirato, *Dell' Istorie Fiorentine*, Florence 1647, part II, p. 180 (Lib. XXVI) : " Il soldano di Babbillonia mandato doni molto magnifici." Further references to the giraffe, which aroused considerable curiosity among European writers, are to be found in L. Thuasne, *Djem-Sultan : étude sur la question d'Orient à la fin du XVe siècle*, Paris 1892, 175 n. 1.

[8] The Egyptian embassy to the " king of the Catalans " departed from Cairo in Dhu'l-Ḥijja 883/Feb.–Mar. 1479, according to Ibn Iyās, *Badā'i' al-Zuhūr*, ed. Kahle-Mustafa, Istanbul 1935, III, 145–6, the title and name of the envoy being " al- Khwāja (Muḥammad) ibn Maḥfūẓ al-Maghribī ". In Dhu'l-Qa'da 889/Dec. 1484 " Malfota " had just returned to Cairo from Florence, according to a letter from Qā'itbāy to Lorenzo, in M. Amari, *I Diplomi Arabi del R. Archivio Fiorentino, Appendice*, Florence 1867, p. 46 (Ser. II, doc. 31). Finally, in a letter from the Mamlūk Sultan to Florence in Jumādā II 901/Feb. 1496 (date uncertain) is a recommendation for one " Khwāja Ibn Maḥfūẓ ", Amari, *Diplomi*, p. 212 (Ser. I, doc. 41).

[9] For the details of Mamlūk embassies to Europe, of which Muslim chroniclers tend only to record the departure and return, if that, one has frequently to rely on European sources and thus accept the probability of a biassed account. See my article " A Mamluk ambassador to Venice in 913/1507 ", *BSOAS*, 1963, pp. 513–4.

the death in Cairo of a Florentine ambassador, one Paolo da Colle.[10] This report is confirmed by the discovery of a letter in the Florentine archives from the Signoria to the Mamlūk Sultan, dated 3 June 1486 and recommending its citizen and merchant to him (" civis ac mercator noster Paulus Collensis ").[11] Before this date Florentine commerce in Egypt appears to have suffered a long period of very little activity, for the Signoria's letter to Salvuccio in Pera makes clear a fresh turning in the Sultan's attitude towards Florence (" L'anno passato, trovandosi apresso al Soldano Paulo da Colle, et faccendo con la sua Signoria qualche parola della mercatura nostra in quello suo regno, la sua Signoria molto liberalmente ne offerse ogni commoditâ ad imitatione de' Venitiani ").[12] The date of Paolo's death in Cairo is not recorded, but the seventeen months which elapsed between his introduction in Cairo and the arrival of Malfota in Florence were, as we shall see, sufficient time for drafting a preliminary treaty, which the latter brought with him.[13]

On 18 November 1487, a week after his arrival, Malfota was introduced to the Signoria ; on 25 November he was granted an audience with Lorenzo, communication on both occasions being established by means of an interpreter.[14] Within a few days a group of Florentine merchants who had either read the draft treaty brought by Malfota or who might

---

[10] G. Müller, *Documenti sulle relazioni delle città toscane coll' Oriente cristiano et coi Turchi fino all' anno* 1531, Florence 1879, p. 237 (doc. 203), located now in the Archivio di Stato di Firenze (ASF), under Diplomatico, Signori, Missive, Ia Cancelleria, filza 49, fol. 177. The Florentine consul at Pera was instructed to allay any suspicions which the Ottoman Sultan Bāyezīd II might have had of an Egyptian embassy to Florence.

[11] ASF, Signori, Missive, Ia Cancelleria, filza 49, fol. 173.

[12] Müller, loc. cit. For a concise but reliable sketch of Florentine commercial activities in Egypt and Syria under the Mamlūks, see W. Heyd, *Histoire du commerce du Levant au moyen-âge*, Leipzig 1885–86, II, 478–80, 487–90. Commercial relations between the two states are attested by documents dating from 1422 to 1510. The pattern of these relations and the question of their dependence upon Venetian precedents will be examined in a study of mine now in preparation, entitled " Venice and Florence in the Mamlūk Commercial Privileges ".

[13] In the letter to Salvuccio in Pera the Signoria describes Malfota as having been sent " con una giraffa et uno lione et con capitoli, secondo che dal decto Paulo era stato richiesto ", Müller, loc. cit.

[14] Landucci, *Diario*, pp. 52–3 ; Rinuccini, *Ricordi*, II, p. 143, the latter mentioning that the interpreter was Sicilian. The use of an interpreter would suggest that Malfota had not, unlike his well-known contemporary Taghrīberdī, been chosen by the Sultan for an embassy because of his linguistic ability or acquaintance with European manners. His title *khwāja* indicates rather, pre-eminence in the world of commerce, see D. Ayalon, *L'Esclavage du mamelouk*, Jerusalem 1951, pp. 1–2 ; and G. Wiet, *Les marchands d'épices sous les sultans mamlouks*, Cairo 1955, p. 124.

even have been in Cairo for its negotiation, presented a petition to the Signoria suggesting certain additions and emendations. Apart from the Signoria's letter to their consul in Pera the next document relevant to the Egyptian embassy is dated 10 June 1488: a letter from Lorenzo to Qā'itbāy recommending to the Sultan's favour a Florentine ambassador, one Luigi della Stufa, being sent to Cairo in the company of Malfota to explain the position of the Florentine merchants, by which apparently was meant their additions and emendations to the draft treaty brought to Florence by the Egyptian envoy (" Ceterum quae ad mercaturam nostrorum pertinent: ut versari et negociari Fiorentini per loca tui Regni possint, et Malphet ipse coram renuntiabit, quae nobis venerint in mentem, et Luisius Stufa, quem ad Te legatum delegimus, cum advenerit, explicabit planius ").[15]

Following upon the embassies of Paolo da Colle and Malfota, Della Stufa's mission to Cairo represents then the third stage of the negotiations out of which the commercial treaty of 1489 grew.[16] Departure from Florence appears however not to have been a matter of urgency, for the Signoria's instructions to their envoy are dated 10 November 1488, five months after Lorenzo's letters to Cairo and Rome, and a year after Malfota's arrival in Florence.[17] Besides the customary admonition to speed and efficiency these instructions contain mention of credentials to the Pope and the King of Naples, gifts for the Sultan, and the following points of business: to express pleasure at the draft treaty brought to Florence by Malfota (" Ma quello che sopratutto ne dette singulare piacere furono e' capitoli i quali ne portò per parte della sua excellentia, acciòche i nostri mercatanti potessino usare la mercatura per le terre del suo gloriosissimo regno "); to deliver a signed copy of them to the Florentine consul in Alexandria (" Li quali, dopo molto examina, furono approvati da noi, et tu ne harai uno instrumento in forma valida sottoscripto come noi usiamo, il quale potrai lasciare nelle mani là del nostro consolo affine che li mercatanti ne possino havere notitia "); to try to persuade the sultan to accept the enclosed list of modifications to the

[15] Epist. Barth. Scalae, in A. M. Bandini, *Collectio veterum aliquot monimentorum*, Arezzo 1752, pp. 12–13. At the same time Lorenzo wrote to the Florentine ambassador in Rome, G. Lanfredini, informing him of the passage of Della Stufa and Malfota on their way to Cairo. ASF, Archivio Mediceo avanti il Principato, filza 59, no. 181, dated 27 June 1488.

[16] Biographical details of the ambassador are to be found in Gismondo di Gismondo di Agnolo della Stufa, Memorie della Casa della Stufa, in Fr. Ildefonso di San Luigi, *Delizie degli eruditi toscani*, Florence 1781, XV, 330 ff.

[17] Amari, *Diplomi*, pp. 372–3 (Ser. II, doc. 46).

treaty, and to return to Florence with one copy of the resulting articles authenticated by the sultan, and to leave a copy of these with the Florentine consul for the information of the merchants (" Harai anchora con questa commissione una nota di consultatione si fece qui sopra certi capitoli come vedrai: ingegnera'ti di obtenere dalla excellentia del soldano tutte quelle chose o quello più che potrai che sono scripte in quella nota, et arrecherai in qua la copia de' capitoli tutti insieme con questi agiunti autentichati secondo la forma loro, et un'altra copia lascerai nelle mani del consolo per la cagione sopradetta ").

Information on the progress of the embassy after November 1488 is meagre. In a letter from Naples, dated 17 January 1489, Della Stufa wrote to Lorenzo de' Medici of difficulties in loading a consignment of weapons for the purchase of which Malfota had got Papal permission during their visit to Rome after leaving Florence. Owing to these complications the envoy expected their departure to be delayed until at least 6 February.[18] In a second letter, from Messina and dated 22 April 1489, he described to Lorenzo further difficulties over the weapons, due to a naval blockade in the Straits, his last message until after his arrival in Egypt.[19]

The Florentine mission to Cairo coincided with the presence there of a Venetian embassy led by Piero Diedo and Marco Malipiero to negotiate the transfer of Cyprus from the House of Lusignan to the Republic.[20] The preoccupation of both Sultan Ḳā'itbāy and the dragoman Taghrīberdī with what was without question more pressing business may in part have accounted for the pathetic letter which Della Stufa wrote to Lorenzo from Cairo, dated 14 November 1489. There he describes his dependence upon the whim of the Sultan and his helplessness without the intercession of the dragoman (" Et non mi posso dispacciare et non ne facenda nessuna salvo che havere licenza da quello Gloriosissimo Signor Soldano . . . et non si puo andare senza il turcimanno et quello gran turcimanno è primo idolo de Veniziani et per questo facto io mi sto qui a perdere tempo ") ; of his desertion by Malfota (" Il nostro magnifico Malfott poi che m'ebbe condotto qua non lo mai potuto rivedere et ha seminato tanto male che non

---

[18] ASF, Archivio Mediceo avanti il Principato, filza 49, no. 120. For the Papal ban on shipment to the Levant of weapons and other strategic materials, see Heyd, *Commerce*, II, 23 ff.

[19] ASF, Archivio Mediceo avanti il Principato, filza 32, no. 178. In both these letters Malfota's preference for commerce over diplomacy is conspicuous.

[20] In a letter to the Doge, dated 24 November 1489, Piero Diedo noted the arrival of the Florentine ambassador, Archivio di Stato di Venezia, Archivio Proprio Egitto I, fols. 13–14 ; and see the references in " A Mamluk ambassador to Venice ", *BSOAS*, 1963, pp. 508–9.

si potrebbe dire piu ") ; of a lack of sympathy with the cause of Florentine merchants (" Et poi ha detto et dice che la Signoria non ha galee ne ne puo fare mandare qua et che noi habiamo dilegiato quello Gloriosissimo Signor Soldan et infinite altre chose vituperose ") ; and finally, that he had no money (" Non so che altro dirmi salvo che io sto malissimo et sanza danari et che sono le spese grande ").[21]

But Florentine prospects were not quite so bleak as the envoy made out. In a letter dated four days after Della Stufa's, 24 Dhu'l-Ḥijja 894/18 November 1489, Qā'itbāy reported to Lorenzo that he had acknowledged and granted the petition (*kitābat al-fuṣūl*) of his envoy and had ordered the writing of commercial privileges (*al-shurūṭ*) for them.[22] According to Diedo's letter cited above Luigi della Stufa must have returned to Alexandria from Cairo on 24 November ; at the end of the month he sailed from there to Modon aboard a Venetian galley, accompanied by a Papal envoy to Egypt on his way home and a Mamlūk embassy to the Pope.[23] Though the first leg of the journey had required only six days, Della Stufa wrote again to Lorenzo on 19 December from Corfu to describe a very tempestuous voyage and to enclose a list of the Sultan's gifts for the Florentine ruler.[24] According to Venetian records the galley bearing Della Stufa and the envoys bound for Rome arrived in Venice on 19 January 1490, approximately fourteen months after the embassy's departure from Florence.[25]

II

In the Signoria's instructions to Luigi della Stufa there are references to four documents : [26]

1. The draft treaty brought to Florence by Malfota (" E' capitoli i quali ne portò per parte della sua excellentia ").

---

[21] ASF, Archivio Mediceo avanti il Principato, filza 41, no. 384.

[22] Amari, *Diplomi*, pp. 181–3 (Ser. I, doc. 39).

[23] ASF, Archivio Mediceo avanti il Principato, filza 41, no. 401. The Mamlūk embassy to Rome was in connexion with Jem, the son of the Ottoman Sultan Meḥemmed II, see *Encyclopaedia of Islam*, second ed. s.v. *Djem*, especially the references there to L. Thuasne, *Djem-Sultan*, pp. 174–6, 199, 254, 262, 337 ; and more recently F. Babinger, *Spätmittelalterliche fränkische Briefschaften aus dem grossherrlichen Seraj zu Stambul*, München 1963, pp. 29, 42–8 (Italian translation in *Archivo Storico Italiano* 1963, pp. 349–56). Both Malfota and Luigi della Stufa could have carried verbal instructions relating to Jem, though in neither case does it appear to have been the envoy's principal mission. I am indebted to Dr. V. L. Ménage for the references to the works of Thuasne and Babinger.

[24] ASF, Archivio Mediceo avanti il Principato, filza 41, no. 407.

[25] ASV, Consiglio di Dieci, Misti, filza 3, no. 233.

[26] See above, p. 43, n. 17.

2. A copy of these authenticated by the Signoria (" Uno instrumento in forma valida sottoscripto come noi usiamo ").

3. A list of modifications to them (" Una nota di consultatione si fece qui sopra certi capitoli ").

4. The final treaty authenticated by the Sultan, in two copies: one for the Signoria and one for the Florentine consul in Alexandria (" la copia de' capitoli tutti insieme con questi agiunti autentichati secondo la forma loro, et un'altra copia lascerai nelle mani del consolo per la cagione sopradetta ").

The first document, undated, is a copy in Italian of commercial privileges probably granted by the Sultan to Paolo da Colle in 1486.[27] It is the earliest example of a Florentine treaty with the Mamlūk Sultan which is based upon a Venetian paradigm.[28] It consists of two parts: the first contains 29 articles pertaining to commerce in Syria (" Circa il traffico di Damascho et Baruti "), and the second 11 articles in addition to those copied from the Venetian privileges (" Agiunti dipoi per nostra adimanda ultra quelli de' Vinitiani "). In the upper left margin of the first folio of the document appears the observation that these articles were a draft for those subsequently obtained by Della Stufa (" Conceptione dei capitoli rifati per M. Luigi della Stufa ").[29] Since the Florentine treaty in its final form has principally to do with commerce in Alexandria mention in the heading of " Damascus and Beirut " can almost certainly be ascribed to carelessness in the adaptation of the Venetian paradigm.

The second document mentioned in Della Stufa's instructions is more difficult to identify. In a note to the printed edition of Lorenzo's letter to the Sultan, dated 10 June 1488, we learn of a treaty concluded between the Republic of Florence and the Mamlūk Sultan, sealed and signed by Bartolomeo Scala, dated 20 November 1488, and deposited in a Florentine museum (" In museo nostro Pacta inter Flor. Remp. dictumque Sultanum inita autographa adservantur sigillo Reip. signata, ac subscripta a celebri Barpth. Scala die XX Nov. MCCCCLXXXVIII, cum hoc titulo: Capituli intra lo Illustrissimo Sig. Soldano e la excelsa Signoria di

[27] Amari's conjectural date (Ser. II, doc. 45) of 1487–88 is probably correct, though according to his dating of the preceding document in his collection (*Diplomi*, pp. 361–2, Ser. II, doc. 44, and p. 485), the draft treaty ought to have been dated 1481 (see Heyd, *Commerce* II, 488, n. 4).

[28] See above, p. 42, n. 12.

[29] This marginal note, in a later hand, provides evidence of a connexion between this document and the embassy of Della Stufa, a link substantiated by an examination of the contents of the treaty, as will be shown below. For the technical term *conceptione*, see H. Bresslau, *Handbuch der Urkundenlehre*, Berlin, 1931, I, 88.

Firenze ").[30] While from this note it could be inferred that a commercial treaty had been finally concluded between the two rulers on 20 November 1488, a fortunate discovery has shown the document in question to be merely a further step in the negotiations begun by Paolo da Colle in 1486. At the Biblioteca Nazionale in Florence (Fondo Del Furia, cod. no. 49) is a copy of a document which fits in every particular the description cited above, including Scala's signature accompanied by the motto " Priores libertatis et vexillifer iustitia populi Florentini ". It consists of 21 folios (31·5 × 21·5 cm.) containing: the " capitoli " brought by Malfota to Florence (fols. 2r–17r), four additional articles (fols. 17r–18r), and finally, the additions and emendations to Malfota's treaty presented to the Signoria by a group of Florentine merchants shortly after the arrival of the Egyptian envoy in Florence (fols. 18v–20r).[31] The significance of the document lies in the relationship which it indicates between Malfota's draft treaty, the merchants' petition, and the embassy of Luigi della Stufa; though it is likely that the document in the Biblioteca Nazionale is a copy and not the original of the " instrumento " mentioned in Della Stufa's instructions.

The third document, like the first undated, is a petition containing 32 requests which the Signoria instructed Della Stufa to put to the Sultan.[32] Its contents (" domande ") are modifications of the articles in the second document, described above, and became, almost article for article, the basis for the final treaty obtained by Della Stufa from the Sultan in Cairo.[33]

The fourth document mentioned in the Florentine envoy's instructions is the Sultan's commercial privilege itself, of which two copies were to be requested. The history of this document is rather confused. In Buonazia's catalogue of the Arabic manuscripts in the Biblioteca Nazionale entry

---

[30] A. M. Bandini, *Collectio veterum*, footnote, p. 12. Bartolomeo Scala was head of the Prima Cancelleria from 1464–94, 1494–97, see D. Marzi, *La cancelleria della Repubblica di Firenze*, Rocca San Casciano, 1910, p. 514.

[31] The merchants' petition is published separately in Amari, *Diplomi*, pp. 361–2 (Ser. II, doc. 44) and dated 27 November 1481 (see above, p. 46, n. 27). The document, preserved in ASF, bears unmistakably the date 27 November 1487, and is clearly based on a Venetian paradigm, to which in fact the first five emendations refer, while the next three refer to Malfota's " capitoli " and the last two are simply additions. For the Venetian document in question see Amari, op. cit., pp. 347–59 (Ser. II, doc. 42), and above, p. 42, n. 12.

[32] Amari, *Diplomi*, pp. 374–81 (Ser. II, doc. 47).

[33] For the role of the petition in treaty negotiations and the manner in which it was employed in drafting the final form, see my article " A Moroccan amir's commercial treaty with Venice of the year 913/1508 ", *BSOAS*, 1962, p. 466, notes 2, 6.

no. 72 is a commercial treaty concluded between the Republic of Florence and the Mamlūk Sultan, dated 6 Dhu'l-Ḥijja 894/31 October 1489[34]. The manuscript (Fondo Del Furia, cod. no. 50) contains 21 folios (29·7 × 21 cm.), fols. 8–1 in Arabic, fols. 9–17 in Italian, the remainder blank. The Arabic is clearly that of an amateur hand (see Plate XX) and the text full of errors, some of which the copyist noticed and struck out. In addition to instances of marginal and interlinear commentary referring to specific words in the text there are two notes of some interest for the documentation of Della Stufa's embassy. The first of these, in Italian at the bottom of folio 7v, is a reference to the footnote in the printed edition of Lorenzo's letter to the Sultan, dated 10 June 1488, thus indicating that the copyist had some knowledge of the historical background to his work.[35] The second note, in Arabic at the end of the text on folio 1r, informs us that the original document, from which the present manuscript was copied, bearing the seal of Francesco I, Duke of Lorraine, Grand Duke of Tuscany and Emperor, will be found in the Biblioteca Laurenziana, to which it had been transferred from the Biblioteca Imperiale Palatina :

والختم مكتبة فرنشيسكو الاول دوكا دي لورينا غران دوكا دي توسكانا يمبراتور
مكتبة يمبريالى پالاتينو ثم انتقل الى مكتبة لللاورنسيانية

Before turning to the Laurenziana document, which represents the last step in the negotiations whose course we have been tracing, there are three observations to be made about the Italian translation which accompanies the Arabic copy of the treaty in the Biblioteca Nazionale. On folio 18r the translator, who may also have been the copyist,[36] has begun a list of words of Arabic origin, together with their transliterations and Italian translations, which occur in the commercial vocabularies of both languages. On folio 17r a marginal note, possibly a later insertion, refers to the original Arabic document in the Laurenziana. Finally, a note at the top of folio 9r, which may also be a later insertion, mentions yet

---

[34] L. Buonazia, *Catalogo dei codici arabi della biblioteca nazionale di Firenze,* Florence, 1878, p. 36 : " Serie del Furia 49 (sic). Cartaceo, di fogli 8, alto 13c (sic), largo 21c, a 15–23 linee ; naskhi grande del secolo XVIII." Buonazia corrected the obvious error in the date, from 294 to 894 (" errato certo nel copiare "), but restricted his notice to the Arabic folios of the manuscript. Notwithstanding his conjecture there is no evidence in either Arabic or Italian parts of the manuscript from which the date or the identity of the copyist/translator might be inferred.

[35] See above, p. 47, n. 30.

[36] In this respect it is worth noting that the date is correctly given in the translation as " il dì 6 del Mese Del Hage Anno 894 ".

another Italian translation of the treaty, published in Pagnini, *Della Decima*, II, 213–7.[37]

This second translation, of which only the version in Pagnini appears to be extant, is a curious document. It is a less faithful rendering than the translation in the Biblioteca Nazionale: where one article has been omitted in the latter, two are missing here; errors are frequent throughout, including the date (" 6 mensis Moharra, anno Egira 894 ") and the name of the Sultan.[38] There is nothing in the document to indicate when or where the translation was made: on somewhat questionable grounds Amari has suggested Stephanus Assemani (1708–82), thus making the work a product of antiquarian interest rather than a matter of juridical and practical moment.[39]

The original Arabic treaty granted by Sultan Qā'itbāy to Luigi della Stufa on 6 Dhu'l-Ḥijja 894/31 October 1489, is not in the Florentine State Archives but, as we have seen, in the Biblioteca Mediceo-Laurenziana.[40] How it came to be there is not clear. As was the practice for commercial privileges, the form employed in the Mamlūk chancery for this document was the *marsūm*, addressed not to the Florentines but to members of the Egyptian administration whose task it was to deal with European merchants. Of the several copies of the document which must have been made for the officers in Alexandria and the Syrian ports it is not unlikely that Della Stufa asked for and got two, as he had been instructed to do. Of these he left one with the Florentine consul in Alexandria, and brought the other with him to Florence, where it was probably of less value as a state-paper than the Italian documents upon which, as we have seen, it was based. Della Stufa's embassy was an important move in the course of commercial relations between Egypt and Florence. When Sultan Qānṣūh al-Ghawrī renewed the Florentine commercial privileges in 911/1506, it was the treaty of 894/1489 to which he referred.[41]

---

[37] Pagnini Dal Ventura, *Della Decima e delle altre gravezze, della moneta, e della mercatura dei Fiorentini fino al secolo XVI*, Lisbon-Lucca, 1775–76; reprinted, with emendations, by Amari, *Diplomi*, pp. 382–6 (Ser. II, doc. 48).

[38] The sultan's name was corrected by Amari, op. cit., p. 486, and his conjecture as to the date is now shown to have been correct.

[39] Amari, loc. cit.

[40] Listed as Or. 455 A, which also contains a second Mamlūk-Florentine commercial treaty, dated 902/1497, of which an edition is included in my study now in preparation, cited above, p. 42, n. 12. These documents were probably transferred from the Palatina to the Laurenziana in July 1771, cf. G. Gabrieli, *Manoscritti e carte orientali nelle biblioteche e negli archivi d'Italia*, Florence 1930, p. 15.

[41] See Amari, *Diplomi*, pp. 214–7 (Ser. I, doc. 42); other privileges had meanwhile been granted in 901/1496 (date uncertain) and 902/1497.

Following is a list of the documents in Florence related to the commercial treaty of 894/1489 and a schema of their relationship to one another:

A. Malfota's draft treaty, undated (Amari, *Diplomi*, pp. 363–71, Ser. II, doc. 45).

B. Emendations proposed by Florentine merchants, dated 27 November 1487 (Amari, *Diplomi*, pp. 361–2, Ser. II, doc. 44).

C. Luigi della Stufa's instructions, dated 10 November 1488 (Amari, *Diplomi*, pp. 372–3, Ser. II, doc. 46).

D. Authenticated copy of Malfota's draft treaty together with the merchant's proposed emendations and four additional articles, dated 20 November 1488 (Biblioteca Nazionale, Fondo del Furia, cod. 49).

E. Della Stufa's petition to the Sultan, undated (Amari, *Diplomi*, pp. 374–81, Ser. II, doc. 47).

F. Original Arabic treaty, dated 6 Dhu'l-Ḥijja 894/31 October 1489 (Biblioteca Mediceo-Laurenziana, Or. 455 A).

G. Italian translation of Document F, dated 6 Muḥarram 894/10 December 1488 (Pagnini, *Della Decima* II, 213–7; Amari, *Diplomi*, pp. 382–6, Ser. II, doc. 48).

H. Arabic transcription of Document F, dated 6 Dhu'l-Ḥijja 294 = 894/31 October 1489 (Biblioteca Nazionale, Fondo del Furia, cod. 50).

J. Italian translation of Document H, dated 6 Dhu'l-Ḥijja 894/31 October 1489 (Biblioteca Nazionale Fondo del Furia, cod. 50).

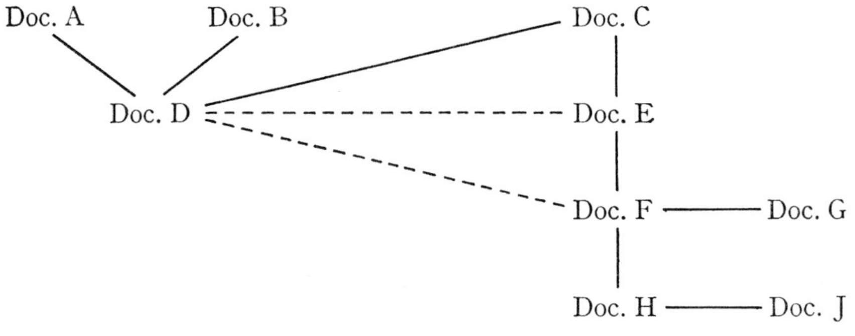

The Arabic text of the original treaty (Document F) is offered here, with an English translation and commentary. The document is a scroll of heavy yellowish paper with no watermark, 16·5 cm. wide and 586 cm. long. It consists of 26 pieces each approximately 24 cm. long pasted together with overlapping joints of about 0·5 cm. The top piece, which is outside when the document is rolled, is somewhat worn; it contains no writing but has two seals: of the House of Lorraine and of the Biblioteca Mediceo-Laurenziana. Except for the end of the last piece, which is also slightly frayed, the roll is well-preserved, showing only occasional brownish flecks towards the edges. The document is contained when rolled in a sheath of light paper, cut to fit the width and bearing the Habsburg seal in black wax. On this covering, which is of European origin and was probably designed to preserve the document in its place of storage, is written, in three different hands:

Trattato di commercio fra i Fiorentini col Soldano di Egitto.

A.

La sua traduzione esatta si vede al numero XII.

Questa non si è trovata.

The writing, in black ink and contained in 268 lines, begins 1 cm. below the paste-joint between the first and second pieces. For the first seven lines, about 1 cm. apart, there is a regular right margin of 1·5 cm. and an irregular left margin of about 1 cm., the seven lines covering rather less than half the second piece (Plate XXI). The remainder of the second and all of the third piece is blank. Just below the paste-joint between the third and fourth pieces are two lines, with a right margin of 4·5 cm. The next line is 3 cm. from the bottom edge of that piece, the space between being filled by the sign manual of Qā'itbāy, which is 15 cm. high and 10·5 cm. wide (Plate XXII). Thereafter follows the remainder of the protocol, 17 lines in all including the sign manual, with a regular right margin of about 4·5 cm. and an irregular left margin of 0·5–1 cm. (Plates XXIII–XXVI). Towards the left margin the writing inclines slightly upwards, and the lines are separated by regular intervals of 6 cm. The actual text of the document begins with the word *faṣl* in line 25, with thereafter a right margin of 3–4 cm. and a left margin of 0·5–1 cm., and an interval of 1 cm. between the lines. The whole text consists of 32 such *fuṣūl*, written in 232 lines. The concluding formulae revert to the dimensions of the protocol given above, and consist of 12 lines of which the last seven are nearly centred on the paper, the last line being at the end of the roll (Plates XXVII–XXIX), where the seals of Lorraine and Laurenziana again appear.

TEXT

1 الاسم الشريف   بما رسم به

مرسُوم شَرِيف لكل واقف عليه ومستمعه وناظر اليه من جميع النواب

والحكام وولاة امور الاسلام والنظار والمباشرين والمتصرفين

بممالكنا الشريفة الاسلامية وثغر الاسكندرية المحروس والمين

5 والسواحل اعزّهم الله تعالى بان يتقدموا باعتماد ما تضمنه هذا

المرسُوم الشريف من الفصُول المشرُوحة فيه والعمل بها وعدَم

الخروج عن شىء منها   على ما شرح فيه

بسم الله الرحمن الرحيم

رُسم بالامر الشريف العَالي المولوي

10 قايتبَاى

السلطانى الملكى الاشرفى السَيفى

اعلاه الله تعالى وشرفه وانفَذَهُ وصرفه ان يُسْطَّر

هَذا المرسُوم الشريف الى كل واقف عليه ومستعمه وناظر

اليه من جميع النواب والحكام وولاة امور الاسلام

15 والنظار والمباشرين والمتصرفين بممالكنا الشريفَة

الاسلامية وثغر الاسكندرية المحروُس والمين والسواحل

اعزّهم الله تعالى نوضّح لعلمهم ان المحتشم لويز دلصتوفا قاصد

حضرة الملك المحتشم حاكم الفرنتيين حضر الى ابوابنا الشريفة

وتمثل بمواقفنا المعظمة وأنهى الينا على لسان مُرسله ما

20 يتعلق بطائفة الفرنتيين وتجارهم من الشروط الصادرة

من المُلُوك السالفة وسُوال صدقاتنا الشرِيفة تجديد مرسُوم

شريف بذلك والعمل بما شرح فيها من الفُصُول فرسمنا بذلك

وسُطّرت الفُصُول المشروحة ادناه إجابة لما سأل فيه

ليكون العمل بها وعدَم الخروج عنها وهي

25 فصل   I

أنهى لويز القاصد المذكور ومن معه من التجار الفرنتيين ان مراكبهم منها

مُربع واغربة وطرائد وغير ذلك وسألوا صدقاتنا الشريفة

انه اذا حضرت الى مينا من المين الاسلاميّة او سَاحلٍ من السواحِل
او ثغر من الثغور الاسلامية مركب من المراكب المذكورة وبها
30 وكلائهم وبضائعهم وأقامُوا بما جرت به عادتهم من الحقوق الديوانية
لا يتعرض اليهم احدٌ بعد ذلك ببلص ولا يُجدّد عليهم حَوَادث
لا فى البر ولا فى البحر لا فى الثغر السكندرى المحروُس ولا فى غيره من
الثغور ولا يعارضهم احد بغير طريق أُجيبُوا الى ذلك ورسمنا به
ورسمنا به [1]

II فصل

35 سأل المذكورون ان احداً من تجار الفرنتيين او من جماعتهم
اذا حضر الى الثغر السكندرى المحروس او غيره من الثغور الاسلامية
ونزل ببضاعته من جوخ او حرير او صابون او زيت او بندق
او كُحل او كبريت او مرجان او غير ذلك من الاصناف يكون
المُحضِر بذلك امنا على نفسِه وبضاعته وان يبيع لمن يختار
40 بالنقد او بالقياض ولا يتعرض اليه احدٌ ولا يكلفه الى الدرهم
الواحد اجيبوا باجرائهم على جارى عادتهم فى ذلك
ورسمنا به

III فصل

أنهى المذكورون لمواقفنا الشريفة ان قبل هذا التاريخ اذا حضر
45 لتجار الفرنتيين بضاعة الى الثغر السكندرى المحروس يفتحها المباشرون
بالخمس ويفتشونها ويصير كل واحدٍ منهم ياخذ منها شيئاً ويقول
انا اشتريه ويُعطل المباشر اشغالهم وينقص بضاعتهم ويعوقها
عليهم حتى يشترى منها وسَـألوا صدقاتنا الشريفة انه اذا
حضر احد من تجار الفرنتيين او وكلائهم ببضاعة الى الثغر السكندرى
50 لا احد من النايب ولا من المباشرين ولا من جمـاعتهم ياخذ بضاعتهم
بغَير رضآئهم وتمكين المذكورين من اخذ بضاعتهم وان يخزنونها
فى مخازنهم او فى فنادقهم ويحضر المباشرون ويعلّدوا العدّة ويقبنوا

---

[1] Sic; the second *wa-rasamnā bihi* is in the same line as *faṣl*.

حتى لا يحصل تفريط للديوان فى شىء من ذلك اجيبوا الى ذلك ورسمنا به

IV فصل

سأل المذكورون صدقاتنا الشريفة انه اذا حضرت البضائع المتعلقة بالفرنتيين ودخلوا بها المخازن والفنادق ومضى ثلاثة ايام ولم يحضر المباشرون من الديوان لاخذ العدّة والقبانة وتعطل حالهم من تأخير المباشرين المذكورين يطالعوا النايب بالمكان الذين هم به بذلك ويقومُون بما جرت به العادة فى ذلك من المَصَاريف وتوضع تحت يد النائب وحيث اقاموا بذلك على جارى عادتهم والمانع من تأخير المباشرين يمكنوا من بضائعهم ولا يحدث عليهم شىء خارج عن عادتهم اجيبوا الى ما سألوه من ذلك ورسمنا به

V فصل

سأل المذكورون صدقاتنا الشريفة انه اذا حضر اليهم قطارة الى الثغر السكندرى المحروس او ثغر من الثغور الاسلامية وأُخِذ اشرفى فى كل برميل على العَادة لا احد يبلصهم ولا يكلفهم الى الدرهم زايدا عن العادة أُجيبُوا بان يبيعوا ذلك لتاجر الذخيرة الشريفة بالثغر السكندرى على جارى العادة فى ذلك

VI فصل

سأل المذكُورون صدقاتنا الشريفة انه اذا حضر جماعة الفرنتيين الثغر السكندرى المحرُوس او الى ثغر من الثغور الاسلامية وحضرُوا ببضاعتهم الى فندقهم او مخزنهم يبيعون بضاعتهم بالقياض او بالنقد لمن يختاروه وبَعد ذلك يقوم المذكورون للديوان الشريف باربعة عشر دينار[2] فى المائة دينار وان يوزنوا بضاعة بقيمة ذلك او نقداً من غير السمسرة والتراجمة واذا اقامُوا بذلك وتاخر عندهم بضاعة او لم يبيعوا بضاعتهم ووزنوا ما عليهم من ذلك واختارُوا ان يُسَافروا ببضاعتهم الى القاهرة المحروسة لا يتعرض اليهم احد حيث وزنوا ما هو

---

[2] For *dīnāran*.

عليهم مما جرت العادة فى ذلك بضاعة [3] وذلك خارج عن القطارة لا من النواب ولا من الحكّام ولا من المباشرين واذا وزنوا الاربعة عشر دينار [2] فى المائة دينار يكون ذلك بضاعة [3] من سآئر ما معهم من الاصناف بالسويّة اجيبُوا عن ذلك باجرآئهم على جارى العادة فى ذلك ورسمنا به من غير احداث حادث

VII فصل

سأل المذكورون انه اذا وقع بيع بين تاجر فرنتيّ وبين المسلمين فى بضاعة من البضائع بعد النظر والتقليب ونزل ذلك فى ديوان القبان لا احد من المسلمين ولا تجار الفرنتيين يقلب شيئاً على شىء ولا يردّ البيع لا بحيلة ولا بشىء اجيبوا عن ذلك الّا بطريق شرعى ورسمنا به

VIII فصل

سألوا صدقاتنا الشريفة انه اذا كان لاحدٍ من التجار الفرنتيين قرضاً [4] على احدٍ من مباشرين الديوان [5] وحضرت بضاعة للتاجِر الذى لهُ القرض وطّلب قرضه ممن هو عليه يُدفَع له قرضه على الوجه الشرعى ولا يحتج عليه بأمر البضاعة ولا بغيرها ويُودي القرض اجيبُوا الى ذلك ورسمنا به

IX فصل

سأل المذكورون صدقاتنا الشريفة انه اذا هلك احد من التجار الفرنتيين بثغر الاسكندرية او غيره وكان كتب وصية لا يعارض فيها احدٌ من المسلمين ولا غيرهم وان وضع بضاعته تحت يد من يختار ويُوصّي من يختار لا يُعارَض الوصي بطريق من الطرق ولا يكلّف لنواب ولا لحكام ولا لمباشرين حتى ولا الدرهم الواحد واذا هلك عن غير وصيّةٍ يكون بضاعته وموجوده جميعه تحت يد قنصل الفرنتيين المذكورين الى حين يحضر المستحقون لميراثه واذا كان لاحدٍ من التجار المذكورين وكيل او قاصد وعلى يده بضاعته وحضر بها الى ثغر من

[3] For *tilka 'l-baḍā'a*.

[4] Sic; presumably for *qarḍ*^{un}.

[5] For *mubāshirī 'l-dīwān*.

الثغور الاسلامية وتصرف فى البضاعة ببيع او كان عليه دين وأوفى من ذلك دينه ثم هلك وحضر بعد ذلك التاجر صاحب البضاعة الى الثغر الذى هلك فيه الوكيل المذكور او القاصد واثبت ان ذلك عين رجله لا يعارضه فيه احدٌ وياخذ بضاعته ممن اخذها من الهالك من غير معارضة لهُ فى ذلك على حكم الشريعة المطهرة بالطريق الشرعى اجيبوا الى ذلك ورسمنا به

X فصل

سأل المذكورون صدقاتنا الشريفة بروز امرنا الشريف انه اذا لم يُقطع سعر فى البهار او غيره من البضائع وحضر تاجر من تجارهم واراد البيع والشراء لا يُعارضه احد من المسلمين ولا غيرهم من خلق الله تعالى اجيبوا باجرائهم فى ذلك على ما جرت به العادة ورسمنا بذلك

XI فصل

سأل المذكورون صدقاتنا الشريفة بروز امرنا الشريف ان احداً من المسلمين لا يشتكى احداً من تجار الفرنتيين الا من حاكم الثغر الذى هو به واذا حضر الشاكى قدام نائب الثغر وحرر الامر بينهما بالطريق الشرعى ولم ينفصل امرهم يُحمَل مع غريمه الى ابوابنا الشريفة اجيبُوا الى ما سالوه من ذلك ورسمنا به

XII فصل

سأل المذكورون انه اذا حضر قنصل من طائفة الفرنتيين الى الثغر السكندرى المحروس او الى ثغر من الثغور الاسلامية يجرى على عادة قنصل البنادقة من المعلوم والجامكية والحقوق الجارى بها العادة اجيبوا الى ذلك اجرآ على العادة ورسمنا به

XIII فصل

سأل المذكورون صدقاتنا الشريفة بروز امرنا الشريف ان احدا من تجار الفرنتيين اذا حضر الى مينا بيروت وغيرها وقصد البيع والشراء لا يعارضه احدٌ ويُجرى على جارى عادة البنادقة فى بيعهم وشرائهم وان كان تجار الفرنتيين تشترى قِليا من بيروت او من دمشق المحروسَة يقومُون بما يقوم به طائفة البنادقة من غير

زايد على ذلك اجيبُوا الى ذلك ورسمنا به

XIV فصل

سأل المذكورون صدقاتنا الشريفة بروز امرنا الشريف انه اذا كان بين طائفة الفرنتيين ضراب او شرور او لاحدٍ منهم حقٌ على احد من طايفته لا يحكم بينهما احد من النواب ولا من الحكام ولا من التجار الا قنصل طائفتهم على ما جرت به عادتهم او برضاهم بذلك اجيبُوا الى ذلك ورسمنا به

XV فصل

أنهى المذكورون ان جرت عادتهم اذا قَصَد احد منهم السفر من بلادٍ الى بلادٍ وقصد تغيير حليته وان يلبس ملبوُس المماليك خوفا من الطمع فى جانبهم فى الطرقات لا يتعرض اليهم احد ولا يتعرض لاكلهم ولا لشربهم ولا يكلفهم الى الدرهم الفرد بسبب ذلك اجيبوا باجرائهم فى ذلك على عادتهم من غير احداث حادث ورسمنا به

XVI فصل

سأل المذكورون صدقاتنا الشريفة بروز امرنا الشريف ان احداً من تجار الفرنتيين اذا حضر الى السواحل الاسلامية او الى الثغور الاسلامية فى مراكب مربعة او غيرها وقصد اصلاح المركب الذى حضر فيه واحتاج الى شرآء ما يتعلق بذلك من جميع الاصناف يُمكن من ذلك ولا يُعَارض فيه جملة كافة بغير طريق ولا وجه اجيبوا الى ذلك ورسمنا به

XVII فصل

سألوا صدقاتنا الشريفة بروز امرنا الشريف انه اذا حضر مراكب[6] من مراكب الفرنتيين الى البلاد الاسلامية بغير بضاعة ومع من بها ما يتعلق بهم من اكلهم وشُربهم لا يعارضهم احدٌ ولا يكلفهم الى الدرهم الفرد بغير طريق اجيبُوا الى ذلك ورسمنا به

XVIII فصل

سألوا صدقاتنا الشريفة بروز امرنا الشريف انه اذا كان على احد من تجارهم او من طائفتهم وعليه حقوق شرعية لاحدٍ من

[6] For *markab* ?

المسلمين او كان بينهما ضراب او مشاجرة لا يُلزَم غيره من طائفته
وابنآ جنسه بذلك حتى ولا الابن بالاب ولا الاب بالابن
الا بطريق شرعى   اجيبوا الى ذلك ورسمنا به

XIX فصل

سألوا صدقاتنا الشريفة بروز امرنا الشريف ان احداً من
تجار الفرنتيين اذا اراد سَفَرَ سعاة او قصاد بكتبهم واشغالهم
لاحدٍ لا يُعارضه احد ولا يشوش عليه ولا يعوقه ولا يفتح
كتبهم اجيبوا باجرآئهم فى ذلك على ما جرت به العادة ورسمنا به

XX فصل

سأل المذكورون صدقاتنا الشريفة بروز امرنا الشريف انه
كان لاحد من تجار الفرنتيين تعلقات او حقوق شرعية على احدٍ
من المسلمين ولم يُحضره الحاكم ليقوم بما عليه من الحق وامتنع عن اعطآ
الحق بالطريق الشرعى وقصد التاجر الفرنتى الحضور الى خدمة
ابوابنا الشريفة بسَبَب ذلك لا يعارضه نايب ولا احد من الحكام
ولا تاجر ويُمكَّن من الحضور من غير ان يتكلف الى الدرهم الفرد ليُخلص
حقه على الوجه الشرعى   اجيبوا الى ذلك ورسمنا به

XXI فصل

سأل المذكورون صدقاتنا الشريفة بروز امرنا الشريف ان احدا من
تجار المسلمين اذا عمل البيع مع احد من تجار الفرنتيين ووقع بينهما
قياض ببهار او غيره من البضائع وادعى احد غير البايع ان ذلك
بضاعته فلا يُقبل منه ولا يوخذ من البضائع شىء بعد دخول
ذلك فى ديوان القبان ولا يعارضه احد فى ذلك الا بطريق شرعى
اجيبوا باجرآء الامر فى ذلك على ما جرت به عادة التجار

XXII فصل

سألوا صدقاتنا الشريفة بُروز امرنا الشريف ان طائفة الفرنتيين
اذا أحضُروا ذهباً طيباً خالصاً يصرفوه على حكم ذهب
البنادقة   اجيبوا الى ذلك ورسمنا به

XXIII فصل

أنهى المذكورون ان تجار الفرنتيين اذا حضروا الى الثغر السكندرى

المحروس او الى ثغر من الثغور ببضاعةٍ واقاموا بما عليهم من الحقوق الديوانية واستقر غير المتكلم على الجهات وتغير المباشرون والمتحدثون فى الديوان لا يقوم احد من التجار الفرنتيين بما اقام به ثانياً وسألوا انه اذا تغير احد من المباشرين والمتحدثين لا يطلب منهم ذلك ثانى مرّة اجيبوا بالاجرآء فى ذلك على ما جرت به العادة حيث كان ذلك عن قرب عهدٍ فى المدّة ورسمنا بذلك

XXIV فصل

سأل المذكورون صدقاتنا الشريفة بروز امرنا الشريف اذا قصد احد من تجارهم/توجهه/[7] الى بلاده ببهار من جميع الاصناف من الثغر السكندرى المحرُوس او غيره من الثغور بعد قيامه بما عليه من الحقوق الديوانية يمكن من السفر ولا يعارضه احد فى ذلك حيث لم يكن عليه تبعة اخرى ولا طريق اجيبوا الى ذلك ورسمنا به

XXV فصل

سألوا صدقاتنا الشريفة بروز امرنا الشريف انه اذا قصد احد من تجارهم التوجه الى بلاده فى مراكبهم او فى مراكب غير طائفتهم لا يعارضه احدٌ فى شىء من غلمانه ولا فى اكله ولا شربه ولا فرشه ولا لبيسه ولا شىء من حاله ولا يكلف بسَبَب ذلك بغير طريق
اجيبوا الى ذلك ورسمنا به

XXVI فصل

سألوا صدقاتنا الشريفة بروز امرنا الشريف بانه اذا كان احدٌ من طائفة الفرنج من اى جنس كان تعرض الى طائفة الفرنتيين فى البر او البحر واخذ لهم شيئا او حصل لهم منه تشويش او كان لَهُم عليه حقوق او ديون او دَعوى وحضروا الى البلاد الاسلامية يخلص الحاكم بالمكان الذى هم فيه حقهم واذا لم تَخلُص حقهم او كان مركب من مراكب الفرنتيين شوش على احدٍ يحملوا الى ابوابنا الشريفة ليخلص حق كل منهم على حكم الشرع الشريف
اجيبوا الى ذلك ورسمنا به

[7] Inserted between lines 198 and 199, above *ilā*.

XXVII فصل

سأل المذكورون صدقاتنا الشريفة بروز امرنا الشريف انه اذا وقع حساب بين احدٍ من تجار الفرنتيين وبين احدٍ من المسلمين وصدر بينهما براءة لا يرجع احد منهما يتقلب على احدٍ بعد ذلك الّا بطريق شرعى اجيبُوا الى ذلك ورسمنا به

XXVIII فصل

سأل المذكورون صدقاتنا الشريفة بروز امرنا الشريف بانه اذا حضر الى المين الاسلامية مركب للفرنتيين بثابوتٍ واقام بما تعين على ما به من الحقوق الديوانية بالمينا من جميع ما يلزمه لا يعارضه احدٌ ويمكن من السفر من غير كلفة على جارى عادة البنادقة فى ذلك وقاعدتهم اجيبوا الى ذلك ورسمنا به

XXIX فصل

سأل المذكورون صدقاتنا الشريفة ان يعين فندق بثغر الاسكندرية المحروس لقنصلهم ولتجارهم على العادة فى ذلك وكما هو لغيرهم من طوائف الفرنج اجيبُوا الى ذلك ورسمنا به

XXX فصل

سأل المذكورون صدقاتنا الشريفة ان التاجر من الفرنتيين اذا حضر الى ثغر الاسكندرية المحروس بما صحبته من البضائع وباع واشترى وقايض واقام بما عليه من العشور والحقوق الديوانيّة والمصاريف الجارى بها العادة وقصد التوجه من الثغر المحروس والسفر الى جهة بلاده لا يُعارضه الشاد بباب البحر ولا غيره بسبب شىء ياخذه زيادة على ما اقام به التاجر المذكور حتى ولا ما قيمته الدرهم الواحِد ابداً اجيبُوا الى ذلك ورسمنا به

XXXI فصل

سأل المذكورُون صدقاتنا الشريفة انه اذا حضر احد من الفرنتيين فى مركب لغير طائفته من اى جنس كان الى المين الاسلامية الثغر السكندرى وغيره وكان بها احدٌ من الفرنتيين

وعليه طلب من جهة حرامٍ او مفسَدةٍ او حقٍ لا يطلب به غيره من الفرنتيين ممن حضر فى المركب المذكور الّا ان كان ضامناً او كفيلاً   اجيبوا الى ذلك ورسمنا به

XXXII فصل

سأل المذكورون صدقاتنا الشريفة انه اذا حضر احد من تجار الفرنتيين الى الثغر السكندرى المحروس او غيره من المين الاسلامية وحضر اليه من يبتاع منه شيئا من بضائعه الواصلة صحبته يمكن من ذلك ولا يعارض التاجر الفرنتى بسبب ذلك حيث اقام بما عليه من العشور والحقوق الديوانية الجارى بها العادة   اجيبُوا الى ذلك ورسمنا به

ومرسُومنا لكل واقف عليه ان يتقدم باعتماد ما رسمنا به فى الفصُول المشرُوحة اعلاه والعمل بها وعدم الخروج عن شىء منها قولاً واحدا وامرا جازما فليُعتَمد هذا المرسُوم الشريف ويُعمل بحسبه ومقتضاه من غير عدُول عنه ولا خروج عن معناه والخط الشريف اعلاه الله تعالى اعلاه حجة فيه   ان شاء الله تعالى

فى سادس ذى الحجة الحرام
سنة اربع وتسعين وثمانمائة
حسب المرسوم الشريف
الحمد لله وحده وصلى الله على من لا نبى بعده
وحسبنا الله ونعم الوكيل
حر

TRANSLATION

The noble name—by which has been decreed a noble decree for all whom it may concern, who hear it and see it among the viceroys, magistrates, and officeholders of Islam, the inspectors, officials, and authorities of our noble Islamic provinces, the God-guarded port of Alexandria and the harbours and coasts, may God Almighty strengthen them: that they proceed on the basis of the articles contained and set out in this noble decree, to the execution of them, and the avoidance of any departure whatever from them, in accordance with what is here set out. (1)

In the name of God the Merciful the Compassionate.

It has been decreed by the noble command, the lofty, the lordly, the sultan, Al-Malik Al-Ashraf Sayf [al-Dīn] Qā'itbāy, may God Almighty elevate and ennoble it, and grant it effectiveness and power of disposition: that this noble decree be written to all whom it may concern, who hear it and see it among the viceroys, magistrates, and officeholders of Islam, the inspectors, officials, and authorities of our noble Islamic provinces, the God-guarded port of Alexandria and the harbours and coasts, may God Almighty strengthen them. We would bring to their attention that the honourable Luigi della Stufa, ambassador from his presence the honourable king, ruler of the Florentines (Lorenzo de' Medici), has arrived at our noble portals and appeared at our glorious station, and has informed us from him who sent him of the privileges issued by former kings which relate to the Florentine nation and their merchants, and has requested of our noble benevolence a renewal of the noble decree to that effect and the execution of the articles contained in it. So we have decreed that, and the articles are set out in writing below, in response to what he has requested: that they be executed and departures from them be avoided. And they are the following: (2)

I. The aforesaid ambassador Luigi and the Florentine merchants accompanying him have informed (us) that their ships include sailing vessels, galleys, cargo vessels, and others. And they have requested of our noble benevolence that when one of the aforesaid ships arrives at one of the Islamic harbours or coasts or ports with their agents and goods aboard, and they have paid their customary administrative dues, no one shall trouble them after that with extortion or impose innovations upon them, either ashore or at sea, either in the God-guarded port of Alexandria or in any other of the ports, nor shall anyone oppose them without due process. They have been answered in that and we hereby decree it. (3)

II. The aforesaid have requested that when one of the Florentine merchants or (one) of their community arrives at the God-guarded port of Alexandria or another of the Islamic ports and discharges his goods, such as cloth or silk or soap or olive oil or hazel nuts or antimony or sulphur or coral or other than that of such commodities, that the importer of those be secure in respect of his person and of his goods, and that he may sell for cash or by barter to whom he chooses, and no one shall trouble him nor extort from him even a single dirham. They have been answered according to their custom in that and we hereby decree it. (4)

III. The aforesaid have informed our noble station that prior to this date when goods arrived at the God-guarded port of Alexandria for Florentine merchants, the officials of the fifth would open them and inspect them, and each one would begin to take something from them, saying " I will buy it ". Thus the official impairs their business and damages their goods, holding them back to their (owners') disadvantage so that he can buy them. And they have requested of our noble benevolence that when one of the Florentine merchants or their agents brings goods to the port of Alexandria, no one such as the viceroy, nor the officials nor anyone of their (own) community shall take their goods without their consent, and (that) the aforesaid be permitted to take their goods and to store them in their warehouses or in their *funduqs*, while the officials are present to count and to weigh so that the dīwān suffer no loss in that. They have been answered in that and we hereby decree it. (5)

IV. The aforesaid have requested of our noble benevolence that when goods arrive belonging to the Florentines and they have put them in their warehouses and *funduqs*, and three days pass without the officials coming from the dīwān to take the count and weight, their circumstances being thus impaired by the delay of the aforesaid officials, they may inform the viceroy of the place(s) where they happen to be of that, and pay the customary expenses for that while (the goods) are deposited with the viceroy. And where they have paid that which is customary and delay by the officials has been prevented, they shall be allowed their goods, and nothing new imposed upon them beyond their custom. They have been answered in what they have requested in that respect and we hereby decree it. (6)

V. The aforesaid have requested of our noble benevolence that when syrup arrives for them at the God-guarded port of Alexandria or any other of the Islamic ports and an *ashrafī* has been taken for each cask according to the custom, no one shall extort from them nor oppress them for even a dirham more than the custom. They have been answered that they shall sell that (syrup) to the merchant of the Royal Stores in the port of Alexandria according to the custom in that respect. (7)

VI. The aforesaid have requested of our noble benevolence that when the Florentine community is in the God-guarded port of Alexandria, or (comes) to any other of the Islamic ports and bring their goods to their *funduqs* or their warehouses, they may sell their goods by barter or for cash to whom they choose, after which the aforesaid will pay to the noble dīwān 14 dīnārs per cent ; and that they pay in kind to that amount or in cash excluding brokerage and interpreters' (fees). And when they have paid that and some goods remain in their hands, or they have not sold their goods but have paid what they owe in that respect and choose to travel to God-guarded Cairo with their goods, no one of the viceroys nor magistrates nor officials shall trouble them where they have paid what they owe of that which is customary for those goods, which is exclusive of the syrup. And when they have paid the 14 dīnārs per cent those goods shall be considered the equivalent of the rest of what they have in the way of commodities. They have been answered that such shall not happen, according to their custom in that, and we hereby decree it so without innovations. (8)

VII. The aforesaid have requested that when a sale takes place between a Florentine merchant and Muslims, of any kind of goods, after examination and inspection and entry of that in the weigh-house neither Muslim nor Florentine merchant shall alter anything nor repudiate the sale by any device or other means. They have been answered that such shall not happen except by due legal process, and we hereby decree it. (9)

VIII. They have requested of our noble benevolence that when one of the Florentine merchants has a credit against one of the officials of the dīwān and goods arrive for the merchant who has the credit while he is seeking repayment from his debtor, his credit shall be paid him according to holy law and not claimed against him so far as the goods are concerned nor exchanged for it, but the credit shall be paid. They have been answered in that and we hereby decree it. (10)

IX. The aforesaid have requested of our noble benevolence that when one of the Floretine merchants dies in the port of Alexandria or anywhere else and had written a testament no one of the Muslims nor anyone else shall oppose it, and that his goods be deposited with whomever he chooses and bequeathed to whomever he chooses, and the executor shall not be opposed in any way whatever nor oppressed by viceroys nor magistrates nor officials for even a single dirham. And should he die intestate his goods and all his estate shall be deposited with the consul of the aforesaid Florentines until the claimants to his legacy appear. And should one of the aforesaid merchants have an agent or envoy in charge of goods who brings them to one of the Islamic ports and disposes of them by sale or to pay a debt of his, and then dies, after which the merchant who owns the goods comes to the port in which the aforesaid agent or envoy died and it is confirmed that the latter was in fact his man, then no one shall oppose him in it and he shall take his goods from whoever took them from the deceased, without opposition to him in this in accordance with the holy undefiled law, with due legal process. They have been answered in that and we hereby decree it. (11)

X. The aforesaid have requested of our noble benevolence promulgation of our noble command that when a price has not been fixed for spices and other goods and one of their merchants arrives and wishes to buy and sell no one of the Muslims or any other of God's creatures shall hinder him. They have been answered according to their custom in that and we hereby decree it. (12)

XI. The aforesaid have requested of our noble benevolence promulgation of our noble command that no one of the Muslims shall bring a complaint against any one of the Florentine merchants except by way of the magistrate of the port in which he (the Florentine) happens to be. And when the plaintiff comes before the viceroy of the port the matter shall be composed between them with due legal process, and (if) their matter has not been decided he shall be brought with his litigant to our noble portals. They have been answered in what they have requested in that respect and we hereby decree it. (13)

XII. The aforesaid have requested that when a consul from the Florentine nation arrives at the God-guarded port of Alexandria or another of the Islamic ports he shall be treated according to the custom of the consul of the Venetians in respect of salary, stipend and customary rights. They have been answered in that according to custom and we hereby decree it. (14)

XIII. The aforesaid have requested of our noble benevolence promulgation of our noble command that when one of the Florentine merchants arrives in the harbour of Beirut or in another (harbour) intending to buy and sell no one shall oppose him and he shall be treated according to the custom of the Venetians in their buying and selling. And if the Florentine merchants buy potash from Beirut or from God-guarded Damascus they shall pay what the Venetian nation pays and not in excess of that. They have been answered in that and we hereby decree it. (15)

XIV. The aforesaid have requested of our noble benevolence promulgation of our noble command that when there is within the Florentine nation dispute or quarrels or one of them has a right against another of his nation no one of the viceroys or magistrates or merchants shall adjudicate between them except the consul of their nation according to their custom or to their satisfaction in that. They have been answered in that and we hereby decree it. (16)

XV. The aforesaid have informed (us) that it is their custom when one of them intends to travel from country to country to change his costume and wear the clothing of the Mamlūks out of fear of rapacity against them on the roads. No one shall trouble them nor interfere with their victuals and their drink nor because of that oppress them for even a single dirham. They have been answered according to their custom in that without innovations and we hereby decree it. (17)

XVI. The aforesaid have requested of our noble benevolence promulgation of our noble command that when one of the Florentine merchants arrives at the Islamic coasts or Islamic ports in sailing ships or other kinds seeking to repair the ship he is in and requiring to buy whatever of the many articles related to that, he shall be allowed to do so and not opposed at all by any means whatever. They have been answered in that and we hereby decree it. (18)

XVII. They have requested of our noble benevolence promulgation of our noble command that when any Florentine ships arrive in the Islamic lands without goods and those aboard have what they require in the way of victuals and drink, no one shall oppose them nor oppress them for a single dirham without due process. They have been answered in that and we hereby decree it. (19)

XVIII. They have requested of our noble benevolence promulgation of our noble command that when one of the Muslims has legal rights against one of their merchants or (one) of their nation, or there is between them a dispute or strife no one else of his nation or fellow countrymen shall be held liable for that, even a son for his father or a father for his son, except with due legal process. They have been answered in that and we hereby decree it. (20)

XIX. They have requested of our noble benevolence promulgation of our noble command that should one of the Florentine merchants wish to despatch couriers or envoys with their letters and business to anyone, no one shall oppose him nor make difficulties for him nor impede him nor open their letters. They have been answered according to what is customary in that and we hereby decree it. (21)

XX. The aforesaid have requested of our noble benevolence promulgation of our noble command that (should) one of the Florentine merchants have concerns or legal rights against one of the Muslims and the magistrate has not summoned him (the Muslim) to pay what he owes and he has refused payment with due legal process, and the Florentine merchant seeks audience in the service of our noble portals because of that, neither viceroy nor merchant nor anyone of the magistrates shall oppose him, and the audience shall be permitted without (his) being oppressed for a single dirham, that his right be discharged with due legal process. They have been answered in that and we hereby decree it. (22)

XXI. The aforesaid have requested of our noble benevolence promulgation of our noble command that when one of the Muslim merchants contracts a sale with one of the Florentine merchants and it is between these two a matter of barter for spices or any other goods, and someone not the seller claims that these are his goods, it shall not be accepted from him nor shall any of the goods be taken after entry in the weigh-house. And no one shall oppose him in that except by due legal process. They have been answered in that according to the custom of the merchants. (23)

XXII. They have requested of our noble benevolence promulgation of our noble command that when the Florentine nation imports good, pure gold they shall exchange it at the rate of Venetian gold. They have been answered in that and we hereby decree it. (24)

XXIII. The aforesaid have informed (us) that when the Florentine merchants arrive at the God-guarded port of Alexandria or another port with goods and have paid what they owe of the administrative dues, and another spokesman has been appointed in the offices, and the officials and the authorities in the dīwān have been changed, no one of the Florentine merchants shall pay what he has (already) paid a second time. And they have requested that when one of the officials or authorities has been changed that will not be demanded of them a second time. They have been answered according to custom in that, in respect of what happened recently during the " muda ", and we hereby decree it. (25)

XXIV. The aforesaid have requested of our noble benevolence promulgation of our noble command (that) when one of their merchants intends to repair to his country with spices and any other commodities from the God-guarded port of Alexandria or another of the ports after having paid what he owes of the administrative dues, travel shall be permitted and no one shall oppose him in that, where there is no other prosecution or process against him. They have been answered in that and we hereby decree it. (26)

XXV. They have requested of our noble benevolence promulgation of our noble command that when one of their merchants intends to repair to his country in their ships or in ships not belonging to their nation no one shall oppose him in anything pertaining to his servants or his victuals or his drink or his bedding or his clothing, nor in any of his personal effects. Nor shall he be oppressed because of that without due process. They have been answered in that and we hereby decree it. (27)

XXVI. They have requested of our noble benevolence promulgation of our noble command that should anyone of the Frankish nation of whatever race have troubled the Florentine nation ashore or at sea and taken anything from them or caused them difficulties, or should they have rights against him or debts or claims when they arrive in the Islamic countries the magistrate in the place where they happen to be shall discharge their right. And when their right has not been discharged or (when) a Florentine ship makes difficulties for another, they shall be brought to our noble portals in order that the right of each of them be discharged in accordance with the noble holy law. They have been answered in that and we hereby decree it. (28)

XXVII. The aforesaid have requested of our noble benevolence promulgation of our noble command that when there has been an account between one of the Florentine merchants and one of the Muslims and an acquittance has been issued by them one of them may not go back upon the other after that except by due legal process. They have been answered in that and we hereby decree it. (29)

XXVIII. The aforesaid have requested of our noble benevolence promulgation of our noble command that when a cargo ship belonging to the Florentines arrives in the Islamic harbours and has paid what has been assigned it in the way of administrative dues in the harbour and everything for which it is liable, no one shall oppose it and it shall be permitted to proceed without oppression in accordance with the custom and practices of the Venetians in that respect. They have been answered in that and we hereby decree it. (30)

XXIX. The aforesaid have requested of our noble benevolence that a *funduq* be assigned to their consul and merchants in the God-guarded port of Alexandria in accordance with custom in that and as is the case for other of the Frankish nations. They have been answered in that and we hereby decree it. (31)

XXX. The aforesaid have requested of our noble benevolence that when a Florentine merchant arrives in the God-guarded port of Alexandria with what he has in the way of goods and buys and sells and barters, and has paid what he owes of the tithes and administrative dues and customary expenses, and seeks to withdraw from the God-guarded port and to make for his own country, neither the superintendent of the harbour entrance nor anyone else shall oppose him for any reason by taking from him more than that which the aforesaid merchant has paid, not even to the amount of a single dirham. They have been answered in that and we hereby decree it. (32)

XXXI. The aforesaid have requested of our noble benevolence that when one of the Florentines arrives in a ship belonging to a nation other than his of whatever race at the Islamic harbours—the port of Alexandria or another—in which one of the Florentines is sought for a crime or misdemeanour or right against him, no other Florentine, such as he who arrived in the aforesaid ship, shall be detained in his stead unless he is surety or guarantor. They have been answered in that and we hereby decree it. (33)

XXXII. The aforesaid have requested of our noble benevolence that when one of the Florentine merchants arrives in the God-guarded port of Alexandria or in another of the Islamic harbours, and one approaches him to buy from him some of the goods which arrived with him, that shall be permitted and the Florentine merchant shall not be opposed because of that where he has paid what he owes of the customary tithes and administrative dues. They have been answered in that and we hereby decree it. (34)

And our decree is for everyone whom it may concern to proceed on the basis of that which we have decreed in the articles set out above, to the execution of them, and the avoidance of any departure whatever from them, punctiliously and resolutely. So let this noble decree be authoritative, and executed in its intention and its prescription with neither deviation from it nor departure from its sense.

And the noble signature above, may God Almighty exalt it, is its authentication, God willing.

On the 6th of Dhu 'l-Ḥijja in the year 894 (31 October 1489).

In conformity with the noble decree.

Praise be to God Alone, and God bless him after whom there is no prophet.

And God is our sufficiency, and how excellent a guardian is He! (35)

COMMENTARY

1. From the point of view of Mamlūk chancery practice the commercial treaties were related in principle to safe-conducts (*amānāt*) and armistices (*hudan*) but in form to an administrative order or decree (*marsūm*, pl. *marāsīm*) of the kind originally employed for lesser officials in the Mamlūk administration, see al-Qalqashandī, *Ṣubḥ al-Aʿshā*, Cairo 1913–20, XIII, 321–51, XIV, 2–78, XI, 107–12, respectively. While al-Qalqashandī does not mention the commercial treaty as a recognized class of chancery document he includes under armistices provision for a " commercial clause " by which merchants of either party to the contract were free to trade in the lands of the other (op. cit., XIV, 10), a provision also explicit in his observations on the safe-conduct (op. cit., XIII, 322). Examples of the *marsūm* are abundant among the documents preserved from the Mamlūk chancery, only a few of which are commercial privileges see especially H. Ernst, *Die mamlukischen Sultansurkunden des Sinai Klosters*, Wiesbaden 1960, passim; Amari, *Diplomi*, pp. 214–17 (Ser. I doc. 42), 226–9 (Ser. I, doc. 45); G. Elezović, *Turski Spomenici*, Beograd 1952, I/ii, 175–82 (doc. 135); B. Moritz, " Ein Firman des Sultans Selim I. für die Venezianer," *Festschrift Eduard Sachau*, Berlin 1915, pp. 429–36 (heading incomplete, cf. p. 428). The extant examples correspond in most respects to al-Qalqashandī's description of the class (op. cit. XI, 107–12, esp. p. 111, and also VIII, 21–4): the abstract of its contents written in the top margin (*ṭurra*) of the document (in our document lines 1–7, see Plate XXI), two pieces (*waṣl*, pl. *awṣāl*) left blank between the *ṭurra* and the *basmala*, and followed by the formula *rusima bi'l-amr al-sharīf* and the name of the originator (see Plate XXII, and below, n. 2). Because of the brevity of the abstract the Mamlūk officers are addressed generally in it, a closer delineation of their functions appearing in the

articles of the treaty, see in general M. Gaudefroy-Demombynes, *La Syrie à l'époque des mamelouks*, Paris 1923, pp. lv–lxxx ; D. Ayalon, "Studies on the structure of the Mamluk Army III," *BSOAS*, 1954, pp. 57–70 ; and W. Popper, *Egypt and Syria under the Circassian Sultans* I, Berkeley 1955, pp. 90–120. For the uses of the term *mubāshir*, of which *mutaṣarrif* appears here to be a synonym (cf. Ernst, *Sultansurkunden*, pp. 160, 182), see Ibn Iyās III, 151 (where it is a general term for administrative officials), 159, 219 (where it is employed in contradistinction to *umarā'* and *mamālīk*, respectively), and further references in Moritz, "Firman," p. 437, n. 3. *Mubāshir* appears also in Italian documents occasionally, as "Bassarini", see C. Marin, *Storia civile e politica del commercio dei Veneziani*, Venice 1808, VII, 288–321, part II, article 7. *Ḥākim* may here be simply a synonym of *qāḍī* (cf. Moritz, "Firman," p. 438 n. 18), but more likely refers to a magistrate with jurisdiction in the customary law which governed the markets and transactions with European merchants, see Elezović, *Turski Spomenici* I, ii, 175 and J. Sauvaget, "Décrets mamelouks de Syrie," *BEO*, II, 1932, p. 26 (where *ḥukkām* and *quḍāt* appear together) ; and for this application of the term in other parts of the Muslim world, Amari, *Storia dei Musulmani di Sicilia*, ed. Nallino, Catania 1933–39, II, 5 n. 1 ; H. Idris, *La Berbérie orientale sous les Zirides*, Paris 1962, II, 548, 550 ; and U. Heyd, *Ottoman Documents on Palestine* 1552–1615, Oxford 1960, p. 49, n. 6.

2. The mark of authentication in our document is the name of the Sultan, who was the originator of the document, referred to here as *al-ism al-sharīf* (line 1) and *al-khaṭṭ al-sharīf* (line 261). The development of signatures employed in Islamic chancery practice is the subject of a detailed historical investigation by S. M. Stern in his study, *Fāṭimid Decrees*, London 1964, pp. 123–65, and for the Mamlūk chancery especially pp. 157–9. For other published facsimiles of Qā'itbāy's signature see the references in "A Mamluk letter", *BSOAS*, 1961, p. 201, n. 1. The general form of the preamble or expositio, which follows the *basmala* and introduces the text of the document (see Plates XXIII–XXVI), corresponds to al-Qalqashandī's description (op. cit., XI, 111). *Ṭā'ifa*, *jamā'a*, and *jins* appear to be used interchangeably with reference to the Florentines, and are rendered in the contemporary Italian translations as "nazione" or "generazione" without consistent distinction, but see Amari, *Diplomi*, p. 438 n. i, and M. van Berchem, *Matériaux pour un Corpus inscriptionum Arabicarum*, Cairo 1894–1930, II, i, Jerusalem ville, p. 382 n. 2. The terms *shurūṭ* (sing. *sharṭ*) and *fuṣūl* (sing. *faṣl*) both refer to the contents of a commercial treaty ; while the former might designate

specifically the contents of the treaty (i.e. conditions or privileges) and the latter the form in which these are cast (i.e. items or articles), they are in fact used interchangeably, see Amari, *Diplomi*, p. 182; Moritz, "Firman," p. 433 art. 16, and above pp. 10–11). The use of *ḥākim* for the ruler of Florence is arbitrary, the same being called *malik* and *ṣāḥib* in other contemporary documents (cf. Amari, *Diplomi*, pp. 182, 222, 225), while al-Qalqashandī has examples of the application of *ḥākim* to other European rulers (op. cit., VIII, 46, and XIV, 51).

3. Cf. Doc. D, pt. 1, 1; Doc. E, 1; Doc. G, 1; Doc. H, 1; Doc. J, 1, for the corresponding article (similar cross-references are given below for each of the articles). The three kinds of ship named here are attested in Arabic sources but with such diversity of application that it is difficult to know which kind of Italian ship is meant. Doc. G has "navi fiorentini quadre o lunghe ovvero di qualunque struttura" (Amari, *Diplomi*, p. 382), while Doc. J has "Navi, galere, galeazze, fuste ed altri legni", and Doc. H an interlinear note "navi — quadrireme — galera". Though it is not impossible that the term *murabba'* (or *murbi'*) refer to a ship's size or structure (cf. H. Kindermann, "*Schiff*" *im Arabischen*, Zwickau i. Sa. 1934, p. 94 s.v. *muthallatha*), it is more likely a reference to a sailing ship as opposed to a galley, see Ibn Taghrībirdī, *al-Nujūm al-Zāhira*, ed. Popper, VI, 607, 608, where the expressions *murabba'at al-qilā'* and *markab murabba'* (or *murbi'*) are used especially for European ships (cf. ibid., Glossary, p. xxx). Such distinctions are however of limited value. While for example, the terms *aghriba* (sing. *ghurāb*) and *ṭarā'id* (sing. *ṭarīda*) often designate respectively light galleys and heavy transports, they are frequently used interchangeably, see Kindermann, op. cit., pp. 68–71, 56–9; and "A Moroccan amir", *BSOAS*, 1962, p. 451 n. 8. *Ḥuqūq dīwāniyya*, which also appear in article XXIII, were very likely extralegal taxes levied by the administration, as distinguished from the canonical taxes, *ḥuqūq shar'iyya*, mentioned in articles XVIII and XX, see Ernst, *Sultansurkunden*, pp. 178, 200, 212, 252; H. Lammens, *Remarques sur les mots français dérivés de l'arabe*, Beirut 1890, p. 100; and for the corresponding Ottoman term *'awāriḍ-i dīwāniyya*, R. Mantran and J. Sauvaget, *Règlements fiscaux ottomans*, Paris 1951, p. 33 n. 7. While the grammatical structure of the articles, based upon the expressions *wa-sa'alū ṣadaqātinā al-sharīfa* and *ujību ilā dhālik wa-rasamnā bihi*, belongs to a chancery tradition, it demonstrates the role of the petition in treaty negotiations and at the same time the importance of the Italian documents in the final casting of the Arabic, see above p. 47, n. 33, and below note 35.

4. Cf. Doc. E, 2; Doc. G, 2; Doc, J, 2; Doc. H, 2. The commodities (*baḍā'i'* or *aṣnāf*) listed here, which are Florentine imports into Egypt and Syria, made up together with spices and slaves, the bulk of mediaeval Mediterranean commerce, see B. Pegolotti, *Pratica della Mercatura*, ed. Evans, Cambridge, Mass. 1935, Index; and Heyd, *Commerce*, II, 553–711. For *qiyāḍ* (= *muqāyaḍa*) see *EI*, second ed., s.v. "Bay' ".

5. Cf. Doc. D, pt. 1, 7; Doc. E, 3; Doc. G, 3; Doc. H, 3; Doc. J, 3. The references to *makhāzin* (sing. *makhzan*) and *fanādiq* (sing. *funduq*) are further evidence of the dependence of the Florentine commercial privileges upon those granted to nations longer established in the Levant, and especially Venice. It is not indeed clear whether the Florentines were ever allotted their own *funduq*, see article XXIX, and Heyd, *Commerce* II, 490. The expression *bi'l-khums* is probably a reference to the *ḥuqūq dīwāniyya*, see above note 3, Ernst, *Sultansurkunden*, p. 200, line 7, and note p. 286, and Amari, *Diplomi*, p. 203, art. 25, though it is worth noting that Doc. J has " aprire la quinta parte ". Counting (' *adda*) and weighing (*qabāna*) must have been among the most important aspects of transactions in Alexandria, and it is not unlikely that the dīwān mentioned here and throughout the treaty (articles I, III, IV, VI, VIII, XXIII, XXVIII, XXX, XXXII) is the *dīwān al-qabbān*, so designated in articles VII and XXI, see below note 9.

6. Cf. Doc. E, 4; Doc. G, 4; Doc. H, 4; Doc. J, 4.

7. Cf. Doc. E, 5; Doc. G, 5; Doc. H, 5; Doc. J, 5. For *qiṭāra* (*quṭāra* ?) Docs. E, G, and J have " melazi ", " vino o rosolio ", and " una quantita di vetture " (= botte), respectively, see Dozy, *Suppl.* s.v. (where it is described as a mixture of honey and sugar). *Barmīl* is rendered " barile ", " charatello ", and " vettura " in the Italian documents; according to Pegolotti the Florentine " barile " contained in the 14th century 45·6 litres (op. cit., p. 191). *Ashrafī*, rendered in Docs. G and J as " sarafo " and " surifo ", and in Doc. E simply as " ducato " was a gold coin (*dīnār*) minted at the order of Sultan al-Malik al-Ashraf Barsbāy in 829/1425 in a move to limit the circulation of European currency, chiefly the Venetian ducat, in Egypt and Syria. Not a full dīnār in weight (3·45 gr. instead of the traditional 4·25 gr.) the *ashrafī* had nevertheless the weight of the European coin it was meant to replace, and became during the 15th century almost synonymous with dīnār, see Popper, *Egypt and Syria* II, 45, 49–50; and Mantran-Sauvaget, *Règle-*

ments, p. 11 n. 1. *Al-dhakhīra*, which may have been the point of control for regalian monopolies, appears frequently in Italian documents as " dachieri " or " dachiera ", see " A Mamluk ambassador ", *BSOAS*, 1963, p. 528 n. 3, and also Ernst, *Sultansurkunden*, pp. 182, 184, 188 ; Elezović, *Turski Spomenici*, p. 176 ; Moritz, " Firman," p. 441 n. 39 ; " A Mamluk letter," *BSOAS*, 1961, p. 211 n. 7.

8. Cf. Doc. E, 6 ; Doc. G, 6 ; Doc. H, 6 ; Doc. J, 6. For *wazana* in this usage : to pay an impost (after weighing ?), see Dozy, *Suppl.*, s.v., to which may be added examples in M. Alarcón y Santón and Ramón García de Linares, *Los Documentos árabes diplomáticos del Archivo de la Corona de Aragón*, Madrid-Granada, 1940, p. 373, arts. 2, 3, 5. Apart from customs fees for brokerage (*samsara*) and interpreters (*tarājima*) were regularly levied in Muslim ports, see Pegolotti, *Pratica*, pp. 28, 44 ; Moritz, " Firman," p. 443 n. 52 ; Mas Latrie, *Relations et commerce de l'Afrique septentrionale*, Paris 1886, pp. 351–3 ; " A Mamluk ambassador," *BSOAS*, 1963, p. 526 n. 6.

9. Cf. Doc. D, pt. 1, 2 and pt. 2, 1 ; Doc. E, 7 ; Doc. G, 7 ; Doc H, 7 ; Doc. J, 7. *Dīwān al-qabbān* appears in Italian documents both translated (e.g. Doc. G : " tribunale del pesatore," Amari, *Diplomi*, p. 383) and transliterated (e.g. Doc. E : " dogana del chapanno," Amari, *Diplomi*, p. 376), see also article XXI and note 5 above, and for the word *qabbān*, Dozy, *Suppl.*, s.v. ; Heyd, *Commerce* II, 451 n. 4 ; Amari, *Diplomi*, p. 441 n. tt ; Pegolotti, *Pratica*, pp. 57, 92 ; Mantran-Sauvaget, *Règlements*, pp. 13–4 ; and the references in " A Mamluk ambassador ", *BSOAS*, 1963, p. 526 n. 7. The functionaries of the dīwān were called *qabbāniyyūn*, see Ibn Iyās III, 262, 268 ; E. Lane, *Modern Egyptians*, London 1908, p. 62 ; and note the verbal noun *qabāna* in article IV of our document. In view of the frequency with which this office is mentioned in the commercial documents of the late Mamlūk period (e.g. Amari, *Diplomi*, pp. 197, 202 ; Alarcón-García, *Documentos*, pp. 375–6 ; Elezović, *Turski Spomenici*, p. 178) it is surprising not to find it listed with the other dīwāns in al-Qalqashandī, or in Khalīl al-Ẓāhiri's *Zubdat Kashf Al-Mamālik*, ed. Ravaisse, Paris 1894, pp. 93–110.

10. Cf. Doc. D, pt. 1, 27 ; Doc. E, 8 ; Doc. G, 8 ; Doc. H, 8 ; Doc. J, 8.

11. Cf. Doc. D, pt. 1, 9 and pt. 4, 4 ; Doc. E, 9 ; Doc. G, 9 ; Doc. H, 9 ; Doc. J, 9. For the legal problem involved in protecting the rights of a third party, see *EI*, second ed., s.v. " 'Akd ". Here is the first mention

in the treaty of a Florentine consul, whose rights are further delimited in articles XII and XIV.

12. Cf. Doc. D, pt. 1, 10 ; Doc. E, 10 ; Doc. G, 10 ; Doc. H, 10 ; Doc. J, 10. The expression *qaṭa'a si'r fi'l-bahār* appears in Italian documents as " rompere (fare, mettere, stabilire) la voce (il pretio) de spetie ", and would seem in context to indicate an arbitrary fixing of prices by the administrative authorities and thus, perhaps, the regalian monopoly of spices, see " A Mamluk ambassador ", *BSOAS*, 1963, p. 528 n. 4, but cf. the Arabic terms in Sauvaget, " Décrets mamelouks," *BEO* XII, 1947–48, pp. 22–7.

13. Cf. Doc. D, pt. 1, 11 ; Doc. E, 11 ; Doc. G, 11 ; Doc. H, 11 ; Doc. J, 11.

14. Cf. Doc. D, pt. 1, 13 ; Doc. E, 12 ; Doc. G, 12 ; Doc. H, 12 ; Doc. J, 12. Here is the first mention in our document of a Venetian precedent, which occurs again in articles XIII, XXII, and XXVIII. The distinction, if any, between *ma'lūm* and *jāmakiyya* is not clear ; the latter is attested frequently in the Mamlūk commercial privileges, and appears to have been a fixed stipend of 200 ducats paid to the consul by the Sultan out of the revenues in Alexandria, see the references in " A Mamluk ambassador ", *BSOAS*, 1963, pp. 529 n. 4, 525 n. 2. The consul's rights (*ḥuqūq*) are left undefined, though the term may be a reference to his jurisdiction in disputes among his compatriots (see article XIV), suggested by the rendering in Doc. G (Amari, *Diplomi*, p. 384), though this jurisdiction was in practice limited (cf. the passage in al-Ẓāhirī, *Zubda*, p. 41, in which the European consul is described as a hostage—*rahīna*—for his nation in Alexandria).

15. Cf. Doc. D, pt. 1, 14, 24 ; Doc. E, 13 ; Doc. G, 13 ; Doc. H, 13 ; Doc. J, 13. Potash (*qalī* or *qilī*) was a major European export from Syria, and provision for its handling appears in most of the Mamlūk commercial privileges, see Pegolotti, *Pratica*, pp. 296, 428 (sale arcali) ; Mantran-Sauvaget, *Règlements*, pp. 22–4, 69 (*bals*) ; Heyd, *Commerce* II, 459.

16. Cf. Doc. D, pt. 4, 8 ; Doc. E, 14 ; Doc. G, 14 ; Doc. H, 14 ; Doc. J, 14. See above note 14.

17. Cf. Doc. D, pt. 1, 17 ; Doc. E, 15 ; Doc. G, 15 ; Doc. H, 15 ; Doc. J, 15. The expression *malbūs al-mamālīk* is not clear, but it is doubtful whether by it is meant the clothing of the Mamlūk amīrs (*ziyy al-atrāk*).

More likely is a reference to a garment worn by the natives of Egypt and Syria and perhaps by some ranks of amīr as well. A few marks of distinction in their clothing were preserved at all times by the ruling class of the Mamlūk state, see L. A. Mayer, *Mamluk Costume*, Geneva 1952, pp. 24, 25, 32 n. 12. This provision does not appear often in the Mamlūk commercial privileges, only three times in the 15th century, though it may have been merely desultory recognition of a widely established practice.

18. Cf. Doc. D, pt. 1, 19; Doc. E, 16; Doc. G, 16; Doc. H, 16; Doc. J, 16. For *marākib murabba'a* (or *murbi'a*) see above note 3.

19. Cf. Doc. D, pt. 1, 22; Doc. E, 17; Doc. G, 17; Doc. H, 17. In Doc. J this article has been omitted, while in Docs. D and E a customs-duty of 3 and ⅓ per cent is specified on goods for the personal use of Florentine merchants.

20. Cf. Doc. D, pt. 1, 15; Doc. E, 18; Doc. G, 18; Doc. H, 18; Doc. J, 18. *Ḥuqūq shar'iyya*, mentioned again in article XX, are attested elsewhere (e.g. Amari, *Diplomi*, p. 195; Moritz, " Firman," p. 436 art. 30), and may be identical with the tithes (*'ushūr*) in articles XXX and XXXII, see also above note 3, and below note 33.

21. Cf. Doc. D, pt. 1, 26; Doc. E, 19; Doc. H, 19; Doc. J, 19. This and the following article were omitted in Doc. G.

22. Cf. Doc. D, pt. 1, 18; Doc. E, 20; Doc. H, 20; Doc. J, 20.

23. Cf. Doc. D, pt. 1, 28 and pt. 2, 8; Doc. E, 21; Doc. G, 19; Doc. H, 20; Doc. J, 20. The usual dispositio *wa-rasamnā bihi* was omitted by the scribe. For *dīwān al-qabbān* see above note 9.

24. Cf. Doc. D, pt. 1, 29 and pt. 2, 10; Doc. E, 23; Doc. G, 20; Doc. H, 22; Doc. J, 22.

25. Cf. Doc. D, pt. 2, 2; Doc. E, 24; Doc. G, 21; Doc. H, 23; Doc. J, 23. *Mutakallimūn* and *mutaḥaddithūn* appear in Mamlūk documents as generic designations of " officials ", much as *mubāshirūn* and *mutaṣarrifūn* (see above note 1), e.g. Amari, *Diplomi*, pp. 214, 215, 223; Ernst, *Sultansurkunden*, pp. 218, 222, 226. For the two former terms see Dozy, *Suppl.*, s.v., to which the use of *taḥadduth* in al-Qalqashandī, *Ṣubḥ*, XIV, 7, might be added. The appearance of the term *mudda* in the

dispositio may be evidence to support the conjecture of Moritz, " Firman," p. 443 n. 52, that the mediaeval Italian word " muda " is thence derived, rather than from the Latin " mutare ", see " A Mamluk ambassador ", *BSOAS*, 1963, p. 526 n. 1. Heyd's derivation from " mutare " in the sense of to exchange or barter (*Commerce*, II, 453) is not impossible though it does not appear quite to cover the synonymous expression " tempo de galie " which occurs so often in the Italian sources, e.g. passages in the Venetian records such as " dicte galee habeant mutam in Alexandria " and " propinquat tempus mutarum galearum Alexandriae " (Terminazioni ed incanti di galere 1469–89, *Archivio Veneto*, Ser. 5, II, pp. 250–51), and article 9 in the Mamlūk-Venetian treaty of 913/1507 (" A Mamluk ambassador "), p. 523 ; but cf. Du Cange, s.v. no. 7 : " *Muta*, dici videtur de navibus, quae securitatis causa simul navigant."

26. Cf. Doc. D, pt. 2, 6 ; Doc. E, 27 ; Doc. G, 22 ; Doc. H, 24 ; Doc. J, 24.

27. Cf. Doc. D, pt. 2, 5 ; Doc. E, 26 ; Doc. G, 23 ; Doc. H, 25 ; Doc. J, 25. In the Italian documents " personal effects " (*shay' min ḥālihi*) is generally rendered " roba ", and servants (or slaves ?) are not usually included in the provision.

28. Cf. Doc. D, pt. 4, 9 ; Doc. E, 28 ; Doc. G, 24 ; Doc. H, 26 ; Doc. J, 26.

29. Cf. Doc. D, pt. 4, 10 ; Doc. E, 29 ; Doc. G, 25 ; Doc. H, 27 ; Doc. J, 27. *Barā'a* is a financial or administrative discharge, called in the Italian documents " polizza " or " licentia ", and could in this article be translated " receipt ", see C. Becker, *Islamstudien*, Berlin 1924, I, 262 ; Amari, *Diplomi*, p. 416 n. j ; and the references in " A Mamluk ambassador ", *BSOAS*, 1963, p. 526 n. 2.

30. Cf. Doc. E, 30 ; Doc. G, 26 ; Doc. H, 28 ; Doc. J, 28. This article appears to be a repetition of the provision in article I but with particular reference to the *markab bi-thābūt*, which would thus not have been included among the ships' types enumerated there. While Docs. G and J have simply " navi ", Doc. E contains the expression " navilio di ghaggia " (Amari, *Diplomi*, p. 380), providing further evidence of the use of Della Stufa's petition in the drafting of the Arabic treaty. *Thābūt* (or *tābūt*) and " ghaggia " (commonly " gabbia ") designate a crow's-nest (and by extension top-sail) or a storage place aboard ship, see Dozy, *Suppl.*, s.v. *tābūt* ; R. Brunschvig, *La Berbérie orientale sous les Hafsides*, Paris

1940–7, II, n. 4 on pp. 97–8; H. and R. Kahane and A. Tietze, *The Lingua Franca in the Levant,* Urbana 1958, pp. 236–7, no. 315. Since all masted ships could have had a crow's-nest, including thus the *murabba'at al-qilā'* in article I (see above note 3), it seems likely that here *thābūt* refers to storage or hold and, perhaps because of the cargo carried therein, received special attention in the commercial privileges. In the Mamlūk-Venetian treaty of 918/1512 the expression " nave a magazen ultra le galie ", also uncommon in the commercial documents of the period, may be a reference to the same kind of vessel, see Marin, *Storia civile e politica del commercio dei Veneziani,* VII, 288–321, pt. 1 art. 6.

31. Cf. Doc. D, pt. 1, 11; Doc. E, 32; Doc. G, 27; Doc. H, 29; Doc. J, 29. See above note 5.

32. Cf. Doc. D, pt. 4, 7; Doc. G, 28; Doc. H, 30; Doc. J, 30. *'Ushūr* may be taxes levied on the goods of merchants in accordance with the prescriptions of the holy law, and therefore possibly identical with *ḥuqūq shar'iyya* in articles XVIII and XX, though the application of the term *'ushr* may be a legal fiction, see " A Moroccan amir ", *BSOAS,* 1962, p. 460 n. 5; and cf. the expression *al-mūjib wa'l-'ushr al-sulṭānī* in Amari, *Diplomi,* p. 189. For the Mamlūk official *al-shādd bi-bāb al-baḥr,* see Gaudefroy-Demombynes, *Syrie,* p. 223 n. 4; Popper, *Egypt and Syria* I, 106; Moritz, " Firman," pp. 441 n. 38, 442 n. 49.

33. Cf. Doc. D, pt. 1, 15; Doc. E, 18; Doc. G, 29; Doc. H, 31; Doc. J, 31. This article, supplementary to the provisions of article XVIII, is contained in principle in all of the Mamlūk commercial treaties of the 15th century, underlining the importance in the eyes of the Mamlūk administration of the notion of collective responsibility with regard to the foreign merchant communities resident in their territory. Abuses on both sides were frequent, and the inclusion of this provision could have been a comfort to the Europeans since the question of responsibility among their own number was determined by their consul. For *ḍamān,* in its broadest application a synonym of *kafāla,* see *EI,* second ed. s.v., though it is not unlikely that the Arabic terms are merely renderings of European notions of legal responsibility, explicit in such terms as " piezo o principal ", " plezius vel appacator ", " piezo per carta ", " in caso de piezaria ", " principal o piezo, over chel habi scripto carta a dosso ", which invariably appear in the Latin and Italian commercial documents, see Brunschvig, *La Berbérie* I, 431–40; and J. Schacht, " Droit byzantin et droit musulman." in *Convegno Volta* XII, Rome 1957, pp. 205–6.

34. Cf. Doc. D, pt. 4, 6; Doc. E, 25; Doc. G, 30; Doc. H, 32; Doc. J, 32. In Docs. D and E the corresponding article has an additional provision for sales aboard ship.

35. Like the protocol, the concluding formulae and the terminal sigla *ḥr* (see Plates XXVII–XXIX) correspond closely to the prescriptions of al-Qalqashandī for all chancery documents (op. cit., VI, 232–5, 262–70; VIII, 21–2) of which abundant examples have been preserved (e.g. Amari, *Diplomi*, pp. 209, 212–3, 217, 220, etc.; Ernst, *Sultansurkunden*, pp. xxxiii–xxxix and passim). Cast substantially in the form of a *marsūm* the Mamlūk commercial privileges as such offer the conventional chancery forms for the introductory and concluding parts of the document (*fawātiḥ* and *khawātim*). In the text (*matn*) clearly marked divisions (*fuṣūl*) opening with a verbatim statement of the petitio and closing with the dispositio *wa-rasamnā bihi*, follow, too, a chancery convention for letters of reply, employed as a safeguard against omission of details (al-Qalqashandī, op. cit., VII, p. 207). If, however, the form of the commercial treaties adheres closely to a Muslim tradition it is not unlikely that the juridical principle upon which they were based was an introduction from European practice, see *EI*, second ed., s.v. *amān*, and the references to the studies of Brunschvig and Schacht in note 33 above.

I should like to thank the directors and staff of the Biblioteca Mediceo-Laurenziana, the Biblioteca Nazionale, and the Archivio di Stato in Florence for their kindness; the Central Research Funds Committee of the University of London for material assistance; and Professor B. Lewis and Dr. N. Rubinstein for their helpful advice during the preparation of this study.

SEVEN OTTOMAN DOCUMENTS FROM THE REIGN OF MEḤEMMED II

by

V. L. Ménage

When, on 28 July 1463, Venice declared war on the Ottoman Empire, she embarked on a struggle that was to drag on for nearly sixteen years and to result, with the loss of Euboea and northern Albania, in a grievous weakening of her power in the Aegean and an increase in the Ottoman threat to the Adriatic. Venice had not sought the war: to protect her wealthy commerce by means of an accommodation with the "foes of Christendom" had always been her policy, a policy which, piously reprehended by other Christian powers, was to leave her now bereft of powerful allies. Nor was the Sultan, Meḥemmed II, inflexibly determined to maintain a state of war. Although he had, by his conquest of Bosnia and by provocation in the Morea, forced the war on Venice, more than once during the long hostilities the Sultan himself set on foot negotiations for peace and on several occasions showed himself prepared to receive a Venetian embassy. Indeed hardly one of the sixteen years passed without a peace-feeler being extended by one side or the other.

The seven documents here presented concern various of these abortive negotiations. They were discovered by my colleague Dr. John Wansbrough (who has most kindly put photographs of them at my disposal) in Busta 161 of the series *Procuratori di San Marco, misti* in the Venetian State Archives. This file is labelled "Commissaria di Angelo Malipiero, capitano de galere di Barbaria", with no hint that Ottoman documents are included in it, so that they are mentioned neither in Professor Bombaci's handlist available at the Frari nor in his article [1] on the Turkish documents preserved there.

Of the seven, six emanate from the Sultan, two of these being drawn

[1] A. Bombaci, "La collezione di documenti turchi dell' Archivio di Stato di Venezia," *Rivista degli Studi Orientali*, xxiv (1949), 95–107.

up in Italian, the other four in Turkish ; the seventh, in Greek, is a lette sent by an Ottoman general to a Venetian ambassador.[2]

THE DOCUMENTS

1. 24 May 1471, Constantinople. Letter in Italian from Meḥemmed II to th Doge Cristofero Moro stating the terms on which he is prepared to mak peace. Plate XXX. [50 cm. × 32 cm., 15 + 1 lines

Text :

[invocatio] (none)

[*ṭughrā*] محمد بن مراد خان مظفر دايما

(1)Mahameth dey gra(tia) turchie et grecie Imp(er)ator. Illust(ri)ssim e exellentissimo domino cristofaro (2)mauro duci ueneciano Salutem Alla porta della segnoria n(ost)ra sono venuti li ambasiaturi dell ex(ellentia) v(ostra) (3)liquali anno praticato la paxe secundo lo t(em)p passato. laqual la segnoria n(ost)ra liberame(n)te c(on)cede de (4)aue bona paxe c(on)la ex(ellentia) v(ostra) cosi damar cho(me) da terr c(on)li modi e c(on)dicio(n)e frascripti. v(idelicet) ch(e) la segnori (5)v(ost)ra sea obligata restituir allo dominio n(ost)ro la isola de stalimn ch(e) fo n(ost)ra occupata p(er) vui i(n) questa (6)guerra / e simeleme(n)t tuti li lochi tolti da noi i(n) lo brazo de maina : remanendo a vui maluasi laqual (7)auiti tolto dal mano de alt(ri) e similit(er) debiati restituir anu croia occupata p(er) vui dapoi lamorte (8)de schender. dello rest ueramente ogni una delle p(ar)te tengna quello ch(e) allo presente ten e possede. (9)dechiarando ch(e) la mea segnoria se obliga de exocupa tuto quello territorio fosse ocupato p(er) li (10)mei delle iuridicio(n) passade de modono e coro(n) neapoli de romania e de tuti alt(ri) u(ost)r lochi. Li am (11)basciadori della illust(ri)ssima u(ost)ra Segnoria m anno p(re)gato p(er) parte della ex(ellentia) v(ostra) ch(e) debia la se (12)gnoria n(ost)ra fare paxe c(on) rodo e c(on) cipri. Veniendo l ambasiaturi loro la signoria n(ost)ra fara (13)paxe c(on)li dicti a com piacentia u(ost)ra. li altri v(ost)ri recomandati usati senumereran(n) i(n) li capituli ch(e) (14)sonno usitato p(er) lo passato. della moneta tolta alla segnoria n(ost)ra da bartolomei giorgi li ambasiatu (15)ri della ex(ellentia) v(ostra) ve informeran(n)o quello ch(e) la segnoria n(ost)ra li aue dicto ecosi delli capituli passati.

Data c(on)stantineopoli Anno n(ost)re fidei · dccclxxv die xxiiij madii

[2] Only a few of the questions which they raise can be touched on here : I limit mysel to presenting the documents, with a brief commentary, and setting them in their historica context.

Translation :

[*tughrā*] Muḥammad son of Murād Khān, ever victorious

Meḥemmed, by the grace of God Emperor of Turkey and Greece, to the most renowned and distinguished lord Cristofero Mauro, Doge of Venice, greeting.

To the Porte of Our Majesty have come Your Excellency's ambassadors, who have treated for peace as in the former time ; the which Our Majesty freely grants, to have good peace with Your Excellency, both by sea and by land, on the terms and conditions hereunder written, namely :

That your Signory be obliged to restore to our dominion the island of Lemnos, which was ours and has been occupied by you in this war, and likewise all the places seized from us in the Braccio di Maina, there remaining to you Malvasia, which you seized from the possession of others ; and likewise you must restore to us Croia, occupied by you since the death of Iskender. Beyond this, indeed each of the parties is to hold that which he holds and possesses at the present time, with the declaration that My Majesty undertakes to evacuate whatever territory may have been occupied by my people of the former jurisdictions of Modon and Coron, Napoli di Romania, and of all other places of yours.

The ambassadors of your most renowned Signory have prayed me, on behalf of Your Excellency, that Our Majesty should make peace with Rhodes and Cyprus. Upon their ambassadors presenting themselves Our Majesty will, to give you satisfaction, make peace with the aforesaid.

Your other customary submissions will be set out in detail in the capitulations which have been in force in the past.

Concerning the money seized from Our Majesty by Bartolomeo Giorgi, Your Excellency's ambassadors will inform you of what Our Majesty has said to them, and likewise concerning the former capitulations.

Given at Constantinople, in the year of our faith 875, on the 24th day of May.

2. Middle decade of Rabīʿ I 882/23 June–2 July 1477, Constantinople. *Fermān* to the sanjak-beys of Rumeli, ordering them to grant passage and protection to a Venetian ambassador travelling to the Porte. Plate XXXI.

[dimensions not recorded, 9 lines]

Text :

[invocatio] هو

[*tughrā*] (as in Doc. 1)

مفاخر الامراء الكرام روم ايلى سنجاقلرى بكلرى دام عزهم

توقيع رفيع واصل اوليجاق معلوم اولا كم شمدكيحالده

ونديكك ايلچسى دركاه فلك اشتباهمه كلمك استرمش
ايله اولسا بيوردم كى ذكر اولنان ايلچى هر قنقكوزك
تحت حكومتندن چقوب كلمك استرسه مانع ومتعرض
اوليوب بيلهسنجه يرار آدملر قوشوب كوندرب
دركاه معلامه ايصال ادهسز شيله بلاسز
علامت شريف ازره اعتماد قلاسز
تحريراً فى اواسط ربيع الاول سنه اثنين وثمانين وثما<نمائه>

بمقام
قسطنطنيه

Translation:

[invocatio] He!

[*ṭughrā*] (as in Doc. 1)

The ornaments [3] among the noble commanders, the begs of the sanjaks of Rumeli, may their glory endure!

When the exalted sign arrives, be it known that at this present the ambassador of Venice wishes to come to my Porte, lofty as the Heavenly Sphere; this being so, I have commanded that through the jurisdiction of whichever of you the afore-mentioned ambassador may wish to come up you are not to prevent or molest him but to depute competent men as his escort and send him on his way and enable him to reach my exalted Porte.

Thus you are to know; you are to place reliance upon the noble sign.

Written in the middle decade of Rabīʿ I in the year 882.

In the residence
of Constantinople

3. 25 February [1478], Constantinople. Safe-conduct in Italian issued by Meḥemmed II, permitting the Venetian ambassador Tomaso Malipiero and his suite to travel to the Porte and return to Venetian protection. Plate XXXII

[42·7 cm. × 15·2 cm., 41 + 2 lines]

Text:

[invocatio] (none)

[*ṭughrā*] (as in Doc. 1)

[3] Literally: "objects of pride."

(1)Mehemet / dei gratia turchie gretieq(ue) Imp(er)ator &c.

(2)p(er) la auctorita et / tenor dile p(rese)nte do / concedo / et / tribuisco (3)pleno / amplo / ualido / et / securo saluo conducto / et / fede (4)ampla / ualida / et / secura / alo M(agnifi)co ambasiator dela ll(ustrissi)ma (5)Signoria d(i) venetia mis(ser) tomasio malipiero ch(e)l ossa (6)uegnir libera / et securam(en)te p(er) tuti luoci et / te(r)re del 7)Imp(er)io mio et / ala porta mea Imp(er)ial / p(er) te(r)ra cu(m) tutala 8)cometiua c(om)pagnia / et / famegli sui / chauali / chariazi / dena(r)i 9)argenti robe et / beni del ditto M(agnifi)co ambasiator et d(i) tuta 10)la c(om)pagnia sua d(i) ch(e) c(on)dictio(ne) s(e) fossi coma(n)dando tutili (11)Capitanei / sanzachi / timarati / chadie / eschiaui mei / et / 12)atutili offitiali d(i) ch(e) natura se fossi ch(e) sutto pena (13)dila disgratia t / Indignatio(ne) mea ch(e) alo ditto amba (14)siator c(om)pagnia et / amegli sui cu(m) li beni loro no(n) li fossi (15)fatto pu(n)cto d(i) Inpacio / nzi ogni fauore schorta ecur- (16)tixia bexogna(n)doli sia p(ro)uisto p(er) ina ch(e) uegna ala (17)porta mea. Euegna(n)do ala p(rese)ntia mea et / la Imp(er)ial (18)p(re)fata po(r)ta / o / facando paxi cu(m) lo Imp(er)io neo / o / no(n) (19)facando paxi / cusi anch(e) libera / et / honoratam(en)te 20)cu(m) tutili fauori sup(ra)scripti sene possa partir zenza (21)alchuno mpedim(en)to ni d(i) p(er)sone ni d(i) hauer loro (22)echaminar p(er) utili luoci et / te(r)re mee come di sup(ra) (23)escrito p(er)fina ch(e) sene a al suo paexe seguro. (24)Coma(n)dando atuti sup(ra)ditti ch(e) sia fato usi al to(r)nar (25)honor / ecurtixia come al uegnir alo ditto mis(ser) 26)tomasio ambasiator ut / sup(ra) dela p(re)fata Ill(ustrissi)ma S(ignoria) 27)di venetia Equesta tal scriptura fede esaluoconducto (28)escrito p(er) oma(n)damento del mio Imp(er)io p(er) ma(no) d(i) vno deli (29)mei criuani Latini Ep(er) fede eroborazio(ne) del p(re)no(m)i(n)ato saluo 30)co(n)ducto segnato / e del mio Imp(er)ial solitto signo ep(er) sigurta 31)echautella d(e)l p(re)fato faco sagramento p(er) lo S(ignor) Idio ch(e) 32)acreato cello ela te(r)ra Ep(er) lo n(ost)ro propheta mahomet / 33)ep(er) li cento euinti quat(tr)o milia p(ro)pheti d(i) dio / ep(er) lo hamin (34)euie ch(e) facemo / ep(er) la cimittara ch(e) me cenzo / ep(er)la 35)fede musromana qual credimo nui musromani ch(e) (36)questa p(re)messa fede / esaluo ‸ conducto ‸ fato dal coma(n)dam(en)to mio 37)sia fermo / Rato / eualituro ech(e) p(er) nullo modo i(n) alchuno 38)pu(n)cto sera contrafato cusi dala mia p(er)sona p(ro)pria (39)come da tutili mei viziri basse et / officiali d(i) che (40)c(on)dicti(ne) s(e) fossi Anzi onfermato i(n) tuto ep(er) tuto come (41)escrito nel suo tenore :

(42)Dat(a) / In Residentia mea Imp(er)iali Ciuitatis constanti 43)nopolis die vigesimo quinto Mensis Februarij :—

Translation:

[*ṭughrā*] (as in Doc. 1)

Meḥemmed, by the grace of God Emperor of Turkey and Greece, etc.

By the authority and content of these presents I give, grant and assign full, comprehensive, binding and secure safe-conduct, and a comprehensive, binding and secure guarantee to the excellent ambassador of the most renowned Signory of Venice, Messer Tomasio Malipiero, that he may come freely and safely through all places and lands of My empire and to My Imperial Porte, by land, with all his retinue, company and servants, [and with] the horses, carriages, money, silver, gear and goods of the said excellent ambassador and of all his company of whatever rank they be; commanding all My captains, sanjak-beys, timariots, kadis and slaves, and all officers of whatever character they be, under pain of My displeasure and anger, that not the slightest difficulty be caused to the said ambassador, his company and his servants, together with their goods, but rather that every favour, protection and courtesy of which they stand in need be supplied, so that he may come to My Porte.

And when he comes to My presence and to the Imperial Porte aforesaid, whether he makes peace with My Majesty or does not make peace, so too freely and honourably, with all the attentions above-written, he may depart thence without any obstruction either to their persons or to their possessions and travel through all the places and lands belonging to Me as is written above, so that he may depart to his land in safety; commanding all those above-named that on his return just as on his coming honour and courtesy be shown to the said Messer Tomasio, ambassador, as aforesaid, of the said most renowned Signory of Venice.

And this document, guarantee and safe-conduct has been written by My imperial command by the hand of one of My Latin clerks.

And as guarantee and confirmation of the safe-conduct abovementioned, it is signed with My customary Imperial sign; and as assurance and security of the aforesaid, I make oath by the Lord God Who created heaven and earth, and by our prophet Muḥammad, and by the 124,000 prophets of God, and by the road and paths which we follow, and by the sword with which I gird myself, and by the Muslim faith which we Muslims profess, that this guarantee and safe-conduct aforesaid made at My command be fixed, confirmed and binding, and that in no way in any detail will it be infringed, either by My own person or by any of My viziers, pashas and officers, of whatever rank they be, but rather maintained in its entirety and by all, as is set out in its content.

Given in My Imperial residence at the city of Constantinople, on the 25th day of the month of February.

4. Last decade of Dhu'l-Qaʿda 882/24 February–5 March 1478, Constantinople. *Fermān* to the Venetian ambassadors [Tomaso Malipiero and his secretary Alvise Manenti] urging them to come to the Porte without hesitation. Plate XXXIII. [44 cm. × 14·5 cm., 10 lines]

Text:

[invocatio] هو

[*ṭughrā*] (as in Doc. I)

مفاخر امراء خلاف الملّه ونديك ايلچيلرى ختمت عواقبهم بالخير
توقيع رفيع واصل اوليجاق معلوم اولا كم شمدكيحالده ونديك
بكلرى قبلندن رسالت وجهيله دركاه عالمپناهمه توجّه ادب بونده
كلملك بابنده استيذان اتمش‌سز امدى چون كى
رسالت طريقيله كلورسز تردّد واحتياط چكميوب
كلوب استان سعادت آشيانمه واصل اولوب قضايا ومصالح
نيسه پايۀ سرير اعلامه اعلام ادەسز شيله بلاسز
بونلك كبى امر محل خوف وتوهّم دكل ادكى خود هر عاقله
معلومدر شيله بلاسز علامت شريف ازره اعتماد قلاسز
تحريراً فى اواخر ذى القعده سنه اثنين وثمانين وثما<نمائه>

بمقا
قسطنطني

Translation:

[invocatio] He!

[*ṭughrā*] (as in Doc. I)

The ornaments among the commanders of the lands outside the [Muslim] community, the ambassadors of Venice, may they come to a good end!

When the exalted sign arrives, be it known that at this present you have asked for authorization in the matter of setting out for My Porte, the refuge of the world, and coming here on an embassy on behalf of the lords of Venice; now therefore, since you are coming here as ambassadors you need feel no hesitation or caution, but may come and present yourselves at My threshold, the abode of felicity, and make known to the foot of My lofty throne whatever business and affairs you have.

Thus you are to know—indeed that a matter like this is not an occasion for fears and fancies is known to every intelligent man.

Thus you are to know; you are to place reliance upon the noble sign.

Written in the last decade of Dhu'l-Qa'da in the year 882.

In the residence
of Constantinople

5. First decade of Muḥarram 883/4–13 April 1478, Constantinople. *Nishān* ordering the kadis and sanjak-beys to afford passage and provide an escort to Venetian ambassadors travelling to and from the Porte. Plate XXXIV.

[dimensions not recorded, 13 lines]

Text:

[*ṭughrā*] (as in Doc. I)

نشان همایون ومثال میمون انفذه الله تعالی الی یوم یبعثون حکمی اول درکی
مصالحه امریچون
شمدکیحالده وندیکك بکلرندن عتبهٔ علیامه ایلچی کلملك ایچون استیذان
ولنوب ایلچان نامه[6] طلب اتدکلری سببدن اجازت ویرب بو حکم
شریفی آنلاره ویردم وبیوردم کی آنلرك ایلچیلری هر قچن که
وجه وعزیمت ایدب ممالك محروسمدن هرنه محله چقسلر اول ییرك
سنجاغی بکلری وقاضیلری بونلاره آدم ویولداش قوشوب کوندرب
عتبهٔ علیامه ایصال ادهلر کندولره ومال‌لرنه واسباب‌لرنه بوجهٍ من الوجوه
تعرض اولمیلر آنلار دخی کلوب قضایادن ومصالحدن نه وارسه
رکاه عالمپناهمه رفع ادب کتملو اولیجاق کرو ارسال اولنلر
صالحه امری اتمام اولنسه ویا اولنمسه کلملك‌لرنده وکرو کتملك‌لرنده
نلاره کمسنه تعرض اتمیه ومانع اولمیا اختیارلریله وارب

كلدكلرى يره واصل اولالر شيله بلالر علامت شريف ازره
اعتماد قلالر تحريراً فى اوايل محرم الحرام سنه ثلث وثمانين وثما<نمائه>

بمقام
قسطنطنيه

Translation:

[invocatio] (none)

[*tughrā*] (as in Doc. 1)

The order conveyed by the Imperial sign and the felicitous device—may God Almighty preserve its validity “ until the day when they are raised ” ! [4]—is this, that :

< for the business of making peace > [5] At this present, since authorization has been sought for ambassadors to come to My lofty Porte from the lords of Venice and since they have requested a letter of safe-conduct,[6] I have granted permission and have given them this noble command ;

And I have commanded that at whatever time their ambassadors may set forth and proceed, and at whatever place in My well-protected dominions they may appear, the beys and kadis of the sanjak in which that place is found are to provide men to travel with them as escort and send them on their way and enable them to reach My lofty Porte, and they are not to interfere in any way at all with them or their possessions or their gear. And when they for their part have come and have submitted to My Porte, the refuge of the world, whatever business and affairs there may be [to transact] and are due to return, they are to be sent back, whether the business of making peace is concluded or not : both on their coming and on their returning back no-one is to molest or hinder them, but they are to travel freely and arrive at the place from which they first came.

Thus they are to know ; they are to place reliance upon the noble sign.

Written in the first decade of the sacred Muḥarram in the year 883.
In the residence
of Constantinople

---

[4] Koran, VII, 13, XV, 36, etc.

[5] These words have been added as an afterthought, see p. 95 below.

[6] I.e. *éljān-nāme*, see pp. 96–8 below.

6. First decade of Rabīʿ I 883/2–11 June 1478, Egri Dere. *Fermān* to the kadis of Rumeli, ordering them to permit a Venetian ambassador to come freely to the Porte and to return. Plate XXXV.

[dimensions not recorded, 11 lines]

Text:

[invocatio] هو

[*ṭughrā*] (as in Doc. I)

مفاخر القضاة والحكام مبينو الشرايع والاحكام روم ايلى قاضيلرى دامت فضايلهم
توقيع رفيع واصل اوليجاق معلوم اولا كم شمدكيحالده ونديك
ايلچيلرى بونده كلوب اجازت ويرلوب كرو اول جوانبه
توجّه ايدب مصالحه امرى اچون ايلچيلرى ويا آدملرى
كلَجك اولدغى سببدن بيوردم كى مصالحه مصلحتى اچون
اول طرفدن ايلچى ويا آدم كلوب عتبۀ عليامه توجه ادب
هر قنقكوزك تحت حكومتندن چقوب كلملك استرسه
كمسنه‌كوز مانع اولميه وبوندن اجازت ويرلوب
كرو اول طرفه كتملو اوليجاق عايق ودافع اولمياسز
شيله بلاسز علامت شريف ازره اعتماد قلاسز تحريراً
فى اوايل ربيع الاول سنه ثلث وثمانين وثمانما<ئه>

بيورت
اكرى دره

Translation:

[invocatio] He!

[*ṭughrā*] (as in Doc. I)

The ornaments among the kadis and judges, exponents of the Sharīʿa laws and the decrees, the kadis of Rumeli, may their virtues endure!

When the exalted sign arrives, be it known that at this present, since the ambassadors of Venice have come here and been given leave to depart and have set out back for those parts, and since their ambassador or their agent is going to come for the business of making peace, I have commanded that if, for the affair of making peace, an ambassador or agent comes from that direction and sets out for My lofty Porte, through the jurisdiction of whichever of you he may wish to come up, none of you is to prevent him ; and when he is given leave to depart from here and is due to go back there, you are not to impede or repel him.

Thus you are to know ; you are to place reliance upon the noble sign.

Written in the first decade of Rabīʿ I in the year 883.

In the camp
at Egri Dere

7. No date [? June 1478], no place of issue [? the Ottoman camp outside Scutari]. Letter in Greek from an Ottoman officer [? Dā'ūd Pasha, beylerbey of Rumeli] to a Venetian ambassador [? Tomaso Malipiero] ; the sender acknowledges the ambassador's letter, which reported that he had reached Alessio, that Aḥmed Bey [? Evrenos-oghlu Aḥmed, sanjak-bey of Albania] had given him an escort, but that he had been robbed by the *martolos* ; the sender promises to do his best to recover the stolen property and urges the ambassador to proceed on his mission. Plate XXXVI.
[23 cm. × 11·2 cm., 20 lines]

Translation : [7]

[*penche*] Dā'ūd b. ʿAbd Allāh [8]

To the most honourable, renowned and wise ambassador, worthy of all honour. Let me inform you that I have received your letter and acquainted myself with what you write to me. You write to me that because of the weather and because of the rain you were delayed in reaching Lesi. You write to me, however, that you met with Ahmat Beg, and he sent his *voyvoda* to accompany you and [. . . ?] [9] to [?] return from you. The *amartoloi* appeared and wounded their men and seized both your horses and your baggage, and they took baggage of yours to the value of five to six hundred ducats.

As soon as I saw your letter, I sent a slave and an order that they should seek for it, and I trust in God that I shall find it. Do not feel distress or anger ; but just [. . .] [10] do all that you can and carry out the service as the Grand Signior commanded you.

---

[7] To give a confident transcription of this document and to comment on it fall quite outside my competence. In the hope that a specialist will subject the text to detailed study, I confine myself to giving a tentative translation ; for this I am indebted to Mr. V. Demetriades, whose help I most gratefully acknowledge.

[8] For this reading of the name in the *penche* see p. 100 below.

[9] Obscure : is a word missing after *των*?

[10] ἀντίληψις (" perspicuity " or " help ") appears to be used here as a respectful address, " your honour " or " your excellency ".

NOTES
DIPLOMATIC AND LEXICAL [1]

Document 1.

This is apparently the oldest known original Ottoman document drawn up in Italian. Unless the document was refolded when it was filed away in Venice, the faint " mirror-image " of the *ṭughrā* in its top fold suggests that the paper had, contrary to Ottoman practice,[2] been folded from the top downwards. Neither on this document, nor on Doc. 3, is there any *invocatio* (although the fact that they are written in Italian does not preclude the presence of an *invocatio* in Arabic).[3] The salutation is similar to that of Meḥemmed II's letter of 25 March 1466, also in Italian, to the same Doge : [4] " Mahumeth Dei gratiâ Imperator Turciae atque Graeciae &c. Christophoro Mauro Serenissimo Duci Venetiarum salutem " ; the salutation in his letter of 24 April 1480,[5] after the conclusion of peace, is more cordial : " Sultan Mohamet dei gra(tia) totius Asye et grecie Imperator etc. Serenissimo principi ac Illustrissime d(omi)nationi venetiarum pacem amoris plenitudinem Gratiam et sinceram uoluntatem." " Turcia / Asya " and " Grecia " stand for the two beylerbeyliks of Anadolu and Rumeli. In documents

---

[1] Works cited more than once in this section are referred to by the following abbreviations :—

Anhegger and Inalcık = R. Anhegger and H. Inalcık (edd.), *Ḳānūnnāme-i sulṭānī ber mūceb-i 'örf-i 'Osmānī : II. Mehmed ve II. Bayezid devirlerine ait yasaḳnāme ve ḳānūnnāmeler*, Ankara (TTK) 1956.

Beldiceanu = N. Beldiceanu, *Les actes des premiers sultans . . . , i : actes de Mehmed II et de Bayezid II du ms. fonds turc ancien* 39, Paris–The Hague 1960.

Elezović, i/1, i/2 = G. Elezović, *Turski spomenici*, i/1 (translations and commentary), Belgrade 1940, and i/2 (facsimiles and index), Belgrade 1952.

Kraelitz = F. Kraelitz, *Osmanische Urkunden in türkischer Sprache aus der zweiten Hälfte des 15. Jahrhunderts* (Sitzungsberichte Ak. Wien, 197/3), Vienna 1922.

Miklosisch and Müller, iii = F. Miklosisch and J. Müller, *Acta et diplomata graeca medii aevi sacra et profana*, iii, Vienna 1865.

Truhelka = Ć. Truhelka, *Tursko-slovjenski spomenici Dubrovačke arhive*, Sarajevo 1911.

Uzunçarşılı = I. H. Uzunçarşılı, " Tuğra ve pençeler," *Belleten*, v (1941), 101–58.

[2] See *EI*², art. *Diplomatic* (by J. Reychman and A. Zajaczkowski), 315b.

[3] The letter of Meḥemmed II to the Doge, in Italian, dated 24 April 1480, has the *invocatio* " *Huwa'l-Ghanī* ", see A. da Mosto, *L'Archivio di Stato di Venezia*, i, Rome 1937 (Bibl. des Annales Institutorum, vol. v), plate xiv.

[4] Its text is quoted by M. Sanuto, *Vite de' Duchi di Venezia*, in L. A. Muratori, *Rerum Italicarum scriptores*, 1723–51, vol. xxii, 1184. Cf. also the salutation of Bāyezīd II's letter to Ragusa (Truhelka, no. 153) : " Sultan Paiasit chan dei gra(tia) Imperator maximus Asie Europeq(ue) etc. . . . s(alutem) p(lurimam) d(icit)."

[5] See n. 3 above.

written in Greek the equivalent of the "dei gratia" formula does not appear until the reign of Bāyezīd II.[6] Similarly, the equivalent of the phrase "alla porta della segnoria nostra" appears (as a calque ?) in a slightly later letter in Greek.[7] In the final date, the day and month (24 May) are recorded by the solar calendar, but the year is that of the Hijra (875, beg. 30. vi. 1470). The same combination is found in documents of this period written in Slavonic, e.g. Truhelka, no. 38: 24 September 877 (= 1472); no. 40: 8 July 879 (= 1474); no. 41: 24 September 879 (= 1474). An example of this hybrid dating in a document in Greek, Bāyezīd II's letter of 30 November 893 (= 1488), is found in the "Liber Graecus", where there is a further example for a document in Italian, his letter of 10 February 892 (= 1487).[8]

Document 3.

The wording of this safe-conduct, presumably based on European diplomatic practice, may be compared with that of the safe-conduct in Latin, issued by Meḥemmed II to Christians wishing to enter Ottoman territory to ransom their enslaved relations (Truhelka, no. 69), in which are echoed numerous phrases of Doc. 3.[9] This Latin document, like our Doc. 3, is dated merely by the (solar) day and month,[10] as is a letter of Bāyezīd II to Ragusa (Truhelka, no. 153) in Latin, and some of Meḥemmed II's letters in Slavonic (Truhelka, nos. 20, 22, 23, etc.). Where the Latin safe-conduct has merely "(Datu)m ex chancelarijs imperii nostri signoque nostro solito [i.e. the *ṭughrā*] sign(atum)", the

---

[6] See the *'ahd-nāme* of September 1481 (Miklosisch and Müller, iii, 310) and the Sultan's letter of April 1485 (op. cit., p. 332).

[7] Op. cit., p. 294: *εἰς τὴν Πόρταν τῆς αὐθεντίας μου.* The "Porte", of course, is no specific locality, but the "presence" of the Sultan, wherever he may be: this is nicely illustrated by a phrase in the instructions of the Venetian ambassadors Capello and Cocco, of Nov. 1470 (for which see p. 102 below): "... dirrigite vos ad portam turci ubi illum esse intellexeritis."

[8] See A. Bombaci, "Il 'Liber Graecus', un cartolario veneziano comprendente inediti documenti in greco (1481–1504)," in *Westöstliche Abhandlungen* (Festschrift R. Tschudi), Wiesbaden 1954, pp. 288–303 at p. 296.

[9] E.g.: "... jussimus ac imperauimus scribere presentes apertas et manifestas litteras ac fidem et plenum, amplum, tutum, validum et securum saluum conductum omnibus et singulis cuiuscumque nationis aut conditionis sint ...," "... Volentes et mandantes ... omnibus capitaneis terre, sançachis, timaratis, chadijs et alijs quibuscumque offitialibus, cuiuscumque conditionis sint, et sclauis nostris, quatenus presentem saluum conductum obseruent et obseruari fatient sub pena indignationis nostre."

[10] The place of issue also is expressed in the Latin document in terms similar to those of Doc. 3: "Datum in nostra residentia ciuitatis Constantinopolis."

corresponding sentence of Doc. 3 is preceded (lines 28–9) by the reference to " mei scrivani Latini ", attesting the existence at the Porte of a special staff of clerks for correspondence in Latin and Italian. Doc. 3 has further, unlike the Latin document, the corroborating oath.

There is as yet no study on the oath employed by Ottoman rulers.[11] Examples are to be found in documents of this period written in Greek and in Slavonic,[12] while a contemporary example in Turkish appears in a *berāt* of Meḥemmed II, probably of 1463, granting protection to the Franciscan monks of Bosnia and permitting brethren from outside Ottoman territory to come and go freely.[13] An oath usually (but not invariably) corroborates a treaty (*'ahd-nāme*) ; as it appears also in the *berāt* for Roman Catholic monks and (here) in a safe-conduct,[14] it seems to be associated particularly with the conferring of *amān*.[15] In Doc. 3 the Sultan swears by (1) God the Creator, (2) the Prophet, (3) the 124,000 prophets of God, (4) the " way " (= *sabīl Allāh* ?) which he follows, (5) his sword, and (6) the Muslim faith. All these clauses are found in other contemporary oaths, (4), however, being rare [16] ; this oath lacks two clauses usually found : the " seven *muṣḥaf* ", and the " soul " or " life " of the Sultan's ancestors, himself or his children. The forms " musromana " and " musromani " (line 35) appear to be a Slavism : " musroman- " is found in the Slavonic text of the *'ahd-nāme* granted by Murād II to Ragusa in 1442. It appears indeed, as in Doc. 3, in the course of the oath.[17] Was the " scrivano Latino " translating from a model formula in Slavonic ?

---

[11] See for the moment the notes at Elezović, i/1, 1140–1 ; and at p. 253 of F. Babinger and F. Dölger, " Mehmeds II. frühester Staatsvertrag," in *Orientalia Christiana Periodica*, xv (1949), 225–58 (= F. Dölger, *Byzantinische Diplomatik*, 1956, p. 286) ; and also Elizabeth Zachariadou, *Μία ἑλληνόγλωσση συνθήκη του Χηδὴρ 'Αϊδίνογλου*, in *Byzantinische Zeitschrift*, lv (1962), 254–65 (especially 259–60).

[12] In Greek : in the treaty of 1446 (see preceding note), and Miklosisch and Müller, iii, 286 (of 1450), 287 (of 1453), 290 (of 1454), 295 (of 1479), 313 and 318 (of 1482) ; in Slavonic : Truhelka, no. 6 (of 1442), no. 15 (of 1459), no. 71 (of 1481).

[13] Elezović, i/1, 1139–45 = i/2, 223. For the circumstances in which this document was issued see F. Babinger, *Mehmed der Eroberer und seine Zeit*, Munich 1953, p. 240.

[14] A safe-conduct issued by Shihāb al-Dīn Pasha to Ragusan ambassadors in 1441 (Truhelka, no. 4) is also ratified by an oath.

[15] I refrain the more readily from following up this question here since Dr. Wansbrough is, I understand, preparing a study on *amān* which will involve this point.

[16] It appears in Truhelka, no. 71 (p. 65, lines 12–13), the *'ahd-nāme* of 1481 in Slavonic.

[17] Truhelka, no. 6, line 4 (three further references in the index, s.v. *musromanin*)—but *musloman-* later in the document (p. 10, l. 19). The equivalent passages in the oaths of no. 15 (l. 4) of 1459 and no. 71 (p. 65, l. 15) of 1481 have *musloman-*.

Documents 2, 4, 5, 6.

For only one of these documents (4) have I a note of the dimensions: 44 cm. × 14·5 cm., but the similar proportions of the others indicate that they too are of about the same size, and thus fall within the limits of those of "everyday" *fermān*s of this period.[18] Only for Doc. 2 are the foldings visible: the paper is folded 11 times. Docs. 2 and 4 have the brief invocatio *huwa*, the tail of which is just visible also on the upper (trimmed?) edge of Doc. 6. The photograph of Doc. 5 shows only a shallow space above the *ṭughrā*, which suggests that the top few cm. of the document have been lost, perhaps taking with them an *invocatio.* The *ṭughrā*s are all bold and wide, with the converging loops extended to, or nearly to, the right-hand edge. All four documents, and especially Doc. 2, are carelessly written, very possibly by the same clerk.[19] Little attention has been given to making the lines start precisely beneath one another. In Doc. 5 the words *muṣālaḥa emrichün* are squeezed in as an afterthought at the end of the first line and thus, contrary to normal practice, interrupt the introductory formula: ... *ḥükmi oldur ki / shimdiki ḥālde.* Similarly in Doc. 4 it is surprising to find the concluding formula "*Shöyle bilesiz* ..." interrupted by the afterthought: "*bunuŋ gibi emir maḥall-i khawf u tewehhüm değül idüği khod her ʿāqile maʿlūmdur.*" In these dealings with representatives of the enemy the Ottoman chancery evidently felt no obligation to produce attractive and faultless documents. The introductory formula of the *nishān*, Doc. 5, demands no comment,[20] nor, so far as its wording is concerned, does the address which fills the first line of Doc. 6, a *fermān* to the kadis of Rumeli.[21] It is perhaps a little surprising that the *fermān*, providing for the protection and escort of the enemy's ambassador, is addressed only to the kadis (unlike Doc. 2, to the sanjak-beys, and Doc. 5, for the attention of both sanjak-beys and kadis); the explanation may be that the clerk, himself on active service in the Ottoman camp, knew well that the sanjak-beys

---

18 Namely 40–47 cm. × 14–17 cm., see Kraelitz, 8.

19 Compare the writing in Docs. 2, 4, 6 of *tewqīʿ-i refīʿ wāṣil olïjak maʿlūm olakim*, in Docs. 2, 5, 6 of *buyurdum ki*, and in all four of *shöyle bile-siz(-ler) ʿalāmet-i sherīf üzre iʿtimād kïla-sïz(-lar)*. Compare also (Doc.) 2, (line) 6 *adamlar*, 5,6 *adam*, 6,4 *adamlar*; 4,6 *maṣāliḥ*, 5,1 and 10 *muṣālaḥa*, 6,4 and 5 *muṣālaḥa*; 5,9 and 6,9 *gitmelü olïjak*; 5,2 and 6,6 *ʿatebe-i ʿulyāma*; 2,4–5 and 6,7 *her kankïŋuzuŋ taḥt-i ḥukūmetinden*; 2,5 and 5,8 *mutaʿarriż*, 5,11 *taʿarruż*; 4,4 and 5,2 *istiʾdhān*; 5,11 and 6,8 *kimesne*; 4,3 and 6,4 and 6 *tewejjüh*; 2,7 and 4,7 *edesiz*, 5,7 *edeler*; 5,3 and 6,5 *sebebden*.

20 Cf. Kraelitz, no. 4 (of 874/1469) and Anhegger and Inalcık, nos. 1, 2, 3, etc.

21 Cf. Kraelitz, no. 9 (of 883/1478–9) and no. 11 (of 891/1496).

were at this time (June 1478) all under arms, encamped before Scutari.[22] The address of Doc. 2, to the sanjak-beys of Rumeli, is in the shortest possible form: already in a document of 898/1493 (Kraelitz, no. 21) is added the honorific phrase *dhawu'l-qadr wa'l-iḥtirām*. The address of Doc. 4 is (so far as I know) unique: *mafākhir umarā' khilāf al-milla Venedik elchileri khutimat 'awāqibuhum bi'l-khayr*. In general it corresponds to the address on documents to the " begs " of Ragusa: *mafākhir umarā' al-milla al-masīḥiyya Dubrovnik begleri khutimat 'awāqibuhum bi'l-khayr* [23]; but where we should expect *al-milla al-masīḥiyya* we find the phrase *khilāf al-milla*. That this phrase, literally " the opposite of the community [of Allāh] ", means " non-Muslim lands " is apparent from a parallel use in Sa'd al-Dīn's *Tāj al-Tawārīkh* (ii, 33, line 10), where in describing Jem's reception in Rome (in 1489) Sa'd al-Dīn makes the Pope ask him what his intention was in coming *khilāf-i millet arasîna*.[24] The use of the phrase, less courteous than *al-milla al-masīḥiyya*, in our document may have been prompted by the existence of a state of war, so that the normal protocol did not apply. Whereas the *fermāns* (Docs. 2, 4, 6) have the older formula *ma'lūm ola kim*, in the *nishān* (Doc. 5) we find . . . *oldur ki*, with the *ki* written as a loop,[25] as in the *buyurdum ki* of Docs. 2, 5 and 6, and in the *chun-ki* of Doc. 4, line 4 (but not the *kachan-ki* of Doc. 5, line 4).

In the content of the Turkish documents, one point only calls for extended comment: the term *él-jān*, which, with its appearance in Doc. 5, is attested for the fourth time in published contexts.

Its earliest appearance is in a document issued at Istanbul by Maḥmūd Pasha, then Grand Vizier and beylerbey of Rumeli, in Jumādā I 867/January 1463 (Elezović, i/1, no. 13 = i/2, no. 5 = Uzunçarşılı, pp. 137–8 and pl. 36). According to the *expositio*, the bearer, Franco

---

[22] See below, pp. 110–11.

[23] Elezović, i/2, no. 81 of 908/1503, no. 93 of 911/1506, and (with *ümerālarî* for *begleri*) no. 127 of 920/1514.

[24] The phrase is reproduced in works depending on Sa'd al-Dīn: Solak-zāde, p. 286; Ḥüseyn, *Badā'i' al-Waqā'i'*, Moscow 1961, p. 688. The meaning " non-Muslim lands " is confirmed when the wording of Sa'd al-Dīn's source is compared; he is here following, in a close paraphrase, the *Wāqi'āt-i Sulṭān Jem* (*T'OEM*, *'ilāwe*, p. 22), which has *ghayr-i millet arasîna gelmekden maqṣūdîn sordîlar*, and continues: *Merḥūm dakhi eyitdi Ghayr-i millete gelmek maqṣūd değül idi, belki Rūm-iline gechmeğe Rodos qawmîndan yol istedim*, " [Jem] replied: ' To come to non-Muslim lands was not intended; on the contrary I asked the people of Rhodes to provide passage for me to pass into Rumeli.' "

[25] For this " Schleifenform " and its development see P. Wittek's note at p. 111 of his " Zu einigen frühosmanischen Urkunden (V) ", in *WZKM*, lvii (1961), 102–17.

(?)Bobanič, had requested an *él-jān mektūbî* [26] so that he might come from Ragusa and settle at Novabrdo [27]; the *dispositio* states that " this *ḥükm* " has been issued to him so that he and his people, being treated as *ra'āyā*, may live unmolested on the Imperial *khāṣṣ* there.[28]

The term appears again in a group of four documents, very similar to one another, preserved in MS. fonds turc ancien 39 of the Bibliothèque Nationale. All four—nos. 4, 8, 9, 10 in the edition of R. Anhegger and H. Inalcık and the translation of N. Beldiceanu—are *nishān*s giving authority to and laying down the powers of the government supervisors (*yasakchî*) of silver-mines in Serbia and Bosnia. Only the last is dated : Rabī' II 880/August 1475. Among the provisions is one whose common text can be reconstructed thus : *We-buyurdum ki él-jān verüb kuyujîlarî ve charkhchîlarî ve ma'dene münāsib olan kishileri* [+ (no. 8 only) *ki kharāja we-kimesneye ra'iyyetde yazîlmamîsh ola*] *getürdüb ma'denleri sheneldeler* : " And I have commanded that he [i.e. the supervisor, *yasakchî*], is, by giving *él-jān*, to cause to be brought in miners and engineers and people qualified at mining [+ not being enregistered as payers of *kharāj* or as anybody's *ra'āyā*], who may make the mines prosper." [29] The addition in no. 8, most probably a gloss, makes it clear that the miners who are to be recruited are immigrants from the *dār al-ḥarb* : hence the *él-jān* by virtue of which they can enter Ottoman territory is *amān*.

In commenting on this passage Anhegger and Inalcık adduce from Kemāl's *Selāṭîn-nāme* (completed in 895/1490) the couplet : *Kili'yi jebr-ile ol shah-i dewrān / aluban verdi küffārîna él-jān* : " That ruler of the age [i.e. Bāyezīd II] took Kilia by force and granted *él-jān* to its infidels." [30] This passage, when compared with other accounts of the campaign, confirms the meaning of *él-jān*, for it is used here as a synonym

---

[26] Elezović translates " *list* " (" letter, document "), without comment. Uzunçarşılı reads *il-khān*, without comment : the point of the *jîm* is to be detected, however, as a small excrescence below the stroke of the *lām*.

[27] One word seems to be lacking. I am inclined to read : *Dubrovnikden chîkub ḥażret-i khilāfet-penāhî . . . nüŋ Novabrdadaghî* < *khāṣṣlarînda* > *gelüb mütemekkin olmaghichün . . .* " to come and settle on the Sultan's < *khāṣṣ*-lands > at N." (cf. l. 6 : *gelüb medhkūr khāṣṣlarda otura*).

[28] Franco is returning to the district, for the order provides that he is not to be called to account for his actions " in the time of the Despot ", i.e. before the definitive Ottoman occupation of the region in 1455.

[29] Dr Beldiceanu interprets the passage in this sense, and no doubt correctly, in spite of the awkward change of subject. He renders *él-jān* " permis de séjour ".

[30] Anhegger and Inalcık, p. 7, n. 19. Kemāl seems to be contradicting himself, for Kilia, surrendering on terms, was not taken " by force ".

for the *amān* mentioned by 'Āshiqpasha-zāde (ed. F. Giese, p. 187, l. 13) and in the *fetḥ-nāme* (Ferīdūn, *Munsha'āt al-Salāṭīn*², i, 296, line 1).

The word was unfamiliar to the copyist of the Paris MS. ; only in no. 8 does he write ايلجان, the other three contexts having ايلرجان, with the vocalization *īlerjān* indicated. The latter spelling is certainly incorrect, for Kemāl's metre demands a dissyllable, and other Paris MSS. which give the texts of nos. 8 and 10 read here *īljān*,[31] the spelling found also in 15th-century *taḥrīr*-registers.[32] The misspelling however, most easily explicable as a misreading of ايلوجان, does suggest a possible etymology : *él u-jān*, usually contracted to *él-jān*,[33] " peace [34] and [guarantee of] life." Be that as it may, the meaning of the phrase *éljān-nāme* found in Doc. 5, parallel to the *éljān mektūbî* mentioned in the document issued by Maḥmūd Pasha, is clear : it is " a letter conferring *amān* ", i.e. a safe-conduct.

In Ottoman usage there seems to have been no single term regularly employed for " safe-conduct ". In Ottoman documents of this period the safe-conduct issued by a European ruler is referred to as *amān kāghîdî* (? a calque of *litterae securitatis*) [35] and that of the Sultan, in words put into the mouth of an Italian, as *vére kāghîdî* [36] ; and the author of the

---

[31] Beldiceanu, p. 162, n. 8.

[32] Anhegger and Inalcık, p. 8, n. 19.

[33] The simple juxtaposition of two nouns is a normal feature of Turkish, needing no illustration ; but it is worthwhile to point out the parallel provided in Elezović, i/2, no. 32, line 5 *él-gün*, but line 11 *él-u-gün*.

[34] This (? extended) meaning of *él*, first attested by Maḥmūd Kāshgharî (*Dīwān Lughāt al-Turk*, ed. Kilisli Rif'at, i, 50 = B. Atalay's translation, i, 49 : *al-ṣulḥ bayna 'l-malikayn*) and given also by Abū Ḥayyān (*Kitāb al-Idrāk . . .*, ed. A. Caferoğlu, Istanbul 1931, p. 20) is not itself found in Ottoman but lies behind the well-attested meaning " at peace " (as opposed to *yaghi*, cf. *Tanıklariyle Tarama Sözlüğü*, i and ii, s.v. il (el) 3, and iv, s.v. il olmak), whence *éllik*, " peace " (*TTS*, i–iii, s.v. illik).

[35] In the report of the Ottoman agent Barak published by Ş. Turan, in *Belleten*, xxvi/103 (1962), 547, referring to the passport of the Duke of Savoy. The term, with the meaning " safe-conduct ", was known to Meninski and (? hence) Zenker. Zü'l-Fiqār Efendi, who went on a diplomatic mission to Vienna in 1099/1688 (in time of open war) uses the terms *emn kāghîdî* and *pasaporto kāghîdî* for the safe-conduct sent him by Maximilian of Bavaria (Siliḥdār, ii, 653). An Ottoman report of about 1780 (*Belleten*, xxvi/101 (1962), 154) uses the term *amān buyruldusu* for the document which the authorities at Jedda sent out to European ships wishing to enter harbour.

[36] So I interpret *warā kāghîdî* in the report of another Ottoman agent published by I. H. Uzunçarşılı (see *Belleten*, xxiv/95 (1960), 462 and 476). The terms *amān* " [grant of] security " and *vére* " submission [under promise of security] " were, it appears, in common parlance already overlapping in meaning : in later texts (e.g. Pechevī, ii, 194) *amān* and *vére* are practically synonymous and *amān kāghîdî* means " terms of surrender ".

Wāqi'āt-i Sulṭān Jem explains a *salvo condotto* as being a *mīthāq-nāme*,[37] which Sa'd al-Dīn in his turn paraphrases (ii, 23) as *'ahd-nāme*. In the later Ottoman safe-conducts of 966/1559 and 989/1581 published by J. H. Mordtmann,[38] no specific term is used : the documents themselves are called merely *ḥükm* or *fermān*, and they are conferring *ijāzet* or *idhn*.[39] Perhaps no specific term was necessary, for the conditions under which a *harbī* might travel in Muslim lands were already covered by the ancient doctrine of *amān*, for which the locution *él-jān* seems to be no more than a transient synonym.[40]

Document 7.

The use of Greek in correspondence emanating from Ottoman statesmen is well attested, the earliest example being Saruja Pasha's letter of 1431 to the inhabitants of Yanina ; Doc. 7, however, appears to be the earliest known original letter.

---

[37] *T'OEM*, *'ilāwe*, 7 (cf. *Gurbet-nâme-i Sultan Cem*, ed. I. H. Danişmend, in *Fatih ve İstanbul*, ii/7–12 (1954), 211–71, at p. 217).

[38] J. H. Mordtmann, " Zwei osmanische Passbriefe aus dem XVI. Jahrhundert," in *Mitteilungen z. osm. Geschichte*, i (1921–2), 177–201.

[39] The letter of protection issued by 'Īsā Beg to a " Latin " merchant in 868/1464 (Elezović, i/1, no. 16 = i/2, no. 7) is called merely *mektūb* ; a document issued to Transylvanian merchants by the beylerbey of Buda in 987/1579 is called in its text *temessük* (M. Guboglu, *Paleografia şi diplomatica Turco-osmana*, Bucharest 1958, p. 173, facs. 15; Guboglu lists also, at p. 55, the terms *amān-nāme* and *yol-fermānī* for " safe-conduct ").

[40] There is a problem of terminology here. The " Geleitbrief " of 898/1493 published by Kraelitz (no. 21), a *fermān* ordering the sanjak-beys, kadis, and *su-bashis* of Rumeli not to hinder a Ragusan agent nor to permit his horses to be seized for the courier-service, is similar in form and content to the " safe-conducts " in Turkish published here, but strictly speaking it is not quite of the same class, for Ragusa did not belong to the *dār al-ḥarb* : the Ragusans were *kul* and *kharāj-güẕār* (Kraelitz, no. 2), regarded as *dhimmī* (Kraelitz, no. 7; Elezović, i/1, 293), the tribute which they paid was *jizya* (Kraelitz, no. 3), and they are on occasion even given the *du'ā* : *zīda 'izzuhum* (Elezović, i/2, no. 37), usually reserved to Muslims. The *fermān* was no doubt a great convenience to the Ragusan agent, and he would not in practice (for practice and theory may differ) have ventured on the journey without it, but juridically it was not essential to his safety. Similarly the five Tīmūrid " Passbriefe " published by H. R. Roemer (*Staatsschreiben der Timuridenzeit*, Wiesbaden 1952, pp. 96–104 and 179–82) are no more than letters of recommendation, issued by a Muslim ruler to be carried by Muslims travelling through Muslim lands : they are " passports " in the modern sense, in that the sovereign " requests and requires " that his own subject be protected and assisted. The documents borne by the Venetian ambassadors are on a different footing, for here the hostile power guarantees a temporary protection to which the ambassador as such was in theory entitled, but which might not otherwise embrace his attendants.

The ungainly stiffly-drawn *penche*, like some others of the period, imitates the Sultan's *ṭughrā* and appears at the head of the document.[41] Not without hesitation I read the name "Dā'ūd bn 'Abd Allāh", as follows: the lowest horizontal stroke with the short vertical stroke to its right gives *dāl*; the left-hand *hasta* gives *alif*; the next horizontal stroke, with the loop to its right, gives *wāw*; immediately above it, to the left, is a second *dāl*. The wide loop to the left swinging right across the paper stands for *bn*, as does one of the two loops of the *ṭughrā*. The prominent *'ayn* is followed by a "tooth" (for *bā*) at the foot of the right-hand *hasta*, and then by a *dāl*; the right-hand *hasta* is the initial *alif* of *Allāh*, the *llh* filling the central space. With this reading, I identify the sender as the Dā'ūd Pasha who was in 1478 [42] beylerbey of Rumeli and was later, for most of the first half of Bāyezīd II's reign, Grand Vizier. At first sight this identification is precluded by the fact that the same Dā'ūd Pasha signed himself, as Grand Vizier, "Dā'ūd b. 'Abd al-Wadūd"; my reasons for maintaining the identification are set out in an excursus (pp. 112–8 below).

To comment on the Greek text is not my province, and I note only a few points in passing. The spelling is almost entirely phonetic.[43] The spelling of *ἀποκρισιάριος* "ambassador" with a *lambda* (line 2 *απωκλεισιαρη*) is a Slavism (cf. Serbo-Croat *poklisar*). The spelling *αμαρτολη* (lines 9–10 = *αμαρτολοι*) in this relatively early attestation of the word prompts the question whether Turkish *martolos* might not after all derive from Gk. *ἁμαρτωλός* "sinner", as Hammer proposed, rather than from *ἁρματωλός* (from Ln. *armatus*), as has gained general acceptance.[44] *ῥοῦχα* (lines 11–12), literally "clothes", has the more general

[41] To the examples reproduced by Truhelka, Kraelitz ("Studien zur osmanischen Urkundenlehre, i: die Handfeste (Penče) der osman. Wesire", in *Mitteilungen z. osm. Geschichte*, ii (1923–6), 257–68) and Uzunçarşılı, is now to be added that of Khāṣṣ Murād published by F. Babinger, in *Documenta Islamica inedita*, Berlin 1952, pp. 197–210 = *Aufsätze*, i, 344–54.

[42] My reasons for dating the document to June 1478 are given below (pp. 110–1).

[43] E.g. (line 1) *τοιμης* for *τιμῆς*, (l. 2) *ηστων* for *εἰς τὸν*, (l. 3) *γραφης* for *γράφεις*, (l. 6) *αλομος* for *ἀλλ' ὅμως*, (l. 15) *ωρησμον* for *ὁρισμὸν*, (l. 17) *εβρω* for *εὕρω*, etc.

[44] For this much-discussed term see R. Anhegger, "Martoloslar hakkında," in *Türkiyat Mecmuası*, vii–viii/1 (1940–42), 282–322, especially 284–5 and references there, and idem, art. Martolos in *IA*. Assuming that 'Āshiqpasha-zāde's references to "*martoloz*" in the 14th century are anachronistic, the word first appears in a document in Slavonic issued by 'Īsā Beg (Truhelka, no. 8), in the form *martoloz-*. It is perhaps significant that in the Ottoman register of 835/1432 for Albania (H. Inalcık, *Hicrî 835 tarihli sûret-i defter-i sancak-i Arvanid*, Ankara 1954) the word does *not* appear.

meaning of "gear, possessions"[45] (cf. Ital. *roba* and also, at this period in Turkish, *qumāsh*).[46] The *voyvoda* was a subordinate officer of the sanjak-bey, whose duties at this period are obscure. That he held some territorial jurisdiction, however, is apparent from a document of 912/1507 (Elezović, i/1, no. 140 = i/2, no. 97 = Uzunçarşılı, 138–9), in which the sanjak-bey of (?)Herzegovina orders "Rüstem voyvoda" to protect Ragusan ambassadors from bandits in all parts of his *voyvodalîk* and to give them an escort to the frontier—a situation similar to that which lies behind Doc. 7.

HISTORICAL COMMENTARY[1]

Document 1 concerns the negotiations of 1471, conducted by Francesco Capello and Niccolò Cocco. These, the Venetians believed, had been initiated by the Sultan's stepmother, the Serbian princess Mara, who was

---

[45] G. Meyer, *Neugriechische Studien, II* (SBAk. Wien, 130, 1894), 55.

[46] See for example *Ibn Kemal : Tevârih-i Âl-i Osman, vii. defter*, ed. Ş. Turan, Ankara 1954 (facsimile), p. 176, l. 14, p. 299, l. 15 = Ankara 1957 (transcription), 171, 283.

[1] Works cited more than once in this section are referred to by the following abbreviations :—

Babinger, *Aufsätze*, i = Franz Babinger, *Aufsätze und Abhandlungen zur Geschichte Südosteuropas und der Levante*, i, Munich 1962.

Babinger, *Conquérant* = Franz Babinger, *Mahomet II le Conquérant et son temps*, Paris 1954.

Babinger, *Darius* = Franz Babinger, *Johannes Darius (1414–1494), Sachwalter Venedigs im Morgenland, und sein griechischer Umkreis*, (Bay. Ak. Wiss., Phil.-hist. Kl., Jg. 1961, Heft 5), Munich 1961.

Babinger, *Eroberer* = Franz Babinger, *Mehmed der Eroberer und seine Zeit*, Munich 1953.

Barletius = M. Barletius, *De obsidione Scodrensi*, in P. Lonicerus, *Chronicorum Turcicorum . . .*, iii, Frankfort 1578.

Cippicus = C. Cippicus (Cepio), *De Petri Mocenici imperatoris gestis libri tres*, Basle 1544.

Cornet = E. Cornet, *Le guerre dei Veneti nell' Asia, 1470–1474*, Vienna 1856.

Da Lezze = Donado da Lezze, *Historia turchesca*, ed. I. Ursu, Bucharest 1910.

Lopez = R. Lopez, "Il principio della guerra Veneto-Turca nel 1463," in *Archivio Veneto*, xv (1934), 45–131.

Malipiero = Domenico Malipiero, *Annali Veneti*, in *Archivio Storico Italiano*, vii/1, Florence 1843.

Nagy and Nyáry = I. Nagy and A. Nyáry, *Magyar diplomacziai emlékek Mátyás király korából*, 4 vols. (= *Monumenta Hungariae Historica, Acta Extera*, iv–vii), Budapest 1876–8.

Navagero = A. Navagero, *Historia Veneta . . . usque ad 1498*, in L. A. Muratori, *Rerum Italicarum scriptores*, 1723–51, vol. xxiii.

Romanin = S. Romanin, *Storia documentata di Venezia*, Venice 1853–61.

then living in seclusion near Mount Athos.[2] Her intervention with the Sultan would have received a ready hearing: with the storming of Negroponte in July 1470 he had achieved a major objective, the possession of Venice's principal naval base in the Aegean, and he was no doubt aware of the efforts being made by Pope Paul II to promote a coalition against him and of the Signory's attempts to expose him to a war on two fronts by embroiling him with Uzun Ḥasan.

Early in October 1470[3] the agents of the Princess and her sister Catherine arrived in Venice, and towards the end of the following month the ambassadors were elected and given their instructions[4]: they were to wait at Corfu for their safe-conduct, and travel by sea or by land as it prescribed; they were to visit the Princess[5] in order to present the Signory's thanks and to discover from her what their reception was likely to be; and on being received at the Porte they were to propose peace on the basis of *uti possidetis*—the Venetian authorities were resigned to the loss of Negroponte.

Almost immediately afterwards, however, the situation appeared to change in Venice's favour, for on 22 December the Pope's endeavours were rewarded by the signature of the League of Lodi. New instructions dated 2 January 1471,[6] were sent post-haste to catch the ambassadors before they left Corfu or to overtake them on their journey. The main item of their instructions was now that they were to attempt to negotiate the recovery of Negroponte, offering, if necessary, up to 250,000 ducats for it; but if it appeared from their reception that it would be imprudent to mention the subject, they were at liberty to refrain. In the peace were to be included Venice's allies, the Lusignan King of Cyprus, the Knights of Rhodes, the despot of Santa Maura, and other princelings of the Aegean. The ambassadors were instructed to report back by letter on the progress of the negotiations and to await, in the Ottoman dominions, the Signory's reply.

---

[2] Malipiero, p. 67. For this lady see F. Babinger, "Ein Freibrief Mehmeds II . . . ," in *Byzantinische Zeitschrift*, xliv (1951), 11–20 (= *Aufsätze*, i, 97–106) and idem, "Witwensitz und Sterbeplatz der Sultanin Mara," in *Κανίσκιον Φαίδωνι Ι. Κουκουλέ*, Athens 1953, pp. 240–44 (= *Aufsätze*, i, 340–43), and references there given. She acted as the intermediary again in 1472 (embassy of Marco Aurelio) and in 1474–5 (embassy of Geronimo Zorzi).

[3] Babinger, *Eroberer*, p. 309 = *Conquérant*, p. 346.

[4] The instructions, dated 27 November 1470, are reproduced in Cornet, pp. 15–7.

[5] In 1475 also the ambassador got in touch with the Princess before proceeding to the Porte (Malipiero, p. 112).

[6] Cornet, pp. 19–20.

For what followed we have to depend mainly upon the reports—largely based on rumour—which were sent to the Duke of Milan by his ambassador at Venice, Gherardo de Collis. He heard that the ambassadors sailed to Crete, where there was some delay because their safe-conduct covered only one ambassador, and a new document, covering two, had to be sent to them.[7] Having visited the Princess they travelled overland through Thrace,[8] to be held up again at Edirne, for the Sultan refused to receive them until they communicated to him what they were empowered to offer.[9] They arrived in Istanbul on 12 March 1471.[10] Throughout May and June news was being eagerly awaited in Venice,[11] but it was not until 3 July that an Ottoman envoy arrived.[12]

Document 1, dated 24 May (just on six weeks earlier), is evidently the letter he brought with him. The Sultan's terms—at least so far as they are specified in the letter—are not unreasonable. Lemnos, which he demands, had been granted by him in 1453 to the Gattelusi and in 1460 to the deposed despot Demetrius Palaeologus; at the outbreak of the war it had been held by a Greek corsair, but on the approach of the Venetian fleet in the first months of hostilities the leading men of the island had induced him to submit to the Admiral, who installed a

---

[7] Nagy and Nyáry, ii, no. 150 (dispatch of 22 April 1471).

[8] Cippicus, pp. 6–7: "conscensa navi, primum ad Despotae filiam . . . inde terrestri itinere Byzantium se conferunt." De Collis was told by the Doge that the princess and her sister had accompanied the ambassadors to Istanbul (Nagy and Nyáry, ii, no. 157, of 14 June).

[9] Nagy and Nyáry, ii, no. 155 (31 May).

[10] Op cit., no. 158 (25 June).

[11] Op. cit., no. 152 (3 May): "li lor Orator sono andati dal Turcho per la pace et si aspecta per tuto questa mese sentir, como haverano facto. Cadauno spera et brama pace . . ."; no. 153 (27 May): "Da li soy Oratori del Turcho non ano poy novella alcuna . . ."; no. 156 (6 June): "la Signoria sta in grande dubio et pagura . . ."; no. 159 (30 June): ". . . da li soy Oratori de Constantinopoli, non lie cosa alcuna, ma ala zornata si aspecta uno gripo . . ."; no. 164 (27 June): ". . . de di in di si aspecta una gripa con novelle da Constantinopoli".

[12] Op cit., no. 160 (3 July). Babinger, apparently regarding the arrival of this Ottoman envoy as a new démarche, does not link up the incidents relating to this embassy (*Eroberer*, pp. 309 and 320–22 = *Conquérant*, pp. 346–7 and 358–60); but at this time Capello and Cocco were staying at the Porte, in obedience to their instructions (Cornet, p. 20): "Et de omnibus rebus et difficultatibus occurrentibus nobis per vestras litteras distinctam et particularem date noticiam, reducendo vos interim ad eum locum qui aut per turcum vobis fuerit ordinatus a(u)t vobis visus fuerit, et ibi responsionem et mandatum nostrum expectate."

garrison.[13] The Braccio di Maina (now Mani), the rocky arm of the Peloponnese which ends in Cape Matapan, was then, as for centuries before and since, the home of intractable mountaineers and pirates; upon the arrival in the Peloponnese in the summer of 1463 of the Venetian expeditionary force under Bertoldo d'Este, the Mainiotes had rebelled and massacred the Turkish garrisons in the vicinity.[14] Croia (Krüje in Albania), the hereditary seat of George Castriota ("Iskender Beg") and his principal base throughout his long resistance to the Ottomans, had been formally surrendered to Venice after his death in January 1468 by his son John; but it had in effect been a Venetian outpost for some years before, and a Venetian garrison had held it during Meḥemmed's campaign of 1466.

To Malvasia (Monemvasia), the impregnable "Gibraltar of Greece" off the east coast of Laconia, the Sultan makes no claim for, unlike Lemnos, Maina and Croia, it had never been occupied either by himself or by one of his vassals. It had held out during the Ottoman campaign of 1460 when the other possessions of the despots Thomas and Demetrius were lost, but the city-fathers, not trusting entirely in their wealth and the natural strength of their island-fortress, had placed themselves under the protection of the Pope; then, with the outbreak of the war, they too had invited Venice to station a garrison there.[15]

There is in the letter no mention of Negroponte. Either the Sultan regarded the demand as too far-fetched to deserve a reply (a report was current in Venice that he had dismissed the ambassadors as soon as the subject was raised)[16] or the ambassadors found the atmosphere so unpropitious that, as their instructions permitted them to do, they refrained from mentioning it. The Sultan agrees to include Cyprus and Rhodes in the peace, and is willing to renew the capitulations (i.e. of April 1454).

The last sentence of the letter concerns a complaint which was raised at every discussion and was finally disposed of in the treaty of 1479. When Venice declared war, her Bailo at Istanbul and many of the Venetian merchants there were arrested and their goods were confiscated; but among those who managed to flee were Bartolomeo Giorgi (Zorzi) and

---

[13] Lopez, p. 74.

[14] Lopez, p. 72 (referring especially to Navagero, p. 1122).

[15] Lopez, p. 57 (referring especially to W. Miller, "Monemvasia," in *Journal of Hellenic Studies*, xxvii (1907), 229–41 and 300–1 = *Essays on the Latin Orient*, Cambridge 1921, pp. 231–45).

[16] Nagy and Nyáry, ii, no. 158 (25 June): "... altri dichano, che luy [scil. the Sultan] quando intese, che li domandaveno Negroponte, subito li face comandamento, che in fra hore XXIIII havevano spagato Constantinopoli ...".

Girolamo Michiel, who held the concession for working the alum-mines. The Sultan claimed that they owed the Treasury 150,000 ducats.[17] The question of this debt had arisen in 1468, when Leonardo Boldù was conducting negotiations,[18] and was to be discussed again in 1475. The sum of 100,000 ducats which Venice undertook to pay by the terms of the treaty of 1479 was, it is true, described in the actual instrument [19] as a general indemnity for all losses sustained by the Sultan and his subjects; but it was recognized in Venice as being the settlement of the Sultan's claim against the concessionaires.[20]

Unless the last words of the letter—" The ambassadors will inform you of what I have said . . . concerning the former capitulations "—conceal a demand for heavy tribute, the Sultan's terms are by no means so outrageous as public opinion was allowed to believe. The otherwise well-informed Domenico Malipiero, who knows of the principal demand, the cession of Lemnos, pretends that the Sultan demanded the ludicrous sum of 100,000 ducats a year as *kharāj* (*100,000 ducati all'anno de carazo*) [21]; and Gherardo de Collis, pressed by his Duke to discover what the Sultan's terms were, made three reports between 25 June and 3 August,[22] each shown by our document to be inaccurate and exaggerated: he too had heard that there was a demand for heavy tribute, 50,000 ducats a year.[23]

---

[17] Navagero, p. 1122.

[18] Navagero, p. 1133.

[19] Miklosisch and Müller, p. 297.

[20] Navagero, p. 1160: " che fra'l termino d'anni due la Signoria dar debba al Signor Turco Ducati 100000 a conto de' Ducati 150000 del debito degli Allumi . . . ," and cf. Sanuto, *Vite de' Duchi* (in Muratori, xxii), p. 1210: " Secondo: Ducati 100000 pel debito di Ser Bartolomeo Giorgi dell' Appalto, ovvero dargli la sua persona nelle mani."

[21] Malipiero, p. 67. Malipiero claims that the ambassadors replied " that the Signoria would rather see the earth destroyed to its foundations than pay tribute to anyone ", which is absurd: under the earlier capitulations the Venetian authorities had readily paid " tribute " (χαράτζιν)—on a small scale, it is true, but conceding the principle that in respect of the territories concerned they were the vassals (*kharāj-güẕār*) of the Sultan.

[22] Nagy and Nyáry, ii, no. 158 (25 June), no. 160 (3 July), no. 165 (3 August). Babinger makes de Collis report that the Sultan was demanding the cession of Crete, Corfu and other islands (*Eroberer*, pp. 320–1 = *Conquérant*, p. 358), but so excessive a demand was not even rumoured; de Collis wrote: " . . . che la Signoria lassa al Turcho Napoli de Romania et Croya . . . , et che per lo resto de terra firma et de le isole Candia, Corfu et Stalimini et certe altre isolete de lo arcipelago, andro stimo etc. che la Signoria si paga de Caragio sive tributo ducati L mille l'anno," i.e. Venice was to retain these places but against payment of tribute.

[23] See preceding note. By the treaty of 1479 which ended the war Venice was obliged to pay no more than 10,000 ducats annually.

The Venetian authorities, knowing that public opinion was all in favour of peace,[24] were perhaps not unwilling that inflated rumours should circulate. The protraction of the negotiations gave them a full year's breathing-space, with no hostilities undertaken by either side,[25] and during this year the tide seemed to be turning in their favour. They may not have attached great hopes to the schemes which they were fostering for procuring the Sultan's assassination [26]; but the Treaty of Lodi was signed, and the courting of Uzun Ḥasan seemed at last to promise results: while Capello and Cocco were still on their way to Istanbul, Quirini had returned from Tabriz, and by April 1471 Caterino Zeno was in Tabriz and Uzun Ḥasan's envoy was in Venice seeking munitions.

The terms of the Venetian reply to the Sultan's letter are not known, but they amounted to a rejection.[27] Nevertheless the Sultan, concerned at the threat offered by the alliance with Uzun Ḥasan, approached Venice again the very next spring with the invitation to send an embassy.[28] Venice was in no hurry to accept. An ambassador was appointed and given his instructions, but was kept waiting at Corfu throughout the year, evidently because the Signory was hoping for good news from the East. The first reports were encouraging: a detachment of Uzun Ḥasan's troops, having tricked the Ottoman beylerbey into allowing them passage through the Sultan's territory, sacked Tokat and stirred up trouble in Karaman. But later in the year this force was destroyed near Konya; and with Meḥemmed's defeat of Uzun Ḥasan in August 1473 the hopes which Venice had reposed in the alliance came to nothing.[29]

---

[24] See p. 103, n. 11 above.

[25] Cippicus, p. 7: "Dum legati proficiscuntur, dum de conditionibus agitur, in mittendis etiam atque remittendis literis, tota aestas effluxit."

[26] For these plots see F. Babinger, "Ja'qûb Pascha, ein Leibarzt Mehmed's II," in *Rivista degli Studi Orientali*, xxvi (1951), 87–113, and idem, *Eroberer*, pp. 309–10 = *Conquérant*, p. 347.

[27] Cippicus, p. 7: "Et quum de conditionibus non convenirent, legati per literas, quas pacis conditiones Turcus offerret Senatum certiorem reddunt. Veneti reiectis conditionibus, ex Senatus decreto legatos domum revocant." Cippicus, as well as Malipiero (p. 67), reports what happened to the ambassadors: "Interim Franciscus Capellus febri correptus moritur, Nicolaus alter legatus, primum piscatoria navicula Lemnum, inde nactus Venetam triremem, Cretam se contulit."

[28] The course of this embassy, with the procrastinations of the Venetian authorities, is now fully set out by F. Babinger, *Darius*, pp. 61–70.

[29] There remains the question how Doc. 1, the original letter to the Doge, came to be lodged in the Malipiero file at the Archives (see p. 81 above). Perhaps Tomaso Malipiero, with whose embassies in 1477–8 the remaining documents are concerned, took this letter with him on those missions, as a reminder of the terms offered earlier, and on his return filed it away with the other, more personal, papers.

Documents 2–6, and probably *Document 7* as well, belong to the peace negotiations of 1477–8, conducted by Tomaso Malipiero. These too had been initiated by the Sultan, who sent a Jewish emissary to Croia, then invested by an Ottoman army under the command of Evrenos-oghlu Aḥmed Beg (sanjak-bey of Albania), some time in the late summer or autumn of 1477. From the Ottoman camp the emissary sent word to the Admiral Antonio Loredano asking for a safe-conduct to travel to Venice. The Admiral detached a galley to carry him, but when it was off Capo d'Istria the emissary died.[30] Nevertheless the démarche was known in Venice—the messenger's papers would have been sent on—and in November 1477, after long discussions, the Senate decided to reply to the Porte's overtures. They appointed as their representative (ostensibly to inform the Sultan of the death of his agent) the *provveditore* of the fleet Tomaso Malipiero, to whom word of his commission was taken by a secretary, Alvise Manenti.[31]

Document 2, issued at Istanbul in June–July 1477, is a safe-conduct—as brief as such a document could well be—in the form of a *fermān* ordering the sanjak-beys of Rumeli to protect and assist on his way a Venetian envoy travelling to the Porte. There is no record of any embassy actually travelling in the latter half of 1477, but all the same the existence of this safe-conduct is easily explained : on other occasions when there were similar initiatives such unofficial agents were employed to obtain a safe-conduct, the essential preliminary to the sending of an embassy [32] ; and this document must have been among the papers carried by the Jewish emissary in case the Signory was willing to respond, and forwarded after his death to Venice. Malipiero could, presumably, have travelled under the protection of this document, but it seems that he did not.

Document 3, in Italian, and dated only " 25 February ", is a much

---

[30] Navagero, p. 1149, according to which the Jew died " nel principio di Gennajo [scil, 1478, N.S.] " and the Senate took the decision to send an embassy in the same month ; but this date must be wrong. It means, if Document 2 of June–July 1477 was (as I suggest) written to be taken to Venice by this agent, that he took six months over the journey ; and the Senate, presumably in response to this initiative, had decided what terms it would accept early in November (Romanin, p. 378). Malipiero seems to be referring to this incident of the Jewish agent when he says (p. 117) : " A' 22 de Novembrio ditto [scil. 1477], Turchi ha tentà el General [i.e. Loredano] de far pace."

[31] Navagero, p. 1151.

[32] In 1466 the Venetian authorities had sent a Jewish agent to the Porte to procure a safe-conduct (Babinger, *Darius*, pp. 56–7) ; in 1467 they asked the Albanian lord of Drivasto to act for them (op. cit., p. 58) ; in 1475 an agent of the Princess Mara brought the necessary document to Venice (op. cit., p. 81, n. 1).

more elaborate safe-conduct in the form of letters patent, setting out in full detail the immunities of the ambassador—named as Tomaso Malipiero—and his entourage, and ratified by an oath. Though the year of issue is not given, it must be contemporary with *Document 4*, in Turkish, issued between 24 February and 5 March 1478. This is in the form of a *fermān*, addressed to the Venetian ambassadors—in the plural. Its wording is somewhat unconventional: after the *dispositio* has emphasized that they may travel with confidence, the formulae of corroboration are interrupted after *shöyle bilesiz* by a curt postscript, which says in effect: "There is no need for all this suspicion and fuss."

It is not difficult to reconstruct what had happened. Venetian ambassadors, travelling in time of open war, were well aware of the necessity to ensure that their safe-conducts were precisely worded: we have noticed the report that Capello and Cocco made difficulties in 1471 because their safe-conduct covered only one ambassador,[33] and in 1475 Girolamo Zorzi sent his safe-conduct back for revision three times.[34] Malipiero cannot have been satisfied with Document 2: it was six months old and it was very laconic in its expressions, with no extended statement of the immunities guaranteed, no mention of the ambassador's companions, and no reference to his return from the Porte to Venice. Before finally leaving Venetian protection he must, from somewhere along the Adriatic coast, have asked for a more precise document.[35] He received in return the lengthy Document 3, written in Italian so that he could satisfy himself of its content, and promising in the most elaborate detail immunity for himself and all his retinue and their goods, both for the outward journey and the return, regardless of the issue of the negotiations.

---

[33] P. 103 above. In their instructions of 27 November 1470 they were warned (Cornet, p. 16): "Verum habeatur ab omnibus vobis deligens consideratio et advertentia, ut salvusconductus sit bene amplus et sufficiens ultra personas vestras et familie vestre, etiam pro galea et zurma, et omnibus qui in ea fuerint, eundo, stando, et redeundo." When at one point they were ordered not to set out from Corfu at all they were advised to excuse themselves either by a diplomatic illness or by finding fault with the safe-conduct: "aut cum tarditate ipsius salviconducti . . . , aut cum simulatione infirmitatis alterius vestrum, aut denique cum dubitatione alicuius articuli salvi conducti predicti" (Cornet, p. 18).

[34] Malipiero, p. 112.

[35] Cf. Navagero, p. 1151: "[Malipiero] nel principio dell' anno susseguente 1478 [by which presumably, *more Venetiano*, he means March] avuta la commessione dal Senato, mandò a dimandare salvocondotto per andare a Constantinopoli." Hammer (*GOR*, ii, 153) makes Malipiero *arrive* in Istanbul early in January and obtain a truce *until* mid-April, which is a complete misunderstanding.

Any remaining scruples were to be removed by the inclusion of the oath. With Document 3 came a testy " covering-note ", Document 4, telling him to stop quibbling : why, said the Ottoman authorities in effect, was he not content with Document 2 ?

Malipiero, accompanied by the secretary Manenti,[36] duly arrived in Istanbul (probably early in April) and opened negotiations. Finding however that the Porte's demands were higher than he was empowered to accept, he asked for a truce of two months to permit him to return to Venice for consultations. This was conceded, and he left Istanbul on 15 April,[37] still travelling under the protection of Documents 2, 3 and 4.

He took with him also *Document 5*. This is a *nishān* instructing the sanjak-beys and kadis to provide protection and escort to Venetian ambassadors travelling to and from the Porte. Dated 4–13 April 1478—and thus issued a few days before Malipiero's departure—it is less elaborate than the very precise Document 3 in Italian, but considerably more detailed than the bald Document 2 : it specifies protection both to the persons of the embassy and to their goods, and guarantees a safe return even if the negotiations fail. This document, it is clear, was issued as a safe-conduct for Malipiero or whoever else should resume negotiations after the consultations in Venice.[38]

Malipiero reached Venice on 3 May. Two days of discussion ensued, and on the 5th Malipiero set out again, protected now by Document 5, with authority to accept the Sultan's terms.[39] Crossing to the Albanian coast, he set out overland from Scutari,[40] which he must have left only a few days before the *akinji*s under Mikhāl-oghlu ʻAlī Beg, appearing in the countryside around,[41] heralded the approach of the Ottoman army for the last campaign of the war. Malipiero was intending no doubt to travel via Üsküb, Filibe and Edirne,[42] but he needed to make less than half the

---

[36] Da Lezze, p. 99 (one of the passages of this text which evidently incorporates the account of Angiolello ; taken prisoner at Negroponte, he was at this time in the service of the Sultan and was present on the Scutari campaign of 1478).

[37] Navagero, p. 1152.

[38] A safe-conduct was, in other words, a " return ticket " *to* and *from* the Porte : the date of issue is no indication of when the document was actually used.

[39] Malipiero, p. 117 ; Babinger, *Eroberer*, p. 395 = *Conquérant*, p. 440.

[40] Da Lezze [Angiolello], p. 100.

[41] According to Barletius, fol. 238v., the *akinji*s arrived on 14 May, the date given also (and with the correct day, Thursday) by Da Lezze [? Angiolello], p. 103.

[42] According to Angiolello, however (Da Lezze, p. 99), Malipiero had learned on his first embassy that the Sultan was preparing, truce or no truce, to march against Scutari, so perhaps it was no surprise to him to meet the Ottoman army on the road.

journey, for he found the Sultan, already on the march to Albania, encamped outside Kustendil.[43] His protests at the breaking of the truce were brushed aside, and he was informed that once more the Sultan's terms had been raised: the cession of Scutari, Drivasto and Alessio was now demanded. Once again Malipiero had to return to Venice for new instructions.

Still covered by Document 5, he took with him this time also *Document 6*, a safe-conduct, in the form of a *fermān* to the kadis of Rumeli, for the Venetian envoy who should return after these further consultations. It was issued, between 2 and 11 June, at "the camp at Egri-dere". Egri-dere ("crooked stream", Slavonic Kriva Reka) is the name of the river along whose valley runs the main route from Kustendil to Üsküb after the crossing of the Deve-bayîrî Pass (now on the frontier between Bulgaria and Yugoslavia); in the 17th century there was built near the head of the valley a fortified station called Egridere Palanka, now the township Kriva Palenka.[44] Here or hereabouts (as the document reveals), some 30 km. south-west of Kustendil and two or three stages further on his road to Albania,[45] the Sultan was encamped when Malipiero took his leave, to hasten back to Venice.

Document 7 suggests that his journey was not uneventful. This letter is written in barbarous Greek, and is undated; the addressee is not named, and the identity of the sender not beyond doubt. It may indeed have no connection at all with Malipiero's journeys. But the fragments of internal evidence—the names Dā'ūd, Aḥmed Beg and Alessio, and even the reference to bad weather—all fall into place on the assumption that it was sent by Dā'ūd Pasha to Malipiero on this, his second, journey home.

---

[43] According to Navagero (p. 1152) "in Sofia", but this is an approximation; Angiolello, who was in the Ottoman camp, is precise (Da Lezze, p. 100): "[Malipiero] gionto a una città chiamata la Bana, dove sono molti bagni caldi, su'l piano di detta città trovò il Gran Turco accampato con grand' essercito . . .". "Bana" (or "banya") is the normal Bulgarian word for a hot-spring (cf. Ewliyā Chelebi, *Seyāḥat-nāme*, iii, 399: *bu diyārda îlîjaya bānā derler*), and stands as or forms part of numerous place-names; but the town "Banya" *par excellence* was Kustendil.

[44] Ewliyā Chelebi, *Seyāḥat-nāme*, v, 564 (= H. Šabanovič's translation, *Evlija Čelebija putopis*, ii, Sarajevo 1957, 46 f.), and cf. M. F. Thielen, *Die europäische Türkey*, Vienna 1828, p. 75.

[45] When Süleymān I marched this way in 944/1537, he spent two nights at the *konak* of "Kustendil îlîjasî" and reached Üsküb in five stages (Ferīdūn, *Munsha'āt al-Salāṭīn*[2], i, 599; here the name "Egri-dere" is not mentioned).

Dā'ūd Pasha was at the time of this campaign beylerbey of Rumeli. Sent on with his sipāhīs ahead of the Sultan, he had arrived before Scutari a few days after the *akinjis*, in the latter half of May,[46] to begin preparations for the siege by casting guns and building a bridge over the Boyana. Over this bridge, completed on 1 June, he had planned to send a raiding-force to ravage the countryside beyond, but heavy rainstorms obliged the raiders to return empty-handed and suspended all activity for some days.[47] Meanwhile the siege of Croia, some 70 km. to the south, was drawing to an end. For more than a year the fortress had been closely invested by an Ottoman force under the command of the sanjak-bey of Albania, Evrenos-oghlu Aḥmed. Upon the approach of the Sultan the garrison abandoned all hope; on 15 June they surrendered on terms, only to be massacred.[48] The Sultan then turned north, reaching Scutari—where Dā'ūd Pasha had meanwhile been joined by the Beylerbey of Anadolu and the Janissaries—on 2 July.

Through this turbulent scene, in early June, Malipiero had to make his way. The letter suggests that on entering Albania he got in touch with Evrenos-oghlu Aḥmed, who, as sanjak-bey, was responsible for his safety on these last stages of his journey. Aḥmed Bey sent him an escort under the command of his *voyvoda*, but the unseasonable storms which had hindered Dā'ūd Pasha held them up, and they were attacked and robbed by the *martolos*—the irregular bands, half-soldier and half-brigand, that infested these districts. Alessio, at the mouth of the Drina, midway between Scutari and Croia, was still in Venetian hands (it was to be taken, plundered and burnt by the two beylerbeys towards the end of August). Before dismissing his escort, to enter Alessio and take ship for Venice, Malipiero must have written a letter of complaint to Dā'ūd Pasha, Aḥmed Bey's superior officer, who was encamped only two or three hours' riding away. Document 7, on this reconstruction, is Dā'ūd Pasha's placatory reply.

Document 6, the safe-conduct for a third journey which Malipiero brought away from Egridere, did not go unused, for in spite of the Sultan's

---

[46] According to Barletius, fol. 239r., " Taut Gaiola [?], novae Romae Bassa generalis " arrived " ad nonum Calend Iunias " (= 24 May); Da Lezze [Angiolello], p. 103 gives 18 May, a Monday.

[47] Barletius, fol. 239v.

[48] The European accounts make much of Ottoman bad faith on this occasion; they receive confirmation from the rather embarrassed apologia of Tursun (*T'OEM*, *'ilāwe*, 169) and Kemālpasha-zāde (facsimile, ed. Ş. Turan, pp. 491 f.); Sa'd al-Dīn (i, 563), who is following Idrīs, records that the garrison were granted *amān* but makes no mention of the massacre.

uncompromising attitude the Venetian authorities retained a faint hope of saving Scutari by negotiation. Some time in July, when the siege was at its height, Malipiero returned, accompanied (as on his first embassy) by the secretary Alvise Manenti.[49] Coming up the Boyana in a light galley as far as a place called San Celso,[50] he himself stayed aboard and sent the secretary on into the Sultan's camp, escorted by 40 Ottoman horsemen (and evidently protected by Document 6). Needless to say this final attempt was fruitless, and it was only with difficulty that Manenti escaped Meḥemmed's wrath and regained the galley. Malipiero, it seems, immediately resumed his duties with the fleet,[51] for it was Manenti who in Venice, on 27 July, reported the failure of the mission.[52]

Though reduced to the most desperate straits, Scutari held out. The Sultan withdrew on 8 September, followed shortly by the Anatolian troops and later by the troops of Rumeli; but the investment was rigorously prosecuted by Evrenos-oghlu Aḥmed Bey, to whom had been entrusted all the siege-material. On 4 January 1479 Venice finally took the hard decision to admit that Scutari could not be saved, and despatched Giovanni Dario to Istanbul to make the best terms he could.

THE PATRONYMICS OF CONVERTS

In the Ottoman Empire, as in other Islamic societies, it was the practice that a convert to Islam whose natural father remained an infidel adopted as his father's name 'Abd Allāh, " slave of Allāh," or a name formed by substituting for the name of God one of the " beautiful names " (*al-asmā' al-ḥusnā*)—'Abd al-Laṭīf, 'Abd al-Qādir, etc. Thus the historian finds in the patronymic used by an Ottoman dignitary a

---

[49] Da Lezze [Angiolello], p. 107.

[50] No locality of this name is mentioned by K. Jireček in his " Skutari und sein Gebiet im Mittelalter ", in L. von Thallóczy, *Illyrisch-Albanische Forschungen*, i, Munich 1916, pp. 94–124; behind the " San Celso " of Da Lezze stands perhaps " San Serzi " (S. Sergius), the regular landing-place for Scutari, situated two-thirds of the way up the Boyana (Jireček, pp. 117–18).

[51] Malipiero was sent in command of ten galleys to attempt to defend Alessio (Navagero, p. 1155); and on 18 September the Senate wrote to him and to the Admiral Loredano urging them to do their utmost to hold Scutari (Romanin, p. 380).

[52] Malipiero, p. 119. Angiolello implies (Da Lezze, p. 107) that Manenti was received by the Sultan, but Malipiero says: " non ha possudo negociar co'l Signor Turco, ma ha trattà con un Bassà."

criterion indicating whether the personage was Muslim-born or recruited, through the *devshirme* or otherwise, into Ottoman service.[1]

These patronymics were in fact rarely used. Ottoman historians and biographers, knowing them to be fictitious, ignore them. They are found occasionally in *penches*, on gravestones, and on seals, but commonly only in legal documents, so that the most fruitful source for determining the patronymic of an individual is a *waqfiyye* for an endowment made by himself or one made by a colleague which he attested as witness.[2] The examination of the sources easily accessible to me has revealed some peculiarities, which have a bearing on the reading " Dā'ūd b. 'Abd Allāh ", which I have proposed for the *penche* of Document 7.

In the middle of the 9th/15th century the use of " b. 'Abd Allāh " seems to have been almost universal: this was the patronymic used by the great Maḥmūd Pasha,[3] by Murād II's viziers Saruja, Isḥāq [4] and Shihāb al-Dīn,[5] by the beylerbey Dayî Karaja, who was killed at Belgrade,[6] by another Isḥāq, who was beylerbey in 861/1457,[7] by an Ibrāhīm, who was *lala* to Meḥemmed II,[8] and by a certain Doghan, who was Yenicheri Aghasî at Varna [9]; and later in the century the defterdār " Tütünsüz "

---

[1] Even so, caution is needed: Ayās Pasha (d. 946/1539), for example, an Albanian recruited through the *devshirme*, calls himself in his *penche* and is called on his tombstone " b. Meḥemmed " (*IA*, s.v. " Ayas Paşa ", col 44a [M. Cavid Baysun]). The explanation of this anomaly is perhaps that his natural father, encouraged by his prosperous son, embraced Islam and took the name Meḥemmed. This did occur during the 10th/16th century: the fathers of " Maqtūl " Ibrāhīm Pasha (d. 942/1536) and Sokollu Meḥemmed Pasha (d. 987/1579), invited by their sons to join them, took the names Yūnus and Jemāl al-Dīn Sinān respectively (*IA*, s.v. " Ibrahim Paşa ", 914b, and s.v. " Mehmed Paşa ", 596a).

[2] Originals or verbatim copies are necessary; in register-entries the final section listing the witnesses is omitted.

[3] As witness to a *waqfiyye* of Meḥemmed II in 861/1457, see *Fatih Mehmet II vakfiyeleri*, Ankara 1938, p. 339 (first signature).

[4] As witnesses to a *waqfiyye*, dated 850/1446, of Murād II, see H. Inalcık, *Fatih devri üzerinde tetkikler ve vesikalar*, i, Ankara 1954, p. 212 and pl. iv[7], also *Vakıflar Dergisi*, iv (1958), 1–17 (by I. H. Uzunçarşılı) and pl. facing p. 19. It is not without interest that whereas the signature of the Muslim-born Khalīl b. Ibrāhīm (Chandarlî) is followed by the du'ā *'ufiya 'anhumā*, in the dual, that of Saruja b. 'Abd Allāh is followed by *'ufiya 'anhu*—with no prayer for the infidel father.

[5] H. Inalcık, *Fatih devri*, p. 84, n. 71.

[6] Op. cit., p. 113, n. 196.

[7] Op. cit., p. 83, n. 67.

[8] Op. cit., p. 112, n. 195.

[9] Op. cit., p. 117, n. 223.

Aḥmed is called in his *waqfiyye* (of 888/1483) " b. 'Abd Allāh ".[10] But among the witnesses to the *waqfiyye* of Tütünsüz Aḥmed, the (third ?) vizier Mesīḥ signs himself " b. 'Abd al-Ḥayy " and the (second ?) vizier Dā'ūd as " b. 'Abd al-Wadūd " [11]; the same Dā'ūd Pasha, now Grand Vizier, is again " b. 'Abd al-Wadūd " in a document of 901/1496,[12] and his two convert-colleagues are " 'Alī b. 'Abd al-Ḥayy " (i.e. Khādim 'Alī Pasha) and " Iskender b. 'Abd al-Ghaffār ".

It seems to have become the fashion for viziers to use more recherché patronymics; and throughout the following century the same fashion is found: Hersek-zāde Aḥmed Pasha is named " Aḥmed b. 'Abd al-Ḥayy " in his *waqfiyye* of 917/1511, and his witness, Khādim Sinān Pasha, is " Sinān b. 'Abd al-Ḥayy " [13]; Luṭfī Pasha, in his *Āṣaf-nāme*, calls himself " b. 'Abd al-Mu'īn " [14]; Güzelje Qāsim Pasha, in a document of 951/1545, is " b. 'Abd al-Ḥayy " [15]; the architect Sinān (not a vizier, but certainly a person of consequence) is " b. 'Abd al-Mennān " [16]; Pertew Pasha signs himself " b. 'Abd al-Ṣamed " [17]; in 980/1572–3 the viziers sign themselves " Meḥemmed " *tout court* (i.e. Sokollu, the Grand Vizier), " Piyāle b. 'Abd al-Raḥmān ", " Aḥmed b. 'Abd Allāh " (an exception), " Maḥmūd b. 'Abd al-Mu'īn " and " Muṣṭafā b. 'Abd al-Ḥayy " [18]; ten years later the Grand Vizier Siyāwush again uses no patronymic but his colleagues are " Mesīḥ b. 'Abd al-Qādir ", " Meḥemmed b. 'Abd al-Melik " and " Ibrāhīm b. 'Abd al-Wahhāb ".[19]

Thus after about 1480 the great men seem only rarely to have been " b. 'Abd Allāh ". One explanation might be that there was a general change of fashion and that newly-recruited converts, formerly dubbed indiscriminately " b. 'Abd Allāh ", were now given a variety of patronymics. Against this however is the fact that relatively obscure converts continue to appear almost invariably as " b. 'Abd Allāh ". A *waqfiyye* of Meḥemmed

---

[10] M. T. Gökbilgin, *XV.–XVI. asırlarda Edirne ve Paşa Livâsı*, Istanbul 1952, appendix p. (280) and p. (282), l. 4.

[11] M. T. Gökbilgin, *Edirne*, appendix, p. (283).

[12] Kraelitz, pp. 102 and 106, and Tafel xiiia (Kraelitz's misreading "'Abd al-Wuḥūd" is corrected by Elezović, i/1, 277).

[13] *The Waqfiyah of Aḥmed Pāšā*, ed. and tr. Muhammed Ahmed Simsar, Philadelphia 1940, § 16, § 68.

[14] R. Tschudi, *Das Aṣafnâme des Luṭfî Pascha* (Turk. Bibl., xii), Berlin 1910, p. 3.

[15] M. T. Gökbilgin, *Edirne*, p. 435, n. 690.

[16] Sā'ī, *Tadhkirat al-Bunyān*, Istanbul 1315 (Iqdām series, no. 13), p. 22.

[17] *Vakıflar Dergisi*, ii (1942), 233.

[18] Op. cit., p. 240.

[19] *Fatih Mehmet vakfiyeleri*, pp. 324–5.

II, of 875/1470–1, presents the names of numerous property-holders in Istanbul [20]; the fathers of 18 of them are called " 'Abd Allāh ", with no other compound in 'Abd represented. A *waqfiyye* of the Muslim-born Isḥāq Pasha,[21] drawn up in 891/1486, bears the signatures of 35 witnesses [22]: 21 of them have patronymics suggesting that they are converts, and in every case it is " b. 'Abd Allāh "; another *waqfiyye* of the same Isḥāq drawn up in the following year has 10 witnesses,[23] of whom seven are " b. 'Abd Allāh ", with no other name in 'Abd. Of these 28 " b. 'Abd Allāh's " only the first—Meḥemmed Pasha—is a person of rank: the rest are freedmen of Isḥāq or officers of his household. A selection of names published from a *waqfiyye* of Khādim Ibrāhīm Pasha, of 968/1560,[24] contains six persons called b. 'Abd Allāh, with no other compound. An examination of the names of witnesses in five *waqfiyyes* published by Elezović similarly reveals that humble folk are always " b. 'Abd Allāh ": of 34 patronymics in 'Abd the only " recherché " ones are borne by the vizier 'Alī Pasha (" b. 'Abd al-Ḥayy ") and the beylerbey Ḥasan Pasha " b. 'Abd al-Selām ".[25]

A similar random collection of names is provided by the admirable index to M. T. Gökbilgin's *Edirne ve Paşa Livâsı*. Here are listed (admittedly perhaps with some doublets) 111 persons, named in documents of the fifteenth and sixteenth centuries, whose fathers' names are compounds in 'Abd. Twenty-two of them are women, the personal names of most of them (Benefshe, Chichek, Injü, etc.) clearly revealing them to be slave-girls. Of these 22 all but one are " bint 'Abd Allāh "; the exception is " Gülbahār bint 'Abd al-Ṣamed ", a consort of Bāyezīd II and the

[20] Op. cit., pp. 271–6.

[21] Isḥāq b. Ibrāhīm, who had been vizier as early as 861 (*Fatih Mehmet II vakfiyeleri*, p. 339, and cf. H. Inalcık, *Fatih devri*, p. 83, n. 67); he acted as Grand Vizier for a short period immediately after the death of Meḥemmed II.

[22] *Vakıflar Dergisi*, iv (1958), 118.

[23] Op. cit., p. 124.

[24] *Vakıflar Dergisi*, i (1938), 32–3.

[25] The figures are :—

Elezović, i/1	date	patronymics in 'Abd	of which 'Abd Allāh
no. 24, pp. 79–126	874/1469	11	11
appendix no. 4, pp. 1145–9	882/1477	4	4
no. 138, pp. 420–525	912/1506	7	5
no. 157, pp. 653–81	919/1513	8	8
no. 163, pp. 713–813	920/1514	4	4

The second of these is the *waqfiyye* of a sanjak-bey of Bosna, who calls himself " Ayās b. 'Abd al-Ḥayy ".

mother of Selīm I.[26] Of the 89 men, 72 are " b. 'Abd Allāh ", and these are nearly all obscure individuals. Of the 17 others, five are probably Muslim-born in spite of the patronymic,[27] and eight are probably pashas or beys.[28] Only four of the 89 are inconspicuous people with patronymics in 'Abd + a " beautiful name ".[29]

These samples indicate that throughout the fifteenth and sixteenth centuries Muslim converts who do not rise to greatness are almost invariably called " b. 'Abd Allāh ", and so are the great men too until about the reign of Bāyezīd II ; but from then onwards the great men are rarely " b. 'Abd Allāh " but almost always use a patronymic incorporating a " beautiful name ".

Since all boys and young men who had been forcibly taken into Ottoman service necessarily started their careers in obscurity, it seems to follow that an officer who eventually achieved high rank must at some stage have signalized his rise in the world by abandoning the " b. 'Abd Allāh " which he shared with thousands of his fellow-converts and adopting a rarer patronymic. If the change were made late in the officer's career, after he had begun to make his mark, we might expect to find indications of it in the documents ; and indeed there are, from the reign of Bāyezīd II (with which particularly we are here concerned), three fairly conclusive examples.

1. Yaḥyā Pasha. Sa'd al-Dīn knows of only one Yaḥyā Pasha to flourish in this reign, whose career he summarizes as follows (ii, 220–1) : having been beylerbey of Rumeli at the end of the reign of Meḥemmed II [30] he was dismissed (in favour of Dā'ūd Pasha) in 887 ; from 893 until 897 he was again beylerbey of Rumeli, and then sanjak-bey of Bosna until

[26] M. T. Gökbilgin, *Edirne*, p. 46, n. 46.

[27] Ḥusām b. 'Abd al-Raḥmān and Meḥemmed b. 'Abd al-Qādir are both kadis of Edirne ; Muḥyī al-Dīn Meḥemmed b. 'Abd al-Laṭīf is also a kadi ; Meḥemmed b. 'Abd al-Raḥīm and Meḥemmed Chelebi b. 'Abd al-Laṭīf have grandfathers named Ibrāhīm and Ismā'īl respectively.

[28] Namely Derwish Sinān b. 'Abd al-Ḥayy (*waqfiyye* of 907/1502) ; Ḥasan Beg b. 'Abd al-Mu'īn (so at p. 515, but " b. 'Abd al-Mu'min " in the index) ; Qāsim Pasha b. 'Abd al-Ḥayy (*waqfiyye* of 951/1545) ; Sinān Agha b. 'Abd al-Ḥayy (p. 451 ; perhaps the kapudan Sinān Pasha, brother of Rüstem Pasha) ; Iskender Pasha b. 'Abd al-Qādir Muṣṭafā Pasha b. 'Abd al-Kerīm, Muṣṭafā Pasha b. 'Abd al-Mu'min, and Yaḥyā Pasha b. 'Abd al-Ḥayy : to these four names I return.

[29] They are : Ferrukh Ketkhudā b. 'Abd al-Ḥalīm (flor. c. 950), Ḥājjī Minnet b. 'Abd al-Kerīm (flor. 880–910), Ḥüseyn b. 'Abd al-Ḥayy (flor. 927, and probably not Muslim-born for he is called *'atīq*), and Yūsuf b. 'Abd al-Raḥmān (flor. 912, who is *nā'ib* of a kadi).

[30] This is confirmed by Kemālpasha-zāde (facs., ed. Ş. Turan, p. 623).

907, when he became beylerbey of Anadolu; in Rajab 909 he became beylerbey of Rumeli for the third time, and in 911 was appointed vizier. In documents of this and the following years, his name does indeed appear, as vizier [31]; and in 912/1506 he is named in one of his *waqfiyye*s "Yaḥyā Pasha b. 'Abd al-Ḥayy".[32] Who then is the beylerbey (*amīr umarā' al-mu'minīn*) Yaḥyā Pasha b. 'Abd Allāh, whose name appears twice in Bāyezīd's *waqfiyye* of Dhu'l-Qa'da 898/August 1493? [33] No other Yaḥyā Pasha is known who at this time could have been mentioned in the *waqfiyye* as beylerbey.[34] It would appear that Yaḥyā Pasha, having been content to be "b. 'Abd Allāh" in 898, later—perhaps upon his promotion to the vizierate in 911—adopted the rarer patronymic "b. 'Abd al-Ḥayy".

2. Iskender Pasha. Sa'd al-Dīn similarly knows only one Iskender Pasha (ii, 218). At the death of Meḥemmed II he had been sanjak-bey of Bosna; in 888, when Khiḍr-Beg-oghlu Meḥemmed Pasha was promoted to the vizierate, he succeeded him as beylerbey of Rumeli, holding office until 890; from 894 to 904 he was a vizier, when he again became sanjak-bey of Bosna, to remain there until his death in 912. Documents do indeed show him as fourth vizier in 895, 896 and 898 [35]; and in 901/1496, still fourth vizier, he signs himself "Iskender b. 'Abd al-Ghaffār".[36] In the Sultan's *waqfiyye* of 898/1493, however, two Iskenders are named: *emīr-i kebīr, wezīr-i khaṭīr, ḥażret-i Iskender Pasha ibn 'Abd al-Qādir* and *'umdat al-wuzarā' Iskandar Pasha ibn 'Abd Allāh*.[37] The three other viziers in this year were Dā'ūd, Ibrāhīm (Chandarlî) and (Khādim) 'Alī. All three Iskenders—b. 'Abd Allāh, b. 'Abd al-Qādir, and (later) b. 'Abd al-Ghaffār—must, it would appear, be one and the same man.

3. Muṣṭafā Pasha of Üsküb. At least three Muṣṭafā Pashas flourished

---

[31] M. T. Gökbilgin, *Edirne*, pp. 93, 95 (year 911), 379 (year 912), 92, 103, 132 (year 914), 135 (year 915).

[32] Elezović, i/1, 428–9 and cf. M. T. Gökbilgin, *Edirne*, pp. 456–8, especially n. 729, and *Vakıflar Dergisi*, iii (1956), 158–9 (E. Hakkı Ayverdi).

[33] M. T. Gökbilgin, *Edirne*, p. 362, lines 5 and 15–16, and cf. appendix, p. (184), lines 3 and 26–7.

[34] Sa'd al-Dīn, it is true, implies that Yaḥyā Pasha had been made sanjak-bey of Bosna already in 897, but this must be a slight error; or did Yaḥyā retain the rank of beylerbey?

[35] M. T. Gökbilgin, *Edirne*, pp. 139, 302, 113.

[36] Kraelitz, pp. 102 and 106.

[37] M. T. Gökbilgin, *Edirne*, p. 362, lines 4–5 and 15, and cf. appendix, p. (184), lines 1–2 and 26.

in this period, and are very difficult to distinguish. One of them [38] is the founder of one of the principal mosques of Üsküb. In the inscription on his *türbe* beside the mosque (he died in 925/1519) he is called simply " Muṣṭafā Pasha ",[39] but in the foundation-inscription, dated 898/1492, over the principal door of the mosque he is called " Muṣṭafā b. 'Abd Allāh ".[40] The *waqfiyye* for this mosque and other pious foundations was drawn up 22 years later, in 920/1514 ; but here the founder is called " Muṣṭafā Pasha b. 'Abd al-Kerīm ".[41]

Here then are three persons who, having been called " b. 'Abd Allāh ", reappear with more elaborate patronymics.[42] This small problem deserves further investigation, and perhaps one of our Turkish colleagues, with the resources of the archives at his disposal, will pursue it. It can however already be said that although Dā'ūd Pasha, as vizier, signs himself " b. 'Abd al-Wadūd " in 888/1483 and 901/1496, this does not necessarily exclude the identification of the Dā'ūd b. 'Abd Allāh named in the *penche* as the same Dā'ūd, who in 883/1478 had been beylerbey of Rumeli.

---

[38] Certainly not, as Ewliyā believed (*Seyāḥat-nāme*, v, 556), " Koja " Muṣṭafā Pasha as is shown by E. Hakkı Ayverdi in *Vakıflar Dergisi*, iii (1956), 157. Koja Muṣṭafā Pasha had, as *kapîji-bashî*, gone on a mission to Italy in connection with the custody of Prince Jem (and was popularly believed to have poisoned him) ; becoming Grand Vizier in Shawwāl 917 (Ç, Uluçay, in *Tarih Dergisi*, vii/10 (1954), 122), he was executed shortly after Selīm's accession on suspicion of being a partisan of Prince Aḥmed ; he is buried at Bursa (K. Baykal, *Bursa ve anıtları*, Bursa 1950, p. 180, no. 46). This must be the " shehīd " or " maqtūl " Muṣṭafā Pasha who appears in land-registers as " Muṣṭafā Pasha b. 'Abd al-Mu'īn " (M. T. Gökbilgin, *Edirne*, pp. 441–8, especially 441, last line).

[39] Elezović, i/1, 1088–9 = i/2, 202, and cf. *Vakıflar Dergisi*, iii (1956), 158 and *resim* 23.

[40] Elezović, i/1, 261 = i/2, 83, and cf. *Vakıflar Dergisi*, iii, 157 and *resim* 22.

[41] Elezović, i/1, no. 163, pp. 713–813, see especially at p. 721, l. 164 and p. 803, l. 106.

[42] The case of Iskender Pasha raises the further question whether some dignitaries chose to use two (or more ?) " beautiful names " indiscriminately.

THREE LETTERS FROM THE OTTOMAN "SULTANA" ṢĀFIYE TO QUEEN ELIZABETH I.

by

S. A. Skilliter.

The first of the three Turkish letters which are the subject of this study was sent to England in 1593 by Ṣāfiye, then Murād III's Khāṣṣekī—that is to say, as mother of his son and heir Meḥemmed, first-lady in the Sultan's harem. She had great influence over the Sultan and in the contemporary European reports she is usually called the "Sultana". After the death of Murād III (1574–95), throughout the reign of her son Meḥemmed III (1595–1603), she enjoyed the all-powerful position of Wālide Sulṭān—"Sultana Mother".[1] It was at this time, in 1599, that our second and third letters were written to Queen Elizabeth.

In order to provide comparison with the letters sent to England, a letter of the Khāṣṣekī Ṣāfiye to the Signoria of Venice has been added as an appendix to this article, together with the copy of a letter written to the Doge and Signoria by a Wālide, perhaps by Nūr Bānū, the Venetian mother of Murād III.[2]

The first letter became famous, soon after its arrival in England, when Richard Hakluyt printed it in Italian and English translations in the 1598–1600 edition of *The Principal Navigations, Voyages, Traffiques and Discoveries of the English Nation.*[3] Its Turkish original, which is preserved in the British Museum, is published here for the first time.[4]

---

[1] For *Khāṣṣekī* and *Wālide Sulṭān* see *s.v.* in *EI* (articles by Cl. Huart and J. Deny).

[2] I found the Venetian letters when searching for the two "Sultana" letters noted by Hammer (*GOR*, ix, 396–7, nos. 781, 786) as being in the Archivio di Stato, Venice. They do not appear to be the same as his, which may still await discovery. Further "Sultana" letters, from Suleymān I's Khāṣṣekī Khurrem Sulṭān and his daughter Mihrimāh to Sigismund Augustus of Poland, are catalogued by Z. Abrahamowicz in *Katalog dokumentów tureckich*, i, 103–4, 106–7.

[3] Vol. IIi (1599), 311–12 = Glasgow reprint, vi (1904), 114–18.

[4] P. Wittek was the first to point to the possibility of its existence in the B.M., in an article published during the last war, when verification was impossible; see his "The Turkish documents in Hakluyt's 'Voyages'", *Bulletin of the Institute of Historical Research*, xix, 57 (1942), 121–39. I should like to thank Professor Wittek here for all his advice and assistance to me.

The second and third letters were discovered by Professor Akdes Nimet Kurat in the Public Record Office and were published by him ; [5] I now publish them again and study them in a wider context. The contemporary Italian translations of all three letters, sent with them from Constantinople, are also included. Finally, an Italian letter addressed to Queen Elizabeth by the Sultana's Jewish agent, the Kira Esperanza Malchi, and sent to England with the Sultana's letters of 1599, is studied on the basis of the text published by Henry Ellis,[6] and here translated anew.

I make grateful acknowledgement to the Trustees of the British Museum for permission to publish the documents which are in their collection, and also to the Controller of H.M. Stationery Office, who has allowed me to publish transcriptions and photographs of State Papers in which Crown Copyright is reserved.

DOCUMENT I

A letter in Turkish from the Khāṣṣekī Ṣāfiye to Queen Elizabeth, written in the first decade of Rabīʿ I, 1002/25 November–4 December 1593. Britsh Museum, Cotton Ms Nero B. viii, ff. 61–2, see plate XXXVII.

Summary :

After elaborate praises of God and eulogies of the Prophet, Ṣāfiye, mother of the heir-apparent Meḥemmed, sends greetings to the Queen of England. Briefly alluding to the Queen's gifts, she acknowledges the letter which the Queen's ambassador delivered with them to the Qapuagha who, for his part, had handed them all to her personal attendant. The letter has been read to her and its message understood ; further correspondence is encouraged so that the Queen's requests to the Sultan may be transmitted to him by Ṣāfiye in person.

Description :

The Turkish original and an Italian translation have been preserved in the British Museum since 1753 when the Cotton collection, to which our document belongs, was incorporated into the Museum's library at its foundation. The printed catalogue of the collection describes the two documents, among those which constitute the miscellaneous volume

---

[5] *Türk–İngiliz münasebetlerinin başlangıcı ve gelişmesi* (*1553–1610*), 209–10 (Documents XIVi, ii).

[6] H. Ellis, *Original letters, illustrative of English history*, iii (1824), 52–5 : letter ccxxxvi

Nero B. viii, where they occupy folios 61–3 of the new foliation, as follows:

"40. A paper in Arabic. 55.

41. The Sultana, wife of Amurat III, to queen Elizabeth; complimental. (an Italian translation, perhaps of the preceding article.) 57*b*." [7]

It is well known that the great antiquary Sir Robert Cotton (1571–1634), in his zeal to enrich his collection of historical records, was accustomed to use his influence in Court circles to convey a large quantity of State papers into his private library, and this may explain why we find the Sultana's letter and its translation there. The collection remained with his family until it was acquired by the State at the beginning of the eighteenth century and in 1729, after some temporary homes, it was moved for greater safety to Ashburnham House, Westminster. There, however, it suffered on 23 October 1731 the ravages of a great fire after which of the original 958 volumes 861 remained, many of those left in a pitiful state from the effects of fire and water. Nero B. viii is one of the volumes so damaged; it has badly charred edges and much of its contents, including the Sultana's letter, is ruined by water.[8]

The document is a single sheet of Oriental paper, which at first sight resembles parchment and is thick, yellowish and inclined to break at the folds. There is no watermark. The paper is 31½ cm. wide and now 57½ cm. long. The rough upper edge, however, suggests that something is missing from the top and indeed, as we shall see, the original length must have been about 63 cm. The side used for writing has been smoothed and liberally flecked with gold. The upper half is empty except for a brief *invocatio*, placed to the right of the centre and now very near the top but originally at some distance from it. The twenty-four lines of the text occupy 28 cm. of the lower half, reaching down to the bottom of the paper. Each of them begins at a distance of 7½ cm. from the right edge, where a still-discernible impressed line runs from top to bottom. The lines are horizontal and, contrary to the usage observed in Imperial letters, they do not curve upwards at the end, neither are they made to reach the left edge, nor are their final letters elongated. The script is a beautiful calligraphic *naskh*, partially vocalized. It may be noted that the *i* of the

[7] *Catalogue of the manuscripts in the Cottonian library deposited in the British Museum*, (1802), p. 226. The folio numbers refer to a superseded foliation. It is from this entry that P. Wittek concluded (see above, p. 119, n. 4) that item 40 was probably the original of which item 41 was the translation.

[8] For a history of the Cotton collection see A. Esdaile, *The British Museum Library* (1946), pp. 26–7, 226–31.

iḍāfe is sometimes expressed by a small perpendicular stroke. In every line except the last the scribe changes the ink at least three times, using altogether five colours, black, blue, crimson, gold, and scarlet. In these changes of colour purely aesthetic considerations seem to have prevailed; thus the last line is written entirely in black, suggesting an intention to stress the closing. Damp, resulting from the 1731 disaster, has mottled the paper with patches of purple mould and has so much affected the passages in blue ink that they have become to a great degree illegible and have in some places entirely disappeared. The original way of folding, over and over from bottom to top, as is usual in Ottoman documents, can still be seen from the faint marks which remain. Of the resulting rectangles, of which twelve are preserved, the lowest is 4 cm. high. The height of the following rectangles increases in proportion to the progress of the folding, the uppermost being 5 cm. high. As has already been observed, the upper edge is rough and must be regarded as representing the thirteenth fold, so that the loss of a rectangle measuring at least 5 cm. may be assumed. Possibly this rectangle was torn off because of the valuable jewel-studded seal which it bore on its verso. This seal which has not been traced, is described in the inventory which accompanied the letter and gifts (see below, p. 148) : it must have been removed together with the strip, some time after the letter had been presented to the Queen.

This loss, however, was not the worst mutilation the document was to suffer. Before its upper strip was removed, the sheet of paper had been folded in half horizontally and remained so even after the loss of the strip. Later it was folded in half again, this time across, and it was in this condition when the document suffered the soaking. As its lower half was no longer covered by the upper half, the two halves of the final lines (19–24) offset over on to themselves, whereas the remaining major part of the text (lines 1–18) offset on to the blank upper half of the document the *invocatio* at the same time leaving its impression on the lower part of the text, in line 18. This enables us to establish the approximate height of the missing strip. Due to these vagaries of fortune, with its text damaged and in parts irrevocably lost, the Sultana's letter, once an outstanding specimen of Turkish calligraphy, today affords only a pitiful reminder of its beauty and colour at the hour of its presentation to Queen Elizabeth.

Just as the letter is beautiful from the point of view of decoration and calligraphy, so is it elaborate in its style, being composed in a very involved and flowery rhyming prose (*saj'*) with many poetical comparisons (*tashbīh*). In this showpiece of rhetoric, the actual communication which the Sultana has to make occupies less than half of the twenty-four lines—i.e. lines 14–23. Here and there the writer reproduces, more or less faithfully, established formulas of Imperial letters—so, for example, the long series of titles of the Sultan (lines 7–10) and of the Queen of England (lines 12–13). The use of an archaism in line 17 can be noted: – سوريو from سوريمك instead of the usual سورو from سورمك. Also noteworthy is the خدمتلرى used in line 11 as a form of address to the Crown-prince, instead of the expected حضرتلرى.

In the following transcription of the Turkish original the sections written in blue ink have been rendered, as far as they could be deciphered, from the faint marks still to be seen on the manuscript, although not visible on the photograph, or sometimes reconstructed with the help of the Italian translation. Sections offered by the latter but no longer legible on the original are left blank in the transcription but appear between square brackets in my English rendering. In order to simplify printing, the vocalization which is used occasionally in the original has been omitted altogether from my transcription.

Transcription [plate XXXVII]

[a]هو المعين[9]

1 افتتاح كلام صدق انجام وفاتحهٔ مقال عزّت اختتامْ [b] عالم عناصرْ واشباحْ وجملهٔ
اجساد وارواحي [c] يوق ايكن وار طقوزْ فلكي دوّارْ [d] ويدي يري

2 [e]برْقرار ايدن سلطان بي وزير وخلّاق بي نظيرْ [f] صانع اكوان مبدع اشكال
والوان احد يكتا [g] معبود بي همتا حضرْت اللّهْ تعالي شانه [h] عن مخلوقاته

3 (. . . ? 3 words . . .) خالق وستار وبيچون تعالي عما يصفون [i] حضرْتلرينك•
توحيد جلال [j] وتمجيد عظمت وكمالي ايله مزيّن وانك جميع افريدهْسنكْ

4 [k]ايوسي وبرْكزيدهْسي انبيانك سرْوري [l] وجود صدفنك كوهري سعادتْ
باشنك تاجي [m] (. . . ? 7 words . . .)

a–b black, b–c blue, c–d crimson, d–e black, e–f gold, f–g crimson, g–h black, h–i blue, i–j gold, j–k scarlet, k–l black, l–m crimson,

b–c just decipherable on the original. h–i the first words invisible, then three words which can just be seen. تعالي etc.—Koran vi, 100—suggested by the translation, line 6: "... che non ha similitudine si come e descrito dalli proffetti."

[9] *Invocatio* (not included in plate).

5 [n] انبيانك خاتمي باغ جنانْ عكْس جمالي محمّدكْ [o] عرْش عظيمْ وصْف كمالي محمّدكْ حبيب خدا شفيع يومْ جزا [p] نبيّ كزينْ رسول ربّ العالمينْ محمّد

6 [q] (. . . ? 8 words . . .) [r] حضْرتنكْ جان پاكي وترْبهٔ عطرناكي سلامي ايله مـْعنونْ [s] اولمقْدن صكْره بو زمان سعادتْ

7 نشانـْده [t] يدي اقليمك خاني درتْ كوشهٔنك صاحبْ قراني [u] اقليم روم وعجم وانكروسْ ولايت تاتار [v] وافلاق (. . . ? 5 words . . .)

8 [w] قرامان وحبش ودشت قفجاق مشْرق وجوازرْ وشروانْ [x] مغرب وجزايرْ وقيروانْ اقليملرينك شهرياري [y] هندْ وسند وبغداد فرنك وخروادْ

9 [z] وبلغراد ايللرينك پادشاه تاجداري اون اكي ابادن [a′] (. . . ? 8 words . . .) [b′] سايهٔ يزدان پناه دين ودولت خان مراد

10 [c′] داور دوران معزّ سلطنت سلطان مرادْ خلد الله اقباله واجْلاله [d′] حضرتلرينك شهزادهسي [e′] پادشاهلق باغـْجهسنك [f′] سرو ازادهسي لايق تخت دولت

---

m–n blue, n–o scarlet, o–p black, p–q gold, q–r blue, r–s crimson, s–t black, t–u scarlet, u–v gold, v–w blue, w–x black, x–y scarlet, y–z gold, z–a′ crimson, a′–b′ blue, b′–c′ scarlet, c′–d′ black, d′–e′ gold, e′–f′ scarlet,

---

q–r no traces of letters visible but from the translation, line 10, one may tentatively read : مصطفى صلى الله عليه وعلى آله واصحابه وسلّم

v–w the translation, line 14, includes in the list of provinces : "Vulachia, Rossia, turchia, Arabia, Bagdet, Caramania," therefore the lacuna probably contains the words : وافلاق وروس عرب وبغـــدان واتراك حكومت For the translation's "Bagdet" we have to read بغدان rhyming with قرامان instead of بغداد which appears later, and is then omitted in the translation. a′–b′ the translation's "possessor della Corona" suggests تاج آوري (rhyming with تاجداري) at the beginning of the blank, and its "della stirpe di Adam fin hora Imperator fiol de Imperator" probably represents : حضرت آدمدن الى الآن السلطان بن السلطان

11 ولي عهد خلافت وارث سلاطين[g′] درّة التاج خواقين سزاوار عطاي حيّ وديّان
[h′]محمّد خانْ بن سلْطانْ مرادْ خانْ طال بقاه ونال ما يتمنّاه خدْمتلرينك[10]
12 [i′]اناسي طرفنْدنْ عمدة فرقة الخواتين العيسويّات [j′] (. . . 3 words . . .)
المسيحيّات صاحبة دلايل الحشمة والوقار [k′] ساحبة اذيال المجد والاقتدار مطاعة
13 [l′]السّلاطين مهدْ العصْمة والتمكين انْكلتّره ولايتنك[m′] حاكمهسي بانوي تاجْدار
وخاتون مرْيم شعار ختمتْ بالخيرْ [n′] عواقبها وحصلت مطالبها
14 [o′]صوْبنه علي نيّة اتّباعها الهدا برْ سلام پرْ اكْرامْ كهْ كلستانْ [p′] كللري اندن
بروورق و[q′] بـرْكلام صدْق انجام كه بوستانْ بلبللرينكْ درْسي اندنْ برْسبق
15 [r′]بر دعا كه حسن خاتمهي مورث بر ثناكه سعادتْ[s′] دنيا واخرته باعث اولا
مجلس كامرانيلرينك[t′] هديّهْ وارْمغاني عدّ اولنمقدنْ صكْره اعْلام اولنوركهْ
16 [u′]برْ وقت شريفده كهْ هر دمي نيجه سال[v′] وهرْ ساعتي نيجهْ ايّام وليالدنْ
عزيزدرْ[w′] دولتلو وسعادتلو پادشاه اسلام وشهريار مرّيخ المقام حضرتلرينك
17 [x′]سعادتلري اشيكنهْ يوزْ سوريو كلانْ[11] ايلچيلري اليله[y′] باشْقه خيرْخواهْلري
طرفنه[z′] حدّ تعبيردن بيرون ودرجهٔ تقريردن[a″] افزون رعايتي ومحبّتي
18 [b″]اشعار ايدرْ بر مكتوب پر عجايب كه كاغدي[c″] كافور خالص وعنبرْدن
ومركّبي مشك ازفردن[12] [d″] لطيفْ ايدي عفت وادبْ قپوسي اغالري واسطهْ سيلهْ
19 [e″]واصل وپرده عصمت پيش خدمتلري اليلهْ[f″] دايرهٔ وصولنه داخلْ اولوبْ
نامهْلرينك مضموننْده اولانْ ادا[g″] قبول قولاغيله اشعار اولنوب انصاف بودركه

---

f′–g′ blue, g′–h′ crimson, h′–i′ black, i′–j′ scarlet, j′–k′ blue, k′–l′ gold, l′–m′ black, m′–n′ crimson, n′–o′ blue, o′–p′ scarlet, p′–q′ gold, q′–r′ black, r′–s′ blue, s′–t′ black, t′–u′ crimson, u′–v′ gold, v′–w′ scarlet, w′–x′ blue, x′–y′ black, y′–z′ gold, z′–a″ crimson,
a″–b″ gold, b″–c″ scarlet, c″–d″ blue, d″–e″ black, e″–f″ gold, f″–g″ crimson,

---

f′–g′ reconstructed with the help of the translation, sufficiently supported by traces of letters.

---

[10] Professor Wittek will deal with this form of address in his " Zu einigen frühosmanischen Urkunden (vii) ", *WZKM*, lix.

[11] *yüz sürüyü gelen* instead of the expected *yüz sürü gelen* ; cf. 'Āshiqpasha-zāde (ed. Giese), p. 155, l. 4. سلطانمك دولتلو اشكنه يوز سُور يو وارم

[12] Meninski, *Lexicon* (1680), col. 4683 *s.v.* مشك : *müšḱī ezfer* " moschus praestantissimus ".

20 [h″]شمديه°دك اول مهـْد حكومت وايالته° متعلق اولان [i″] اعتبارك زياده° اولماسنه°
سبب° اولمشـْدر° هميشه [j″] بو نوعه° محبّت وصفايي ازدياده° باعث° مكتوب°

21 [k″](. . . ? 2 words . . .) دن خالي اولميه‌لرايسه اعلان بودركه [l″] هربار خبر
صحتـّلري كلنمكـْدن° وخبر صحتّلري بلنمكدن [m″] خالي اولنميه كه اول بانوي
مفخّمه وخاتون

22 [n″]مكرّمه طرفنك خير° عواقب وحصول مطالبـْلرينه [o″] سعـْي اوزره اولوب° دولتلو
وسعادتـْلو پادشاه صاحب° [p″] قران° وخداوند°كار اسكندر° مكان

23 [q″]حضرتلرينك اياقلري طپراغنه بانو طرفنك تربيه [r″] وتعريفلري تكرار اولنوب
مرادلري فلكي [s″] (. . . ? 4 words . . .) جهد اوزره‌در

24 [t″]والسلام الاسني علي من اتـّبع الهدي تحريرا فى اوايل شهر ربيع الاول لسنة اثنى
والف من الهجرة النبويّة عليه الصّلوة والسّلام° [u″]

g″–h″ blue, h″–i″ black, i″–j″ gold, j″–k″ scarlet, k″–l″ blue, l″–m″ crimson, m″–n″ black, n″–o″ gold, o″–p″ black, p″–q″ scarlet, q″–r″ crimson, r″–s″ gold, s″–t″ blue, t″–u″ black.

The official Italian translation (*Public Record Office, S.P. 97/2 ff. 295–6*) [plate XXXVIII]

The translation is written on a single sheet of white paper, 42 × 31 cm., folded to form two leaves, each 31 × 21 cm. The watermark indicates that it is of European, probably Italian, origin.[13] The writing is cursive, in black ink. Folio 295*a* contains the title and first twenty-three lines of the text, folio 295*b* the next twenty-four lines, and the last two lines are on folio 296*a*. Folio 296*b* bears the endorsement: "1594 Translation of the Empress l*ett*ere to the *Q*ueens Ma*jesty*. Receaved at Grenew*i*ch ul*ti*mo Iulii."

This, and not the presentation copy (British Museum, Cotton Ms Nero B. viii, f. 63) which has been preserved with the Turkish original, is the text copied by Richard Wrag in Constantinople and later reproduced by Hakluyt, with some minor variants.[14]

[13] It closely resembles watermark no. 666 (an angel and the initials "N S") in J. Briquet, *Les filigranes*, i (1907). Briquet notes it for a letter written at Salo in 1594.

[14] Hakluyt, Glasgow reprint, vi, 114–16. The variants are indicated in my transcription.

f. 295*a*
Interpretatione della letera che scrive la Ser*enissi*ma Sultana del Gra*n* S*ign*or

Alla Ser*enissi*ma Regina d'Inghiltera

1. Il Principio del Ragionam*en*to nostro sia scritura [15] Perfeta [16] nelle quatro parti del mo*n*do,[17]
2. in nome di quello che ha creato indiferentem*en*te [18] tante Infinite creature che non
3. havevano anima et pur son*no*,[19] et di quello che fa girar li [20] nove cielli,[21] et che la terra
4. sette volte una sopra l'altra fa firmar; Signor et Re senza viceRe, et che non ha
5. comparatio*n* [22] alla sua creatione ne opera, et uno senza precio adorato incomparabilm*en*te
6. l'Altiss*imo* Dio, Creatore, che non ha similitudine si come e descrito dalli proffetti,[23]
7. alla cui [24] grandeza [25] non si ariva,[26] et alla perfecione [27] sua compiuta non si opone; [28]
8. et quel omnipotente creatore, et cooperatore alla grandezza [25] del quale Inclina [29]
9. tutti li proffetti,[23] fra quali el [30] maggior, et che ha ottenuta [31] gracia, orto [32] del
10. paradiso, raggi [33] del [34] sole, Amato dal [35] Altissimo Dio [36] Machemet Mustafa,[37] al
11. qual et suoi adherenti, et Imitatori sia perpetua pace, alla cui sepoltura [38]
12. odorifera si fa ogni honore /
13. Quello che è Imperator de sette clima,[39] et delle quatro Parti del mondo Invincibile
14. Re di Grecia, Agiamia, Ungheria,[40] Tartaria, Vulachia,[41] Rossia, turchia, Arabia,
15. Bagdet, Caramania, Abessia,[42] Giovassir,[43] Sirva*n*, Barbaria, Algieri, franchia,

---

Variants in Hakluyt:

[15] scrittura. [16] perfetta. [17] parte. [18] indifferentemente. [19] ni persona. [20] gli. [21] cieli. [22] comparacion. [23] propheti. [24] a la cui. [25] grandessa. [26] arrive. [27] perfettione. [28] oppone. [29] inchinano. [30] il. [31] ottenuto. [32] horto.

[33] ragi. [34] dal. [35] del. [36] è *added*. [37] Mahomet Mustaffa. [38] sepultura. [39] climati. [40] Ungeria. [41] Valachia. [42] Abessis. [43] Giouasir.

16. Crovacia,[44] Belgrado [45] sempre felicissimo, et de dodici [46] Avoli possessor della
17. Corona, et della stirpe di Adam fin hora Imperator fiol [47] de [48] Imperator con-
18. -servato dalla [49] divina providenza Re di ogni dignita, et honore Sultan
19. Morat,[50] che il S*ign*or Dio sempre augumenti [51] le sue forze,[52] et padre di quello a
20. Cui aspeta [53] la Corona Imperiale, orto,[54] et Cipresso [55] mirabile, degno della
21. sedia Regale, et vero Erede [56] del comando [57] Imperiale, dignissi*mo* Mehemet
22. Kan [58] fiol [59] de Sultan Morat [50] Kan,[58] che Dio compisca li suoi dissegni, et
23. alongha [60] li suoi giorni felici ; Dalla parte della Madre del qual si scrive

f. 295*b*

1. La presente alla ser*enissi*ma, et Gloriosissi*ma* fra le Prudentissime Don*ne*, et Eletta fra li
2. triomfanti sotto il stendardo [61] di Iesu Christo, Potentissi*ma* et Richissima [62] Regitrice,
3. et al mondo singularissi*ma* fra il feminil sesso La ser*enissi*ma Regina d'Inghiltera,[63]
4. che segue le vestigie di [64] Maria vergine,[65] il fine della quale sia con bene et p*er*fecione [66]
5. secondo il suo desiderio / Le mando una salutatio*n* [67] di Pace cossi [68] honorata
6. che no*n* basta tutta la copia de Rossignoli [69] con le loro musiche arivare non che
7. con questa carta per [70] l'amore singulare che è conceputo [71] fra noi, che è simile
8. a un horto de ucelli vaghi,[72] che il S*igno*re [73] Dio la faci degna di salvacione, et il
9. fine suo sia talle [74] che in questo mondo et nel futuro sia con pace.

---

[44] Corvacia. [45] &c. *added.* [46] dodeci. [47] figliolo. [48] del'. [49] de la. [50] Murat. [51] augmenti. [52] forzze. [53] aspetta. [54] horto. [55] Cypresso. [56] herede. [57] commando. [58] Can. [59] filiol. [60] alunga.

[61] standardo. [62] ricchissima. [63] d'Ingilterra. [64] de. [65] virgine. [66] perfettione. [67] salutacion. [68] cosi. [69] rosignoli. [70] "per" *omitted and* ":" *added.* [71] conciputo. [72] di Uccelli vagi. [73] Signor. [74] tale.

10. Doppo comparsi li suoi honorati presenti dalla [75] sedia della [76] ser*eni*ta vostra, sapera
11. che son*no* [77] capitati In un [78] hora, che ogni punto e stato una consolation di lu*n*gho [79] tempo,
12. per ocasione [80] del Ambas*ciato*re [81] di vostra ser*eni*ta venuto alla felice Porta del Imperatore
13. con tanto nostro contento quanto si possi [82] desiderare, et con quello una lettera
14. di vostra ser*eni*ta [83] che ci è stata [84] presentata dalli nostri Eunuchi con gra*n* honore,
15. la Carta della [85] quale odorava di Canfora [86] et Ambracano, et l'Inchiostro
16. di Musco perfetto, et quella pervenuta In nostra man*no* [87] tutta la co*n*tinenza
17. di essa a parte a parte ho ascoltato Intentamente, Quello che hora si co*n*viene
18. è che corispondente [88] alla nostra affecione in tutto quello che si aspeta [89] alle
19. cose atenente [90] alli paesi che son*no* [91] sotto il Comando [92] di v*ost*ra ser*eni*ta, lei no*n* manchi
20. di sempre tenirmi [93] datto [94] noticia, acio [95] che in tutto quello che li ocorera [96] Io
21. possi compiacerla de quello che fra le nostre ser*eni*ta e conveniente, acio che [97]
22. quelle cose che si interprenderano habino il desiderato buon fine, perche
23. Io saro sempre racordevole [98] Al Altiss*imo* Imperatore delle ocorenze [99] di v*ost*ra ser*eni*ta,
24. perche sia in ogni ocasione [100] compiaciuta, con che finendo [101] la pace sia

f. 296*a*

1. con vostra ser*eni*ta, et con quelli che seguitano dretamente la via di Dio ;
2. Scritta alli [102] primi della [103] luna di Rabielavol [104] anno del Proffetta [105] 1002 / [106]

---

[75] da la. [76] de la. [77] sono. [78] una. [79] lungo. [80] occasione. [81] Ambassadore. [82] posso. [83] serenetà. [84] estata. [85] de la. [86] camfora. [87] nostro mano. [88] correspondente. [89] aspetta. [90] attenente. [91] sono. [92] commando. [93] tenermi. [94] dato. [95] *omitted.* [96] occorerà. [97] accioche. [98] ricordevole. [99] occorenze. [100] occasione. [101] " con che finendo " *omitted.* [102] al. [103] dell. [104] Rabie Livol. [105] profeta. [106] " & di Jesu 1594 " *added.*

English rendering of the Turkish text

HE is the Helper ! [107]

line 1 The opening of the sincere speech and the commencement of the glorifying discourse,

lines 1–3 having been decorated with the declaration of the uniqueness of His majesty and with the glorification of the magnificence and perfection of the Lord—High Exalted be He [above (all) that they ascribe (unto Him) !—] [108] the Absolute and the Veiler [109] and the Creator [. . . ? 3 words . . .], Who, when its elements and forms and all its bodies and spirits did not exist, brought the world into existence, caused the nine spheres to revolve and established the seven earths,[110] the Ruler who has no chancellor and the Supreme Creator who is without equal, the Maker of existing things, the Originator of shapes and colours, the Unique One, the Worshipped without peer, the Lord God—exalted be His glory above His creation !—

lines 3–6 and having been ornamented with the salutation of the perfumed sepulchre and the pure soul of Lord Muḥammad [the chosen, upon whom and upon whose friends and followers be perpetual peace !], the apostle of the Lord of the worlds, the chosen prophet, the intercessor at the Day of Reckoning, the friend of God, of Muḥammad who is the perfect eulogy of the Great Throne, of Muḥammad who is the beautiful reflection of the Garden of Paradise, the seal of the prophets [. . . ? 7 words . . .], the crown on the head of happiness, the pearl in the shell of existence, the chief of the prophets, of him who is the best of all His created beings and His elected,

line 6 thereafter,

lines 10–12 on the part of the mother of Sulṭān Murād Khān's son,[111] His Highness Meḥemmed Khān—may he live long and attain that which he desires !—the worthy of the gifts of the Ever-

---

[107] This reference to God as the True Helper is an *invocatio* appropriate to a letter which is essentially a promise of help.

[108] Passages in square brackets are restorations based on the Italian translation.

[109] For *Sattār* see *EI*², i, 717*a* (" Al-Asmā' al-Ḥusnā ").

[110] On the cosmographic ideas expressed here, see E. J. W. Gibb's *A History of Ottoman poetry*, i (1900), chapter 2.

[111] i.e. Ṣāfiye the Khāṣṣekī ; on her see below, pp. 144 f.

Living and Ever-Requiting [112] God, the pearl in the Khāqān's crown, the heir of the Sultans, the heir-apparent of the Caliphate, worthy of the imperial throne, the straight-grown cypress in the garden of kingship, the royal son

ines 6–10 of His Majesty Sulṭān Murād—may God perpetuate his good fortune and majesty!—the monarch of the lands, the exalter of the empire, the Khān of the seven climes at this auspicious time and the fortunate lord of the four corners (of the earth), the emperor of the regions of Rūm and 'Ajam [113] and Hungary, of the lands of the Tatars and Wallachians [and Russians, of the Turks and Arabs and Moldavia, of the dominions of] Karamania and Abyssinia and the Qipchaq steppes, of the Eastern climes and of Jawāzir [114] and Shirwān, of the Western climes and of Algeria and Qairawān, the Padishah bearing the crown of the lands of Hind and Sind and Baghdad, of the Franks and Croatians and Belgrade, [possessor of the crown] from twelve ancestors,[115] [Sultan son of Sultan from all the sons of Adam to this time,] the shadow of God, the protector of faith and state, Khān Murād

ines 12–14 towards the support of Christian womanhood, [the elected of the . . . ? 2 words . . .] who follow the Messiah, bearer of the marks of pomp and majesty, trailing the skirts of glory and power, she who is obeyed of the princes, cradle [116] of chastity and continence, ruler of the realm of England, crowned lady

---

[112] *Dayyān* = no. 135 of the list in J. W. Redhouse's " On the most comely names " . . , *JRAS*, N.S. xii (1880), 1–69.

[113] " Rūm " = the Ottoman empire, especially the lands of the former " Roman ", .e. Byzantine, empire. " 'Ajam " = Persia.

[114] Jawāzir does not usually figure in similar lists of provinces. Ḥājjī Khalīfa *Jihān-numā*, A.H. 1145, p. 465) describes it as a castle situated near the confluence of the Tigris and Euphrates, and indicates its position on the map. He also refers to it as one of the stations on the two routes from Basra to Baghdad (*ib.*, pp. 455–6). The name no longer appears on modern maps of Iraq. When Iraq was conquered by Suleymān I in 1554 Jawāzir became centre of a sanjak of that name in the newly organized beglerbeglik of Baghdad: see Ferīdūn, *Munsha'āt*, 2nd ed., ii (A.H. 1275), p. 406; 'Ayn-i 'Alī, *Qawānīn-i Āl-i 'Othmān* (A.H. 1280), p. 36 = P. A. von Tischendorf, *Das Lehnswesen in den moslemischen Staaten* (1872), p. 84; Ewliyā Chelebī, *Seyāḥat-nāme*, i (A.H. 1314), p. 193; cf. also S. H. Longrigg, *Four centuries of modern Iraq* (1925), p. 26, n. 1.

[115] In fact, Murād III is himself the twelfth Ottoman Sultan.

[116] *Mehd*, " cradle " (used also in l. 20); cf. *Mehd-i 'ulyā*, " most exalted cradle," an honorific title of the Wālide Sulṭān.

and woman of Mary's way—may her last moments be concluded with good and may she obtain that which she desires !—

lines 14–15 with the intention of her following the guidance in the right path, let there be made a salutation so gracious that (all) the rose-garden's roses are but one petal from it and a speech so sincere that the (whole) repertoire of the garden's nightingales is but one stanza of it, a prayer which bestows a fortunate end, a praise which brings forth felicity in this world and the next !

lines 15–19 After Her Felicitous Majesty's presents and gifts have been accounted for, it is to be made known that at an august time whose every moment was more precious than several years and every hour than several days and nights, by the hand of Her ambassador [117] who came to rub his forehead on the threshold of happiness of His Majesty, the fortunate and felicitous Padishah of Islam and the Marslike sovereign, a special letter, full of marvels, whose paper was more fragrant than pure camphor and ambergris and its ink than finest musk, notifying indescribable and immeasurable consideration and love towards (me) Her well-wisher, reached (me) by the good offices of the Agha of the Door [118] of chastity and modesty [119] and entered the circle of arrival by the hand of the highest attendant [120] of the curtain of chastity. What was expressed in the contents of Her letter became recorded by the ear of acceptance, and in justice

lines 20–23 It caused the esteem heretofore attached to that cradle of rule and dominion to increase. If She will never cease from (sending) such [. . . ? 2 words . . .] letters which foster the increase of sincerity and love, this is to be made known : There shall never be cessation from news about Her good health arriving and news about Her good health becoming known, so that while striving for that illustrious princesses's and honoured lady's salvation and Her success in Her desires, I can repeatedly mention Her Highness's gentility and praise at the footdust of His Majesty, the fortunate and felicitous

---

[117] I.e. Edward Barton ; on him see below, p. 143 f.

[118] Probably the famous Hungarian eunuch Ghażanfer (see Hammer, *GOR*, iv, 7), Qapuagha under Murād III and Meḥemmed III. On *Qapuagha* see Gibb and Bowen, *Islamic Society and the West*, i (1950), 78.

[119] I.e. the women's quarters in the harem.

[120] I.e. the *Kāya Qadın* (Gibb and Bowen, i, 74) ; perhaps Jānfedā Qadın (see Hammer, *GOR*, iv, pp. 102, 241).

Padishah, the Lord of the fortunate conjunction and the sovereign who has Alexander's place, and I shall endeavour for Her aims [. . . ? 4 words . . .]

ine 24 And the most sublime salutation be upon whomsoever follows the right guidance! Written in the first decade of the month Rabīʿ al-Awwal of the year one thousand and two of the Hegira of the Prophet—blessings and peace be upon him![121]

DOCUMENTS II AND III

'wo almost identical Turkish letters from the Wālide Ṣāfiye to Queen Elizabeth, ndated [of *circa* 26 November 1599]. Document II is folio 19 and Document III ; folio 5 of Public Record Office, S.P. 102/4, see plates XXXIX and XL.

ummary:

After greeting the Queen, the Wālide notifies the receipt of her letter and romises to act as her intermediary with the Sultan in the matter of the nglish capitulations. She urges the Queen to be firm in friendship. The rrival and acceptance of a coach from the Queen is mentioned and in return he Wālide sends various items of Turkish ladies-costume and certain jewels, ll of which are listed; in this respect only do the two letters differ. The first, elivered by the Bostanjibashı, accompanies a robe, a girdle, sleeves, various andkerchiefs, and a crown of pearls and rubies; the second, delivered by he Kira, accompanies a crown of diamonds and rubies.

)escription:

As has already been noted (see above, p. 120), a transcription of these wo letters has been published by A. N. Kurat.

Document II is a sheet, 41 × $24\frac{3}{4}$ cm., of white European paper, moothed on the written side, with a watermark which I am unable to dentify. The *invocatio* is placed at the top edge, near the centre. The wenty-six lines of text, written in black ink, occupy $20\frac{1}{4}$ cm. of the total ength. The first line is $20\frac{3}{4}$ cm. below the top edge and begins 9 cm. from he right edge, at an impressed line running from top to bottom. When, vith line 15, the bottom of the paper was very nearly reached, the sheet vas turned upside down and the text continued for another ten lines n the margin, these lines reaching from the bottom of the main text to ear line 1. Then the paper was turned again and the final line (26) was vritten the right way up, at the very bottom of the paper, beneath line 15. cm. above the first line and very near the right margin there is an mpression, $16\frac{1}{2}$ × 12 mm., of the Wālide's seal in black ink, the script ppearing as black on white around the central lozenge and as white on

121 = 25 November–4 December 1593.

black inside it. The document, now folded in half, was originally foldec ten times, from the bottom upwards.

Document III is a sheet, $38\frac{1}{4} \times 23$ cm., of white Oriental paper smoothed on the written side. The *invocatio* is placed at the top edge near the centre. The thirty-one lines of text, written in black ink occupy $19\frac{1}{2}$ cm. of the total length. The first line is $18\frac{3}{4}$ cm. below the top edge and begins $8\frac{1}{4}$ cm. from the right edge, at an impressed line running from top to bottom. When, with line 15, the bottom of the paper was very nearly reached, the sheet was turned upside down anc the text continued for another fifteen lines in the margin, these lines reaching from the bottom of the main text to $2\frac{1}{4}$ cm. above line 1. Then the paper was turned again and the final line (31) was written the right way up, at the very bottom of the paper, beneath line 15. This letter also bears an impression of the Wālide's seal, exactly like that of Document II placed $1\frac{1}{4}$ cm. above the first line and $1\frac{1}{4}$ cm. to the left of the margin The document, now folded in half, was originally folded eleven times from the bottom upwards.

The two letters are extremely primitive and crude in appearance and, as shall be seen, also in style. The hand, which is the same in both documents, is awkward and unskilled, the spelling is often incorrect and inconsistent, and the composition is in general poor and even faulty They are personal letters of the Wālide written, as we learn from an English witness, John Sanderson (see below, p. 151), in the harem by one of her women. Comparing them with the letters sent to Venice (see Appendix and plates XLI and XLII), it would seem that they are typica "Sultana" letters and that the beautiful letter of 1593 may be unique of its kind.

Transcription of Document II [plate XXXIX]

هو[1]

[2] [seal

I) افتخار الامراء العظام الملة المسيحيّة اختيار (2) اكبراء الفخّا فى الملة ألمسيحيّة
صلح مصالح (3) ساحب الدّهلايل والوقار صاحب الاديال (4) والافتخار انكلتره

[1] *Invocatio* (not included in plate).

[2] Impression of the Wālide Ṣāfiye's seal (see plate XL). A. N. Kurat's reading of it ma be tentatively completed to:
Around the edge: تو مرادم [يا ساكن آسمان يا خدا يا محمد] فخر جهان
Centre: والدۀ سلطان محمد خان

قرالجهسی ختمت عواقبه (5) بالخیر[3] تحیّات صافیات وتسلیمات وفیات (6) وردیة
الفواحات[4] که محض موالات وفرط (7) مصافاتدن صادر اولور اتحاف واهدی[5]
اولندق (8) دن صکره انها واعلام اولنان بودرکه مکتوبکز (9) کلوب دکدي هرنکه
دمشسز[6] معلومز اولدي (10) انشا الله[7] دیدیکوکز اوزره عمل اولونور بو حصوص
(11) دن[8] اوتوري کوکلیکزي[9] حوش[10] توتهسز[11] اوغلو (12) مز پادشاه حضرتلرینه
دایما تربیّه ایدوب (13) اهدنامه[12]لري موجبنجه عمل ایدهسز دیو (14) سویلمکدن
خالي دکلوز انشا الله[13] بو حصوصدن[14] (15) الم چکمیهسز سزده دایما دوستلق
اوزهرینه[15] (16) صابت[16] اولاسز (17) انشا الله[17] کم اولمز وبزه (18) عرهبه[18]
کندردیکوز[19] کلوب (19) تسلم اولدي مقبولمز اولمشدر (20) بزده سزه بر قفتان بر
قوشاق (21) بر یلك ایکی تانه[20] صرمه[21] دتسمال[22] (22) اوچ مقرمه بر تانه[23] انجلي[24]
(23) فرنك بابلي استفان کندر (24) دوك[25] معزور[26] توتهسز[27] (25) شویله معلوم
اولا (26) باقی الدعا

Transcription of Document III [plate XL]

هو[28]

[29] [seal]

(1) اقتخار الامراء العظام الملة المسیحیّة اختیار (2) الکبراء الفخام فی الملة المسیحیّة
مصلح مصالح (3) ساحب الدّلایل والوقار صاحب الادیال (4) والافتخار انکلتره
قرالحهسي ختمت عوا (5) قبه بالخیر[30] تحیّات صافیات وتسلیمات (6) وفیات
وردیّة الفواحات[31] که محض موالات (7) وفرط مصافاتدن صادر اولور اتحاف

---

[3] This address attempts to be that usually given to a Christian ruler, without taking into account that in this case the addressee is a woman; even so, it is very defective. Its correct form would be : افتخار الامراء العظام العیسویّه مختار الکبراء الفخام فی الملة المسیحیّه مصلح مصالح جماهیر الطایفة النصرانیّه ساحب اذیال الحشمة والوقار صاحب دلایل المجد والافتخار ولایت انکلتره قرالي ختمت عواقبه بالخیر. The usual address to Queen Elizabeth is : افتخار المخدرات العیسویّه مختارة الموقرات فی الملة المسیحیّه مصلحة مصالح الطایفة النصرانیّه ساحبة اذیال الحشمة والوقار صاحبة دلایل المجد والافتخار ولایت انکلتره قرالیچهسی ایلیزابت ختمت عواقبها بالخیر (see A. N. Kurat, *Türk–İngiliz münasebetlerinin başlangıcı*, Document xii).

[4] for فوحات. [5] for اهدا. [6] for دیمشسز. [7] for ان شاء اللّه.

[8] for خصوصدن [9] for کوکلکزی . [10] for خوش. [11] for طوتهسز. [12] for عهد نامه.

[13] cf. n. 7. [14] cf. n. 8. [15] for اوزرینه. [16] for ثابت. [17] cf. n. 7. [18] for عربه.

[19] for کوندردکز . [20] for دانه. [21] for صیرمه. [22] for دستمال. [23] cf. n. 20. [24] for اینجولو.

[25] for کوندردك . [26] for معذور. [27] cf. n. 11. [28] cf. n. 1. [29] cf. n. 2. [30] cf. n. 3. [31] cf. n. 4.

واهدي[32] (8) اولندقدن صكره انها وعلام[33] اولنان بودركه مكتوب (9) كز كلوب
دكدي هر نكم دمش‌سز[34] معلومز (10) اولدي انشا الله[35] مورادیکز[36] اوزره عمل اولو
(11) نور اوغلومز پادشاه حضرتلرينه دايما تر(12) بيّه ايليوب اهدي نامه[37] موجبنجه
عمل(13) ايدەسز ديو سويلمكدن حالي[38] دكلوز بو(14) حصوصدن[39] كوكلوكزي[40]
حوش[41] توته‌سز[42] (15) وسز ده دوستلقكز[43] اوزره سابت[44] اولاسز (16) انشا الله[45]
كم اولمز (17) وبزه عرەبه[46] كنـدرديكز[47] (18) كلوب تسلم اولـدي مقبول (19) مز
اولمشدر بز ده سزه بزم (20) خزمتمزده[48] اولان كرانوك[49] (21) اليله بر تانه[50] استفان
(22) الماس ايله فرنك باب (23) قارشق كنـدردك[51] (24) معزور[52] توته‌سز[53] وبوندن
(25) غيري بوستانجي باشي (26) اليله بر مكتوب وبعضي (27) اسباب بر استفان
انجي (28) لي[54] فرنك باب ايله قارشق (29) كندرمشوزدور[55] شويله (30) معلومكز
اولا (31) باقى الدعا

The Italian translations (*Public Record Office, S.P. 102/61, ff. 74–5 and 78–9*)

The translation of Document II (S.P. 102/61, ff. 74–5) is written on a single sheet of white European paper, 42 cm. long and originally 31 cm. wide (cf. ff. 78–9), but now, having been clipped, only 29½ cm. wide. The paper, which is watermarked with a crown, has been folded to form two leaves, each 29½ × 21 cm. The writing is a fine Italic, in black ink: many examples of this hand may be seen among the letters sent to England by Barton and Lello.[56] There are twenty-seven lines of text, of which folio 74*a* contains twenty-one lines and folio 74*b* six lines. On folio 75*a* is the endorsement: "1599 Emperesse of Turchi to her Ma*j*esty"; folio 75*b* is blank. The original six foldings can still be seen.

The translation of Document III (S.P. 102/61, ff. 78–9) is written on the same kind of paper and by the same hand as that of Document II

---

32 cf. n. 5. 33 for اعلام. 34 cf. n. 6. 35 cf. n. 7. 36 for مرادكز. 37 cf. n. 12. 38 for خالى. 39 cf. n. 8. 40 cf. n. 9. 41 cf. n. 10. 42 cf. n. 11. 43 for دوستلغكز. 44 cf. n. 16. 45 cf. n. 7. 46 cf. n. 18. 47 cf. n. 19. 48 for خدمتمزده. 49 for كرا = κύρα see J. H. Mordtmann, "Die jüdischen Kira im Serai der Sultane," *Mitteilungen des Seminars für orientalische Sprachen*, Berlin, xxxii/2 (1929), 18. 50 cf. n. 20. 51 cf. n. 25. 52 cf. n. 26. 53 cf. n. 11. 54 cf. n. 24. 55 for كوندرمشزدر.

56 It was certainly written by one of the interpreters at the English embassy: for other examples of this hand see H. G. Rosedale, *Queen Elizabeth and the Levant Company* (1904), plates vi–xvii, xx.

but here, however, the paper has broken unevenly into two separate leaves so that folio 78 measures $22\frac{1}{2} \times 31$ cm. and folio 79, $18\frac{1}{2} \times 31$ cm. The outer edge of the wider folio 78 is slightly damaged. There are twenty-seven lines of text, of which folio 78*a* contains twenty-two lines and folio 78*b* five lines. Folio 79 has been bound into the volume back to front, so that folio 79*a* is blank and folio 79*b* has the endorsement: " Emperesse of Turchi to her Ma*jes*ty."

Translation of Document II

f. 74*a*

1. Alla piu Gloriosa fra le Castiss*i*me delli Sig*no*ri grandi che seguitano
2. Iesu, Eletta fra gli Magni & Potenti della legge Christiana,
3. moderatrice delle cosse della natione Nazarena, fulgidiss*i*ma
4. splendidiss*i*ma & Honoratiss*i*ma Sig*no*ra Regina D'Inghilterra
5. la cui fine sia con prosperita & ogni bene. Doppo che a v*ostr*a
6. Ser*eni*ta sarano presentate le n*ostr*e pure & sincere salutacioni &
7. recom*m*andationi, le quale procedono dalla n*ostr*a molta sin-
8. -cera amicitia & benevolenza, a v*ostr*a Ser*eni*ta sara noto &
9. manifesto, qualm*en*te la l*ett*era di v*ostr*a Ser*eni*ta essendo qui venuta
10. & da noi ricevuta, habbiamo inteso tutto quello che la Ser*eni*ta
11. v*ostr*a habbia scritto, & piaccendo a Dio secondo quella da
12. noi sara osservato, della qual osservanza non solamente
13. v*ostr*a Ser*eni*ta sia certiss*i*ma ma anche si assicuri, che non manca-
14. -remo sempre d'essortare il Ser*eniss*imo Re n*ostr*o figliuolo, accio
15. che debba osservare secondo gli suoi privillegii, si che
16. la v*ostr*a Mag*es*ta per questa cossa non habbia nissuna cura, ma
17. degniarsi sempre star ferma nella n*ostr*a mutua amicitia, piac-
18. -cendo a Dio non sara male. La Carozza qual v*ostr*a M*ages*ta
19. habbia mandato essendo a noi stata consegniata hab-
20. -biamo accetato con gratiss*i*mo animo: Noi ancora per la
21. fermezza della n*ostr*a mutua amicitia habbiamo mandato

f. 74*b*

1. a v*ostr*a Ser*eni*ta una Veste, una Cintura, un par di manichi,
2. duo fazzoleti lavorati con fil d'Argento, & tre Sughatori
3. lavorati di seda, & Ghirlanda di perle al modo di
4. franchia, tutte queste preghiamo di degniarsi accetare
5. con buon animo. Cosi alla M*ages*ta v*ostr*a sia noto. Nel
6. restante la salutiamo.

Translation of Document III

f. 78*a*

1. Alla Gloriosiss*i*ma fra le castiss*i*me delli Sig*no*ri grandi che se-
2. -guitano Iesu, Eletta fra li Magni & Potenti della legge
3. Christiana, moderatrice delle cosse della natione Naza-
4. -rena, fulgidiss*i*ma Splendiss*i*ma & Honoratiss*i*ma Sig*no*ra Regina
5. D'Inghilterra, la cui fine sia con prosperita &
6. ogni bene. Doppo che a v*ost*ra Ser*eni*ta sarano presentate le n*ost*re
7. pure & sincere salutationi & recom*m*andationi le quale
8. procedono della n*ost*ra molta sincera amicitia & benevolen-
9. -za, a v*ost*ra Ser*eni*ta sara noto & manifesto qualm*en*te la l*ette*ra di v*ost*ra
10. Ser*eni*ta essendo qui venuta & da noi ricevuta, habbiamo inteso
11. tutto quello che la Ser*eni*ta v*ost*ra habbia scritto, & piaccendo
12. a Dio secondo quella da noi sara oss*erva*to della qual osservan-
13. -za non solamente v*ostr*a Ser*eni*ta sia certiss*i*ma ma anche si assicuri
14. che non mancaremo sempre essortare il Ser*enissi*mo Re n*ost*ro figli-
15. -uolo accio che debba osservare secondo gli suoi privilegii,
16. si che la v*ost*ra Ser*eni*ta per questa causa non habbia nissuna
17. cura, ma degniarsi sempre stare ferma nella n*ost*ra mutua
18. amicitia, piaccendo a Dio non sara male La Carozza
19. qual v*ostr*a Ser*eni*ta habbia mandato, essendo da noi stata con-
20. -segniata habbiamo accetato con gratissimo animo.
21. Noi ancora a v*ostr*a Ser*eni*ta habbiamo mandato, per mano
22. della Kira, che sta nel n*ost*ro servitio una Girlanda

f. 78*b*

1. con diamenti mescolato al modo di franchia, qual acceta-
2. -rete in buona parte. & oltra di questo per mano di Bos-
3. -tangi Bassi la habbiamo mandato, una n*ost*ra l*ette*ra, & alcune
4. robbe & una altra Girlanda mescolato con perle
5. cosi le sara noto. Nel restante la salutiamo.

English rendering: Document II

HE

Seal:	Around the edge;	Thou art my desire (my Murād), O dweller in the heavens! O Lord, O Meḥemmed, glory of the world!
	Centre;	The mother of Sulṭān Meḥemmed Khān.

lines 1–5 *Address, see below n. 57.*

lines 5–9 After the presentation and offering of sincere greetings and abundant salutations, rose-perfumed, which emanate from pure mutual confidence and the abundance of amity, what has to be submitted and notified is this : Your letter has arrived and reached (us) ; whatsoever you said became known to us.

lines 10–15 God willing, action will be taken according to what you said. Be of good heart in this respect ! We do not cease from admonishing our son, His Majesty the Padishah,[58] and from telling him : " Do act according to the treaty ! " [59] God willing, may you not suffer grief in this respect !

lines 16–19 May you, too, always be firm in friendship ! God willing, it will never fail. And you sent us a coach ; it has arrived and has been delivered. It had our gracious acceptance.

lines 20–24 We, too, have sent you a robe, a girdle, a sleeve,[60] two gold-embroidered handkerchiefs, three towels,[61] one crown studded with pearls and rubies.[62] May you excuse (me for it) ! [63]

lines 25–26 Thus may it be known ! Finally, prayer (for you).

---

[57] The Turkish address, as it stands, is too faulty to be translated, therefore the translation of the correct form offered in n. 3 to the transcription is substituted here for it : " The pride of the great Christian princes, the chosen of the illustrious nobles in the Messiah's nation, the supreme mediator of the states of the Nazarene sect, trailing the skirts of pomp and dignity, possessing the tokens of honour and glory, the king of England, may his last moments be concluded with good ! " The usual address to Queen Elizabeth runs as follows : " The pride of the virtuous Christian women, the chosen of the honoured ladies in the Messiah's nation, the supreme mediatrix of the Nazarene sect, trailing the skirts of pomp and dignity, possessing the tokens of honour and glory, Elizabeth, queen of England, may her last moments be concluded with good ! "

[58] I.e. Meḥemmed III.

[59] I.e. the first English capitulations of 1580 ; see Hakluyt, Glasgow reprint, v, 169.

[60] Turkish *bir yen* = " a sleeve ". Sir W. Foster in his *The travels of John Sanderson in the Levant*, Hakluyt Soc., 2nd ser., lxvii (1931), p. 185, misread " a paier of shewes (i.e. shoes) " for " a paier of slewes " = sleeves, in the original of Sanderson's journal.

[61] The Kira in her letter (see below p. 141 f.) describes these more fully.

[62] Turkish *Frenk bāb*, not to be found in any standard dictionary but it can be understood from Sanderson's account (*Travels*, p. 185) and the Kira's letter (below, p. 142 f.) that it means " ruby ". In support of this meaning can be quoted J. A. Vullers, *Lexicon Persico–Latinum etymologicum*, ii (1864), *s.v.* فرنك art. 3, " *met.* rubri coloris ". *Frenk bāb* may have denoted some inferior kind of ruby—Sanderson says that the jewels were " none of the finest ".

[63] The same Turkish expression must underlie the *sia con perdone* in the translation of Nūr Bānū's letter to the Bailo in 1579 (Spagni, " Una Sultana Veneziana," *Nuovo Archivio Veneto*, xix (1900), 313), which the Bailo in his accompanying letter explains as " May you excuse me if the present is not suitable and what is deserved ".

Document III

Invocatio, seal and lines 1–9 are the same as the corresponding parts of Document II.

lines 10–14	God willing, one will act according to your wishes. We do not cease from admonishing our son, His Majesty the Padishah,[58] and from telling him : " Do act according to the treaty ! "[59] Be of good heart in this respect !
lines 15–16	And may you, too, be firm in your friendship ! God willing, it will never fail.
lines 17–30	And you sent us a coach ; it has arrived and has been delivered. It had our gracious acceptance. We, too, have sent you by the hand of the Kira[64] in our service a crown of rubies[62] mixed with diamonds. May you excuse (me for it) ![63] And apart from this we had sent by the hand of the Bostanjibashı[65] a letter and a few articles, a crown with pearls and rubies[62] intermixed. Thus may you know !
line 31	Finally, prayer (for you).

THE KIRA'S LETTER

A letter in Italian from Esperanza Malchi, the Sultana's Jewish agent, to Queen Elizabeth ; dated 16/26 November 1599.

Summary :

After addressing the Queen, the Kira discloses how she has desired to serve her ever since entering the Sultana's employ, and now that the Queen's ambassador has arrived with a present for her mistress he has found her ready to help. She lists the presents sent in return from the Sultana, then advises the Queen about the gifts she should send in future—not jewels, but cosmetics and fine cloth. These should be sent to the Kira who will deliver them herself to the Sultana.

The text of this personal letter of the Kira to the Queen was published, with his own translation into English, by H. Ellis in his

---

[64] I.e. the Sultana's Jewish agent, Esperanza Malchi ; see below, pp. 144 f. Her own letter to Queen Elizabeth follows.

[65] Probably the Bostanjibashı Deli Ferhād Pasha : on him see *Sijill-i 'Othmānī*, iv, 17 ; on his office see Gibb and Bowen, *Islamic Society and the West*, i, 84.

Original letters, illustrative of English history,[1] there introduced as: "Esperanza Malchi, a Jewess, to Queen Elizabeth, accompanying a Present of certain Articles of Dress from the Sultana Mother at Constantinople—from the *Original* in the British Museum." For some reason Ellis, contrary to his usual practice, omitted to quote the press-mark of this document and, unfortunately, the original has not yet been found again. Hence it is necessary to rely on Ellis's transcription, although it seems to contain inaccuracies and at a certain point has even lost a line or two which appear, nevertheless, in his translation. In the text which follows the missing lines are filled in by Ellis's English. Since his translation is to a large extent erroneous, I offer a new and more accurate translation from his text of the original.

Ellis's text of Esperanza Malchi's letter to Queen Elizabeth

Alla serenissima Reggina de Ingelterra, Francia, et Iberna

Como il Solle alumina con soi raggi sopra la terra, la virtu et grandeza di sua maesta si stende per tutto el universo, sin tanto che quelli que sonno di differente nacioni et legge desidreno servir sua maesta. Questo dico io per me, che essendo io Hebrea di legge et nacione diferente di sua maesta, da la prima hora che piache al Sr Iddio di mettere nel cuore di questa nostra serenissima Reggia [2] Madre servirse di me, sempre sonno stata desiderosa che me venisse hocasion di potter mustrar a sua Maesta questa mia vullunta. Fora [3] che S.M. à mandato questo ill[mo]. Imbasiator in questo Regno con un presente per questa serenissima Reggina mia s[a] in quanto si â volluto servir di me mi â trovato prôta.[4] Et hora alla dispidicione di esso ill[mo] Inbasiator la serenissima Reggina vullendo mustrar a sua maesta el amor che gliâ, manda a sua maesta con questo ill[mo] Imbasiatore una veste, et una cintura, et doi faeiolli lavorati de horo, et tre lavorati di seta al

[1] Ser. I, iii (1824), 52–5. Ellis's faulty translation has been reproduced by C. Roth in *Anglo-Jewish letters, 1158–1917* (1938), pp. 38–9 and again in his *The House of Nasi—Doña Gracia* (1947), pp. 107–8.

[2] = "Reggina".

[3] = "Hora".

[4] = "pronta".

uzanza di questo Regno, et un collar di perle et rubini ; il tutto manda la ser^{ma}. Reggina all ill^{mo}. S^{r}. Imbasiator per mano del Sr Bostanggi Basi e' per mia mano gli ho consignato al ill^{mo}. S^{r}. Imbasiator una corona di diamante gioia di sua ser^{ta}. qualli dice piaaera [5] â sua maesta portar per amor di lei et de la receputa dar aviso. Et per esser sua Maesta donna senza vergogna alcuna la posio hocupar con questo aviso il qual ê che trovandosi nel suo regno aque destillati fini de hogne sorte per la facia et hogli hodoriffere per le mani sua Maesta mi favorira mandarne per mia mano [for this most serene Queen ; by my hand as, being articles for ladies, she does not wish them to pass through other hands.] per il medesimo se si trovano nel suo Regno panini di seta ho di lana cosse stravaganti et convenienti per una tanta alta Reggina come lei sua Maesta potra mandarli che piu avera lei caro questo che qual si voglia gioia che sua Maesta gli posia mandar non altro sollo pregar il Sr Iddio gli dia vitoria di soi nemici et sempre sia S.M. prospera et fellice. Amen.
Di Constantinopolli 16 Nov. 1599.

Umilissima di S.M.

Esperanza Malchi.

English rendering

To the Most Serene Queen of England, France and Ireland. Just as the sun gives light with its rays over the earth, Your Majesty's power and greatness extend throughout the whole universe, so much so that those who are of other nations and religion wish to serve Your Majesty. This I say on my own behalf, although being as I am a Jewess by faith and of a different nation from Your Majesty, from the first hour since it has pleased the Lord God to put it into the heart of this our most serene Queen Mother to use me in her service, I have always been desirous that the opportunity might arise for me to be able to show Your Majesty this good will of mine. Now that Your Majesty has sent this most illustrious ambassador to this kingdom with a present for this most serene Queen my lady, in as much as he was wished to make use of me, he has found me ready. And now at the leave-taking of the aforesaid most illustrious

[5] = " piacerà ".

ambassador, the most serene Queen, wishing to show Your Majesty the love she bears you, is sending Your Majesty with this most illustrious ambassador, a robe and a girdle and two handkerchiefs worked with gold and three worked with silk according to the custom of this kingdom and a necklace of pearls and rubies ; all of which the most serene Queen sends to the most illustrious Lord Ambassador by the hand of the Lord Bostanggi Basi and by my own hand I have delivered for you to the most illustrious Lord Ambassador, a crown of diamond gems from Her Serenity which she says it will please Your Majesty to wear for her sake, and to give notice of the receipt. And on account of Your Majesty's being a woman I can without any embarrassment employ you with this notice, which is that as there are to be found in your kingdom rare distilled waters of every kind for the face and odiferous oils for the hands, Your Majesty would favour me by sending some of them by my hand *for this most serene Queen ; by my hand as, being articles for ladies, she does not wish them to pass through other hands.* Likewise, if there are to be found in your kingdom cloths of silk or wool, articles fantastic and becoming such an exalted Queen as she, Your Majesty will be able to send them, for she will hold this more dear than any jewel whatsoever that Your Majesty might send her. No more, only to pray the Lord God that He may grant you victory over your enemies and that Your Majesty may always be prosperous and happy. Amen. From Constantinople, 16 November 1599.

Your Majesty's most humble (servant),
Esperanza Malchi.

COMMENTARY

Anglo-Ottoman diplomatic relations were first established in 1583 when William Harborne arrived in Constantinople as Queen Elizabeth's ambassador, carrying her letters and delivering the royal present, due at the installation of every ambassador, to the Sultan—in this case to Murād III (1574–95). Harborne returned to England in August 1588, leaving behind as agent his secretary, the then twenty-five years old Edward Barton.[6] In spite of this inferior status, Barton at once involved himself in many of the far-reaching diplomatic intrigues which were rife in the Ottoman capital. To further his aims he even sought the support of the Imperial harem, using as his go-between probably the same Jewish

[6] For information on Harborne and Barton see the rewritten *DNB* articles in *Bull. Inst. Hist. Res.*, xix/57 (1942), 158–62.

woman whom we shall later encounter as the co-operator of his successor, Henry Lello—that is to say Esperanza Malchi, the last representative of the series of women who, with the title of Kira, had served the Sultanas as medical advisers, entertainers, business-agents and in all their contacts with the outside world. In order to achieve full ambassadorial status Barton needed to procure a new present and it was only after a long and hard struggle on his part that in 1593 the Queen's second gift left England, so that in the October of that year he was at last able to deliver the royal letters and present to the Sultan. At the same time a special letter and gifts also arrived for the Sultana, sent on the advice of Barton who wished to encourage his good relations with the harem.

Ṣāfiye, the Sultana from whom our three letters emanate, was, according to the Venetian Bailos Morosini and Bernardo, of Albanian origin,[7] a view confirmed by Soranzo, who describes her even more accurately as " nativa di Rezi, villa delle montagne de' Ducagini nell'Albania ".[8] Gerlach, another reliable contemporary informant, writes of her, however, in his Diary in 1575 as a Moldavian and in 1576 as a Bosnian,[9] whereas the Bailo Tiepolo calls her a Slav in 1576 and the Bailo Zane calls her a Circassian in 1594.[10] She must have been born in 1550, or not long after. The French ambassador de Germigny, on the authority of her Kira, says that her age was twenty-nine or thirty in 1583 ; [11] equally relying on information from a Kira, the Portuguese Jew Solomon Usque,[12] in his account for Barton of the events occurring at the death of Murād III, says that Ṣāfiye was then (in 1595) forty-five.[13] He tells us that as a girl of thirteen she became the concubine of the sixteen years old Prince Murād who, since 1562, was Sanjak Beg of Saruhan. She was presented to him by his cousin Humāshāh, then

---

[7] Morosini (1585) in E. Albèri, *Relazioni degli Ambasciatori Veneti*, III, iii, 283, 286 ; Bernardo (1592), ibid., III, ii, 359.

[8] L. Soranzo, *L'Ottomanno* (1598), p. 2. " Rezi " is perhaps the modern Kryezi in the " Ducagini " mountains in the N.W. corner of present-day Albania ; cf. the map in *Enciclopedia Italiana*, " Albania ".

[9] S. Gerlach, *Tage-Buch* (1674), pp. 77, 177.

[10] Tiepolo in Albèri, III, ii, 166 ; Zane, ibid., III, iii, 439.

[11] In his report to Catherine de' Medici, 12 July 1583 ; in Hurmuzaki and Iorga, *Documente privitóre la Istoria Românilor*, xi (1900), 165.

[12] On him see C. Roth, " Salusque Lusitano " . . . , *Jewish Quarterly Review*, N.S., xxxiv (1943–4), 65–85.

[13] For facsimiles of the original (P.R.O., S.P. 97/3, ff. 5–10) of his *Relatione de le cosse occorse in Constantinopoli ne la morte di Sultan Murat, & ne l'intrata del nouo Sultan Mehemet* see H. G. Rosedale, *Queen Elizabeth and the Levant Company*, plates vi–xvii. Rosedale (pp. 19–33) offers a very faulty translation of it. For Ṣāfiye's age see plate vii.

Ferhād Pasha's wife, according to the reports of Gerlach and the Bailo Tiepolo in 1576.[14] In the summer-camp on Bozdagh near Manisa in May 1566 Ṣāfiye bore Murād a son, the future Meḥemmed III.[15] Murād left Manisa in 1574 upon news of the death of his father Selīm II, whom he was to succeed. Ṣāfiye, as his Khāṣṣekī, now took second place in the harem under his mother Nūr Bānū, the Venetian Cecilia Venier-Baffo, who until her death in 1583 ruled the harem as Wālide Sulṭān. It must have been at this time that Ṣāfiye began to be identified with Nūr Bānū, an error of early date, first rectified by Albèri in 1855 [16] and finally discussed and dismissed by E. Spagni in 1900.[17]

Morosini in his report of 27 December 1583 describes Ṣāfiye as a witty and quick-tongued lady, rather haughty and possessing all the bad characteristics of the native Albanian; [18] twelve years later, however, Usque calls her very prudent, wise, clever and most patient.[19] He also remarks that although Murād never made her his legal wife by giving her the " chebin " (i.e. *kābīn*, the " dowry "),[20] he contented himself with Ṣāfiye alone for the first twenty years of the thirty-two years they lived together. Of their many children, besides Meḥemmed, only two daughters survived: 'Ā'ishe, the wife of Ibrāhīm Pasha and Fāṭima, who married first Khalīl Pasha and later Ja'far Pasha.[21]

As Khāṣṣekī, especially after the death of Nūr Bānū, Ṣāfiye enjoyed great influence in the affairs of the Empire; upon the accession of her son Meḥemmed III (1595–1603), however, as Wālide Sulṭān, she became all-powerful. Like her predecessor Nūr Bānū, Ṣāfiye was now corresponding with the rulers of Western states, using her Kira as agent.[22]

---

[14] Gerlach, *Tage-Buch*, 177; Tiepolo in Albèri, III, ii, 166.

[15] Rosedale, pl. xiv, with incorrect birth-date. The date given by Kara Chelebi-zāde, *Raużatu'l-Abrār*, 445 (i.e. during the first decade of Dhu'l-Qa'da, 973/20–29 May 1566) is supported by Selānīkī, *Ta'rīkh*, p. 22, where the birth of the prince is announced to Suleymān I on 13 Dhu'l-Qa'da, 973, when he was encamped at Pazardzhik on the march to his last campaign at Szigetvár. *Sijill-i 'Othmānī* (and its followers) has a wrong date (7 Dhu'l-Qa'da, 974), perhaps based on Munejjim Bashı.

[16] In notes to the *Relazioni*, III, iii, 235, 283.

[17] In " Una Sultana Veneziana ", *Nuovo Archivio Veneto*, xix (1900), 241–348; his findings were largely ignored and had to be reiterated by E. Rossi in " La Sultana Nūr Bānū ", *Oriente Moderno*, xxxiii (1953), 433–41.

[18] Spagni, 348 (Doc. iv).

[19] Rosedale, plates vi, vii.

[20] Ibid., plate ix.

[21] Rosedale, plate vii. On the princesses see *Sijill-i 'Othmānī*, i, 49, 60.

[22] Spagni and Rossi suggest that the partiality both ladies showed for the Republic of Venice was probably the major reason for the subsequent confusion of their identities.

During their revolt in 1600 against the harem tyranny the Spahis demanded Ṣāfiye's exile and the heads of the Qapuagha Ghażanfer and the Bostanjibashı Ferhād Agha, but without success. While her son lived Ṣāfiye's power could not be diminished. Although the two major harem servants escaped, however, she was unable to protect her Kira, who was stabbed to death and torn to pieces by the Spahis on 1 April 1600. This assassination, which provoked many contemporary accounts, will be discussed below. In January 1604, less than a month after her son's death, Ṣāfiye was exiled by her grandson Aḥmed I to the Old Seraglio, where she died in January 1619, during the reign of her great-grandson 'Othmān II.[23]

The ship which carried the Queen's present, the *Ascension* of London, set sail in March 1593 and reached Constantinople in September. One of her passengers was Richard Wrag, to whom we owe a vivid eye-witness account of the ceremony on 17 October during which Barton made the presentation to the Sultan.[24] Ṣāfiye received her gift soon after this and Wrag gives the following description: "The Present sent her in her majesties name was a jewel of her majesties picture, set with some rubies and diamants, 3 great pieces of gilt plate, 10 garments of cloth of gold, a very fine case of glasse bottles silver & gilt, with 2 pieces of fine Holland,[25] which so gratefully she accepted, as that she sent to know of the ambassador what present he thought she might return that would most delight her majestie: who sent word that a sute of princely attire being after the Turkish fashion would for the rarenesse thereof be acceptable in England. Whereupon she sent an upper gowne of cloth of gold very rich, an under gowne of cloth of silver, and a girdle of Turkie worke, rich and faire, with a letter of gratification, which for the rarenesse of the stile, because you may be acquainted with it, I have at the ende of this discourse hereunto annexed, which letter and present, with one from the grand Signor,[26] was sent by M. Edward Bushell, and M. William Aldridge over-land the 20 of March, who passed through Valachia and Moldavia, & so through Poland."

---

[23] Hammer, *GOR*, iv, 354, 509.

[24] In his *A description of a Voiage to Constantinople and Syria* in Hakluyt, Glasgow reprint, vi, 94–118.

[25] Wrag's list of presents to the Sultana agrees exactly with the official inventory in B.M., Cotton Ms Nero B. xi, f. 124*a*.

[26] The text of the Sultan's letter is only known from the entry in Mühimme Defteri, 71, p. 69, no. 141, published by A. Refik in *Türkler ve Kraliçe Elizabet* (1932), pp. 28–9 (Doc. xiv) and again by İ. H. Uzunçarşılı in "On dokuzuncu asır başlarına kadar Türk–İngiliz münasebâtına dair vesikalar, *Belleten*, xiii (1949), 620–2.

The "letter of gratification" which Wrag refers to and appends to his "discourse" is the official Italian translation (see above, p. 126 f.). It must have been made in Barton's house, where the Sultana's letter was received and where Wrag was staying. The writer of the translation—and very probably its author also—was Paulo Mariani, a young and impetuous Venetian merchant who, after having been successively French and English consul in Egypt, was at that time acting as secretary to Barton, whose friend and confidant he was.[27] Comparison of its writing with that of an autograph letter of Mariani's (S. P. 105/109, f.17) immediately shows that both are by the same hand. This translation was sent overland to England together with the original and the Sultana's gifts on 30 March 1594 and, according to the endorsement quoted above, was delivered at Greenwich on 10 August. Though in no way literal and in many cases inaccurate, it renders adequately enough the contents and tone of the letter as a whole.[28]

The other Italian translation, which today still accompanies the Turkish original in British Museum, Cotton Ms Nero B. viii, f. 63, and therefore at first might be regarded as the translation sent from Constantinople, after closer study appears to have been copied in London, with several mistakes, from the Mariani translation. Probably the latter was considered, not without reason, to be too poor in appearance to be presented to the Queen.[29] Therefore, an aesthetically more satisfying copy was produced which, after presentation, remained with the original, whilst the official translation was kept in the State Paper Office among the Turkey papers.

The following inventory of the Sultana's gifts, which gives the value of each article in aspers as well as in pounds sterling, must also have been drawn up in Constantinople under Barton's supervision and sent off with the gifts and letter: [30]

---

[27] This is attested for 1592 when the English merchant John Sanderson arrived in Constantinople; see *The travels of John Sanderson*, op. cit., p. 10. Ibid., 13, the record of Mariani's death in 1596.

[28] The English translation which follows it in Hakluyt was probably made by Hakluyt himself and has been repeatedly reprinted, e.g. in A. von Miltitz, *Manuel des Consuls*, I, ii (1840), 1610–16 (Appendice vi); Rosedale, op. cit., 2; E. Pears, "The Spanish Armada and the Ottoman Porte," *English Historical Review*, viii (1893), 465.

[29] This presentation copy seems to be the work of the then secretary for the Levant correspondence: c.f. the copy of the Queen's letter to the King of Morocco (B.M., Cotton Ms Nero B. viii, f. 71) of 31 March, 1600, which is in exactly the same hand.

[30] P.R.O., S.P. 97/2, ff. 230–1; the text in M. Epstein, *The early history of the Levant Company* (1908), pp. 13–14, is incomplete and inaccurate.

" The perticule*r*s and the value of the Present sent from the Greate
Sultan to hir Mag*e*stie in Anno. 1593. as follow*e*th
  Firste two garment*e*s of cloth of silver might cost
                   aspe*r*s .20000. £68.00.00.
  More one girdle of cloth of silver might coste.
                   aspe*r*s .3000. £10.00.00.
  More two handekerchers wrought w*i*th massy gould
                   aspe*r*s .6000. £22.00.00.
  More one shell of gould w*hi*ch couered the seale of
  her le*tt*ere to her Mag*e*stie uppo*n* w*hi*ch was sett
  ii smale sparkes of Dyamondes and ii small sparkes
  of rubies might bee worth   £20.00.00.
      The vallue of this present is.   li 120.00.00.''

Additional note of *circa* 1599 :

" In Lieu hereof the Comp : doe retorne a coache richelye Furnished
And Crave her Mag*e*sties awnsw*e*r (if yo*u*r ho : soe thinke meete
to the Sultana her le*tt*eres.''

Judging from Barton's letter [to Sir Thomas Heneage ?] of 1 Apri
1595 the present as inventoried above did not include all the article*s*
which the Sultana had intended for the Queen : [31]
  " Concerning that your honour mentioneth in your honours Letter*es*
of the 18th September that the queen of England thinketh itt strang*e*
that the attyre for the head, with the earings which were your honou*r*
saith the principall part of the Sultana her present to the queen of Englan*d*
were imbeazelled ; Indeed I remember to haue advised your honour tha*t*
part of the Sultana her present was reteyned by the mediatrix between*e*
the Sultana and mee, for that I was advertised that the Sultana ha*d*
ordeyned divers gentilesses for the queen of England and being my self*e*
demaunded what were expedient to be sent from the Sultana to th*e*
queen of England I replyed the forme of the Sultana her usuall attyre
upon which was sent mee what I sent into England, but what particula*r*
rityes were deteyned I know not, and though it grieved mee sore to hear*e*
that parte was imbeazelled, and know none could haue itt but th*e*
mediatrix betweene the Sultana and mee, yet because my selfe canno*t*
come to the speech of the Sultana, and all my busines passe by the hande
of the said Mediatrix, loosing her freindshippe, I loose the practick wit*h*
the Sultana, and therefore stirred not in the matter, and now to meddl*e*

---

[31] B.M., Cotton Ms Nero B. xii, ff. 171–2*a*.

therein by your honours order, when I am sure to reape noe gaine, but displeasure, and hinderance to many my affaires, I thinke itt not wisedome: onely it may serue for a warninge to haue knowne her quality and hereafter to deale more warily."

Fynes Moryson, who in 1597 was in Constantinople and Barton's guest, tells the same story:[32] "Yea such is the Corruption of bribery and so generall [i.e. among the Turks at that time] as when the Emperors mother sent a present of a whole linnen attyre richly wrought, to Elizabeth Queene of England, many peeces thereof were detayned by her women, to the utter disgrace of the present, till our Ambassador redeemed them with more mony then they were woorth." A tentative solution to the problem of the missing jewels will be discussed later.

True to her promise, the Sultana soon had an opportunity to use her influence in the interest of the Queen. She asked the Sultan to allow Barton to act as mediator between the Porte and the Emperor in the Hungarian war which had broken out in 1592, but she was unsuccessful, as the ambassador Zane reports on 4 December 1593:[33] "I hear that the Sultana has tried to persuade the Sultan to allow the English Ambassador to mediate for peace, but that his Majesty would lend no ear to her."

Queen Elizabeth did not write to the Sultana again until the time when she at last sent a long overdue letter and present to Meḥemmed III. Such a letter and present had been due since January 1595, to congratulate the Sultan upon his accession and had become still more urgently needed after Barton's death in January 1598, when his secretary Henry Lello had to be introduced as ambassador. Finally, when in March 1599 the royal present, which included the famous organ for the Sultan, left England in the *Hector*, the ship also carried a beautiful coach for the Wālide. Among those on board were the coachman Edward Hale and the organ-maker Thomas Dallam of Lancashire. Another passenger was John Sanderson, newly appointed by the Levant Company as their treasurer in Constantinople; both he and Dallam have left us invaluable journals, of which ample use will be made in the following account.[34]

---

[32] C. Hughes, *Shakespeare's Europe: unpublished chapters of Fynes Moryson's Itinerary* (1903), p. 65.

[33] *Cal. S. P. Ven.*, ix (1897), item 240.

[34] Some parts of Sanderson's day-book (B.M., Landsdowne Ms 241) have been published in *The travels of John Sanderson*, cited above. Dallam's journal is printed as *The diary of Master Thomas Dallam*, ed. by J. T. Bent, in *Early voyages and travels in the Levant*, Hakluyt Soc., lxxxvii (1893). For an entertaining account of this journey, based on Dallam's *Diary*, see S. Mayes, *An organ for the Sultan* (1956).

The *Hector* reached Constantinople at the end of August. It was at first suggested that the coach should be given to the Sultan, since the organ had been sadly spoiled during the long voyage, but this idea had to be abandoned for, as Lello reported to Sir Robert Cecil:[35] "The coache must of necessity be givne to the old Sultana because itt hath byn brutted here longe agone by some out of Ingland thatt hir highnes had ordayned the same,[36] for hir, who longe seince have taken notice ther of and nowe sheweth hir selfe to be glade, havinge alredie sente to me thatt I wold sende for two horses, out of hir owne stable, to drawe the same."

Excitement and curiosity began to mount. On 12 September Ṣāfiye went by water to view the English ship, following the Sultan in his golden caique. By 21 September Dallam had managed to repair the organ and had begun to erect it in the Seraglio; he notes in his Diary:[37] "The same Daye, our Imbassader sente Mr. Paule Pinder, who was then his secritarie, with a presente to the Sultana, she being at hir garthen. The presente was a Coatche of six hundrethe poundes vallue."[38]

The success of the presentation is shown by Lello's report:[39] "The Sultana sente me worde, thatt I should sende hir the Queen's l*ett*ere and the Coatche, w*hi*ch she harde [i.e. heard] was destined for hir to the courte wher shee was w*i*th hir sonne, w*hi*ch accordingly I sente together w*i*th a fanne by my Secrettarie accompanyed w*i*th Ientlemen and M*e*rchanttes of the w*hi*ch she made a greate demostration of Ioy by hir Agent or Aga, and tooke itt very gratfully sendinge to them three vestes of cloath of silver, 300 chequins of gold and 40. chequins to the Coatchman the like have never byn seen or herde here thatt any of these have given any like rewardes, also proferinge hir selfe readye to doe all

---

[35] 25 August/4 September 1599; P.R.O., S.P. 97/4, f. 43*a*.

[36] The person who "brutted" or spread the rumour around was William Aldrich; see Lello's next report of 8/18 September.

[37] Dallam, *Diary*, p. 63.

[38] Thus more valuable than the organ which cost about £550. Dallam adds, enigmatically: "At that time the Sultana did Take greate lykinge to Mr. Pinder, and afterwardes she sente for him to have his private companye, but there meetinge was croste (i.e. crossed)." Pindar was certainly a good-looking man, to judge from a portrait made in 1614, an engraving of which is reproduced in Sanderson, *Travels*, facing p. 222. On him see *DNB*, but no reference is given there to his life in Constantinople before his appointment as ambassador in 1611. Sanderson, not usually quick to praise, writes of him just after he had left for England in 1599: "He is a sensable, wise, jentellmanlike man, and one that hear hath much creadited our nation. I protest to you I am sory of his departure, for hear he will be mist (i.e. missed)." (*Travels*, p. 186.)

[39] Lello to Cecil, 22 September/2 October 1599; P.R.O., S.P. 97/4, ff. 49*b*, 50*a*. For Sanderson's account see *Travels*, p. 181.

the service she could for the Queen and our nation, and thatt I should bouldlye come to hir agent or Aga for any busines w*ha*tsoever, and should finde hir my frinde. The Sultan and she have often tymes byn abroade in the Coache, and seince she have sente to me to sende hir the Queen's picture to behold, w*hi*ch I have her [i.e. here] given order to make by one thatt came with the shipp. '[40]

The *Hector* set sail from Constantinople on 28 October, evidently earlier than Ṣāfiye had expected, since Lello writes :[41] " A day after the dep*ar*ture of the Shipp the Queene mother sent to me lamentinge much that the shipp dep*ar*ted w*i*thout her letter, sainge what an ungratefull woman I shewed my sealf to be, in not writtinge to the sole princes of the world, who voutsafed to write and present me, the messinger[42] Refferringe that she did not eate or drinke that day for sorrow, first I answered that findinge so lyttle favo*ur* I did not seeke any answer, but rather sought meanes to retorne out of the Countrye,[43] yett if shee wold write I Could send the same overland."[44]

Ṣāfiye accepted this suggestion : on 27 November two of the Seraglio servants, the Bostanjibashı Ferhād Agha and Ṣāfiye's Kira Esperanza Malchi, came separately to Lello's house, each carrying a letter and gifts from the Sultana to the Queen. Sanderson writes the next day about what they brought :[45] " The present is com from the Sultana, by the hands of the Bustangi Bassi. It is a gowne of cloth of silver, a paier of slewes,[46] a gerdle like the last she sent, two ritch wraught handkerchers and four other, a steffan of rubies and pearles, with a letter ; none of the finest. Another letter, also written by the sam partie (som woman in the seraglio), is also delivered the secreatary by the hands of the Chara [i.e. Kira], with one from hirself and a ritch stefan of diamonts and rubies, wich also ar to be delivered to Hir Exelent Magistie. With the first wind

---

[40] Probably Rowland Buckett the organ-painter ; cf. Dallam, *Diary*, p. 66. For vivid descriptions of other coach-rides made by Nūr Bānū and Ṣāfiye in 1573 and 1577, see Gerlach, *Tage-Buch*, pp. 29, 334, 391.

[41] Lello to Cecil, 21/31 October 1599 ; P.R.O., S.P. 97/4, f. 53*b*.

[42] Probably the Kira.

[43] In spite of the present, Lello was having no success in his struggle for a new capitulation.

[44] Lello explains Pindar's delay in leaving for England to report personally on the difficult situation in Constantinople, on 4/14 November : " After the dep*ar*ture of the Shipp I determyned to send my Secrettarye for England who heatherto hath byn Reteyned bye the Queen mother saying shee must wright to her majesty." (P.R.O., S.P. 97/4, f. 57*b*.)

[45] Sanderson, *Travels*, pp. 184–5.

[46] See above, p. 139, n. 60.

Master Pinder departeth ; with him Master Conisbie and the workmer of the instrument sent. God prosper them into Ingland." [47] It may be noted that the present of 1599 is almost identical with that sent in 1593

Thanks to her own letter (see above p. 140 f.) we know that the "Chara" mentioned here was Esperanza Malchi, the last of the series of Kiras, whose professional activities are well illustrated by the letter— the trading in jewels, the acquisition of luxury articles for the ladies of the harem, the dealing with European ambassadors. Her long intimacy with Ṣāfiye would seem to have emboldened her to address Queen Elizabeth in rather familiar terms. Sanderson, who knew her, calls her "a short, fat trubkin".[48] The expression calls to mind George Sandys description of Levantine Jewesses, written about ten years later : [4 "They are generally fat, and rank of the savors which attend upon sluttish corpulency. For the most part they are goggle-ey'd. They neither shun conversation, nor are too watchfully guarded by their husbands. They are good workwomen, and can and will doe any thing for profit, that is to be done by the art of a woman, and which sutes with the fashion of these countreys."

In his article "Die jüdischen Kira im Serai der Sultane" [50] J. H Mordtmann gives much information about the only three Kiras who are known at present, although there may well have been more. The first Fāṭima Qadın, a Crimean Karaite as it seems, was Kira to Ḥafṣa Sulṭān the mother of Suleymān I ; she appears to have accepted Islam just before she died in 1548. The second, Esther Handali, probably of a Spanish Jewish family,[51] served Nūr Bānū, Murād III's mother, and died about 1590. The third Kira, Esperanza Malchi, whom we may conclude to have been of Italian origin from the evidence of her name and the language in which she wrote her letter, was probably in Ṣāfiye's service for many years, since before her assassination on 1 April 1600 she had achieved such great influence and acquired so much wealth.

---

[47] The party included Pindar, Conisby, William Hickockes a merchant, Dallam Michael Watson the joiner, Rowland Buckett the painter and the coachman Edmund Hale ; they were accompanied as far as Zante by a renegade Englishman, a certain Finch of Chorley in Lancashire, who served them as dragoman.

[48] Sanderson, *Travels*, p. 86. For "trubkin" see *OED*, *art.* "Trub."-2. "A littl squat woman" ; also, "a slut, sloven ; a wanton ; an opprobrious term."

[49] *Sandys Travailes* (6th ed., 1658), p. 116.

[50] In *Mitteilungen des Seminars für orientalische Sprachen*, Berlin, xxxii/2 (1929), 1–38

[51] Her letter of 1583 to the Doge and Senate (Spagni, op. cit., Doc. ii) is in Spanish and Usque in his report made for Barton in 1595, quoted above, calls her "la B*eata* M*emori* della chiera di Scieres" = Jerez ?

Humphrey Conisby, who was one of the party which accompanied the present to England and was therefore not in Constantinople when the Spahis revolted against the domination of the harem and assassinated the Kira, must have had a correspondent there who sent him the information which he uses in the following account : [52] " They [i.e. the Spahis] drew the Kerah out of her howse (this was a Jew Woman, most deare to the Sultana, who by such grace, with her complices, governed in effect, the whole empire : & was worth at her death Millions). Her they hauled through the streetes, forth at Andrinople gate, & there killing her (after she had offered more for her lyfe then their payes came unto) they cutte her into small peeces, every one, that could get, carrying backe through the streetes to their howses, a peece of her flesh, upon his knives pointe. She was widow, & had 3 sonnes : one (which was chiefe Customer) they caught in the howse with her ; but cut not him so in peeces, only they slew him ; & straight burnt him to ashes. The Seconde fled cleane away, unheard of. The third to save himself turned Turke. I remember her the rather bicause She sent letters, & Presentes of worth (with the Sultanaes) from herself, to her Maiesty."

Pindar's party had left Constantinople on 8 December 1599 and, after travelling overland through Greece and embarking on the *Hector* at Zante, reached England in mid-May 1600. They carried with them Ṣāfiye's letters and presents and the translations, the Kira's letter and present, letters from the Sultan [53] and the Qā'immaqām Khalīl Pasha [54] to the Queen, and Lello's report to Cecil of 27 November.[55] In this report Lello dismisses Ṣāfiye's gifts as " but trifles not princelye or beseeminge her Highnes, yet these their fasshyon and amoungest all in generall estemed a great matter of freindshypp, because it is not their use to send presents to any prynce whatsoever ". At the end of his dispatch he remarks : " After the queene Mother had consyned to me the present aforesaid for the Queen she sent another small thinge w*i*th another Letter, by the handes of the Jew woman her chiefe Kaya to be sent to the Queen w*hi*ch togeather w*i*th the rest I doe send by my said Secretary."

[52] B.M., Cotton Ms Nero B. xi, ff. 7*b*–8*a*, undated but certainly composed late in 1600 and signed " H C ", the initials of Humphrey Conisby ; see Sanderson, *Travels*, p. 185, n. 1. Of the many eye-witness accounts see Sanderson, ibid., pp. 85–6, 201–2, and Lello in O. Burian, *The Report of Lello* (1952), pp. 4–7. The Turkish account in Selānīkī, *Ta'rīkh*, is also to be found in Burian's publication, pp. 75–8 (Appendix i).

[53] B.M., Cotton Ms Nero B. viii, f. 48.

[54] P.R.O., S.P. 102/4, f. 3.

[55] P.R.O., S.P. 97/4, ff. 59–60.

There is some mystery about each of Ṣāfiye's two gifts to Queen Elizabeth : that of 1593 lost its most valuable part, a jewelled head-dress, whereas that of 1599 seems to have been enriched by a head-dress additional to the one already included in the present. Could the Kira have been responsible for both these changes ? Then the second *stafana* would perhaps be the same " attyre for the head, with the earings " which, according to Barton, was stolen from the present of 1593 by his " mediatrix " with the Sultana, i.e. the Kira. That it was the Kira who not only delivered the second *stafana* but was also its donor is explicitly stated by Conisby and Sanderson in the passages already quoted above. Furthermore, the latter remarks in a marginal note to his autobiography, when speaking of the death of the Kira's eldest son on 2 April 1600 : [56] " He was a goodly Gentleman *Iew*, some few dayes before, I had shewed him our Ship, and had talked with him at his Mothers house, and Master *Paul Pinder* and my selfe, were with his Mother, to whom [i.e. to Pindar] shee delivered for the Ambassadour, to send the Queene a *Stafana*, of *Rabines* from the *Sultana*, and another of Diamonds from her selfe, with teares in her eyes I well remember."

The evidence of these two English eye-witnesses, both of them connected with the present, is contradicted, however, by the Sultana's second letter (Document III), by Lello, and by the Kira's own letter. Other perplexing questions remain unanswered. Why should Ṣāfiye have sent her present in two parts, each accompanied by a separate letter of almost identical content ? Why two head-dresses with only one robe ? Finally, why does Document II, the letter delivered by the Bostanjibashı, mention neither its bearer nor the other letter and gifts to be delivered by the Kira, whereas Document III mentions both its bearer, the Kira, and the letter and gifts brought by the Bostanjibashı ?

The gift, poor though it may have been, did not reach England unremarked. The Fugger agent, reporting from Venice on 3 March 1600 writes : [57] " We are advised from Constantinople that the Sultan has sent magnificent gifts of rubies, pearls and diamonds to the Queen of England with a request that she should effect a peace between him and His Imperial Majesty."

---

[56] In S. Purchas, *Hakluytus Posthumus or Purchas His Pilgrimes*, Glasgow reprint, ix (1905), p. 435 ; *Travels*, p. 85. The marginal notes were added by Sanderson himself ; see *Travels*, introduction, p. xxxix.

[57] *The Fugger News-letters*, ed. by V. von Klarwill, 2nd ser. (1926), p. 324.

APPENDIX

Document A

A letter in Turkish from the Wālide Sulṭān to the Doge and Signoria of Venice, undated. Venice, Archivo di Stato, Documenti turchi, Busta XIV. 23 (3).[1]

Transcription [plate XLI]

والده سلطان[2]

1) جناب عزّت مئآب رفعت نساب[3] ونديك دوزي وبكلري كامبنى كامياب[4]
سعادتلوپادشاه 2) عالمپناه حضرتلرينك آستانهءِ سعادتلري ايله اولان دوستلقلريكزه
3) لايق اولان سلام تقديمندن صكره <. . . ؟ . . .> اعلام اولنان اولدوركه 4) حالا
جلوس همايون تهنتى[5] ايچون ارسال ايلدوككز بيوك الجيكز بو جانبه نامه‌كوزي
5) وبعض دوستلق ياديكارلرين كونده‌روب اظهار اتمكين اشبو مكتوبمز 6) جنابكزه
تحرير اولنوب ارسال اولنمشد[ر] انشا الله تعالي مادمكه[6] سعادتلو 7) پادشاه
عالمپنان[7] حضرتلري ايله كمال دوستلق[8] ثابت قدم اولاسز سعادتلو 8) وعزّتلو پادشاه
حضرتلرينك جانب همايونلرندن دخي هر وجهله الجيكزه 9) وبايلوسلريكزه انعام
واحسانلر ايله رعايت اتمك مقرّردور حالا دخي 10) بيوك الجيكزه[9] هر وجهله معسر[10]
ومحترم اولوب اول جانبه متوجّه وروانه اولمشدور 11) سعاديلو[11] پادشاه حضرتلرينك
حضور شريفلرنده دوشن <. . . ؟ . . .> مصالحكزده دوستلغه لايق 12) اولدوغي
اوزره حسن معاونتمز بزل[12] اولنمق مقرّردر شويله معلوم اولا باقى والسلام

English rendering

In the margin ; Wālide Sulṭān

line 1 His Excellency the glorious and eminent Doge of Venice and her Nobles, may you obtain the wishes you cherish !

---

[1] Indexed by A. Bombaci in his *Regesti di documenti turchi*, available in typescript in the Archivio di Stato in Venice. He suggests that the letter may be a copy, and it would indeed seem to be so, probably made by a European. It is perhaps from the Venetian Nūr Bānū and may refer to the accession of her son Murād III in 1574. There is no *invocatio*.

[2] Written downwards in the margin, probably taking the place of the impression of the Wālide's seal on the original.

[3] for نصاب. [4] كامبينى كامياب (?). [5] for تهنيتى. [6] for مادامكه. [7] for عالمپناه. [8] the sense demands دوستلقده.

[9] the sense demands ايلچيكز. [10] probably معتبر is intended. [11] for سعادتلو. [12] for بذل.

lines 1–3 After the offering of greetings befitting your friendship with the threshold of happiness of His Majesty the fortunate Padishah, the Refuge of the world, what has to be notified is this :

lines 4–6 This letter of ours has been written and dispatched to Your Excellencies because your ambassador, whom you dispatched at this time to congratulate upon the Imperial accession, has sent and delivered your letter and some tokens of friendship to us.

lines 6–12 As long as you are steadfast in perfect friendship with His Majesty the fortunate Padishah, the Refuge of the world, then also is certain, God Almighty willing, the treating kindly of your ambassador and bailos, with every kind of favours and graces, on the Imperial part of His Majesty the fortunate and glorious Padishah. Your ambassador also, having been honoured and respected in every way, has now been allowed to leave and depart for those parts. It is certain that our best assistance, as befits friendship, will be exerted in your affairs which occur in the noble Presence of His Majesty the fortunate Padishah.

line 12 Thus may it be known ! Finally, farewell !

Document B

A letter in Turkish from the Khāṣṣekī Ṣāfiye to the Doge of Venice, undated. Date of receipt, 17 March 1589. Venice, Archivio di Stato, Documenti turchi, Busta VII. 2 (4)[13].

Transcription [plate XLII]

هو[14]

[15] [seal]

1) فخر الملة العيسويّه ونديك بكلري خدمتلري[16] عاقبت الخير بعد السلام انها

2) اولنان اولدركه مكتوبكز وارد اولوب اخبـــار سلامتكزي وهرنه ددكوز ايسه

[13] Indexed and summarized by A. Bombaci, *Reg. di doc. turchi*, no. 736.

[14] *Invocatio* (not included in plate).

[15] The impression of the seal is almost entirely illegible ; comparison of its lower edge inscription, however, with that of the seal on Documents II and III (see plate XL) suggests that they are the same, i.e. يا خدا يا محمد فخر جهان

[16] See note 10 to Document I.

3) معلوم اولندي ددي‌قودي‌دن خالي دكل‌سيز مسلمانلره غايت شكوا ايله جفا
4) اولنوردرلر لازم اولن بودركه چونكه پادشاهه باريشلك ودوستليق 5) ايدرسز بر
خوشجه دوستليق ايلكز اوته بري قارشدرميه‌سز 6) نته‌كه سيز تلك دورمزسز پادشاهده
سزي شويله قوه‌يه‌جك[17] د 7) كلدر سز كندو حالكزده اولنجه پادشاه ده سزه
نسنه ايلمز همان 8) سز تلك دورك كه دوستليق دايم وقايم اوله شويله ايده‌سز وبو
9) جانبدن ايكي خلعت وايكي دستمال ارسال اولندي قبول ايده‌سز 10) وبو استانه‌دن
بر مصالحكز اولرسه انشا الله كوريلور باقي والسلام

English rendering

HE

Seal ; . . . O Lord, O Meḥemmed, glory of the world !

line 1 His Highness the Beg of Venice, the glory of Christendom, good ending !

lines 1–4 After the greeting this is what has to be imparted : Your letter having arrived, the news of your well-being and whatsoever you may have said has been understood. You do not keep aloof from false rumours. With exaggerated complaints harm is done to the Muslims. What is necessary is this :

lines 4–8 Since you have made peace with and are friendly towards the Padishah, do practise a proper friendship ! Do not interfere in all kinds of matters, for as much as you do not remain quiet neither will the Padishah let you get away with it like this. As long as you keep within your limits the Padishah for his part will do you no harm. Well then, keep quiet so that the friendship may be lasting and upright ! Thus may you do !

lines 8–9 And from our side two robes of honour and two towels have been dispatched. May you accept (them) !

line 10 And if there should be some matters you are asking from this threshold, God willing they will be dealt with. Finally, farewell !

---

[17] for قويه‌جق (?).

UN SOYURGHAL QARA-QOYUNLU CONCERNANT LE BULŪK DE BAWĀNĀT-HARĀT-MARWAST

(*Archives persanes commentées 3*)

par

Jean Aubin

Quatre documents émanant de la chancellerie du souverain Qara-Qoyunlu Jahān-Shāh ont été à ce jour édités : par A. D. Papazjan deux documents ayant trait à des domaines monastiques arméniens, par H. Busse un *soyurghal* concernant Julfa, par moi-même un acte en faveur d'un sayyid de Qum.[1] A cette brève liste j'ajouterai un deuxième document intéressant les anciennes provinces timourides conquises en 1452 par Jahān-Shāh. Sous la cote E 5427 se trouve aux archives du Musée de Topkapî Saray à Istanbul une donation en *soyurghal* de 859/1455 concernant les cantons de Harāt-ō-Marwast et de Bawānāt, en Fārs.[2] (Voir Planches XLIII–LII.)

(1) عواطف صنع یزدانی و لطایف فضل ربانی که وفاق شکر آن میسر باد

(2) در حقّ ما زیاده از اینست که قوة تحریر بتقریر آن وفا نماید وقدرت زبان حقیقت آنرا

---

[1] A. D. Papazjan, *Persidskie dokumenty Matenadarana*, I, Erevan 1956, doc. no. 1 (incomplet) et no. 2 (facsimile et texte, p. 244–247 ; trad. russe, p. 163–165 ; remarques, p. 196–197). On y joindra les no. 3 (copie d'un *manshūr* de Begum Khātūn, épouse de Jahān-Shāh, daté de 866/1462 et confirmant un *manshūr* de Sulṭān Uways Jalā'ir) et no. 4 (Ḥasan 'Alī, 872/1468).

Heribert Busse, *Untersuchungen zum islamischen Kanzleiwesen an Hand turkmenischer und safawidischer Urkunden*, Le Caire 1959, doc. no. 1, pp. 149–50, pl. I. Un facsimile avait déjà paru dans *Arşiv kılavuzu*, fasc. 2, Istanbul 1950, doc. XVI.

Jean Aubin, *Archives persanes commentées* I, pp. 3–6, pl. I (*Mélanges Massignon*, I, Damas 1956, pp. 125–128).

De plus, les copies de deux *manshūr* de 870/1466 nommant émir du pélerinage un certain Niẓām al-Dīn 'Abd al-Ḥaqq ont été publiées dans le *Tārīkh-ō jughrāfī-ye dār os-salṭane-ye Tabrīz* de Nāder Mīrzā Qājār, pp. 83–5. Les originaux faisaient partie du fonds d'archives en possession de Mīrzā Kāẓim Wakīl, cf. p. 85 et *Yādegār*, II/5 (1323 sh.), pp. 20–1 ; portrait de Mīrzā Kāẓim dans *Nashriyye-ye dāneshkede-ye adabiyyāt-e Tabrīz*, XI/4 (1338 s.), pp. 412–3.

[2] J'ai pu faire photographier le document en 1961, grâce à la bienveillante autorisation de M. H. Örs, Directeur du Musée.

(3) استیفا کند و در ادراك کمیت و معرفت کیفیت آن اوهام در ششدر ابهام نماید و افهام در گشایش

(4) ایهام بیفتد و بنزد عقل دور اندیش اعداد امداد آن بانواع استقصا در حیّز احصا آید

(5) کما قال الله تعالی «و اِن تعدّوا نعمة الله لا تحصوها» فله الحمد علی افاضة الانه والیه الرغبة فی ادامة نعمائه

(6) حمداً یرتقی فی مدارج التحقیق ویمتدی افاویق التوفیق و اکرم این نعم که مارا کرامتست و اجزل این

(7) قسم که نصیب روزگار همایون شده آنکه ریاض بارگاه جهانپناه را بوجود امراءِ نامدار و دولتخواهان

(8) ذوی الاقتدار که هر کدام مهر سپهر کامکاری وجلالت وکوکب سعد فلك بختیاری وایالت اند زین و زینت داده

(9) وجسم دولت و عرصه مملکت بجمال ایشان روشن گردانیده لاجرم همواره خاطر انور و ضمیر ازهر که مظهر اشعه انوار الطاف آلهیست

(10) و مهبط فیض فضل نا متناهی است بر افتتاح ابواب مرحمت واتّساع عرصه مکرمت و انشراح صدور ارکان دولت

(11) و انفساح قلوب اعیان حضرت و اعلاء قدر دولتخواهان صافی نیت و اداء حقوق خدمتکاران وافی طویت که

(12) استیفاء عهود دولت خودرا در استحکام عقود مملکت ما مخصوص دانسته بقدم عبودیت در جادهٔ اخلاص

(13) و جانسپاری راسخ و راسی اند مجبول و مفطور است و چون امیر اعظم اکرم افتخار الامراء فی الزّمان

(14) نتیجهٔ اکابر الحکام و الصنادید فی الاوان المختص بعنایت الملك الرحمن امیر جلالالدین ترخان که

(15) بدین صفات مرضیه اتصاف دارد مدتهاست تا طوق عبودیت بر گردن و حلقهٔ رقیت در گوش و کمر اطاعت

(16) بر میان بمراسم خدمات پسندیده قیام مینماید و در اقسام شجاعت و دلاوری و هنگام عدالت و رعیت پروری

(17) از اقران و اخوان ممتاز است هراینه عنان عنایت و زمام عاطفت بصوب تربیت و تمشیت او معطوف نمودیم

(18) و بلوک هراه و مروست و بوانات که از معظمات بلوکات دار السلطنهٔ شیراز است در بسته از ابتداء لوییل

(19) مطابق سنه تسع و خمسین و مایه خانی باو ارزانی فرمودیم که آنچه از مال و منال و سایر جهات آنجا بدیوان میرسد سوی غله مقاسمه

(20) تصرف نماید و از ابتداء ییلان ییل مقاسمه تعلق بامیر مشار الیه داشته باشد که جهت خود مزروع گردانیده حاصل

(21) متصرف شود و جماعت ایوهٔ آباده و محمد حضر و برادران از احشام ایکدشی فارس و فرزند احمد علی ارعش که

(22) در آن بلوک بزراعت مشغول اند از احشام مفروز شناخته داخل بلوک مذکور دانسته متعلق بامیر مشارالیه باشند

(23) این منشور لا زال منفذاً الی یوم النشور سمت اصدار و شرف نفاذ یافت

(24) تا امراء عظام نامدار و وزراء کرام عالی مقدار و نواب و دیوانیان برینموجب مقرر دانسته هر سال مال و منال

(25) و جهات بلوک و جماعت احشام مذکوره در وجه مواجب امیر اعظم مشار الیه حساب نمایند و اصلاً حوالتی بر آنجا باشد سادات و قضاة و موالی

(26) و مشایخ و اصول و کلانتران واهالی و کدخدایان و ارباب و مزارعان وجمهور مقیمان آن بلوک و جماعت

(27) احشام مذکوره باید که شرایط اطاعت و انقیاد مرعی داشته از اوامر و نواهی امیر مشارالیه و گماشتگان او که هراینه متضمن

(28) معموری و آبادانی ولایت و رفاهیت و جمعیت رعیت خواهد بود تجاوز ننمایند و مراسم تقویت و تمشیت تقدیم نموده مال

(29) و منال و سایر جهات بموجب حواله و براة ایشان جواب گویند و در جمیع امور و قضایا رجوع بدیشان نموده مجال مداخلت

(30) غیر محال شمرند و جهات و رسومی که همیشه متعلق بداروغگان بوده مخصوص او دانند کلانتران احشام تراکمه بتخصیص قنغراد بزرگ

(31) قلم و قدم کوتاه و کشیده داشته بعلت مال و جهات و حق حمایت و خارجیات و قسمات و طرح و قلان و بیگار و غیره مزاحم و متعرض

(32) ایشان نشوند امیر اعظم مشار الیه نیز باید که بساط شفقت بر طوایف خاص
و عام گسترده هر کس را علی
(33) اختلاف طبقاتهم و تفاوة درجاتهم تفقد و تعهد نموده و مستمال و امیدوار
ساخته بزراعت و عمارت ترغیب و تحریص نماید
(34) و هر قضیه که واقع شود بر وفق شریعت غرّا و طریق عدالت غوررسی کرده
بفیصل رساند و دست تعدّی ارباب تغلب
(35) و تسلط از اذیال احوال ضعفا و عجزه کوتاه و کشیده داشته در تعمیر
ولایت و تکثیر زراعت کوشیده مال
(36) و جهات براستی از محل خود مستخلص گرداند و بنوعی مرتکب امور آنجا
شود که صیت نیکک نامی او منتشر گردد از جوانب
(37) برینجمله بروند و چون بتوقیع رفیع اشرف اعلی موشّع و مصحّح و مجلّی
شود اعتماد نمایند
(38) کتب بالامر العالی اعلاه الله تعالی و خلّد نفاذه فی ثالث رجب المرجب لسنه
تسع و خمسین و ثمانمایه
(39) رب اختم بالخیر و الحسن
(marge) پروانچه برساله امیرین اعظمین اعدلین اکرمین نظاماً و شمساً

Fondée sur l'examen d'un nombre de pièces très insuffisant, notre connaissance des usages des chancelleries turkmènes est encore fragile. La diplomatique turkmène emprunte ses règles à la diplomatique chaghatay et il eût fallu, en bonne méthode, étudier d'abord celle-ci pour mieux suivre l'évolution de celle-là, en palliant, comme il est possible de le faire partiellement, la perte des originaux d'époque mongole ou timouride par un recours soigneux aux copies anciennes. L'apport de notre document en cette matière est insignifiant. Il ne présente aucune particularité qui ne soit déjà connue par d'autres publications. L'apprecatio *rabbī ikhtim bi'l-khayr wa'l-ḥusn* est identique à celle du *soyurghal* de Jahān-Shāh édité par M. Busse,[3] et nous trouvons des formules similaires dans les documents timourides (de même pour la formule *bi'l-amr al-'ālī a'lāhu*

[3] Dans sa recension des *Untersuchungen zum islamischen Kanzleiwesen*, M. Fekete, *Der Islam*, 36/3, a corrigé *wa'l-iḥsān*, lecture fautive de M. Busse, en *wa'l-ḥusn* leçon qui apparaît aussi très clairement sur notre document.

Allāh ta'āla wa khallada nafādhahu) ; par exemple : *rabbi ikhtim bi'l-khayr* (Tamerlan à Muḥammad Sulṭān Bahādur concernant Shaykh Dursun Marāghānī, daté de Ūjān, 24 muḥarram 804/3 septembre 1401) ; *rabbī ikhtim bi'l-yumn wa'l-iqbāl* (Pīr Muḥammad-i 'Umar Shaykh à son frère Rustam, portant nomination de Rukn al-Dīn Ṣā'id Qāḍī comme *mutawallī* du *buq'a* du souverain muẓaffaride Shāh Shujā', Ier jumada II 804/6 janvier 1402) ; *rabbī ikhtim bi'l-khayr wa'l-ḥusn* dans un diplôme d'exemption du 12 rabī' I 821/19 avril 1418, etc. A la formule marginale *parvānacha ba-risāla-yi...* ont été consacrées des observations récentes.[4]

L'absence de l'invocatio et de l'intitulatio s'explique par une déterioration probable du rouleau, dont le bord supérieur, ainsi qu'il arrive souvent, aura disparu à la pliure. Daté du 3 rajab 859/19 juin 1455, notre document ne peut émaner que de la chancellerie Qara-Qoyunlu, puisque l'Iran méridional était sous la domination des Turkmènes du Mouton Noir depuis les campagnes du prince Pīr Budāq de 1452 en Iraq et Fārs et de 1454 au Kirmān.[5] Mais notre *soyurghal* anonyme a-t-il été rédigé au divan de Pīr Budāq, gouverneur du Fārs, ou à celui de Jahān-Shāh, son père ? Bien que le district (*bulūk*) de Harāt-Marwast-Bawānāt ait relevé, théoriquement, de la principauté de Chiraz, nous ne savons pas s'il était sous la juridiction de Pīr Budāq, ou si Jahān-Shāh s'était réservé d'en disposer.[6] Nous inclinons à attribuer le *soyurghal* à Jahān-Shāh lui-même. Les deux émirs chargés de la ratification, " Niẓām " et " Shams ", dont les noms figurent en marge, doivent être les vizirs de Jahān-Shāh, Amīr Niẓām al-Dīn Sayyid 'Āshūr [7] et Khwāja Shams al-Dīn Ḥusayn Tabrīzī.[8]

Notre document complète heureusement ce que des références isolées et laconiques nous apprennent sur l'histoire des Bawānāt et du Harāt-ō-Marwast. Au cours de la période d'extension du pastoralisme, le tracé des

---

[4] Cf. Busse, *Untersuchungen*, pp. 70 sq.; H. R. Roemer, dans *Bulletin de l'Institut Français d'Archéologie Orientale*, LIX (Le Caire 1960), 278–9 ; L. Fekete, *Birtakim farsça belgerde bulunan bir ek-formülün açıklaması hakkında*, dans *Németh Armaganı*, Ankara 1962, pp. 389–93.

[5] Cf. Jean Aubin, *Deux sayyids de Bam au XVe siècle*, Wiesbaden 1956, pp. 58–63, 67, 78–9.

[6] En mars 1453 Pīr Budāq envoya de Yazd à Kirmān un *ilchī* nommé Sayyidī Aḥmad, porteur d'un *nishān* nommant Sayyid Sharwānī gouverneur de Kirmān, cf. Ibn Shihāb Yazdī, *Jāmi' al-Tawārīkh-i Ḥasanī*, ms. B. N. Téhéran, p. 837 ; J. Aubin, *Deux sayyids de Bam*, p. 71. Mais nous ne savons pas si la décision avait été prise par lui-même ou par Jahān-Shāh, qui le tenait en position subalterne.

[7] 'Abd al-Razzāq Samarqandī, *Maṭla' al-Sa'dayn*, éd. Shafī', II, Lahore 1949, p. 1177.

[8] Abū Bakr Ṭihrānī *Kitāb-i Diyārbakriyya*, éd. F. Sümer, I, Ankara 1962, p. 258.

voies de communication se diversifie dans les pays iraniens. Le vieux réseau caravanier, axé sur les villes, se double d'un autre réseau de grande circulation, axé sur les terrains de pâture.[9] Comme les armées sont formées de levées tribales, et que les campagnes sont rythmées par les impératifs de la migration et l'alternance des hivernages (turco-persan *qīshlāmīshī*) et des estivages (turco-persan *yāylāmīshī*), les routes du nomadisme sont aussi les routes militaires. Au carrefour du Fārs, du Kirmān et de l'Irāq persan, la région que concerne notre document commande les deux types de trafic.

Relais important de la route Chiraz-Yazd, Abarqūh a capté en partie, dans des conditions que nous ne pouvons décrire ici, le trafic de la route Chiraz-Ispahan, et demeure jusqu'à l'époque ṣafawide la plaque tournante du réseau caravanier.[10] Abarqūh est une ville-clef, dont la prise est indispensable à quiconque veut s'assurer la domination de l'Iran méridional et de Yazd. Les gouverneurs d'Abarqūh tentent parfois d'utiliser cette forte position stratégique et commerciale au profit de leurs ambitions. Dans les années 1390, Pahlawān Muhadhdhab se taille ainsi une petite principauté étirée d'est en ouest, de manière à couvrir l'éventail des routes du Fārs vers l'Irāq, prenant appui à l'ouest sur le château de Sarmāq, à l'est sur celui de Harāt et sur celui de Marwast.[11] En 1503, un gouverneur d'Abarqūh soustrait Yazd à l'autorité de Shāh Ismā'īl.[12]

Située en bordure d'un kavir, Abarqūh dépend pour son ravitaillement des envois de grain que lui font les cantons voisins.[13] Harāt, étape sur la transversale qui relie le Fārs au Kirmān par le nord du lac Bakhtigān, et les Bawānāt sont connus des textes géographiques comme lieux de production céréalière et fruitière.[14] Au début du XIVe siècle des domaines sont mis en valeur aux Bawānāt, à Harāt, à Marwast et à Sarchahān par

---

[9] Pour l'exemple typique du Khurāsān occidental, voir notre étude sur *Les mouvements sociaux en Iran oriental au XIVe siècle* (à paraître).

[10] L'hypothèse selon laquelle Barbaro (1474) serait passé à Arāwirjān, grosse ville, a été avancée inconsidérement par A. Gabriel *Die Erforschung Persiens*, p. 248 ; Barbaro est passé à Abarqūh. Gabriel (pp. 62–3) a également pris dans Sykes l'itinéraire Ormuz-Harāt (du Fārs)-Chiraz de Varthema, lequel n'a jamais voyagé en Iran.

[11] Ḥāfiẓ-i Abrū, " Géographie ", ms. British Museum Or. 1577, fol. 121a.

[12] Ḥasan Rūmlū, éd. Seddon, pp. 54, 82.

[13] Ḥāfiẓ-i Abrū, *l.c.*

[14] Al-Iṣṭakhrī, p. 102 ; al-Muqaddasī, p. 436 ; Ibn al-Balkhī, *Fārs-nāma*, p. 125 ; Mustawfī Qazwīnī, *Nuzhat al-Qulūb*, éd. Le Strange, pp. 122-3 ; Mustawfī Yazdī, dans *Farhang-e Irān Zamīn*, VI/2–3, pp. 169–70 ; Le Strange, *Lands*, p. 287 ; etc. Description moderne des Bawānāt par Sir Aurel Stein, *An archaeological tour in the ancient Persis*, Londres 1936. (*Iraq*, III/2), pp. 206–12.

Rashīd al-Dīn, le célèbre vizir des Ilkhans,[15] qui avait de gros intérêts en Fārs et entretenait les rapports les plus étroits avec les milieux d'affaires de Yazd, Abarqūh et Chiraz. Toutefois, si les noms des oasis éparses au sud et au sud-est d'Abarqūh reviennent fréquemment dans les chroniques du XIVe siècle ce n'est pas la fertilité de terroirs au demeurant restreints qui leur vaut d'être mentionnées. Toutes ces mentions sont liées à l'agitation tribale ou aux entreprises guerrières.

Aux Bawānāt se rejoignent les chemins du nord et de l'est qui permettent l'invasion du Fārs à partir de l'Irāq persan via Abarqūh,[16] ou à partir du Kirmān, traversant le terrain de parcours des nomades, via Marwast et Harāt.[17] Sulṭān Muẓaffar, le fondateur de la dynastie muẓaffaride, chargé par Öljeytü (1304–1316) de la police des voies qui desservent Yazd jusqu'à Harāt, Marwast et Abarqūh, se heurte, comme se heurteront après lui ses descendants, aux tribus arabes qui occupent la région.[18] Le terme générique de " tribus ", *aḥshām*, inclut les tribus bédouines, *a'rāb*, mais paraît désigner plus particulièrement les tribus turkmènes. Vers la fin du XIVe siècle un gouverneur du *bulūk* de Fasā cumule ce poste avec celui de gouverneur des tribus turkmènes, *aḥshām-i tarākima*.[19] Dans la liste des vingt-et-une divisions administratives du Fārs donnée par le *Shams al-Siyāq* (vers 1441), l'ensemble Bawānāt-Harāt-Marwast ne forme, comme dans notre *soyurghal*, qu'une seule circonscription ; Fasā, citée entre les Garmsīrāt et Fīrūzābād, n'est pas jumelée aux *aḥshām*, placées en fin de liste, à la suite de trois circonscriptions territoriales à peuplement nomade, le Shūlistān, le Kūhgīlūy et Jūyum-i Lār.[20] Nous distinguons dans la région Fasā-Jūyum un centre d'habitat turkmène [21] qui doit être la zone d'hivernage d'*aḥshām* estivant dans les " terres froides " (*sardsīrāt*) du nord du Fārs . Entre les Bawānāt et les Garmsīrāt la route de transhumance passait à l'est du lac Bakhtigān.

---

[15] *Mukātabāt-i Rashīdī*, éd Shafī', Lahore 1947, p. 202 et p. 230 (avec des identifications erronées de l'éditeur).

[16] En 742/1341–42, Amīr Ashraf Chūpānī envahit le Fārs en passant par Abarqūh et les Bawānāt, qu'il pille, cf. Ḥāfiẓ-i Abrū, *o.c.*, fol. 104b.

[17] Au IVe s.H., cf. *Simṭ al-'Ula*, éd. Eghbal, p. 15 (Marwast) ; en 1213, cf. *al-Muḍāf ilā Badāyi' al-Azmān*, éd. Eghbal, p. 49 (Harāt) ; à l'époque Aq-Qoyunlu, cf. Faḍl'ullah b. Rūzbihān, trad. Minorsky, p. 31 (Sarchahān).

[18] Kutubī, *Tārīkh-i Āl-i Muẓaffar*, éd. Nawā'ī, p. 6 et *passim*.

[19] Ḥāfiẓ-i Abrū, *o.c.*, fol. 117b.

[20] 'Alī Shīrāzī, *Shams al-Siyāq*, ms. Ayasofya 3986, fol. 127b.

[21] Des Yinallu paraissent établis aux confins du Shabānkārā en 1264 (Waṣṣāf, p. 192), dans la région ou vivent actuellement des Ainallu (sur ce groupe en général, cf. Minorsky, " Ainallu/Inallu ", dans *Rocznik Orientalistyczny*, XVII). En 1299–1300 une tribu turque hiverne près de Jūyum (Waṣṣāf, p. 371 ; cf. *Journal Asiatique*, 1955, p. 496).

Ainsi Sulṭān Muẓaffar poursuit des rebelles jusqu'en pays shabānkāra Ainsi Shāh Manṣūr, après une attaque sur Abarqūh, va faire *qīshlāmīsh* dans les Garmsīrāt en passant par le chemin des Bawānāt et de Dārābjird.[22] Certains groupes se déplaçaient sur un axe différent, entre les " terre froides " du Fārs et les " terres chaudes " du Kirmān. De tels mouvement sont attestés pour l'époque muẓaffaride, et, indirectement (cf. *infra*) pou l'époque Qara-Qoyunlu.

Tandis qu'à l'automne de 1452 les Qara-Qoyunlu occupaient Chira et Yazd, une armée de siège conduite par deux généraux de Pīr Budāq Mīr 'Alī Mamāsh et Mīr Sayyidī 'Alī, bloquait Abarqūh, où deux représen tants du sultan timouride Bābur, Jān Darwīsh Tuwāchī et Mīr Tarkhān organisaient la résistance. L'émir Aḥmad-i Pīrzād, chef d'un secours d cent cavaliers envoyé par Bābur, tua Jān Darwīsh à l'occasion d'un beuverie, fit mettre aux liens Mīr Tarkhān, et se trouva maître de la ville Au bout de dix mois la plus grande partie des citadins étaient morts d faim. D'autres, qui s'étaient échappés, erraient misérablement dans le cantons voisins. Hormis les Chaghatay et d'autres soldats (*'ulūfakhwār*) il ne restait plus dans Abarqūh que quelques habitants. La disette étai telle qu'un *man* de feuilles de vigne et de mûrier se vendait six dinars, et l *man* de noyaux de dattes, quand on en trouvait, dix à douze. On mangeai le cuir et les vieilles toiles. Aḥmad-i Pīrzād ouvrit des pourparlers d reddition. Il fut convenu que le camp des vivandiers (*ordū-bāzār*) serai établi entre la ville et le camp militaire Qara-Qoyunlu, et que les homme des deux partis commerceraient quelques jours, afin que les esprit s'apaisent et qu'on fasse connaissance mutuelle. Ensuite les émir turkmènes entreraient dans Abarqūh. Mais une fois les tentes de vivandiers dressées aux abords des murailles, et les allées et venues et le transactions commencées, Aḥmad-i Pīrzād fit une attaque-surpris nocturne contre l'*ordū-bāzār*, le pilla entièrement, et rentra en ville ave un butin abondant. Les combats reprirent et duraient encore à la date d 30 ramaḍān 857/4 octobre 1453.[23] Il semble que Abarqūh soit tombé avant la fin de 857/1453. Samarqandī place la reddition sous cett année-là.[24] Un des chefs Qara-Qoyunlu chargés du siège, Sayyidī 'Al quittait d'ailleurs bientôt le Fārs pour Bagdad, où il arriva le 3 rabī' 858/3 mars 1454.[25]

Au printemps de la même année le prince timouride Sanjar tentai d'envahir le Fārs. Arrivé à Sarchahān, il dut battre en retraite devan

---

[22] Ḥāfiẓ-i Abrū, *o.c.*, fol. 120b.

[23] Ibn Shihāb Yazdī, ms. cité, pp. 854–5.

[24] Pour le contexte de l'affaire, cf. *Deux sayyids de Bam*, p. 62.

[25] Al-'Azzāwī, *Ta'rīkh al-'Irāq bayn Iḥtilālayn*, III, Bagdad 1939, p. 146.

Pīr Budāq.[26] " Dans chaque vilayat où Pīr Budāq arrivait, Harāt, Marwast, Shahr-i Bābak et autres, il passait au fil de l'épée les *darugha* chaghatay et tous les ennemis qu'il trouvait ".[27] Les renseignements sur la région des Bawānāt et de Harāt-ō-Marwast sont peu nombreux pour le reste de la période Qara-qoyunlu. Lorsqu'en 1462 Jahān-Shāh descendit d'Ispahan sur Chiraz pour en chasser Pīr Budāq en demi-rebellion, la résistance du château de Yazdkhwāst [28] lui fit infléchir sa marche par Abarqūh et les Bawānāt. Il lotit ensuite le Fārs entre trois autres de ses fils, en fonction des besoins de l'économie nomade. Abū Yūsuf reçut la zone des terres froides du Chahārdāng (*ḥadd-i sardsīrāt-i Ch.*). Certains des *garmsīrāt* furent rattachés à Ispahan, afin que la " subsistance " (*khōrash*) de Muḥammadī Mīrzā, qui en était gouverneur, soit égale à celle de ses frères. Les Bawānāt et le Harāt-ō-Marwast furent détachés du Fārs et annexés au Kirmān, apanage de Abu'l-Qāsim.[29]

Le document que nous publions est antérieur de sept ans à l'octroi des Bawānāt et du Harāt-ō-Marwast en *iqṭā'* à Abu'l-Qāsim. Nous ignorons présentement quel avait été le statut de ces deux districts depuis 1455, et si la nouvelle répartition rendit caduques les dispositions prévues en faveur de Jalāl al-Dīn Tarkhān.[30] Le *soyurghal* de 1455 et le partage de 1462 ont ceci de commun qu'ils contribuent à montrer à quel point le régime Qara-Qoyunlu, responsable d'une regression accusée de la vie socio-économique, servait essentiellement les intérêts des tribus qui le soutenaient.

Le document distingue deux catégories de tribus. (1) Des tribus turkmènes, en particulier celle des " grands Qonghirād ", [31] qui ne sont

---

[26] J. Aubin, *Deux sayyids de Bam*, p. 78.

[27] Ṭihrānī, *Kitāb-i Diyābakriyya*, II, Ankara, 1964, p. 338 (où " Marwdasht " est une restitution inappropriée).

[28] Et non du château de Yazd, comme l'a écrit par inadvertance Mükrimin Halil, *Islam Ansiklopedisi*, art. " Cihan Şah " (p. 182 b) ; cf. Ṭihrānī, II, p. 362.

[29] Ṭihrānī, *Kitāb-i Diyārbakriya*, II, pp 366, 401.

[30] Notre document ne portant ni sceau ni endossement, il se peut qu'il n'ait pas été validé.

[31] Je lis *buzurg*, " grand " le mot dépourvu de points diacritiques qui suit le nom " Q.ngh.rād ". Les Qonggirat, qualifiés dans notre document de " turkmènes ", étaient en réalité à l'origine des Mongols. A l'époque Jengiskhanide, le clan mongol des Qonggirat est bien connu pour avoir donné à Jengis-Khan sa première épouse Börte et avoir été dès lors constamment allié au clan Kiyat-Borjigin (voir le décret ordonnant que les filles qonggirat deviennent impératrices et que les garçons épousent les princesses impériales, F. W. Cleaves, *Harvard Journal of Asiatic Studies*, xiii (1950), p. 13. L'existence du clan est attestée au moins un siècle plus tôt parmi les tribus proto-mongoles des Leao : une partie vient en 1123 à la suite de Ye-liu Ta-che fonder l'empire Qara-Khitai (voir Pelliot, *Histoire des campagnes de Gengis-Khan*, Tome 1, (1951), p. 402).

pas mises sous l'autorité de Jalāl al-Dīn Tarkhān, mais qui passent ou séjournent sur le territoire à lui octroyé, et qui continueront d'y passer ou d'y séjourner, puisqu'il est enjoint aux *kalāntar* de ces tribus de ne plus tourmenter ni inquiéter la population du *bulūk* pour motif de taxes (*māl-ō-jihāt*), droit de protection (*ḥaqq al-ḥimāyat*), impositions extraordinaires (*khārijiyyāt*), " parts " (*qasamāt*), achat (ou vente) à prix arbitraire (*ṭarḥ*), *qalān*, corvées (*bīgār*) et autres (lignes 30–32). Encore que la signification exacte de plusieurs d'entre eux reste à préciser, tous ces termes sont connus par d'autres documents.[32] (2) Des tribus qui seront désormais considérées comme " détachées des *aḥshām* et inclues dans le dit *bulūk* ", c'est-à-dire ne seront plus comptées par le fisc au nombre des tribus, à savoir : " la communauté des Īwä de Ābāda ; Muḥammad-i Khiḍr et ses frères, des tribus mêlées (*ighdishī*) du Fārs ; le fils de Aḥmad-i 'Alī Ar'ash, qui s'adonnent à l'agriculture dans ce *bulūk* " (lignes 21–22). Si notre document décernait le pluriel majestatif au détenteur du *soyurghal*, on pourrait supposer que le membre de phrase " qui s'adonnent à l'agriculture dans ce *bulūk* " s'applique au seul fils (sans doute jeune, car non nommé) de Aḥmad fils de 'Alī Ar'ash. Tel n'est pas le cas. C'est donc à tout le moins les deux derniers, et fort probablement les trois groupes énumérés qui travaillent la terre. Toutefois, si le capital humain attribué à Jalāl al-Dīn Tarkhān est grossi de trois groupes détachés des *aḥshām*, nous ne pouvons affirmer qu'ils sont exclus de cette catégorie en raison de leur mode de vie. La mention expresse de leur activité agricole n'implique pas automatiquement un degré de fixation avancé. Les nomades chaghatay rencontrés par Clavijo dans la région de Sarakhs semaient durant leur estivage du grain, du coton et des melons.[33] Faute d'études précises sur les rapports de fait entre nomades et villageois, il serait prématuré de considérer les croisements de sang entre turkmènes et paysans de la contrée comme une conséquence de la sédentarisation des pasteurs. Notre document ne dit pas quelle était la souche des " tribus bâtardes " parmi lesquelles figurait celle de Muḥammad-i Khiḍr. Seule nantie d'un nom de clan, la " communauté (*jamā'at*) des Īwä de Ābāda ", — le mot *jamā'at* ayant ici le sens de communauté tribale plutôt que de communauté villageoise,[34] — se rattache à une tribu oğuz

[32] Cf. en dernier lieu I. P. Petrushevsky, *Zemledelie i agrarnye otnoshenija v Irane XIII-XIV vekov*, Moscou-Leningrad 1960, pp. 369–402.

[33] Clavijo, trad. Le Strange, p. 190.

[34] Cf. ici-même, lignes 27–8. L'expression *jamā'at-i A'rāb* appliquée aux tribus arabes de la région de Harāt-Marwast, cf. Ḥāfiẓ-i Abrū, *o.c.*, fol. 156 b. Sur le *jamā'at* villageois, cf. Petrushevsky, *o.c.*, pp. 298 sqq.

bien connue. Fixés dans la région de Hamadan, les Yïwa/Īwä se sont à l'époque mongole dispersés en direction du nord-ouest. M. Minorsky leur affilie le clan Bahārlū, clan royal de la confédération Qara-Qoyunlu.[35] Rien dans notre document n'atteste le souvenir d'une parenté ancestrale entre les Iwä de Abāda, d'implantation indatable, et le clan de Jahān-Shāh, non plus que l'existence d'un lien spécial entre eux et Jalāl al-Dīn Tarkhān. Si l'on pouvait identifier Ābāda de notre document à l'une des deux bourgades de ce nom connues des textes historiques, soit celle située à l'ouest d'Abarqūh, soit celle située au nord du lac Bakhtigān (ce qui serait ici plus plausible), on aurait la preuve que la communauté des Iwä était encore nomade et ne pratiquait l'agriculture que comme appoint très secondaire dans le *bulūk* de Bawānāt-Harāt-Marwast, puisque l'un des Ābāda est situé dans le *bulūk* de Chahārdāng, et l'autre dans le *bulūk* de Ābāda. Mais il existe un autre Ābāda aux Bawānāt, dans la fertile vallée de Mazayjān,[36] et il est bien probable qu'il s'agit de celui-ci. En tous cas ces groupuscules tribaux ne sont pas assimilés à la population sédentaire autochtone, notre document distinguant de " tous ceux qui résident dans le dit *bulūk* " la " communauté des dites tribus " (l. 27–28).

Bien que le mot *soyurghal* ne figure pas dans le document en faveur de Jalāl al-Dīn Tarkhān, — (la formule employée est simplement " nous lui avons octroyé ", *ba ū arzānī farmūdīm*), — les stipulations sont caractéristiques de ce qu'on appelle un *soyurghal*.[37] Le bénéficiaire reçoit le *bulūk* de Harāt-Marwast-Bawānāt *intégralement* (*dar basta*), " à compter du début de l'année du dragon, qui correspond à l'année 159 de l'ère khānīe, afin qu'il jouisse des biens (*māl*), revenus (*manāl*) et droits (*jihāt*) qui reviennent au *dīwān*, à l'exception du blé du *muqāsama* " ; " à compter du début de l'année du serpent le *muqāsama* reviendra au susdit émir et ayant mis lui-même les terres en culture il s'appropriera la récolte ". (l. 20). Les habitants du *bulūk* " doivent s'adresser en toutes affaires et circonstances aux agents appointés par le dit émir, considérer comme interdite l'immixtion d'une autre personne, reconnaître comme propres à lui les droits (*jihāt wa-rusūm*) qui appartenaient aux *dārūgha*." (l. 29).

En contre-partie il est recommandé à Jalāl al-Dīn Tarkhān de gouverner selon la loi coranique (*sharī'at*) et d'exercer ses pouvoirs avec

---

[35] V. Minorsky, " The clan of the Qara Qoyunlu rulers ", dans *Fuad Köprülü Armağanı*, Istanbul 1953, pp. 391-5 ; F. Sümer, art. " Kara Koyunlu " dans *Islam Ansiklopedisi* ; le même, *Yıva Oğuz boyuna dâir*, dans *Türkiyat Mecmuası*, IX (1951), pp. 151–66.

[36] *Farhang-e Joghrāfyā'ī-e Īrān*, VII, 3 ; cf. Sir Aurel Stein, *l.c.*, p. 207.

[37] Cf. Busse, pp. 97 sqq.; Petrushevsky, pp. 272–4.

équité. Il n'est pas stipulé qu'il s'abstienne des pratiques qui sont désormais interdites aux Qonghirat et aux tribus turkmènes. La procédure fiscale à laquelle le document fait allusion, prélèvement d'une partie de la récolte (*muqāsama*) [38] et assignations (*barāt, ḥawāla*) était une source constante d'abus. Il n'est pas question dans le document du service militaire dû par le bénéficiaire du *soyurghal*. Cette obligation est énoncée dans le *soyurghal* de Jahān-Shāh publié par M. Busse, qui fait suite à un ensemble de pièces timourides concernant Shaykh Dursun Marāghānī, seigneur de Marāghān, Ewoghlī, Julāha/Julfā,[39] etc., dont il sera traité ailleurs en détail.

---

[38] Au sens admis ordinairement de " prélèvement d'une partie de la récolte au titre de l'impôt " (cf. A.K.S. Lambton, *Landlord and Peasant in Persia*, pp. 23, 435), M. Petrushevsky, *o.c.*, p. 372, préfère, pour l'époque mongole celui de " partage préalable de la somme générale (en numéraire) du *kharāj* entre les contribuables ". Pour l'époque qara-qoyunlu cette définition ne convient probablement pas.

[39] Soit sur le bas cours du Qutur Chai et dans la vallée de l'Araxe.

SEVEN ṢAFAWID DOCUMENTS FROM AZARBAYJAN

by

B. G. Martin

The seven documents considered in this chapter cover a time span of approximately a century, from within a few years of the establishment of the Ṣafawid dynasty, to the time of Shāh 'Abbās I. The first and second documents, dated 914/1508–09 and 915/1509–10 respectively, are of Shāh Ismā'īl ; the following pair, dated 952/1545–46 and 959/1551–52, come from the long reign of Shāh Ṭahmāsp (known as " Shaw Thomas " to some of his English contemporaries). Then follows a document of Muḥammad Khudābande of 992/1583–84. The last two documents fall within the period of Shāh 'Abbās I, being dated 1000/1591–92 and 1016/1607–08. These seven documents, with a large number of others, some from the Jalāyirid and Qājār periods, reposed for many years in a Bloomsbury bookshop as " specimens of Persian calligraphy." [1] The first and third documents can be considered government decrees, the others can be loosely called *soyūrghāls*. All of them, in one way or another, have to

---

[1] The original collection, the circumstances of whose arrival in England are not known, contained many more documents, now dispersed. Among these was the famous *firmān* of Aḥmad Jalāyir to Shaykh Ṣadr al-Dīn of Ardabīl, dated 22 Dhū'l-Qa'da 773/26 May 1372, now in the Bibliothèque Nationale, Paris, *Supplément persan 1630*, published by Henri Massé in *Journal asiatique*, 1938, pp. 465–8, and in the Persian magazine *Yādgār*, Azar-Māh, 1323, pp. 25–9. From the bookseller's marks near the top, at the back of this *firmān*, it is clear that it passed through the same hands as the seven documents under discussion here. The original collection also contained a long and spurious *soyūrghāl* of Shāh Sulaymān Ṣafawī, dated 1079/1667–68, concerning certain Ṣūfī landholdings in the region between Ṭālish and Mughān, at Anjarūd and Dashtwand (Dashtāwand ?) ; the author hopes to publish it at some future time. The first two documents, like the fifth one, belong to Dr. A. D. H. Bivar, who has kindly allowed me to publish them ; the remainder are in the writer's collection. The document of 959 A.H. was generously given the writer by Dr. T. Gandjei. The author would like to acknowledge the many suggestions made by Drs. Bivar and Gandjei ; and also the kind help of Mr. G. M. Meredith-Owens, M. Jean Aubin, Dr. R. M. Savory, Prof. A. K. S. Lambton, and Prof. H. R. Roemer.

do with landed properties, the first in Tabrīz, the remainder in the region of Ardabīl and Khalkhāl.[2]

These Ṣafawid documents, like those of earlier periods, tend to be long and narrow, and are often repeatedly folded, which sometimes creates difficulties in reading them.[3] The writing is usually centered toward the left side of the paper, and is deliberately run upwards towards the left edge, becoming more and more crowded as it goes. Seals of rulers (or in the case of Document VI, a copy, a place for a seal) are invariably found at the top centre ; the date at the lower left corner. On the back of these documents, at the top, are various authentication and registration marks, and official seals and signatures. In the middle, on the back, lists of villages and properties are often found (see Doc. VII). The paper, thick white or cream-coloured paper (" Khānbalīgh " paper ?) without watermarks, usually carries a dense black ink, except for textually important formulae, such as *al-ḥukm* (or *al-mulk*) *li'llāh*, *firmān-i humayūn shud*, *firmān-i humayūn sharaf-i nafādh yāft*, or words like *Ṣafawiyye* and *shahāne*, which are often written in red or gold ink.[4] The writing itself ranges from a difficult *shikaste-amīz* in the first document to a clearer *nasta'līq* in the documents of Shāh Ṭahmāsp, or a rolling and often unpointed *shikaste* in the last document, where the scribe lays much emphasis on his broad horizontal pen strokes.

The seals on the first two documents, and the fifth one, are flame or tear-shaped. The remainder have round seals (except for Document Six, a copy). The seal of the first document is unusually interesting, as it seems

---

[2] For a definition of the term *soyūrghāl*, frequently a grant of *waqf* land to " eminent families among the religious classes ", which could then be inherited by the descendants of the original grantee unless revoked by the government, see A. K. S. Lambton, *Landlord and peasant in Persia* (*LPP*), Oxford 1953, pp. 115–16. See also A. D. Papazian, *Persidskie ukaz'i Matenadarana* (*PUkM*), II, Yerevan 1959, p. 452. V. Minorsky, " A Mongol decree to the family of Shaykh Zāhid, 720/1320," *BSOAS*, 1954, p. 516, note 2, gives further references, the most important of which is I. P. Petrushevskii, *Ocherki po istorii feodal'nikh otnoshenyii v Azerbaidzhane i Armenii v XVI—nachale XIX vv.*, Leningrad 1949, chapter IV pp. 145–83, " Soyurghal i mu'afi."

[3] H. Busse, *Untersuchungen zum islamischen Kanzleiwesen an Hand turkmenischer und safawidischer Urkunden*, Cairo 1959, p. 27, suggests that the higher the rank of the recipient of a document, the wider it was, at least under the Qara-Qoyunlu and Aq-Qoyunlu. This may have also been the case under the early Ṣafawids. Furthermore, in many of the documents under discussion here, the lower right corner has been cut off. Busse quotes Chardin, *Voyages du Chevalier Chardin en Perse*, ed. Langlès, Paris 1811, II, 293, who observes that this was done as a sign that " all earthly things are incomplete ".

[4] This paper was imported from Central Asia, if not made in Persia. Under the Qajars, at least from Fatḥ 'Alī Shāh onwards, watermarked Italian laid paper was often employed.

to be the earliest seal of Shāh Ismā'īl so far published. It is not the same as the seal mentioned and read by Rabino from a British Museum *firmān* of 918/1512–13 (B.M. Ms. Or. 4934).[5] It contains a distich, doubtless composed by Ismā'īl himself, and the date 908/1501–02; this same distich is known to have been inscribed on one of Ismā'īl's rings.[6] Perhaps this seal, from a large ring stone (29 mm. wide, 35 mm. long), was reserved for private or semi-private royal correspondence, in contrast to the state seals?

Document Five, of Muḥammad Khudābande, has a flame-shaped seal with a distich in the compartments running around the margin, the name of the ruler in the centre, and *Muḥammad*, *'Alī* and *Allāh* at the top. It has no date; most of it can now be read. The other seals (save for the seal of Document Two) are conventional, and bear the name of the ruler, the date, and the names of the Twelve Imams.[7] All the round seals (Ṭahmāsp I and 'Abbās I) contain the names of the imams in the outer ring, and the name of the ruler in the centre, and in two instances the date—950 and 999 H. The seal of Ṭahmāsp I on Document Three appears to be identical with that published by Papazian (*PUkM*, I, p. 266) in his Document Twelve of 951/1534–44; the other seal with the name of the monarch on Document Four seems to be the same seal as the one illustrated on Plate XXV of Busse's collection, a *firmān* of 972/1563–64. The seal of Document Seven is very much like Busse's edict of 1017/1607–08 (Plate XXVIII), or Rabino's seal of the same date, illustrated at the top of Plate III in the text volume of *Coins, medals, and seals of the Shahs of Iran.*

Apart from Document One (from Tabrīz), these documents are concerned with holdings of land in the region of Ardabīl and Khalkhāl; Documents Two, Three, and Five mention the Ṣafawid *zāwiye* at Ardabīl. In phraseology and in many other details, several of these documents recall

---

[5] H. L. Rabino di Borgomale, *Coins, medals, and seals of the Shahs of Iran, 1500–1941*, London 1945, p. 29. This seal is illustrated in the rare volume of plates accompanying this work, published at Oxford in 1951, Plate XIX.

[6] See V. Minorsky, "The poetry of Shāh Ismā'īl I," *BSOAS*, 1942, p. 1008a, note 4, quoting 'Alī-Qulī Walīh, *Riyāḍ al-Shu'arā'* of 1169 A.H. A similar seal appears on a document of Shāh Ismā'īl dated 910, discussed by Jean Aubin in his "Études Safavides I," *Journal of the Economic and Social History of the Orient*, 1959, p. 75, note 2.

[7] The seal of Document Two, another flame-shaped seal of Shāh Ismā'īl, has been very badly abraded and is only partially legible. It is very much like the seal illustrated in Papazian, *PUkM* I, Yerevan 1956, p. 264 (Document Eleven, of 915 A.H.). In the seal of Document Two, the words *sulṭān, bahādur, al-Ḥusaynī*, and part of the date, 90–, can be read, and perhaps the word *'arsh* or *'arshī*. The full inscription may be one of those listed by Rabino, op. cit., pp. 27–7.

the *firmāns* published as an appendix to Shaykh Ḥusayn ibn Abdāl Pīrzādeh Zāhidī's *Silsilat al-nasab-i Ṣafawiyye.*[8] With four exceptions (Documents One, Three, Four and Five) the name of one Mawlānā Kamāl al-Dīn Ḥusayn Ardabīlī and his descendants are prominent in these documents. There is evidence to suggest that this man, if he was not the *mutawallī* of the Ardabil *zāwiye* in the times of Ismāʿīl, was probably the *khādimbāshī* there, and that certain of his descendants inherited the same office. Mawlānā Kamāl al-Dīn Ḥusayn Ardabīlī is not to be confused with the Qizilbāsh amīr Kamāl al-Dawla wa'l-Iqbāl Ḥusayn Beg Lala, Jumlat al-Mulk, mentioned in the first document, a prominent figure among the Shāmlū and an early adherent of Shāh Ismāʿīl, who later served him as *mīr dīwān, wakīl, and amīr al-umarā.* Ḥusayn Beg Lala was killed at the Battle of Chāldirān in 920/1513–14.

A detailed analysis of these documents follows.

Document I—[plate LIII]

Seal :

بود مهر علی وآل او   جون جان مرا در بر
غلام شاهٔ مردانست   اسماعیل بن حیدر
٩٠٨

Text :

١ هو الله سبحانه
٢ بسم الله الرحمن الرحيم
٣ يا على
٤ الحكم لله
٥ أبو المظفر اسماعيل بهادر سوزوميز
٦ درين وقت مقرر فرموديم كه باغ خان[١] أحمد كه در دار السلطنه تبريز واقعست
٧ وباغات در تصرف جناب سيادت مآب سعادت قباب أخوت حباب
٨ جلالا للسيادة و الدين سيد سليمان ميرزا بوده بهماندستور بدو متعلق دانند
وبتصرف وكلاء او كذارند

[١] جان؟

[8] Shaykh Ḥusayn ibn Abdāl Pīrzādeh Zāhidī, *Silsilat al-nasab-i Ṣafawiyye* (*SNS*), Berlin 1343, H.Q./1923–24, pp. 104–16.

٩ و دیگری در آنجا مدخل ننماید داروغه وکلانتران و متصدیان أمور دیوانی
دار السلطنه مذکور حسب المسطور مقرر دانسته

١٠ ما دام که درین باب علیجناب امارت مآب جملة الملك[٢] کمال [الـ]دولة
و الاقبال حسین بیك لله تصرف نموده با شد

١١ محال مداخلت أحدی ندهند و از فرموده در نکذرند و در عهده دانند تحریرا فی

١٢ درینولا بتصرف ایشان دهند وبیرامون نکردند بیضه

١٣ خامس عشرین شهر صفر أربع عشر و تسعمایه

---

[٢] الملکی

Back :

ثبت بها

بوقوف علیجناب کمال الملك والدوله والاقبال مقررست ملاحظه شد

وقفت علیه اعتصمت بالله اطلعت علیه علمت . . . . غلام . . . . . . است

Document I—Translation

1 He is God, extol Him !

2 In the name of God, the Compassionate, the Merciful !

3 O ʿAlī !

4 Judgement is God's alone !

5 Abu'l-Muẓaffar Ismāʿīl Bahādur, Our Order (*sözümüz*) ! [1]

6 At this time we have decreed that the garden of Khān (Jān ?) Aḥmad, situated in the capital (*dār al-salṭane*) of Tabrīz,

7 and the gardens which have been in the possession of the excellent *sayyid*-like person, auspicious and beloved brother (*janāb-i-siyādat-mā'ab, saʿādat-qibāb-i ukhuwwat-ḥabāb*),

8 Glory of Sayyids and Religion, Sayyid Sulaymān Mīrzā, should belong to him, according to the former precedent (*dastūr*), and should pass into the possession of his representatives (*wukalā'*).[2]

---

[1] See L. Fekete, " Arbeiten der grusinischen Orientalistik auf dem Gebiete der Tuerkischen und der persischen Palaeographie und die Frage der Formel *sözümüz*," in *Acta. Orient. Hung.*, 1957, pp. 10–20 ; also H. R. Roemer, " Le dernier *firmān* de Rustam Bahadur Aq Quyunlu," *Bulletin de l'Institut Français d'Archéologie Orientale* (*BIFAO*), LIX, 1960, p. 276.

[2] *wakīl*—here " representative, advocate, steward " ; see A. K. S. Lambton, *LPP*, p. 442, Papazian, *PUkM*, I, p. 227, and II, p. 439.

9 No other person should enter there. The *dārūghe*,[3] *kalāntars*,[4] and *mutaṣaddīs* [5] of the affairs of the *dīwān* of the aforesaid capital should consider it an established matter, according to what is written here.

10 [In this respect, as long as the exalted and dignified (*'ali-janāb-i imārat-mā'ab*) Jumlat al-Mulk[6], Kamāl al-Dawla wa'l-Iqbāl, Ḥusayn Beg Lala has not taken possession [8]]

Sealed with goodness [7]

11 No person should interfere ; nor should they make any alteration in what has been decreed ; they should consider it their obligation. Written on

12 [It should pass into their possession at this time. Searches must not be undertaken. No further remarks (*bīḍa*) [8]]

13 the 25th of the month of Ṣafar 914/25 June 1508.

Document I—commentary

This *firmān* has lost two small rectangular pieces, one about 7 × 4 cm. at the top left, and another about 3·5 × 4·5 cm. at the top right. Originally, without the loss of these pieces, the dimensions would have been about 22 × 49 cm. The lower right corner has been cut off.

The entire document is written in black ink, save for the formulae at the top : *Huwa Allāhu subḥānahu*, the *basmala*, the words *Yā 'Alī*, and the phrases *al-ḥukm li'llāh* and *Ismā'īl Bahādur* within the *tamghā*—the rectangular monogram immediately above the seal—which are written in gold ink (*āb-i ṭalā'*). In the lower right margin, turned 90° to the direction of the lines of the main text, is the phrase *khutima bi'l-khayr*. This phrase is a survival of a formal concluding prayer, often written in full in Qara-Qoyunlu and Aq-Qoyunlu documents, but progressively shortened and finally dropped in the early Ṣafawid period ; it is doubtful if this practice survived the reign of Shāh Ismā'īl ; Busse gives examples of it.[9] What is more, the use of *khutima bi'l-khayr*, usually written in the margin opposite the last line (see *PUkM*, I, facsimiles opposite p. 258, p. 261, p. 263, and in

[3] *dārūghe*—official in charge of a town or ward, an office somewhat like that of the *muḥtasib* in other parts of the Islamic world. Lambton, *LPP*, p. 426, and Lambton, *Islamic Society in Persia*, London, 1958, has a section on the functions and duties of the *dārūghe*. Papazian, *PUkM*, I, p. 229, and II, p. 441, says the word is of Mongol origin.

[4] *kalāntar*—in this context means the overseer of the wards of a city. See *Tadhkirat al-Mulūk*, p. 148, *LPP*, p. 431.

[5] *mutaṣaddī*—overseer, sub-administrator, or manager of *waqf* properties, *LPP*, p. 435, *PUkM*, I, p. 234, " nadziratel'."

[6] Text : *al-Mulkī*.

[7] In right margin, opposite beginning of line 11. See commentary, paragraph 2.

[8] Interpolated line : see commentary, paragraph 2.

[9] H. Busse, op. cit., p. 34.

Busse *Untersuchungen. . . .* Plate XXI, all documents of Ismā'īl I) appears to be a chancery device to prevent additions to documents by unauthorized persons. As lines 6, 7, 8, 9, and 11 in this document are written with the same spacing, and as lines 10 and 12 seem to violate the usual rhythmic interval and as *khutima bi'l-khayr* stands to the right of line 11, it seems likely that lines 10 and 12 are interpolations. They seem to be in a slightly different hand ; the document reads perfectly well if they are omitted. Furthermore, *dar 'uhde dānand* or *dārand* is a normal termination formula (see Document II—*dar 'uhde dārand* in the last line), and is usually followed immediately by the words *taḥrīran fī*. Whether this interpolation was done in the chancery or not, as an afterthought, or a later and deliberate alteration is not clear ; but at any rate, it was not a part of the original draft. The ownership of the garden is not entirely clear from this document. Another oddity in this document is the word *bīḍa*, at the end of line 12 in the interpolation which according to Fekete means " Ende, keine Bemerkung." [10]

As to the persons mentioned in this document, a Khwāja Khān Aḥmad Beg Ṣafawī is mentioned in the *Silsilat al-nasab-i Ṣafawiyye* (*SNS*).[11] At some time unspecified by this source, this man served as *mutawallī* of the mosque of Shaykh Ṣafī al-Dīn at Ardabīl. He might well have held property in Tabrīz. One of Khwāja Khān Aḥmad's two sons, Ma'ṣūm Beg Ṣafawī (see Document Three) also served as *mutawallī* of the Ardabīl shrine, then became *mīr-dīwān* to Ṭahmāsp I, and was eventually killed in 976/1567–68 while on the pilgrimage. The careers of Ma'ṣūm Beg and his father underline the existence of a second and distinct group of the Ṣafawid family known as the *Shaykhāwand*, distantly related to the ruling line of Ismā'il and his descendants (the ruling line were considered hereditary heads of the *ṭarīqe* and were addressed as *murshid-i kāmil*). The Shaykhāwand, whose lands were in the town of Ardabīl and the vicinity, particularly to the east of Ardabīl, seem to have furnished many of the personnel of the *zāwiye*. At times, however, members of the Zāhidī family, close relations of the Ṣafawids, were chosen for these offices.[12]

[10] Ludwig Fekete, review of H. Busse, op. cit., *Der Islam*, 1961, p. 486. Is *bīḍa* a Persian solecism for *bayāḍ* ?

[11] *SNS*, p. 67.

[12] Naṣr Allāh Falsafī, *Zindigānī-yi Shāh 'Abbās-i Awwal*, I, Tehran, 1332 H.S./1952, p. 182, for the Shaykhāwand. The Shaykhāwand were usually on bad terms with the ruling Ṣafawid group (see commentary, Document Three).

For the early connections of the Ṣafawids and Zāhidīs see the *firmān* of 'Abbās I, dated 1009/1599–1600 appointing Abdāl Begā Zāhidī *mutawallī* of this shrine, *SNS*, pp. 108–110 and V. Minorsky, " A Mongol decree of 720/1320 to the family of Shaykh Zāhid," *BSOAS*, 1954, pp. 515–27.

Sulaymān Mīrzā is doubtless the brother of Ismā'īl mentioned in the *Aḥsan al-Tawārīkh* and elsewhere, who accompanied the *Khāqān-i Iskandar-shān* on his flight from Ardabīl to Rasht in 900/1493–94.[13] Like Ismā'īl, Maḥmūd Mīrzā, Ḥasan Mīrzā, and Dā'ūd Mīrzā, Sulaymān Mīrzā was a son of Shaykh Ḥaydar, perhaps not by Ḥalīme Begum Āghā ('Ālamshāh Begum), but of another wife. Ḥalīme Begum Āghā was the daughter of Ūzūn Ḥasan Aq-Qoyunlu, and the sister of Sulṭān Ya'qūb.[14]

Considerable information is available about Ḥusayn Beg Lala Shāmlū, the tutor of Ismā'īl, and one of the most prominent figures of the pre-Chāldirān period of Ismā'īl's reign. Ḥusayn Beg was a leading member of the *ahl-i ikhtiṣāṣ*, the little group of *amīrs* who kept the Ṣafawid *ṭarīqe* going between the death of Shaykh Ḥaydar and the young Ismā'īl's first successful campaign (against the Shīrwānshāh in 906/1499–1500). Ḥusayn Beg had taken part in the disastrous battle of Ṭabarsārān as a troop commander under Ḥaydar, then aided Ismā'īl and his brothers to dodge Aq-Qoyunlu spies and informers in Gīlān for nearly five years. Later, he served Ismā'īl in all major campaigns, until the battle of Chāldirān, where he was one of a number of prominent Qizilbāsh casualties.

A trusted companion of Shaykh Ḥaydar and *lala* to Ismā'īl, Ḥusayn Beg, Jumlat al-Mulk Kamāl al-Dawla wa'l-Iqbāl, was holding a number of offices at the end of his life.[15] Aside from his influential post of *lala* (the Aq-Qoyunlu and Ṣafawid equivalent of *atābeg*), he was the *wakīl* (or in full, the *wakīl-i nafs-i nafīs-i humayūn*), *amīr al-umarā'*, and *amīr-dīwān*, holding some of these positions simultaneously.[16] Ḥusayn Beg was

---

[13] Ḥasan Beg Rūmlū, *Aḥsan al-Tawārīkh* (*AT*), p. 7.

[14] Iskandar Beg Munshī, *Ta'rīkh-i 'Ālam-arā-yi 'Abbāsī* (*TAA*), lithograph, Tehran 1314 H.Q./1895–96, p. 14.

[15] This title, *Jumlat al-Mulk*, was also held by Mīrzā Shāh Ḥusayn, another *wakīl* of Ismā'īl. See Qāḍī Aḥmad Qummī, *Khulāṣat al-Tawārīkh*, apud. Aubin, loc. cit., p. 72, note 2. It was also an Aq-Qoyunlu title (see Sharaf al-Dīn Bitlīsī, *Sharaf-nāme*, ed. Charmoy, II, 1, St. Petersburg 1873, pp. 501, 505), and was known under the Tīmūrids, *ibid.*, p. 517.

[16] See the interesting comments of R. M. Savory on the offices of *lala* and *atabeg* in his " Principal offices of the Safavid state during the reign of Ismā'īl, I," *BSOAS*, 1960, p. 94, note 2. Ismā'īl was only fourteen on his accession in 907. At that time Ḥusayn Beg was one of the most powerful persons in the Ṣafawid movement.

The office of *mīr dīwān* may well be the same office as that of *dīwān begī*, mentioned by Professor Minorsky in *Tadhkirat al-Mulūk*, p. 50 ff., equivalent to " chief justice ". The *Ta'rīkh-i-Ilchī-yi Niẓāmshāh* (*TIlN*), BM. Ms. Or. 153, f. 14b, specifically refers to the deposition of Ḥusayn Beg from this office in the summer of 915.

The colophon of this same MS. refers to the death of its author, Khurshāh bin Qubād al-Ḥusaynī (see Aubin, loc. cit., p. 39, note 1) as having taken place on 25 Dhu'l-Qa'da

appointed to the *wikālat* in 907/1500–01, and held that office until 914/1507–08, at least until the month of Ṣafar in that year, as this document indicates, when he was deposed in favour of a Persian, Shaykh Najm Gīlānī (*Najm-i Awwal*).[17] Apparently, he retained his posts of *amīr al-umarā'* and *mīr dīwān* (or *amīr-i dīwān*) until 915/1508–09, when he lost them, together with his *ulkā'* and his *nawkars* to Muḥammad Beg Sufrachī Ustājlū, as the *Ta'rīkh-i Ilchī-yi Niẓāmshāh* makes clear.[18] In spite of his apparent demotion, Ḥusayn Beg remained faithful to Shāh Ismā'īl, and continued to be one of his closest collaborators. Savory suggests that the reason for the deposition of Ḥusayn Beg was a change of policy on Ismā'īl's part, to favour Persians rather than the Qizilbāsh Turkoman faction. This was done to check the Turkoman power, and is associated with the coming of Shaykh Najm Gīlānī to power in 914, and was continued with the appointment of Amīr Yār Aḥmad Khūzanī Iṣfahānī (Najm-i Thānī) to the *wikālat* in the following year.[19] Aubin suggests that Ḥusayn Beg may have fallen from esteem because Amīr Najm Gīlānī Zargar had some old scores to settle with him.[20] He was made *ḥākim* of Harāt in 918/1511–12, took part in the Özbeg wars, and was a principal commander at Chāldirān, where he was killed in a desperate charge against the Ottoman artillery.

The final years of Ḥusayn Beg's life, his dismissal and replacement, point up one of the great political problems of the Ṣafawids; a conflict of interests between Qizilbāsh Turkomans and Persians. The new ruling dynasty failed to harness the military energies of the Qizilbāsh, and their enthusiasm, even fanaticism, for the Ṣafawid *ṭarīqe*, or to reconcile the Qizilbāsh with the conservatism of the Persian official and administrative personnel now being recruited to fill posts in the Ṣafawid bureaucracy. No

---

972/1563–64 in the town of Gulkundeh (Golconda), *min a'māl-i Tilang* (Tilingana) in the Deccan of South India. According to I. P. Petrushevskii, *Ocherki po istorii . . .*, pp. 24–5, Khurshāh emigrated from 'Irāq-i 'Ajam to India, where he took service with Sultan Burhān Niẓāmshāh of Ahmadnagar (ruled 1508–53). Niẓāmshāh then sent him back to Persia as his ambassador, where he arrived in 1546. Although the work has no pronounced anti-Ṣafawid tone, the author was doubtless at first an anti-Ṣafawid political refugee, one of many intellectuals, Sunni *'ulamā'*, and officials who fled Persia after the break-up of the Aq-Qoyunlu and Tīmūrid states and the rise of the Ṣafawids, to take up employment at the small Muslim courts near Ḥaydarābād. C. Schefer, *Chrestomathie persane*, II, 55–104, contains extracts from the *Ta'rīkh-i Ilchī-yi Niẓāmshāh*.

[17] *AT*, p. 110, J. Aubin, loc. cit., p. 62, gives full details from other sources.

[18] *TIIN*, BM. Ms. Or. 153, f. 14b.

[19] R. M. Savory, loc. cit., p. 95.

[20] Aubin, loc. cit., p. 67.

durable compromise was ever achieved between the interests of these two factions: the clash between the rival groups appeared as soon as Ismāʿīl had created a state. It was to play a destructive role in subsequent Ṣafawid history.

Document II—[plate LIV]

Seal:

. . . عرشی . . .

. . . اسماعیل بهادر الحسینی . . .

٩٠-

Text:

١ هو الله سبحانه

٢ یا علی

فرمان همیون شرف نفاذ یافت بوقوف غلام شاهٔ عالم نجم ثانی آنکه

٤ بنا بر وفور اعتناء و اهتمام در بارهٔ افادت بناهی زبدهٔ العلماء و المتبحّرین
مولانا کمال الدین حسین أردبیلی مقرر شد که موضع کزج

٥ من أعمال خلخال که از رقبات و مسلمیات زاویه منوره و مقدسه صفویه علیه
عالیه است و بمبلغ جهل و بنجهزار دینار تبریزی نقد و جنس . . .[1]

٦ داخل جمع است در وجه سیورغال آبدی و انعام سرمدی افادت بناه مشار الیه
ارزانی داشته مقرر شناسند و مبلغ شش هزار دینار

٧ که نموده برینوجه آنجانب در وجه قطع شرعی[2] مومی الیه مقرر دانسته و تغییر
و تبدیل بقواعد آن راه ندهند و قریه اومانق

٨ و سلطاناباد من أعمال أردبیل بدستور سابق و قانون استمرار بسیورغال هود بری
مشار الیه مقرر دانسته تعرض نرساند و بعلت اخراجات

٩ حکمی و غیر حکمی بر آن حوالهٔ نشمارند و تعرض نرسانند متولیان و ضابطان
سرکار زاویه منوره مذکوره برینموجب

١٠ مقرر دانسته و در استمرار و استقرار آن کوشیده و از مخالفت محذر و مجتنب
باشند و همه ساله درین أبواب برونجه و نشان عالی طلب ندارند برینجمله روند
تحریرا فی عاشر شهر رجب المرجب[3] سنهٔ ٩١٥

---

[1] 2–3 words unreadable [2] شرعیه [3] الاصب

Back :

حصه کما ما . . .

. . . . . . شد   وقفت علی الله   . . . . . . الله   توکلت علی الله

قلمی شد

ملاحظه شد

Document II—translation

1 He is God, extol Him !

2 O 'Alī !

3 A royal decree has had the honour of despatch, with the cognizance of Najm-i Thānī, servitor of the Shāh of the World, that

4 whereas, because of the abundance of [our] attention and diligence in respect of the Refuge of Benefit (*ifādat-panāh*), Cream of the Learned and Erudite, Mawlānā Kamāl al-Dīn Ḥusayn Ardabīlī, it has been fixed that the locality of Kazaj,

5 one of the tax districts (*a'māl*) [1] of Khalkhāl, and one of the villages (*raqabāt*) [2] and exempted properties (*musallamiyāt*) [3] of the sublime and supreme, holy and radiant Ṣafawid *zāwiye*, and which is assessed in the tax register (*dākhil-i jam'*)[4] at the sum of 45,000 Tabrīzī *dīnārs* in cash and kind . . . (2–3 unreadable words in fold) . . .

6 has been bestowed by us upon the aforementioned Asylum of Benefit as an eternal *soyūrghāl* and permanent favour, and should be deemed established. The sum of six thousand *dīnārs*

7 which has been assigned to that excellent person (*ānjānib*) in this way, should be considered fixed as the legal settlement (*qat'-i shar'ī* : fief, appanage, assigned land ?) of the aforementioned person. The bases (*qawā'id*) of it should not be exposed to change or alteration. [Furthermore], the villages of Umāniq (Awmāniq ?)

[1] *a'māl*—perhaps better translated here as " tax districts ", rather than " cantons or dependencies ". Also may mean " reports of tax districts and their revenue accounts ", *LPP*, p. 423. Perhaps originally meant areas subject to an *'āmil*, pl. *'ummāl*, " financial agents."

[2] *raqabe*, pl. *raqabāt*—" a group of villages in a *bulūk* or district," used as in this case to mean villages forming part of *waqf* or endowment property. *LPP*, pp. 437–8.

[3] *musallamiyāt*—" tax-exempt properties." See also Busse, op. cit., pp. 97 ff.

[4] *dākhil-i jam'*—" tax register," see Roemer in *BIFAO*, loc. cit., p. 284, line 7.

8 and Sulṭānābād, among the tax districts of Ardabīl, have been fixed by former precedent (*dastūr*—revenue assessment ?) [5] and continuing statute (*qānūn*) as the inalienable (*hūdbarī*) [6] *soyūrghāl* of the above-mentioned person and should not be molested. For purposes of taxes,
9 fixed by decree or otherwise, drafts (*ḥawāle*) [7] should not be drawn on this [property]. It should not be interfered with. Administrators (*mutawalliyān*) [8] and tax-receivers (*ḍābiṭān*) [9] of the radiant *zāwiye* mentioned above should consider the manner as settled in this wise.
10 They should endeavour to prolong and maintain it ; they should shun and avoid resisting it. No new *parvanche* [10] or exalted *nishān* [11] should be sought each year. Let this procedure be followed. Written on the tenth of the month of Rajab al-Murajjab 915/ [12] 24 October 1509

Document II—commentary

Like the preceding document, this *soyūrghāl* of Ismāʿīl I has been reduced from its original format, having been torn off irregularly at the top right corner. Hence its present dimensions are slightly less than 19 cm. in width at the top. At the time it was written it was doubtless slightly longer than the present 29 cm. There was certainly more space at the right of the text ; an endorsement on the back ending in the word *shud* has been torn in two. Like the first document, the formulae *Huwa Allāh subḥānahu* and *Yā ʿAlī* appear at the top right above the text in gold ink. The introductory phrase *firmān-i humayūn sharaf-i nafādh yāft* is also in gold, as well as the words *bi-wuqūf* and *ānkih* after the phrase *ghulām-i shāh-i ʿālam Najm-i Thānī.*

---

[5] *dastūr*—aside from its normal meaning of " precedent, plan, arrangement, scheme ", this word may mean " revenue assessment ", see *LPP*, p. 426.

[6] *hūdbarī*—see commentary, paragraph four.

[7] *ḥawāle*—" revenue drafts," see *Tadhkirat al-Mulūk*, p. 84, *PUkM*, I, p. 239.

[8] *mutawallī*—administrator of a *waqf*. See commentary, Document III, note 3, for the functions of the *mutawallī* of the Ardabīl shrine. Busse, op. cit., pp. 125 ff. contains much information about the appointment and functions of the *mutawallīs* of the shrine of *Sittī Fāṭima* at Qumm.

[9] *ḍābiṭ*, pl. *ḍābiṭān*—" tax receiver or collector, bailiff," *LPP*, p. 443.

[10] *parvanche*—in this context, synonymous with " decree ". Earlier, in the Il-Khānid period, the word probably meant " notification " or " money draft ". See Busse, op. cit., p. 39, note 3, and p. 67, note 1.

[11] *nishān*—a type of document, similar to a *firmān*. See Busse, op. cit., p. 67.

[12] See commentary, last paragraph.

Najm-i Thānī was the *wakīl* Yār Aḥmad Khūzanī Iṣfahānī, appointed by Ismā'īl to succeed Amīr Najm al-Dīn Mas'ūd Gīlānī Zargar (Najm-i-Awwal), who in his turn was the successor to Ḥusayn Beg Lala. Aubin describes Najm-i Thānī as an " homme sanguinaire et fastueux . . . plus célèbre par son luxe, sa dûreté, ses cruautés en Transoxiane, que par son justice envers grands et humbles "[13] Ḥasan Rūmlū calls Najm-i Thānī a *rū-siyāh-i nā-ḥaqq shinās* for refusing to spare the lives of some *sayyids* at the siege of Qarshī ;[14] in his remarks Rūmlū accurately reflects the views of Qizilbāsh Turkomans about Persian bureaucrats. When Najm-i Thānī was killed at the battle of Ghujduwān in Ramaḍān 918/November 1512, it was because so many of the Qizilbāsh leaders and their men had deserted him, permitting the Özbegs to defeat his small force.[15]

Since this *soyūrghāl* is dated Rajab 915, it was issued within a few months after the unattractive Najm-i Thānī had assumed office, near the beginning of the year 915, according to Khurshāh b. Qubād.[16] The grantee of the *soyūrghāl*, Mawlānā Kamāl al-Dīn Ḥusayn Ardabīlī, also described as " Zubdat al-'Ulamā wa'l-Mutabaḥḥirīn," is mentioned in the *Tuḥfat-i-Sāmī* of Sām Mīrzā, under the name " Mawlānā Ḥusayn Ardabīlī." This Shī'ī *'ālim* died in 950/1542–43 at about the age of seventy. He was a relative of Shaykh Ḥaydar Ṣafawī, and as a young man, had been in the latter's service. Ḥaydar encouraged him to go to Khurāsān to study. After spending some years there, he returned to Ardabīl, where he became a *khādim* of the *zāwiye*, " where he spent his auspicious life and his hours in the diffusion of learning." He sometimes wrote poetry, and Sām Mīrzā quotes one of his *rubā'īs*, and describes him as a " complete scholar and a witty man." [17] The lands allotted to Mawlānā Kamāl al-Dīn Ardabīlī were in two different areas, some at Kazaj in Khalkhāl (which seems to have been Ardabīlī's *soyūrghāl* prior to the date of this document), and the others at a place called Sulṭānābād, probably the village of that name a few kilometers south of the Ardabīl-Astarā road.[18] It is clear from

---

[13] Jean Aubin, loc. cit., p. 69. In BM. Ms. Or. 153, f. 14b, one of his *nisbas* is given as *Qūzānī*.

[14] *AT*, p. 132.

[15] *AT*, p. 133.

[16] *TIlN*, p. 14b.

[17] See *Tuḥfat-i Sāmī*, BM. Ms. Or. Add. 24362, f. 17a and BM. Ms. Add. 7670, f. 47a, where accounts of Mawlānā Ḥusayn Ardabīlī, with slight textual variations, are given. This notice is found in the printed edition of the *Tuḥfat-i Sāmī*, ed. Waḥīd Dastgirdī, Tehran 1314 H.S. on p. 49. Sām Mīrzā was a brother of Shāh Ṭahmāsp. This same notice on Ardabīlī is also contained in Amīn Aḥmad Rāzī, *Haft Iqlīm*, BM. Ms. Or. 203, f. 384a.

[18] Kazaj in Khalkhāl is 11·5 km. N.E. of Hishajīn and about 30 km. S.W. of Herōābād (formerly called Khalkhāl), the *markaz* of the *shahristān* of the same name, situated on the

the back of Document VII, also concerned with this *soyūrghāl*, that two groups of this man's descendants were living in the time of 'Abbās I, and as some of them are entitled *khādim-bāshī*, that their connection with the shrine was maintained, and that they had inherited their ancestor's office and title. If the original grantee, Mawlānā Kamāl al-Dīn was a relation of Shaykh Ḥaydar, he doubtless belonged to, or had close ties with, the non-ruling Ṣafawid clan of the Shaykhāwand, and if a *khādim*, belonged to the second or third rank of dignitaries attached to the shrine.[19]

Dr. Busse claims that the type of document with the introduction *firmān-i humayūn sharaf-i nafādh yāft* was developed under Shāh Ṭahmāsp. also states that this formula is normally written in red ink. From the evidence of the present document, this claim does not seem to be justified.[20]

The word *hūdbarī*, occurring in the text in line 8, meaning " permanent, inalienable, not to be renewed," also occurs in Niẓām al-Dīn Shāmī's *Ẓafar-nāme*, II, ed. F. Tauer, Prague 1956, p. 199, see Index III, p. 306. The scribe, in the last line, probably meant to write *Rajab al-Murajjab*, but was thinking of Rajab al-Aṣamm, and so finished by writing " Rajab al-Aṣabb'."

On the back of this document, as on the backs of some of the others can be seen pious " mottoes " and phrases, generally of a religious turn (or Koranic quotations) in Arabic. These are usually written under seals. These phrases are the " signs-manual " (*'alāma*) of the various officials who dealt with the document in its passage from office to office. Rulers also used the *'alāma*, in lieu of a signature. The employment of the *'alāma* on chancery documents is an old Islamic practice, see S. M. Stern, *Fāṭimid Decrees*, London 1964, p. 124.

---

other side of the Bozgush range from Ardabīl : see *Farhang-i Jughrāfiyā-yi Irān*, IV, p. 417. When this source was compiled, in 1330 H.S./1950, Kazaj had 946 inhabitants both Shī'īs and Sunnīs, Turks and Kurds. Kazaj is described as being in the malarial *garmsīr*. As for Sulṭānābād, it is probably the place described in the same *Geographical Dictionary* as being 10 km. east of Ardabīl, and 8 km. south of the Ardabīl–Astarā road, in the " *dihistān* of Kalkhūrān " (p. 274). On level land, it had in 1950 a population of 771 people, who were Shī'ī Turks.

[19] See Document VII, back. In the *firmān* appointing a member of the Zāhidī family to the post of *mutawallī* at Ardabīl, *SNS*, p. 109, the ranks of the dignitaries of the *zāwīye* are given in hierarchical order : " (1) *mutawallī* ; (2) great *sayyids* ; (3) *khuddām-i kirām* ; (4) learned *'ulamā* ; (5) the remainder of the servants lower staff, and workmen." The precise rank of the *nāẓir* is not made clear.

[20] H. Busse, op. cit., p. 31–2 ; *EI*², fasc. 27, Vol. II, pp. 308–13, in section on Persian documents in article on " Diplomatic ", pp. 301–16.

Document III—[plate LV]

Seal :

بندهٔ شاهٔ ولایت طهماسب ۹۵۰
اللهم صلی علی محمد المصطفی علی المرتضی حسن الرضا حسین الشهید
زین العابدین محمد الباقر جعفر الصادق موسی الکاظم علی بن موسی الرضا
محمد التقی علی النقی حسن العسکری محمد المهدی

Text :

١ الملك لله
٢ صفویه
٣ فرمان همیون شد آنکه رعایا و مزارعان قریه خرانق بموجبی که جلال الدین معصوم بیك صفوی متولی
٤ آستانه مقدسه قرار حقابه ایشان با رعایا موضع سلطاناباد داده شرطنامجه در آن باب
٥ نوشته عمل نموده اصلا ستم بکسی ننمایند و از مخالفت اندیشه نموده از قاعده مقرره تجاوز نکنند
٦ درین باب قدغن دانسته تقصیر ننمایند و در عهده دارند تحریرا فی
٧ شهر ذی قعده ٩٥٢

Back :

بیضه

ملاحظه شد

Document III—translation

1 Sovereignty belongs to God !
2 Ṣafawiyye
3 A royal command has been issued : that, the peasants and crop-sharing cultivators (*muzāra'ān*)[1] of the village of Kh.rān.q should

[1] For the crop-sharing or *muzāra'e* system, see A. K. S. Lambton, *LPP*, pp. 306 ff., p. 127 and elsewhere ; *TM*, p. 22.

carry out [the conditions] which Jalāl al-Dīn Ma'ṣūm Beg Ṣafawī, the *mutawallī* of the Holy Sanctuary (*Āstāne-yi muqaddase*) had fixed concerning their water rights (*ḥaqqābe*) [2]

4 with the peasants of the locality of Sulṭānābād, and in regard to which a written agreement (*sharṭnāmche*) has been drawn up. They should not oppress

5 any person whatsoever, nor undertake any resistance [to it]. They should not depart from the established regulation.

6 In this matter, any shortcoming on their part is forbidden. They should consider it their responsibility. Written in

7 the month of Dhī('l)-Qa'da, 952/ 4 Jan—2 Feb 1546

Document III—commentary

This short *firmān* of Shāh Ṭahmāsp I, regulating a dispute between two villages over water rights, presents a number of interesting features. As usual, the phrases *al-mulk li'llāh* and *firmān-i humayūn shud* are written in gold ink, also the word *Ṣafawiyye* in the upper right margin. Since the document concerns a member of the Ṣafawid family, Jalāl al-Dīn Ma'ṣūm Beg Ṣafawī, or lands or estates belonging to the Ṣafawid family(?), it can be assumed that the document is a special type of inter-Ṣafawid edict. As far as the writer knows, no other examples of documents marked *Ṣafawiyye* in this same way have been published.

Ma'ṣūm Beg Ṣafawī was a well-known public figure during the reign of Ṭahmāsp I. A son of the Khwāja Khān Aḥmad Beg Ṣafawī mentioned in the *Silsilat al-Nasab-i Ṣafawiyye* (and possibly in the first document), Ma'ṣūm Beg was the grandson of Khwāja Muḥammad, one of the two sons of Shaykh Junayd.[3] Khwāja Muḥammad was the half-brother of Shaykh Ḥaydar, being a son of a Circassian slave woman, whereas Ḥaydar was Junayd's son by Khadīja Begum, the sister of Ūzūn Ḥasan Aq-Qoyunlu.[4] From this document, it is evident that Ma'ṣūm Beg was already serving as *mutawallī* of the Ṣafawid *zāwiye* in 962/1543–45 ; by 964, he had become

---

[2] *ḥaqqābe*—water rights, or share in the water from a *qanāt* or stream. Papazian, *PUkM*, I, p. 239, *LPP*, p. 429.

[3] *SNS*, p. 67. A homonymous Ma'ṣūm Begā (Gīlākī form—see V. Minorsky, *Tadhkirat al-Mulūk*, p. 125) Ṣafawī, a *mutawallī*, mentioned by Zāhidī on p. 65, may be an error of identification. The printed edition of this work (Irānshahr, Berlin, 1343 H.S./1924) contains a great number of typographical errors. A new edition of it with clear genealogical charts would be very useful.

[4] *TAA*, p. 13.

amīr-i dīwān.[5] In 959, he had taken part in a campaign against Arjīsh in Eastern Anatolia; in 967/1559–60 he became *wakīl* of Shāh Ṭahmāsp. Later, he was appointed *lala* to Ṭahmāsp's eldest son, Ḥaydar Mīrzā. Iskandar Munshī gives considerable information about Ma'ṣūm Beg, among other things that Ṭahmāsp called him " nephew " (*'amū oghlī*), and that Ma'ṣūm Beg left on the pilgrimage with one of his sons, Khān Mīrzā, after resigning his offices in 967/1567–68 only to be assassinated by Turks

---

[5] *AT*, p. 315, mentions Ma'ṣūm Beg as being *mutawallī* at Ardabīl in 953 A.H. when he was sent to Shirwān by Ṭahmāsp. Ma'ṣūm Beg is first mentioned in Bitlīsī's *Sharaf-nāme* under the events of 964/1556–67, as *amīr-i dīwān*. See *Sharaf-nāme* ed. Velyaminov-Zernov, Saint Petersburg 1862, II, 209 (Persian text). *TIlN*, BM. Ms. Or. Add. 23513, f. 481b gives an account of his Gīlān and Māzāndarān campaigns.

Ma'ṣūm Beg Ṣafawī was also concerned in the affair of Alqās Mīrzā, a son of Ṭahmāsp who revolted against his father. In his unpublished article, " Six *fatḥnāmās* of the reign of Shāh Ṭaḥmāsp I Ṣafawī," Mr. J. R. Walsh of Edinburgh University, has analysed the victory proclamations issued by Ṭahmāsp during his campaigns against his son, and included other valuable information about the middle years of Ṭahmāsp's reign, from Rūḥ Allāh Munshī's *Sharaf-nāme*, erroneously catalogued in the Lindesiana Collection of the John Rylands Library, Manchester, as the *Inshā-yi Munshī-yi Shāh 'Abbās* (see item 494 p. 156, of the Lindesiana Catalogue). Rūḥ Allāh Munshī, son of Mīrzā Ashraf and grandson of the famous Qāḍī-yi Jihān, died between 985 and 995 A.H., and had served for a long time as secretary to Ibrāhīm Khān Dhu'l-Qadar, governor of Shīrāz. The pagination of this MS. is very confused; the script is a very difficult *shikaste-amīz*. An edition of this important source would be very useful.

A *firmān* of 'Abbās I dated 1009/1599–1600 appointing Abdāl Begā Zāhidī as *mutawallī* of the Ardabīl tekke (*SNS*, pp. 108–110) gives a great deal of information about the functions of the *mutawallī* of this establishment. These functions had doubtless been much the same in the days of Ma'ṣūm Beg, fifty years before. As chief administrator, the *mutawallī* had the final word in all translations made by the *zāwiye*. All of its personnel (with the exception of the *nāẓir* ?)—*mustawfīs*, *mushrifs*, *mudarrises*, *sayyids*, and the various ranks of *khādim* were under his control, and were to recognize him as " independent *mutawallī* ". All financial paper issued by the *zāwiye* was to be authenticated by his seal; all wages, stipends, and salaries were to be paid out under his supervision. The entries in ledgers (*rūznāmejāt*) could only be entered in the registers (*dafātir*) when they had been read and sealed by him. The *mutawallī* was to settle disputes arising among the peasants of the *zāwiye's* lands (as in this document), but only after an inquiry according to the *sharī'a* in the presence of *'ulamā'*. The governor (*ḥākim*) of Ardabīl was not to interfere in the affairs of the *zāwīye*, nor was it or its properties to be subject to taxation or duties. The *mutawallī* was to exercise general supervision over the catering at the shrine, and to inspect it from time to time. In matters of the tax rolls (*ṭūmār*), the *mutawallī* was to follow instructions from the *dīwān*. He was not to deviate in any way from the regulations and instructions of the founders (*wāqifīn*). In important matters, he was to consult with the *nāẓir*, and in general, show constant evidence of his administrative efficiency.

See also I. P. Petrushevskii " Vakfn'ie imeniya Ardebilskogo mazara v XVII v.," in *Trud'i Instituta Istorii im.A. Bakhikhanova AN Azerb. SSR, I*, Baku, 1947.

" disguised as desert Arabs." [6] Sharaf al-Dīn Bitlīsī gives further details of his assassination, suggesting that Ma'ṣūm Beg was dissatisfied at Ṭahmāsp's treatment of him after he had conquered Gīlān and Khurāsān on his master's behalf in 975/1566–67, and was using his pilgrimage as a pretext to assemble pro-Ṣafawid *ṣūfīs* on Ottoman territory, to create trouble there or in Persia. Being suspicious, Sulṭān Salīm II ordered the Governor of Damascus, Darwīsh Pāshā, to liquidate Ma'ṣūm Beg, which Darvīsh Pāshā achieved by an ambush somewhere on the road between Medina and Mecca.[7]

The close connection of Ma'ṣūm Beg with the Shaykhāwand clan of Ṣafawids is well known. Iskandar Munshī records that 'Isā Khān Ṣafawī b. Sayyid Beg Ṣafawī, a son of Ma'ṣūm Beg, was a leader of the Shaykhāwand at the time of 'Abbās I, and classifies the Shaykhāwand as " first among the Qizilbāsh tribes." [8] Elsewhere, Iskandar Munshī notes that Ṣadr al-Dīn Khān Ṣafawī, another son of Ma'ṣūm Beg, was in the service of Sulṭān Ḥusayn Mīrzā (as *lala* ?) ; others of the Shaykhāwand were governors of provinces, *qūrchībāshīs*, *muhrdārs*, etc.[9] Owing to their relationship to the ruling line, they were continually being used as pawns by political forces, and were a centre of intrigue, particularly in succession disputes, and often participated in revolts and conspiracies. Shāh 'Abbās I's relations with the Shaykhāwand were hostile ; Ṣadr al-Dīn Khān had been concerned in the assassination of 'Abbāṣ' mother.[10]

A seal of Ma'ṣūm Beg Safavi can be seen on the back of Document IV, just above the *'alāma: iṭṭala'tu 'ala'llāh*, associated with the counterseal of the *wakīl*.

The village of Sulṭānābād is doubtless the same place as is mentioned in the previous document, as being part of the *soyūrghāl* of Kamāl al-Dīn Ḥusayn Ardabīlī. The village of Kh.rān.q. must have adjoined Sulṭānābād, or been upstream or downstream from it, or fed from the same *qanāt*. The name does not appear in the *Geographical Dictionary*, Azerbayjan, IV.

---

[6] *TAA*, p. 118. After Ma'ṣūm's assassination, his deputy Sirāj al-Dīn 'Alī Qummī assumed his functions. The " independent wazīrship " remained vacant until the appointment of Mīr Sayyid Ḥusayn Farahānī and Khwāja Jamāl al-Dīn 'Alī Tabrīzī as joint *wazīrs*. For further details, see R. M. Savory, " The principal offices of the Safavid state during the reign of Shāh Ṭahmāsp I (930–84/1525–76), *BSOAS*, 1961, pp. 65–85.

[7] Sharaf al-Dīn Bitlīsī, *Sharaf-nāme*, events of 976. See Persian text, II, p. 239.

[8] *TAA*, p. 761.

[9] *TAA*, p. 106.

[10] Naṣr Allāh Falsafī, op. cit., p. 182 ; *TM*, p. 16, note 3.

Document IV—[plates LVI and LX]

Seal :

بندهٔ شاهٔ ولایت طهماسب

اللهم صلی علی محمد المصطفی علی المرتضی حسن الرضا حسین الشهید
زین العابدین محمد الباقر جعفر الصادق موسی الکاظم علی بن موسی الرضا
محمد التقی علی النقی حسن العسکری محمد المهدی

Text :

١ الملك لله

٢ فرمان همیون شد آنکه جون حسب الحکم جهانمطاع همیون مزرعه قزلاقوج ودوزده رود واقعه در کریوه سراب از أعمال دار الارشاد

٣ أرده بیل بر افادت بناه خلیفه درویش محمد معاف ومسلم است که مستوفیان عظام بعد از دایریت بمقدار شش خروار [غله] بوزن تبریز بسیورغال وانعام أبدی

٤ او اعتبار نمایند ودر ینولا افادت دستکاه مشار الیه بعز عتبه بوسی مشرف شده معروض داشت که مزرعه مزبور را بحال عمارت در آورده واستدعاء امضاء

٥ حکم مطاع نمود بنا بر وفور عنایت بیدریغ شاهانه در بارهٔ آن افادت بناه مزرعه مزبوره را بهمانقاعده وبهمانمقدار بسیورغال أبدی او ارزانی داشتیم مستوفیان

٦ رقم این عطیه را در دفاتر خلود مثبت ومرقوم کردانیده از شایه تغییر وتبدیل مصون ومحروس دانند عمال ومتصدیان جهات دار الارشاد مذکوره

٧ والکاء سراب وتراکمه تبه حسب المسطور مقرر دانسته من کل الوجوه قلم وقدم کوتاه وکشیده دارند وبهیج وجه من الوجوه حوالتی ومطالبتی

٨ نکنند بعلت اخراجات وعوارضات بهر اسم ورسم که باشد طلبی وتوقعی نموده رعایت ومراقبت واجب ولازم دانند واز فرموده تخلف وتمرد نورزند

٩ از جوانب برینجمله روند وهر ساله حکم وبروانجه مجدد طلب ندارند تحریرا فی

١٠ شهر ربیع الثانی سنة تسع وخمسین و تسعمایه

Back :

فوضت أمرى الى الله   بندۀ در کاه شاهی محمد   معصوم الصفوی غلام شاه
نوشته شد   توکلت على الله . . . .   اطلعت على الله . . .
توکلت على الله
نوشته شد

Document IV—translation

1 Sovereignty belongs to God !

2 A royal command has been issued : whereas, according to the royal decree to which the entire world is obedient, the *mazra'e* [1] of Qizil Aqūj and Dūzdeh Rūd, situated in the valley (*gerīwe*) of Sarāb, one of the tax districts (*a'māl*) of the

3 *Dār al-Irshād* of Ardehbīl (sic), is granted and rendered exempt from taxation on behalf of the Refuge of Benefit, Khalīfe Darwīsh Muḥammad.[2] [Let] the great *mustawfīs*,[3]

4 after . . . (*dā'iriyat*) recognize the quantity of six *kharwārs* [of grain],[4] Tabrīz weight, as his eternal *soyūrghāl* and favour. At this time, the aforesaid Refuge of Benefit (*ifādat-dastgāh*) who has been honoured with the privilege of kissing the Threshold (*'ataba*), has petitioned that the aforementioned *mazra'e*, which he has

5 brought into a flourishing condition [should be granted to him], and has requested the signature of a [confirmatory] order requiring obedience [in this sense]. Because of the fullness of our ungrudging royal favour, we have bestowed the aforementioned *mazra'e* on the Refuge of Benefit previously mentioned, as an everlasting favour in the same manner and by the same rule. The *mustawfīs*

---

[1] *mazra'e*—this vague term may mean " hamlet, arable or grain-raising land, a farm ", or a " small village or settlement attached to a larger one ". See *LPP*, p. 4, note 2.

[2] *khalīfe*—see *Tadhkirat al-Mulūk*, pp. 125–6 for the office of *khalīfat al-khulafā'* and the *khalīfes* subordinate to him. According to Minorsky, this is a survival of the original Ṣafawid *ṣūfī* organization, later incorporated into the state.

[3] *mustawfī*—" revenue accountant, chief revenue office of a district " ; *mustawfīyān-i 'iẓām* might be translated as " chief intendants ", or high treasury officials. See *TM*, pp. 122–5.

[4] The word *ghalle* in this document has been written in by another hand. The word must mean grain here, although it is synonymous with *bahrche* under certain circumstances (see *PUkM*, I, p. 228). A *kharwār* literally " ass-load ", amounts to 100 Tabrizi *manns*, about 655 lb. See also *LPP*, p. 407.

6 should write and deposit a copy of this gift in the eternal registers, to protect and preserve it from the blemish of change and alteration. *'Āmils* and *mutaṣaddīs* of the quarters (*jihāt*) of the above-mentioned *Dār al-Irshād*

7 and the *ulkā'*[*s*] [5] of Sarāb and Tarākime Tappe should consider the matter settled, according to what has been written [here]. Under all circumstances, they should keep their feet and pens away, and under no conditions should they draw drafts (*ḥawālatī*) or make demands (*muṭālabatī*) [6] nor should they, for any reason whatsoever

8 seek or demand extraordinary taxes (*ikhrājāt*) [7] or tolls (*'awāriḍāt*).[8] They should consider observance and attention [to these stipulations] as necessary and obligatory.

9 They should not disobey nor resist what has been decreed; they should proceed according to their instructions (?). They should not seek a renewed *parvānche* or decree (*ḥukm*) in each year. Written in

10 the month of Rabī' II, 959/27 March—24 April 1552

Document IV—commentary

This well-preserved *soyūrghāl* of Shāh Ṭahmāsp I has the normal introductory phrase and the words *shahāne* and *humayūn* in gold ink; the seal is a well-known one of this ruler (see introduction, p. 173 above).

The farms or hamlets (*mazra'e*) of Qizil Aqūj and Dūzdeh Rūd situated in the *gerīwe* of Sarāb (*gerīwe* meaning " broad valley " or " wide valley between two mountain ranges ") are not listed under these names in the Azerbayjan volume of the *Farhang-i Jughrāfiyā*, nor could they be found on the map of Ardabīl, Khiyāw (Meshgīn Shahr), Sarāb, Miyāne, and Heroābād at the end of this volume (Map II).[9] These hamlets are

---

[5] *ulkā'*—(Turkish *ölgä*, or *ulke*—see Iz and Hony, *Turkish-English Dictionary*, p. 362)—a region or district, often held by a clan or other tribal group. See *TM*, p. 27. Also a district assigned to individual *amīrs*, as in the case of Ḥusayn Beg Lala, see Document I, commentary, *PUkM*, I, p. 235.

[6] *muṭālabatī*—" extraordinary demands," " exigences," see Roemer, *BIFAO*, loc. cit., p. 286, line 15.

[7] *ikhrājāt*—" extraordinary taxes," *LPP*, p. 429, *PUkM*, I, p. 231.

[8] *'awāriḍāt*—" dues or tolls, fees," *LPP*, p. 423, Petrushevskii, *Ocherki . . .*, pp. 278–9, *PUkM*, I, p. 223.

[9] At first sight this place name looks like *Qarlāqūch* or *Qara Lāqūj*. Although this reading is possible, by the addition of a dot to the *ra'*, it can be made into *Qizil Aqūch* or *Aqūj*, Azerī Turkish for the more standard *aghāj*. This seems likely, considering the Azerbayjānī Turkish fondness for place names incorporating the name of an object and its

either too small to be marked on the map, have disappeared, or been renamed. Sarāb is a large place, and was formerly called Sarāv or Sarāt. It lies on the main road between Tabrīz and Ardabīl. The valley of Sarāb is limited on the north side by the Sablān or Sawalān Kūh, on the south by the Bozgush Range.[10] Nor is there any mention in this source of Tarākime Tappe, which appears in line seven of the *soyūrghāl*.[11]

The name of Khalīfe Darwīsh Muḥammad I have not found elsewhere. A minor landowner of the district, or head of a group of *ṣūfīs*, this man received a tax exemption (*mu'āf wa-musallam ast*) for his lands, and beyond that, a *soyūrghāl* of six *kharwārs* of grain. Then, having brought these uncultivated lands under cultivation, the Khalīfe was rewarded by the state when they were granted to him as permanent *soyūrghāl*. If this interpretation of Document IV is correct, then this may be an instance of the unconditional grant of uncultivated crown land by the ruler to an occupier who wanted to cultivate it, as described by Professor Lambton, following Chardin.[12] It was normal Ṣafawid practice to grant such lands to those who had, or planned to improve them.

A seal of Ma'ṣūm Beg Ṣafawī can be seen at the top left of the back of this *soyūrghāl*. It is very much like the seal on the back of H. Busse's Urkunde 7, Plate XXV.

---

colour. The Azerbayjan volume of the *Geographical Dictionary* referred to above includes no less than eleven places called *Qara Aghāj*, thirteen called *Qara Bulāgh*, twenty-four called *Āgh(Āq)-Bulāgh*, etc. There is another and more famous Qizil Aghāj at the mouth of the Kūr (Kura) River. See also V. Monteil, " Sur le Dialecte turc de'l Azerbaydjan Iranien," *Journal asiatique*, 1956, pp. 1–77.

Among other odd spellings, the orthography of *Ardabīl* as *Ardehbīl* was common at this time. In a manuscript of Tawakkulī b. Ismā'īl's (Ibn Bazzāz) *Ṣafwat al-Ṣafā'* in the British Museum (MS. Or. Add. 11745), a magnificent piece of calligraphy by Shāh Muḥammad Kātib with gold and blue headings, written in the days of Ṭahmāsp I, this same spelling, " Ardehbīl " can be seen on f. 388a (p. 776) and elsewhere.

[10] For Sarāb, see *Farhang* . . . , IV, pp. 263–4.

[11] I. P. Petrushevskii, *Ocherki* . . . , pp. 127–34 gives a list of the 17th century *ulkā's* of Azerbayjan, in which neither Tarākime Tappeh nor Sarāb figure. These are : Urumiya, Marāghe, Sawūjbulāgh, Khōy and Salmās, Marand, Makū and Chorṣ, Qaradāgh or Qarājadāgh, Ardabīl, Miyāne, Ṭālish, Nakhjīwān, Arasbār, Qāpān, and Bargushāṭ. Another list of provinces and districts can be seen in *TM*, pp. 101–102.

The recent book of Sarhang Bāyburdī (Bāyburtlū), *Ta'rīkh-i Arasbārān*, Tehran 1342/1962 includes much information about Arasbār and the Bāyburdī clan (see also *TM*, p. 16), who lived in the Ahar district N.E. of Tabrīz, and a number of *firmāns* and *soyūrghāls* from the author's family archives ; the Bāyburdī were an important clan in early Ṣafawid times.

[12] A. K. S. Lambton, *LPP*, pp. 118–19.

Document V—[plate LVII]

Seal :

الله

محمد علی

غلام شاه سلطان محمد بن طهماسب

قدم عالم البیّن بالله رب العالمین و مولای المؤ منینم

علی ابن أبی طالب له وابنائه بجان ودل غلام کمترینم

Text :

١ الملك لله

٢ فرمان همیون شد آنکه جون بهرجه موضع کزج خلخال بموجب نشان علیحده که
در بارس ییل عزّ صدور یافته بسیورغال أبدی

٣ وانعام سرمدی شرافت بناه افادت دستکاه میر شریف خادم باشی آستانه منوره
مقدسه مقررست وتغییری در آن نشده

٤ بنا برین کدخد ایان ورعایا ومزارعان موضع مذکور سال بسال بهرجه مقرری
خود را بمشار الیه داده بقدر موقوف

٥ ندارند درین باب بهیج وجه از فرموده در نکذرند واز مخالفت امر کسی ننمایند
بعهده متولی آستانه منوره مقدسه وداروغه وحاکم خلخال

٦ که درین باب نهایت امداد نمایند مستوفی آنسرکار فیض آثار آنجه بخلاف حکم
از بهرجه موضع مزبور متولیان آستانه منوره صرف آستانه منوره

٧ نموده باشند عوض خیر از جوانب برینجمله روند هر ساله حکم مجدد نطلبند
تحریرا فی شهر ربیع الثانی سنهٔ ٩٩٢

Back :

بیضه   بندهٔ شاه است . . . . سلطان ٩٩٢

بیضه

عبد الله بن هدة ٩٩٢

فوضت بالله

الله　　　　　　　　　　　　صاحبه میر شریف خادم باشی

..... محمد　　　　　　　ملاحظه شد

۹۹۰ علی　　　　　بنده فقیر ...... نوشته شد

بیضه

ملاحظه شد

Document V—translation

1 Sovereignty belongs to God!

2 A royal command has been issued: whereas, the *bahrche*[1] of the locality of Kazaj in Khalkhāl, according to an exalted *nishān* which had the honour of issue during the Year of the Leopard (*bārs-yīl*), has been fixed

3 as the eternal *soyūrghāl* and everlasting favour of the Refuge of Nobility and Loom (*dastgāh*) of Benevolence, Mīr Sharīf, *khādim-bāshī*[2] of the Radiant and Holy Sanctuary, and since no alteration has taken place in that matter,

4 *kadkhudās*, peasants, and crop-sharing cultivators of the locality aforesaid [shall] give the established *bahrche* year by year to the person aforementioned. They are to withhold nothing;

5 they should not deviate in any way from what has been stipulated. No person should seek to oppose this decree. (It is) the responsibility of the *mutawallī* of the Radiant and Holy Sanctuary, and the *dārūghe* and the *ḥākim*[3] of Khalkhāl.

6 to render all possible help in this matter. The *mustawfī* of the department (*sarkār*)[4] bearing vestiges of abundance (*fayḍ-āthār*) [should refrain from] opposing the decree concerning the *bahrche* of the locality aforementioned. *Mutawallīs* of the

---

[1] *bahrche*—(or *bahrije*), a harvest tax, or share in the crops taken at harvest time for the benefit of a *soyūrghāl*-holder or the *dīwān*. *LPP*, p. 424, *PUkM*, II, p. 439. Papazian distinguishes between two types of *bahrche*, *bahrche-i-dīwānī*, " *bahrche* of the dīwān " and *bahrche-yi mālikāne*, " landowner's *bahrche* " calling them both " zemel'naya renta ".

[2] *khādim-bāshī*—" chief servant or attendant," see Document III, commentary.

[3] *ḥākim*—governor of a town or province; sometimes means " judge ". *LPP*, p. 429.

[4] *sarkār-i fayḍ-āthār*—a special department in the tax bureau presided over by an *'āmil*. See *TM*, p. 78, where an example is given for Iṣfahān. The official administered " estates and fields, and secured the prosperous state of gardens, mills, rentable property ", and underground channels. Presumably the *mustawfī-i sarkār-i fayḍ-āthār* dealt with financial side of these matters.

7 Radiant Sanctuary . . . the consumption of the Radiant Sanctuary. Proper compensation (*'iwaḍ*) for the . . . (*jawānib* ?) of the *parwanche* [is to be given.] Let them follow this procedure. A new decree should not be sought every year. Written in the month of Rabī' II in the year 992/12 April—10 May 1584.

Document V—commentary

Document V (the property of A. D. H. Bivar) is one of the few *soyūrghāls* of Muḥammad Khudābande so far published. The large flame-shaped seal, 31 mm. wide and 32 mm. long, has its vertical axis parallel to the centre line of the paper. The top of the seal contains words *Allāh, Muḥammad*, and *'Alī*. The centre reads *Ghulām-i Shāh, Muḥammad bin Tahmāsp.*[5] The distich on the four compartments around the margin is somewhat harder to read, as the royal seal-keeper (*muhrdār-i muhr-i humayūn*) pressed slightly harder to the left of the centre than on the right side, and so got a better impression there. For this reason the first two parts of the distich are not easy to read, although the last two are.[6] Above the seal is the usual phrase *al-mulk li'llāh* in gold, and below, in red, the opening formula.

Mīr Sharīf, the *khādim-bāshī* (" chief servant ", or " head attendant ") of the Ardabīl *zāwiye* must have been a man of standing, and an official of importance, ranking after the *nāẓir, mutawallī, mustawfī, sayyids*, etc. of this large and richly endowed institution. Was he a descendant of Mawlānā Kamāl al-Dīn Ḥusayn Ardabīlī ? It is likely that he was, although no direct evidence exists to show it.

Although the duties of the *khādim-bāshī* of the *tekke* are not specified, it is likely that they involved attendance on the higher officials, and perhaps were concerned with the catering. A passage in the *Silsilat al-nasab-i Ṣafawiyye* (p. 111) throws some light on the charitable catering operations (*shīlān-i khayratī*) and soup-kitchen activities of the *zāwiye*: every day 130 *manns* of rice were consumed (1 *mann-i-Tabrīz* is in the

---

[5] In this context, the word *shāh*, probably means 'Alī. This rhyme is more dignified than the rhymes on the coins of 'Abbās I, who called himself *kalb-i 'Alī* (Rabino, *Coins* . . . , p. 33), or Shāh Sulṭān Ḥusayn Ṣafawī, the " dog of the threshold of 'Alī " (Rabino, p. 40).

[6] Rabino, *Coins* . . . , p. 32, gives a reading of this seal which he later discards for a better one in his article " La sigillographie iranienne moderne ", *Journal Asiatique*, 1951, p. 197. For the gap in his reading, after *'ālam*, the word *al-bayyin* may fit. The seal is illustrated in Rabino's volume of plates, Oxford 1951, from BM. Or. 4935, No. IV, and Busse's plate XXVII (Urkunde 9), but a comparison of seal impressions from other documents must be attempted before a final reading can be made.

region of 6·55 to 7·25 lbs.); 47½ *manns* of meat, 27 *manns* of *rawghan* (clarified mutton fat) had to be prepared to serving " day and night." The kitchen (*maṭbakh, hawījkhāne*) of the *tekke* used up in a single year 50,000 *manns* of rice, 10,300 *manns* of *rawghan*, 20,000 *manns* of meat, 200 *manns* of honey, 5290 *manns* of *dūshāb* (grape syrup ?), 1464 *manns* of peas, 3000 *manns* of salt, 300 *manns* of *mūm* (comb honey ? candles ?), 1464 *manns* of onions, a large quantity of wheat for porridge (*āsh-i herīse*), 36,000 *manns* of flour, 1000 *manns* of *pay* (tendons for stewing ?), 50 *manns* of sugar, and large quantities of firewood. Whether the term *shīlān-khayratī* includes feeding the theological students of the *zāwiye*, travellers, as well as the indigent of the town of Ardabīl is not clear; nevertheless this institution was throughout the entire Ṣafawid period one of the most important intellectual, as well as charitable, centres in Iran. Its library, plundered by General Paskievitch during the war of 1828, forms part of the Persian collection of the library at Leningrad; its carpet is one of the showpieces of the Victoria and Albert Museum. There are plans and a description of what remains of it in F. Sarre, *Denkmaeler Persischer Baukunst*, Berlin, 1910, Textband, pp. 32–52.

The year of the Leopard (*bārs-yīl*) just prior to 992/1584 was 986/1577–78.[7]

Document VI—[plates LVIII and LXI]

الملك لله ١

موضع مهر أشرف ٢

فرمان همیون شد آنکه رعایا متفرقه در کزج خلخال که بسیورغال أولاد مرحوم ٣
مولانا کمال الدین حسین خادم مقررست

در هر جا ونزد هر کس باشد از روی امیدوری تمام بجا ومقام خود ٤
آیند بزراعت ودرویشی ورعیتی

قیام نمایند هیچ آفریده مانع ومزاحم رعایای مذکور نشده کذارند که ٥
بوطن مألوف خود آیند بلوازم

دعاکوی دوام دولت ابد مقرون قیام وقدام نمایند حاکم وکلانتر وداروغه ٦
وعمال ومباشران

---

[7] See H. Busse, op. cit., for the Turkish 12-year animal cycle. Also, E. Chavannes, " Le cycle turc des douze animaux," in *T'oung Pao*, 1906, and Osman Turan, " Onik hayvanli Türk takvimi," *Dil ve Tarih-Cografya Fakültesi yayinlarindan tarih serisi*, 3, Istanbul 1941, or D. C. Phillott, *Higher Persian Grammar*, Calcutta, 1919, pp. 203–4 for a briefer exposition of the matter.

٧ وملكــان ألكــاء خلخــال حسب المسطور مقرر دانسته اصلا ومطلقــا مزاحمت بحال رعايا نرسانيده

٨ بخلاف حكم وحساب طلب وتوقعى از ايشان ننماينــد و بعلت اخراجـــات وعوارضات مسدوده الابواب

٩ بهر اسم ورسم كـه بوده باشد حواله واطـلاقى بديشان ننموده قلم وقدم كشيده وكوتاه دانند

١٠ وجـون معروض شد كـه شاه قلى آقـا سورلـه مبلغى بخلاف حق وحساب از رعاياء موضع مذكور

١١ كرفتـه مقرر فرموديم كه وكـلاى ايالت بنـاه حكومت وشوكت دستكـاه جلالا للايالة والاقبال

١٢ اميره سياوش خان حاكم خلخال آنجه شاه قلى مذكور از رعايا موضع مزبور بغير حق ستاده باشد

١٣ باز يافت نموده بديشان بـاز دهد ونوعى نمايد كـه حق ايشان عايد كشته اظهار شكر نمايند

١٤ ازين باب قدقن دانسته از فرموده در نكذرند در عهده دانند

١٥ تحريرا فى شهر شعبان المعظم سنة الف

Back :

موضع مهر نواب اعتماد الدوله العليه العاليه　　موضع مهر نواب فرحاد خان

موضع مهر مستوفى الممالك　　موضع مهر نواب نظارت بنـاه　　موضع مهر

هو الوهّاب

السواد واصله لاصيـل الاشرف الاعـلى

المطاع المنيع المتيـع سيان ستان

نوشته شد

سبحانه من اعظم
عبده صفى الدين أبو القاسم
محمد الحسينى ٩٨٩

هذا السواد المطابق
الاصل الاعلى حرره
صدر الدين محمد الصفوى
الحسيني

Document VI—translation

1 Sovereignty belongs to God!

2 Place of the royal seal (*muhr-i ashraf*).

3 A royal command has been issued: the dispersed peasants at Kazaj in Khalkhāl, which has been fixed as the *soyūrghāl* of the descendants of the late Mawlānā Kamāl al-Dīn Ḥusayn Khādim,

4 wherever and with whomever they may be, are to return to their places and homes with every good expectation, and occupy themselves with agriculture, piety (*darwīshī*) and husbandry (*ra'yatī*).

5 No person is to impede or create difficulties for the aforesaid peasants; they should be allowed to return to their accustomed dwelling place (*waṭan-i ma'lūf*).

6 They should busy themselves and persevere with the needful things of interrupted prayer for the Everlasting State (*dawlat-i abad-maqrūn*).

7 The governor (*ḥākim*), *kalāntar*, *dārūghe*, *'āmils*, bailiffs (*mubāshirān*),[1] and *maliks* [2] of the *ulkā'* of Khalkhāl should recognize the foregoing (*ḥasb al-masṭūr*) as established. They should in no way whatsoever create difficulties in the condition of the peasants;

8 in contravention of this decree (*ḥukm*) and reckoning (*ḥisāb*) they should not seek or expect anything from them. They should not,

9 for the sake of extraordinary taxes (*ikhrājāt*) or irregular exactions (*'awāriḍāt-i masdūde al-abwāb*),[3] write drafts (*ḥawāle*), or requisitions (*iṭlāqī*) [4] of any sort whatsoever. They should keep their feet and pens [away from this property].

10 And since a representation has been made that Shāh Qulī Āghā Sūrleh has wrongfully and improperly taken a sum of money from the peasants of the aforesaid locality,

11 we have decreed that the representative (*wukalā'*) of the Asylum of Administration, the implement of royal majesty and pomp—glorious ornament of sovereignty—

12 Amīre [5] Siyāwush Khān, the governor of Khalkhāl, shall recover what

---

[1] *mubāshir*—bailiff, tax collector, synonymous with *taḥsildār*. Sometimes a crop-estimator for taxes in kind. See *PUkM*, I, p. 233, and *LPP*, p. 434.

[2] *malik*—elder of a town or village, sometimes concerned with raising of taxes. See *PUkM*, I, p. 233.

[3] *'awāriḍāt-i-masdūde al-abwāb*—irregular tolls or dues? For *'awāriḍāt*, see *PUkM*, I, p. 223, *LPP*, p. 423.

[4] *iṭlāqī*—"requisitions," see *LPP*, p. 430. Papazian, *PUkM*, I, suggests that this word properly *iṭlāq*, may have meant some sort of special tax for travelling officials.

[5] *amīre*—Gīlākī form for *amīr*. *TM*, p. 125, note 6.

the aforementioned Shāh Qulī has wrongfully received from the peasants of the locality in question

13 and give it back to them. He should specify that their rights should be rendered to them, [so that] they can make manifest their gratitude.

14 In this matter, it is forbidden to depart from what has been decreed (here) they should consider [its execution] their responsibility.

15 Written in the month of Sha'bān al-Mu'aẓẓam in the year 1000/ 13 May—10 June 1592

Document VI—commentary

Document Six, a copy of the original, which has doubtless disappeared, has no seal at the top, but the tail of the *'ayn* in the word *mawḍi'* has been curled around to enclose the words *muhr* and *ashraf*, forming a roughly circular shape like the seal it replaces. Other examples of this practice can be seen on documents published by Papazian, *PUkM*, II, in the facsimiles facing pp. 487 and 499. Another interesting point is the procedure for the authentication of a copy—showing that it had been compared with the original and found to be correct—can be seen on the back of the top left, signed by Ṣadr al-Din Muḥammad al-Ṣafawī al-Ḥusaynī, perhaps the son of Ma'ṣūm Beg Ṣafawī of that name (?)—see Document III, commentary. Seals of other high officials, or rather, places for these seals and *'alāmas* can be seen on the back at the top ; in one case the seal of the I'timād al-Dawla, the *Mustawfī al-Mamālik*, the *nawwāb* Farhād Khān, a certain Ṣafī al-Dīn Abu'l-Qāsim Muḥammad al-Ḥusaynī, and others.

As to the " scattered peasants " of Kazaj in Khalkhāl belonging to the *soyūrghāl* of Kamāl al-Dīn Ḥusayn Ardabīlī's descendants, they may well have fled their homes to escape the extortion of officials, or heavy taxation. The grim picture drawn by Miss Lambton of " overtaxation and extortion, corruption and misrule, decay and public disorder " among the lower classes in rural Persian during the Mongol period certainly applied to some areas in Ṣafawid times as well.[6] The existence of a horde of officials whose chief duty was to press the multifarious taxes, dues, tolls and other exactions out of the miserable peasants and crop-sharers must have signified widespread poverty and subsistence-level existence in the countryside. Moreover, in Shāh 'Abbās' time, the peasants of Kazaj were not only subjected to the exactions of men like Shāh Qulī Āghā, but had to contend with the disturbances of an Ottoman invasion.

---

[6] *LPP*, p. 95.

After the death of Shāh Ṭahmāsp I, in 984/1576, Persia was torn apart by Qizilbāsh tribalism, resulting in a long series of succession struggles and battles for influence among Turkoman factions, coinciding with the disastrous reigns of Ismā'īl II and Muḥammad Khudābande. Sultan Murād III, seeking to take advantage of these continual disputes, undertook a series of raids on Persian territory, beginning with the *ghazw* of Muṣṭafa Pasha against Armenia and parts of the Caucasus in 986/1578, the campaign of Farhād Pasha in eastern Anatolia and Azarbayjan in 990/1582, and the invasion of Azarbayjan by Özdemīr-zāde 'Uthmān Pasha, ending in the fall of Tabrīz to the Turks in 993/1585. This long time of troubles and almost uninterrupted military operations could only be harmful to the economic life of Azerbayjan Province and the western Ṣafawid domains. These conditions lasted after the Ṣafawids made a truce with the Turks in 999/1590 ; Persia only recovered its province in 1011/1602 under 'Abbās I. During this decade of Ottoman occupation at Tabrīz, Ja'far Pasha, the Turkish governor of the city, extended Turkish control as far east as Sarāb : it may have been at this time that disturbances of a more than usually drastic sort were taking place in the *soyūrghāl*, now close to the frontier[7].

Amīre Siyāwush Khān, the *ḥākim* of Khalkhāl, was a member of a local dynasty of Ṭālish and Khalkhāl, probably from the Gaskar district. He is first mentioned by Iskandar Munshī as *ḥākim* of Gaskar. In 1001–1591/92, Siyāvush Khān was given the *ulkā'* of Khalkhāl in recognition of his services. In the following year he went on a hunting trip with Shāh 'Abbās.[8] But when 'Abbās made clear his intention to annex the territories of the local kinglets of the *Dār al-Marz*, Ṭabaristān, Gīlān-i-Biyā Pas and Biyā Pīsh, Siyāvush allied himself with the followers of another local " rebel " (as Iskandar puts it), Ḥamza Khān Ṭālish.[9] Captured in

[7] Naṣr Allāh Falsafī, op. cit., pp. 152–3. By the terms of this humiliating peace settlement, Persia lost to the Ottomans " the city of Tabrīz and the western part of Azarbayjan, the *wilāyats* of Armenistān, Shakkī, Gurjistān, Qarabāgh, and a part of Lūristān, including the citadel of Nihāwand ". See also V. Minorsky, *Ta'rīkh-i Tabrīz*, ed. A. Kārang, Tabrīz, 1337 H.S./1957, pp. 52 ff.

A fine bronze cannon, with the name Ja'far Pasha on it, dated 989, can be seen in the main courtyard of the Invalides at Paris.

[8] *TAA*, p. 306 and pp. 312–13 ; for Gaskar, see p. 304.

[9] *TAA*, pp. 299 ff. for the rising of Ḥamza Khān Ṭālish, who rose against 'Abbās when Alwand Sulṭān Dhū'l-Qadar, brother of Farhād Khān, was given his hereditary *ulkā'*. When a large force was sent against him, Ḥamza Khān fled to Shīrwān, at that time Ottoman territory, where he was murdered in 1000/1591–92.

1001, Amīre Siyāwush Khān was executed by ʻAbbās some time afterward.[10]

Shāh Qulī Āghā Sūrleh (Sūrluh ?) belonged to a tribe of Kurds listed by Iskandar Munshī, who mentions a certain Shujāʻ al-Dīn Sulṭān Sūrleh as one of the *amīrs* of Shīrwān, in an enumeration of the great *amīrs* among the Kurds and Lūrs of the time of ʻAbbās I.[11] Shah Qulī Āghā might have been a *dārūghe* or *kalāntar*.

Farhād Khān was a member of the Dhu'l-Qadar tribe and a general of Shāh ʻAbbās. He had participated in the Gīlān campaign mentioned above, and was assassinated by his rivals in 1008/1599–1600.[12]

Document VII—[plates LIX and LXII]

Seal :

بندۀ شاه ولایت عباس ۹۹۹

اللهم صلی علی النبی والوصی والبتول والسبطین والسجاد والباقر والصادق والكاظم
والرضا والتقی والنقی والزكي والمهدي

Text :

١ الملك لله

٢ فرمان همیون شد آنكه جون بموجب فرامین مطاعه لازم الاطاعه هشت تومان
وهشت هزار وسیصد ونود دینار از بابت

٣ مالوجهات محال مذكوره ضمن دار الارشاد آرده‌بیل وخلخال بسیورغال
اولاد افادت بناه مرحوم مولانا كمال الدین حسین أرد مبیلی كه

٤ از جمله خد متكاران قدیم این آستان ولایت نشان اند مقرر ومستمر بوده
وجون از ابتداء سیجقان ییل تسع والف سیورغالات آذربایجان را موقوف

٥ فرموده بودیم درینولا اولاد مزبوررا بعز بساطبوسی سر افراز كشته التماس
حكم تاكید نمودند جون شفقت ومرحمت شاهانه در بارۀ اولاد مرحوم مزبور
خصوصا

---

10 *TAA*, pp. 313–15.

11 *TAA*, p. 763.

12 *TAA*, pp. 396–7.

٦ جماعت ظهر درجه اعلی دارد سیورغـال اولاد مزبوررا بدستور سابق مرحمت فرموده ارزانی داشتیم کدخدایان ورعایا محال مذکوره اولاد مذکور را بدستور سابق

٧ صاحب سیورغـال خود دانسته سال بسال مالوجهـات ووجوهـات وحقوق دیوانی خودرا بدیوان جواب کفته جیزی موقوف ندارند وقضایا سانحه را بدیشان رفع نماید که

٨ موافق حق وحساب بتفصیـل رساند حکام کرام وداروغکـان و عمال وملکـان وکلانتران دار الارشاد أرده‌بیل وخلخال و . . . مزبور محال سیورغال

٩ ننموده بیرامون رعایا ومزارعـان سیورغـال ایشان نکردند وداروغکـان بعلت برسش قضایاء مزاحمت نرسانیده بصاحب سیورغال متعلق دانند وبعلت اخراجات وعوارضات مسدوده الاواب

١٠ از علفه وعلوفه وقنلغا وألام وألاغ وبیکـار وشیکار وسر شمار وطرح ودست انداز وعیدی ونوروزی و بیشکش وسلامی وغیر ذلك بهر اسم ورسم که بوده باشد وحواله

١١ واطلاقی ننموده قلم وقـدم کوتـاه کشیده دارند مستوفیان عظـام دیوان اعـلی رقم این عطیه را در دفاتر خلود ثبت نموده از شوایب تغییر و تبدیل مصون و محروس شناسند

١٢ وجون موضع کزج حسب الحکم جهانمطاع از حشو بنیجه اخراجات موضوع ومستثنی است بدستـور سـابق موضوع مستثنی دانسته در بـاقی اعصار وهر ساله حکم مجدد نخواهند تحریرا فی شهر محرم الحرام سنة ١٠١٦

Back :

اطلعت علی الله . . . .

علت . . . . . .

غلام عباس علي — توکلت علی الله . . . .

بندۀ شاه . . . . .

نوشته شد	مقصود غلام عباس	عباس اهل محمد
. . . النظام	بنظارت شد	بقلم آورد

Document VII—translation

1 Sovereignty belongs to God!

2 A royal command has been issued: whereas, according to [former] *firmāns* to which obedience is rendered and submission made, the sum of eight *tūmāns*, eight thousand, three hundred and ninety *dīnārs*, on account

3 of the revenues (*māl u-jihāt wa-wujūhāt*) of the aforementioned (?) places, including the *Dār al-Irshād* of Ardehbil (sic) and Khalkhāl, has been fixed and made perpetual as the *soyūrghāl* of the descendants of the Asylum of Benefit, the late Mawlānā Kamāl al-Dīn Ḥusayn Ardehbīlī (sic),

4 who was one of a number of former servitors of this court (*āstān*), invested with the sign of sanctity. And since, from the beginning of the Year of the Mouse (*sīchqān-yīl*), [corresponding to the year] 1009, we had decreed.

5 the suspension (*mawqūf*) of the *soyūrghāls* of Azarbayjan, and whereas, at this time, the descendants of the aforementioned person have enjoyed the honour and distinction of rendering homage (*basāṭbūsī*), and have solicited the confirmation of their decree, and since the royal sympathy and compassion has reached a high point in regard to the descendants

6 of the aforesaid person, particularly for the group (*jamā'at*) [listed] on the back [of this document], we have exercised compassion and restored the *soyūrghāl* of the descendants previously mentioned, according to previous precedent (*dastūr-i sābiq*). *Kadkhudās* and peasants of the places in question should recognize them as master[s] of their *soyūrghāl*, as by previous regulation.

7 They are answerable to the *dīwān* each year for their taxes, of every sort, and for *dīwān* dues. They should withhold nothing. Litigation which may

8 arise is to be referred to them, so that it can be settled (*tafṣīl namāyad*) in conformity with right and calculation (*ḥaqq wa-ḥisāb*). The respected *ḥākims*, *dārūghes*, *'āmils*, *maliks*, and *kalāntars* of the *Dār al-Irshād* of Ardehbīl and Khalkhāl and . . . (paper flaked off)

9 [are not to interfere in this *soyūrghāl* ?]. They are not to undertake searches among the peasants and crop-sharing cultivators of their *soyūrghāl*. *Dārūghes* are not to molest [them] for the sake of judicial inquiries; [in such matters] they should depend upon the master of the *soyūrghāl*. In

10 the matter of extraordinary taxes (*ikhrājāt*) and irregular exactions

(*'awāriḍāt-i masdūde al-abwāb*) [they shall be exempt]. [Likewise, they shall be exempt] from levies
for the provisioning of officials (*'alāfe*),[1] providing fodder for the animals of officials (*'ulūfe*),[2] levies for official entertainment (*qunalghā*),[3] forced guide service (*ulam*),[4] levies of animals (*ulāgh*),[5] forced labour service (*bīgār*),[6] service as beaters (*shīkār*),[7] poll-tax (*sar-shumār*),[8] house tax (*khāne-kār*),[9] forced purchase of supplies at high prices (?) (*ṭarḥ*),[10] gratuities (*dast-andāz*),[11] *'īd* and New Year tolls (*'ādī wa-nawrūzī*), gifts (*pīshkesh*),
11 audience dues (*salāmī*),[12] and other [dues and taxes] of all kinds. They shall not write drafts (*ḥawāle*), nor levy requisitions (*iṭlāqī*) ;

---

1 *'alāfe*—see *LPP*, p. 423, *PUkM*, I, p. 224, Petrushevskii, *Ocherki* . . . , pp. 273–4. The question of *'alāfe* and *'ulūfe* is also discussed by A. A. Alizadeh, *Sotsialno-ekonomicheskaya i politicheskaya istoria Azerbaidzhana, XIII-XIV, vv*, Baku 1956, pp. 233–6.

2 *'ulūfe*—*LPP*, p. 442, and references in the previous note.

3 *qunalghā*—*LPP*, p. 437. According to Papazian, *PUkM*, I, p. 231, the word means " haven " or " refuge " in Chagatai Turkish, but according to Pavet de Courteille, *Dictionnaire turk orientale*, Paris 1870, p. 438, *qūnālgha* has the meaning of " frais de sejour, indemnité ". Radloff, *Versuch eines Wörterbuches*, II, 538, has it as " Nachtquartier ", while Petrushevskii, op. cit., p. 274, prefers " quartering rights " (*pravo postoya*) and considers the word " old Özbeg " rather than Chagatai.

4 *ulam*—*LPP*, p. 442, Petrushevskii, op. cit., pp. 275–6, likewise *PUkM*, I, p. 238, a Mongol or Chagatai-Özbeg word meaning " cart " or " bullock cart ", usually associated with *ulāgh*, " quadruped," horse, beast of burden (see Pavet de Courteille, op. cit., p. 74) later coming to mean a guide and transport service for officials who wanted to be taken from place to place.

5 *ulāgh*—see previous note, also Alizadeh, op. cit., pp. 237–8, and the heading of *yam* (" postal station ") in the same source.

6 *bīgār*—forced labour service or *corvée*. Alizadeh has written a special article on this word and *cherik* (auxiliary troops) : " Provinnosti ' bigar ' i ' cherik '," in *DAN Azerb. SSR*, vol. X, No. 7, 1954, which is not available to me.

7 *shīkār*—*LPP*, p. 439. May mean " hunting dues ". *PUkM*, I, p. 241 derives it from *shāh-kār*. See also Petrushevskii, op. cit., pp. 289–90.

8 *sar-shumār*—" head tax, sometimes *sarāne*. See Alizadeh, op. cit., pp. 247–8.

9 *khāne-kār*—possibly the same as *khāne-shumār*, " house tax." See *LLP*, p. 431, Alizadeh, op. cit., p. 248.

10 *ṭarḥ*—*LPP*, p. 85 and p. 103, note 3. Possibly some scheme by which the peasants were forced to buy the government share of the harvest in advance, amounting to a tax. Alizadeh has written an article on the matter, not accessible to me : " K istorii feodal'nikh otnoshenii v Azerbaidzhan v XIII–XIV vv : termin ' tarkh '," *Isvestiya AZFAN SSR*, No. 3, 1942, also his *Socio-economic and political history*, pp. 244–6.

11 *dast-andāz*—" gratuities, irregular minor fees ? " See *PUkM*, I, pp. 228–9.

12 *salāmī*—*LPP*, p. 438, defines this as " dues paid for royal audiences and on receipt of news of ruler's well-being ". Sometimes *sālamāne*. See also *PUkM*, I, p. 237.

they shall keep their pens and feet away from this *soyūrghāl.* The great *mustawfīs* of the Exalted *Dīwān* shall enter a copy of this gift in the eternal registers, to protect and preserve it from the blemishes of change and alteration.

12 And since the locality of Kazaj, according to a royal decree to which the entire world is obedient, is free and exempt from the redundancy of collective assessment (*ḥashw-i bunīche*),[13] according to former precedent, it should be considered free and exempt for the remainder of time. A new decree should not be sought every year. Written in the month of Muḥarram al-Ḥarām in the year 1016/28 April—27 May 1607.

Document VII—commentary

Since the original grant of this *soyūrghāl* (see Document II) in the year 915, or at least that part of it situated at Kazaj in Khalkhāl, the total amount of it nearly doubled, from 45,000 Tabrīzī *dīnārs* to 88,390 in about one hundred years' time. Had other documents concerned with this *soyūrghāl* been available, they might have explained the increase in the size of this grant. At a guess, the natural growth in numbers of the descendants of Mawlānā Kamāl al-Dīn Ardabīlī, who continually pressed the state for larger sums to support themselves, may have had something to do with the matter. Alternatively, it is possible that continual inflation was going on during this century. Little evidence on this point is available, but it is clear from this document that the clan of Mawlānā Kamāl al-Dīn continued to keep the good will of the government, to the point that they were able to press successfully for a renewal of their rights to their former domains and the revenue deriving from them, after a suspension of seven years.

One can only speculate as to why Shāh 'Abbās suspended the *soyūrghāls* of Azerbayjan in 1009/1599–1600. This move may have been associated with some plan to increase revenue—perhaps for the expenses of 'Abbās's new-style, non-Qizilbāsh army. It is equally possible that Shāh and government were becoming alarmed at the proliferation of *soyūrghāls* and other types of tax exemptions in Azerbayjan and the resulting diversion of revenue into private hands and away from the treasury. By suspending the grants, 'Abbās may have believed that he could get more funds for the exigencies of the day. If this is the correct interpretation of the Shāh's decision, the plan did not work—at least in

[13] *bunīche—LPP,* p. 425, " group assessment of a village."

this case—and the Shāh had eventually to give in to the pressures brought to bear by the hereditary grant-holders. Professor Minorsky has referred to the "... the evils of the *soyūrghāls*, which kings distributed with much arbitrariness [being] fully realized by the responsible authorities, but the interests at work were too mighty for anything to be done. We know of a catastrophic end of the tentative efforts made under Sultan Ya'qūb Aq-Quyūnlu to suspend the *soyūrghāls* at Iṣfahān and Shīrāz." [14] And it is a notable fact that in later Ṣafawid times the religious classes obtained very large landholdings, in comparison with earlier periods. Professor Lambton notes that "originally they probably held this land as *mutavallis* of *ouqaf*, or by way of hereditary grants or *soyūrghāls*. In due course, much of this land became private property. In certain parts of the country, notably Azerbayjan and Isfahan, the religious classes have continued to form an important element in the landowning class." [15]

The back of this *soyūrghāl* is laid out in two vertical columns. In many places, the paper has flaked off, making an accurate reading difficult (see Plate LXII). The right column shows, at the top, the name Khalīfa Yūsuf (?) Khādim, the left column the names Mawlānā Ibrāhīm Aghā ... and Muḥyī al-Dīn (?) Khādim-bāshī. In the left column, above these names, the word *awlād* can be read, suggesting that Mawlānā Kamāl al-Dīn's descendants were divided into two groups at the beginning of the 17th century, and that the lands and villages of Ibrāhim and his group are listed on the left, and Khalīfa Yūsuf (?) on the right. The numerous horizontal lines no doubt represent an extension of the letter *yā* in the word *qarya* (village), which is drawn out over a number of place names, including Sulṭānābād at the right, Kazaj on the left. The sub-totals of the revenues to be gathered are in both cases the same and are written just under the names of the two groups, in *siyāq*. This suggests that the total sum of the *soyūrghāl* was divided evenly between both groups, amounting in each case to 44,180 dīnārs. Other sums and figures, like *alif* are readable elsewhere in this document, but as Ṣafawid *siyāq* of the 17th century is a specialized study, any further attempts by the present writer to read them would be mere speculation. At any rate, the connection of the family of Mawlānā Kamāl al-Dīn was maintained with these lands for a hundred years after the beginning of the Ṣafawid period, and very probably longer. It is unfortunate that more documents relating to these lands have not survived—or have been dispersed so that they are no longer available for analysis.

---

[14] *TM*, p. 27.

[15] A. K. S. Lambton *Landlord and Peasant* ..., pp. 126–7.

I

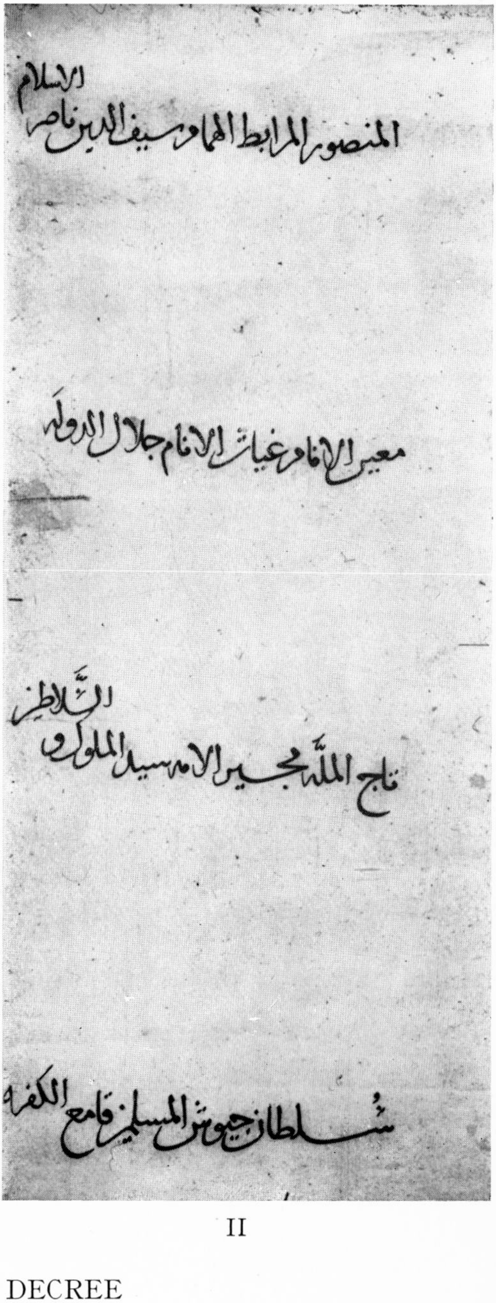

II

AL-'ĀDIL'S DECREE

lines 1–3 *lines 4–7*

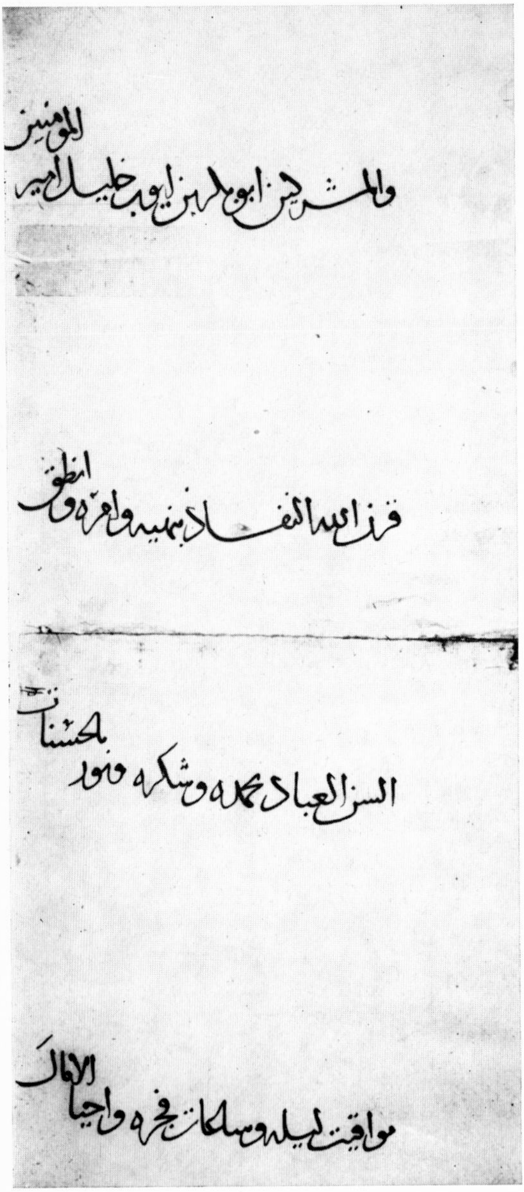
والمشرقين ابو محمد بن ايوب خليل امير المومنين
قرن الله النفاذ بنهيه وامره واطلق
السن العباد بحمده وشكره ونوه بالحسنات
مواقيت ليله وسلكات فجره واحيا الامال

III

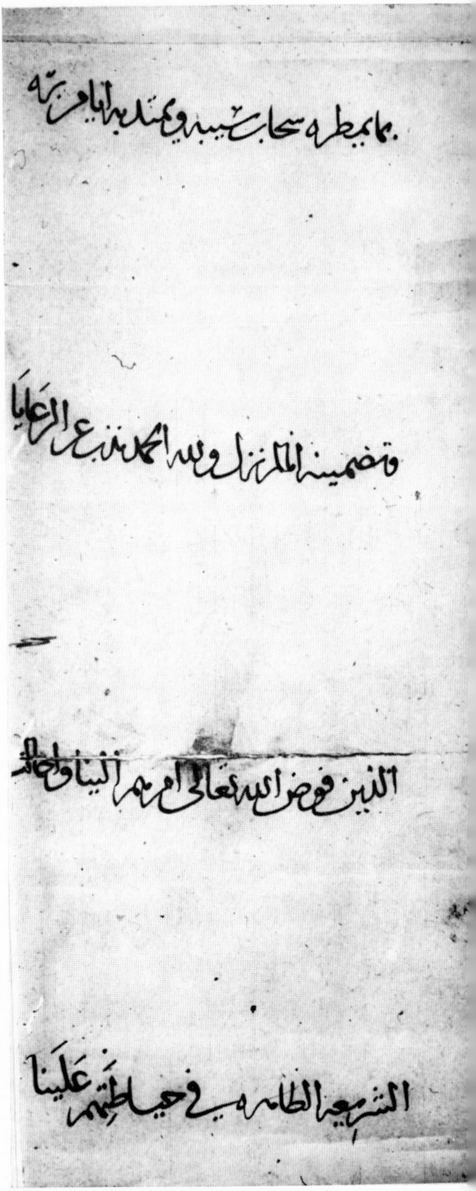
بما يمطره سحاب سيبه ويمحله بايام ربه
وتضمينه الملك نزل وبالله الحمد نزع الرعايا
الذين فوض الله تعالى امورهم الينا واحالهم
الشريعة الطاهرة في حياطتهم علينا

IV

AL-ʿĀDIL'S DECREE

lines 8–11

lines 12–15

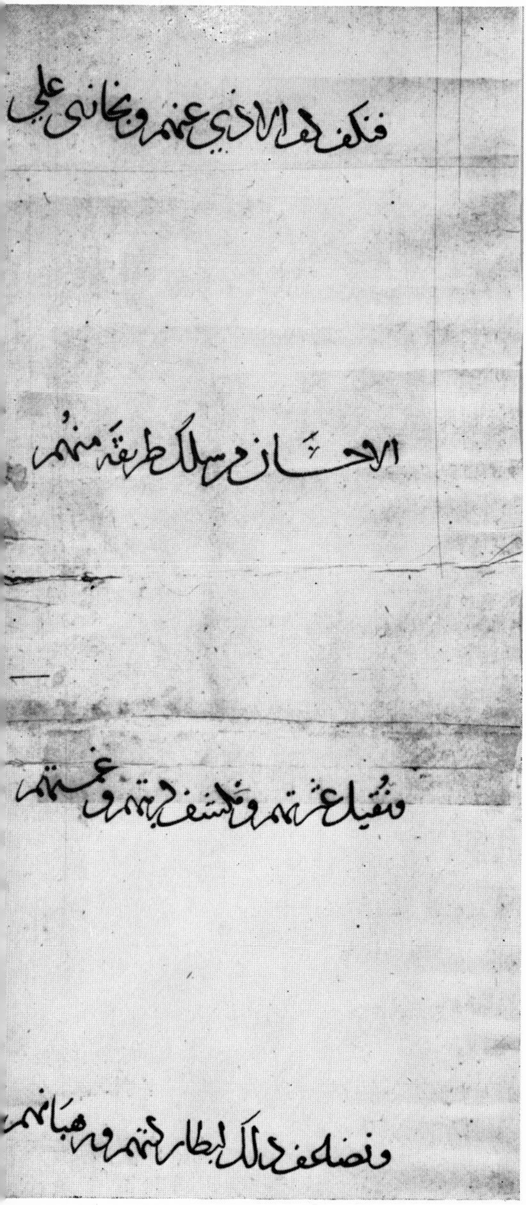
فنكف ايدي الاذى عنهم ونتجافى على

الاحسان من سلك طريقه منهم

ونقيل عثرتهم ونكشف كربتهم وغمتهم

ونضاعف ذلك لبطاركتهم ورهبانهم

V

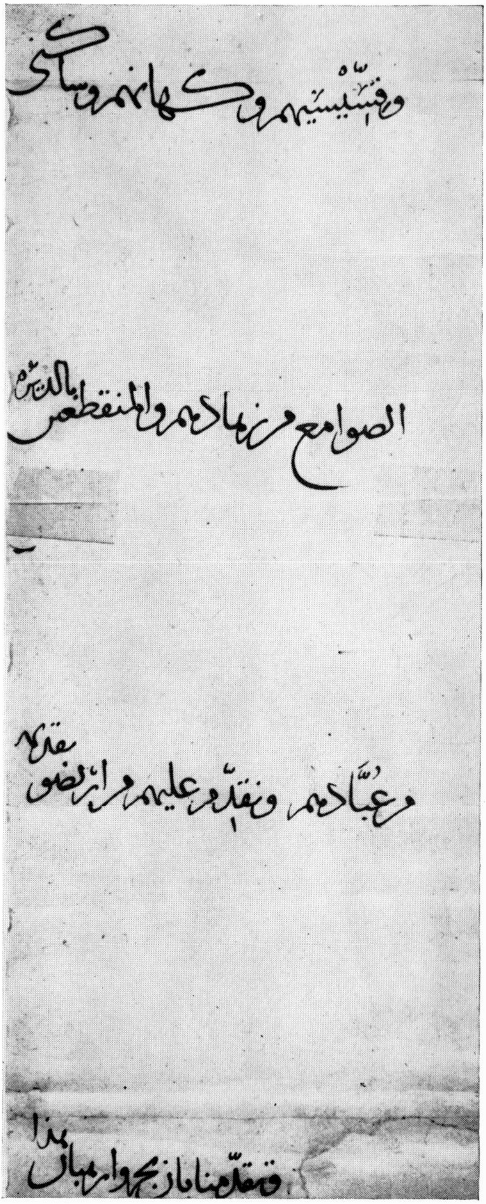
وقسيسيهم وكهانهم وساكني

الصوامع من زهادهم والمنقطعين بالكلية

من عبادهم ونقدم عليهم

VI

AL-'ĀDIL'S DECREE

lines 16–19

lines 20--23

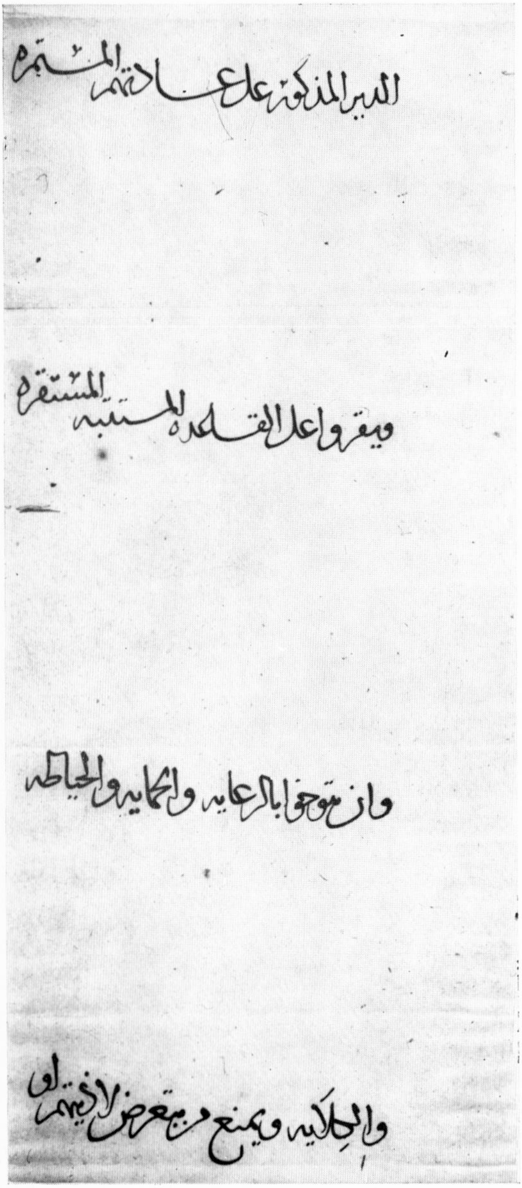

الكبير المذكور على عادتهم المستمره
ويقروا على القاعده المستتبه المستقره
وان يتوخوا بالرعايه والحمايه والحياطه
والكلايه ويمنع من يتعرض لاذيتهم او

VII

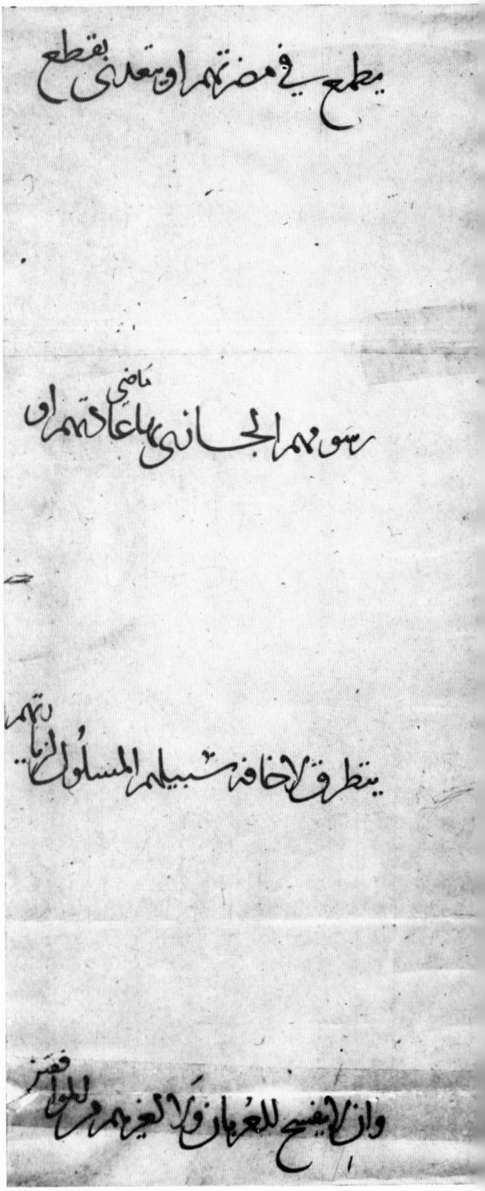

يطمع في مضرتهم او يتعدى بقطع
رسوم لهم الجاري على عادتهم او ماضي
يتطرق لاخافة سبيلهم المسلوك الى زيارتهم
وان لا يفسح للعربان ولا لغيرهم من الطوائف

VIII

AL-'ĀDIL'S DECREE

lines 24–27

lines 28–31

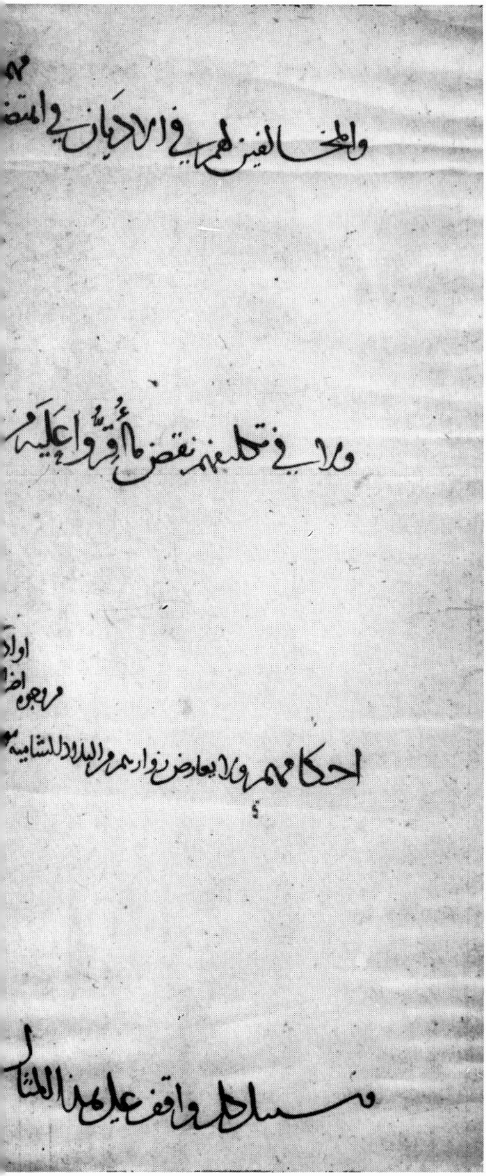

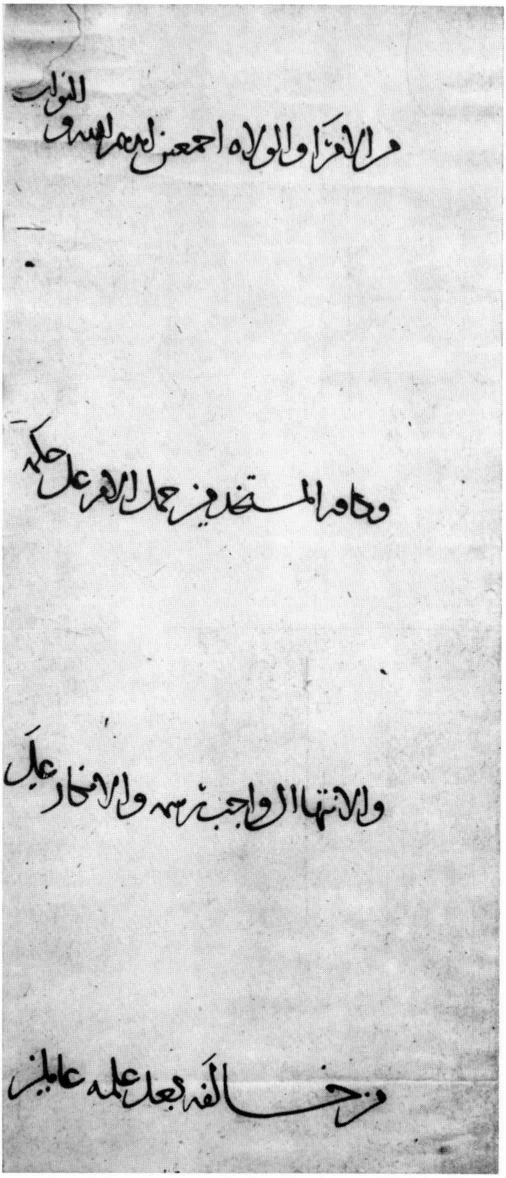

IX

X

AL-ʿĀDIL'S DECREE

lines 32–35

lines 36–39

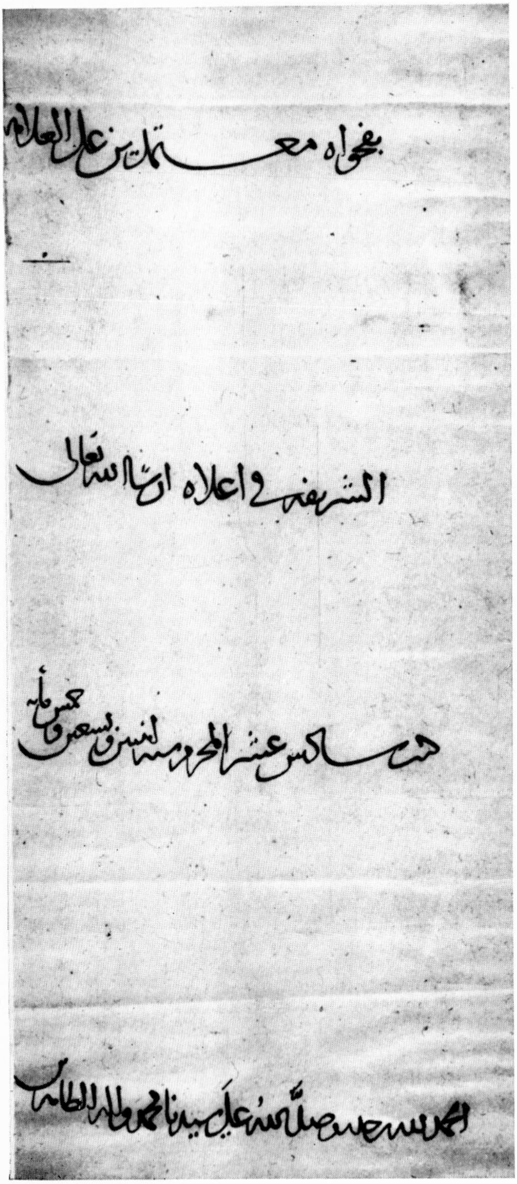

XI

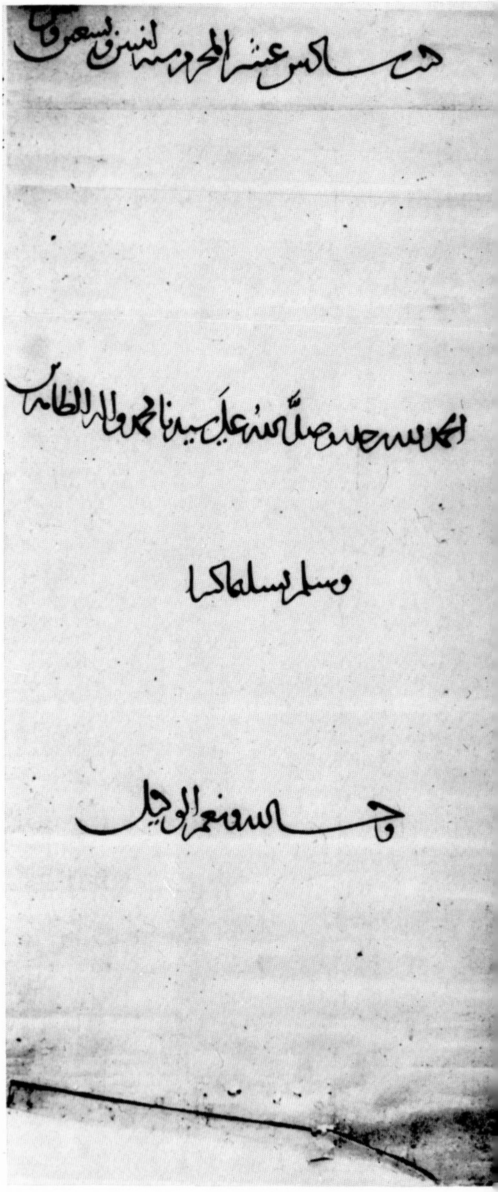

XII

AL-ʿĀDIL'S DECREE

lines 40–43

lines 42–45

بسم الله الرحمن الرحيم
خرج الأمر العالي المولوي
السلطاني الملكي الأفضلي زاده الله

XIII

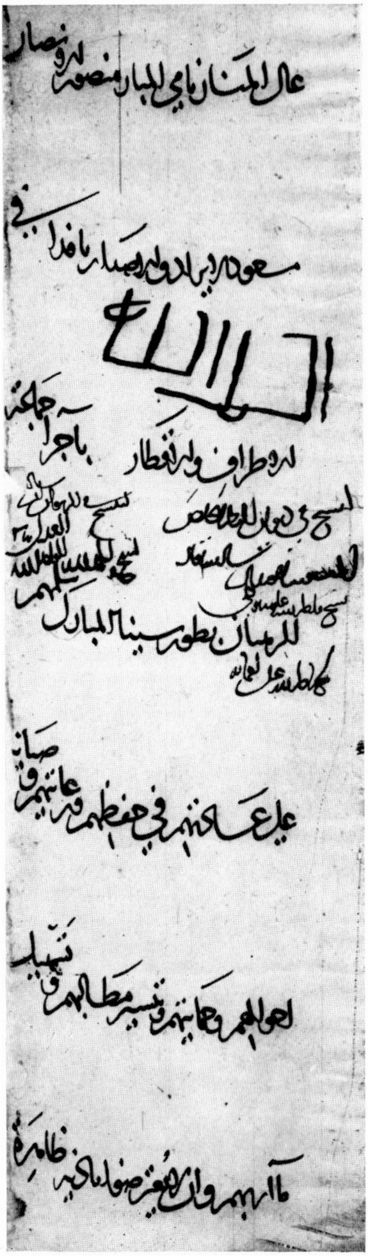

للرهبان بطور سينا المبارك
على عادتهم في حفظهم ورعايتهم وصيانتهم
لهم وحمايتهم وتيسير مطالبهم وتسهيل

XIV

AL-AFḌAL'S DECREE

lines 1–3 *lines 4–10*

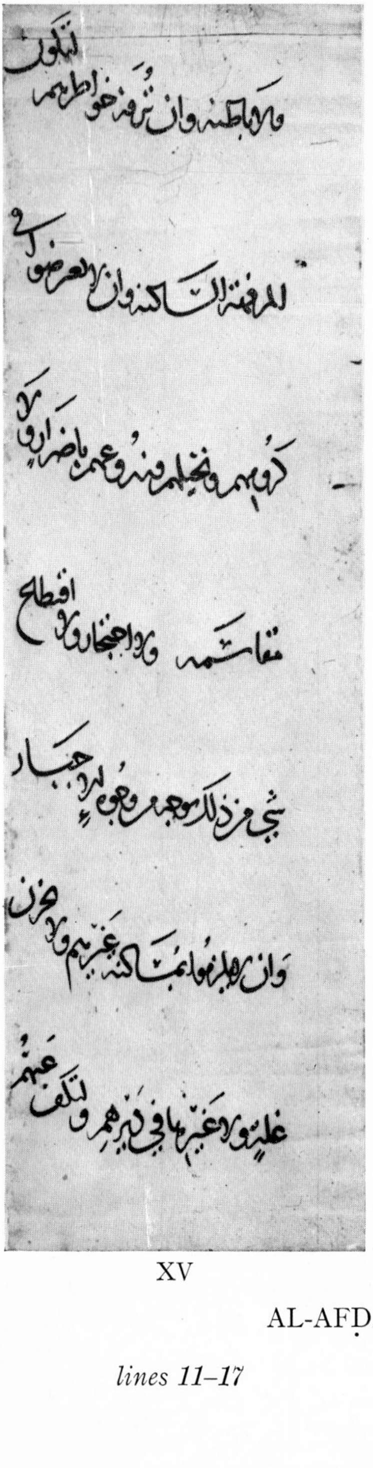

XV

lines 11–17

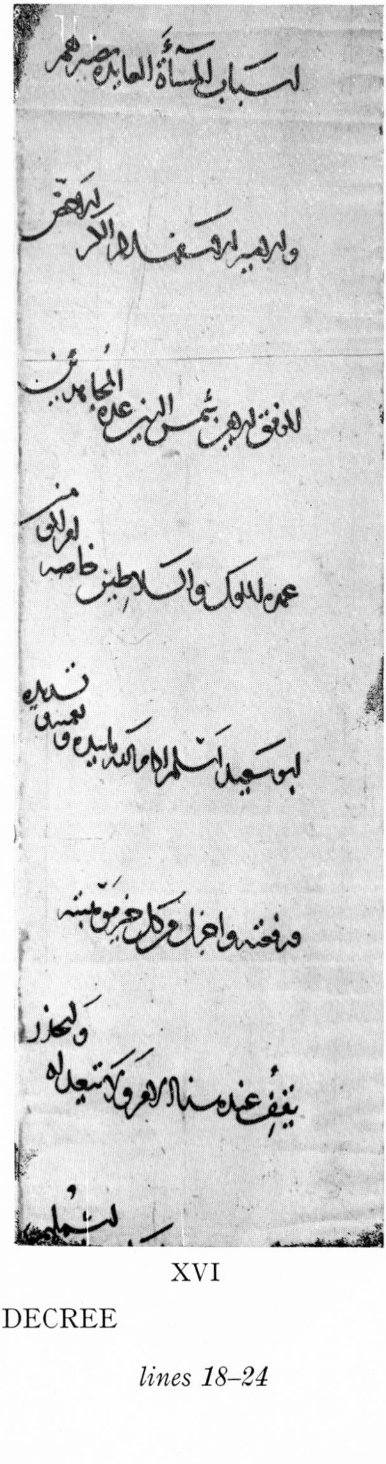

XVI

lines 18–24

AL-AFḌAL'S DECREE

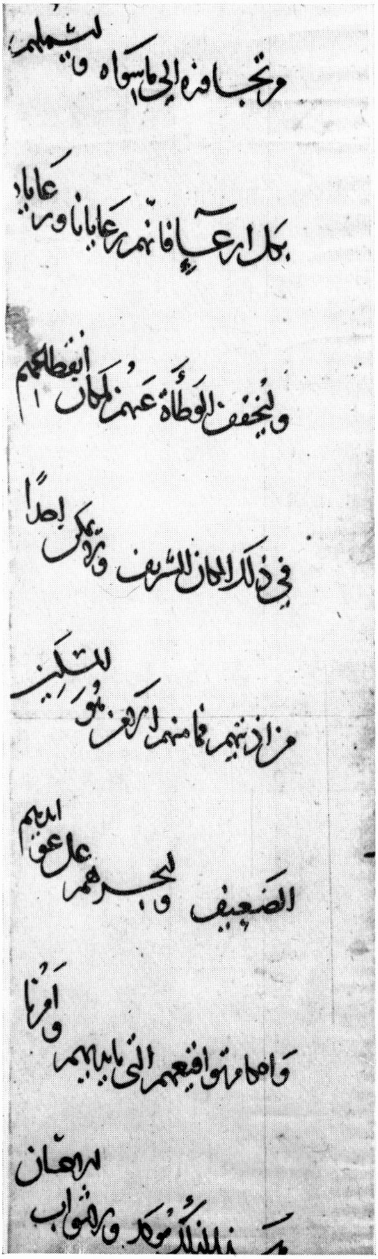

XVII

lines 25–31

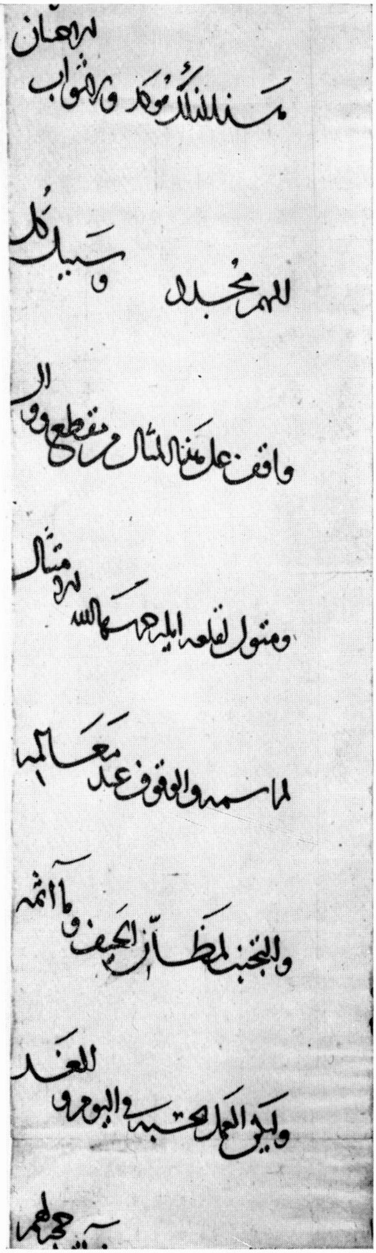

XVIII

lines 32–37

AL-AFḌAL'S DECREE

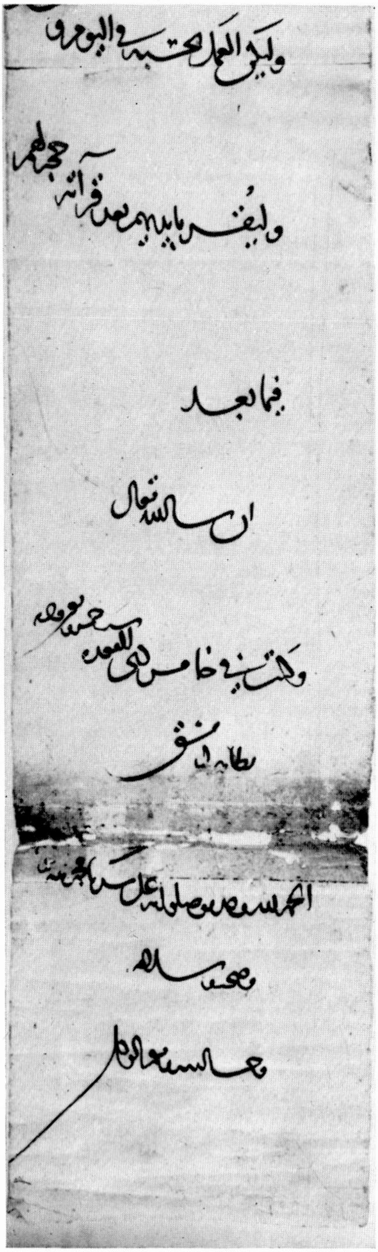

XIX

AL-AFḌAL'S DECREE

lines 38–46

RENCE, Biblioteca Nazionale *Fondo Del Furia, no. 50*

XX

BEGINNING OF ARABIC COPY AND ITALIAN TRANSLATION OF QĀ'ITBĀY'S DOCUMENT

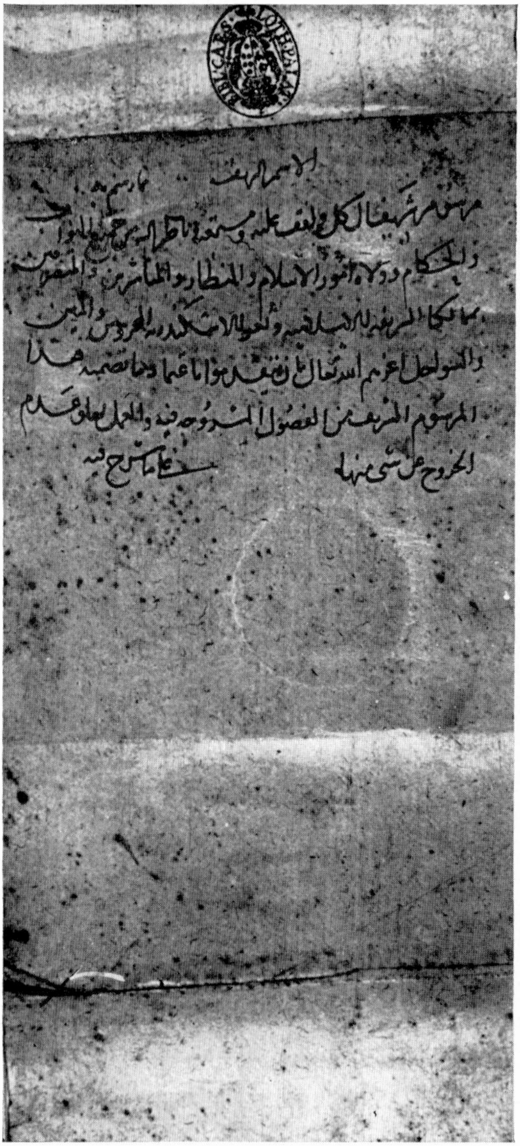

XXI

بسم الله الرحمن الرحيم
رسم بالامر الشريف العالي المولوي
السلطاني الملكي الاشرفي السيفي

XXII

QĀ'ITBĀY'S DOCUMENT

lines 1–7 *lines 8–12*

XXIII

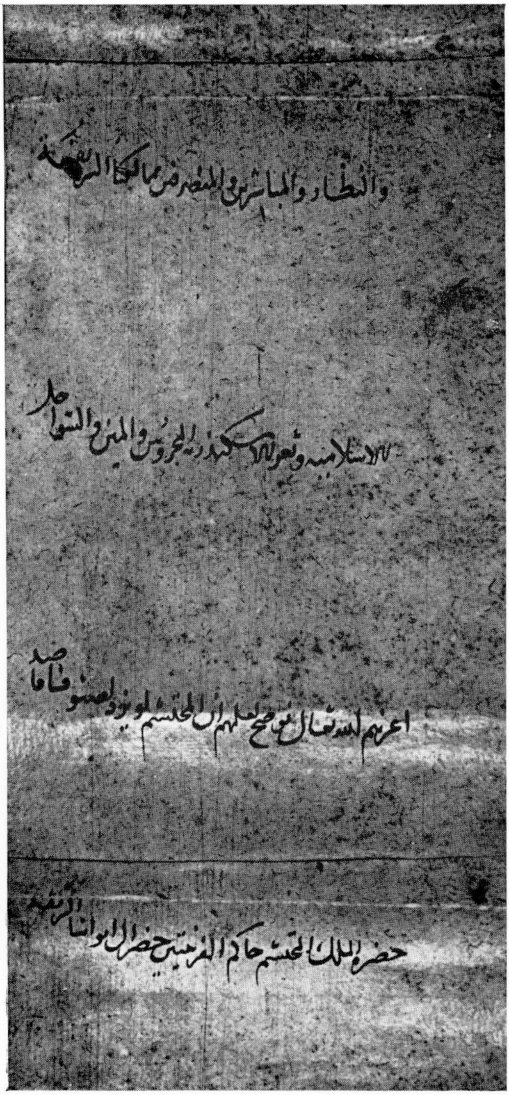

XXIV

QĀ'ITBĀY'S DOCUMENT

lines 12–15

lines 15–18

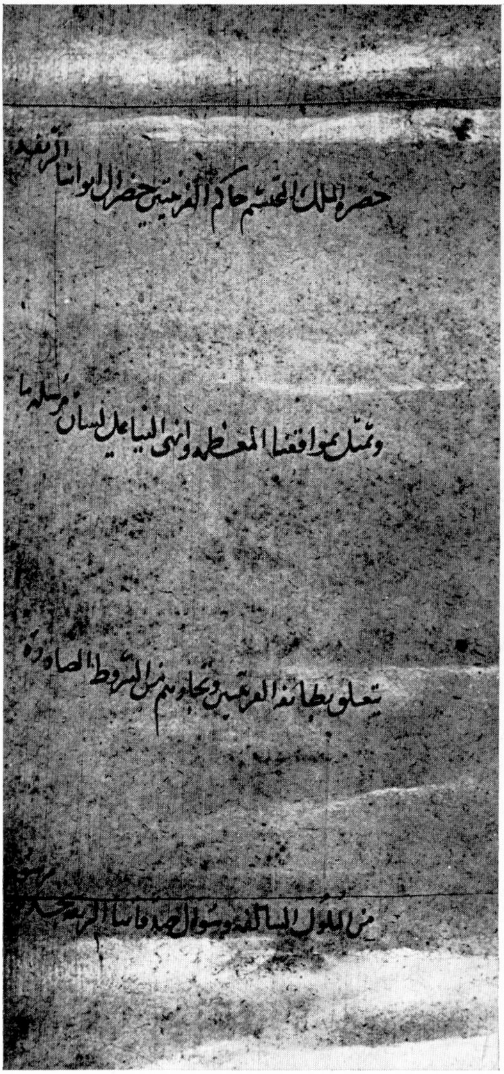

XXV

XXVI

QĀ'ITBĀY'S DOCUMENT

lines 18–21

lines 21–28

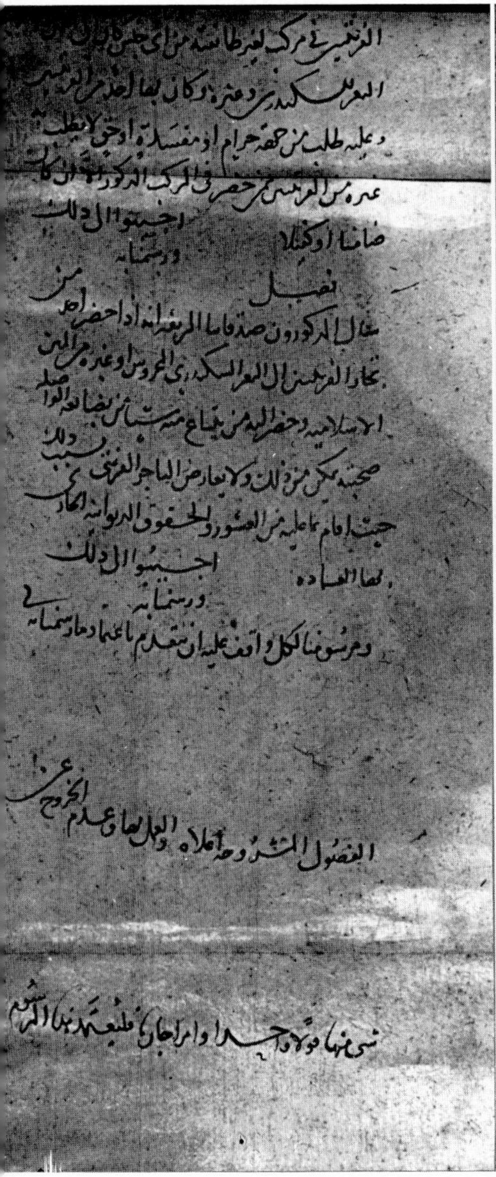

XXVII

lines 245–59

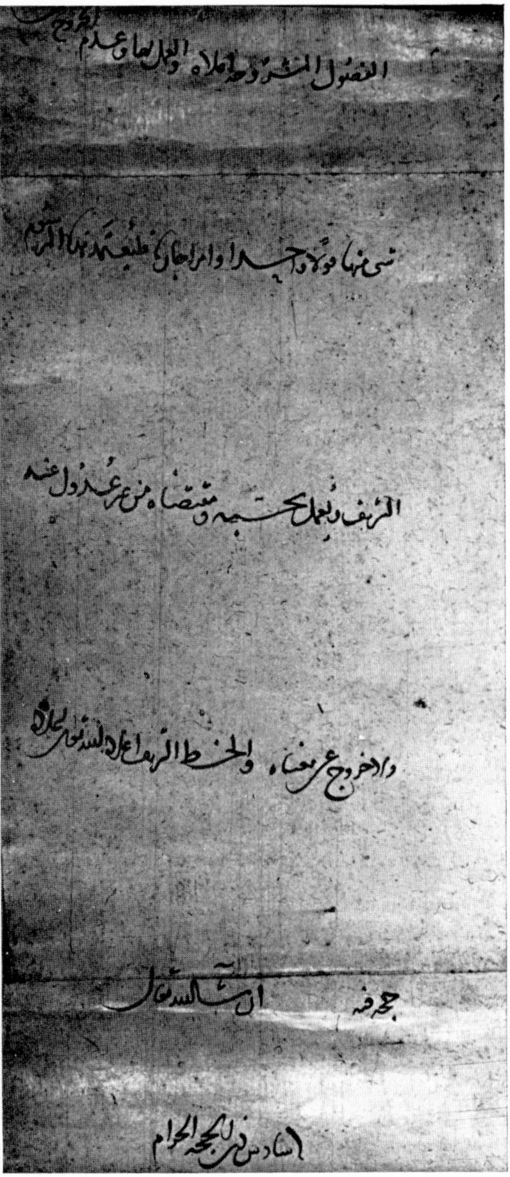

XXVIII

lines 258–63

QĀ'ITBĀY'S DOCUMENT

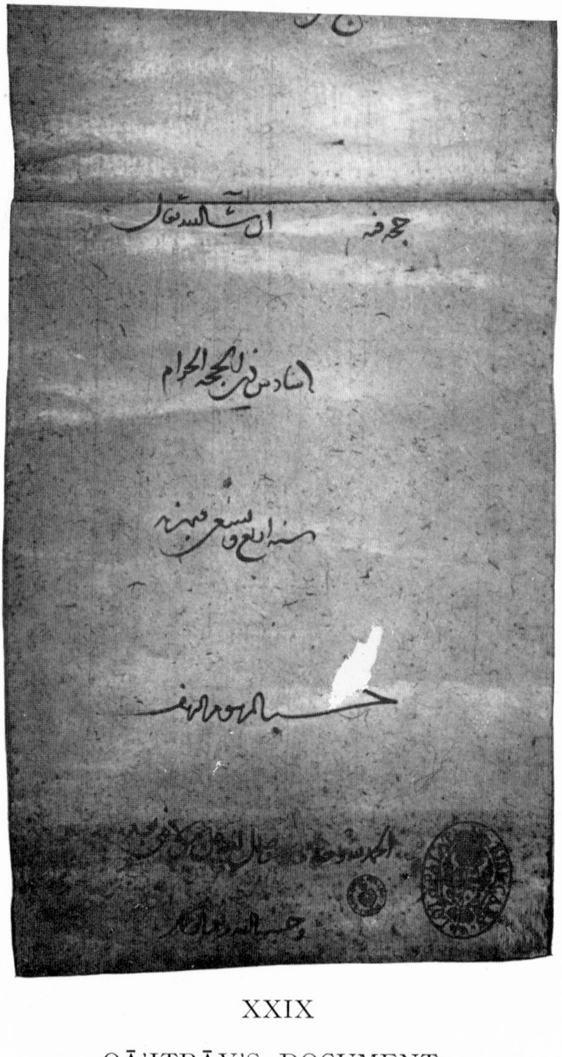

XXIX

QĀ'ITBĀY'S DOCUMENT

lines 262–68

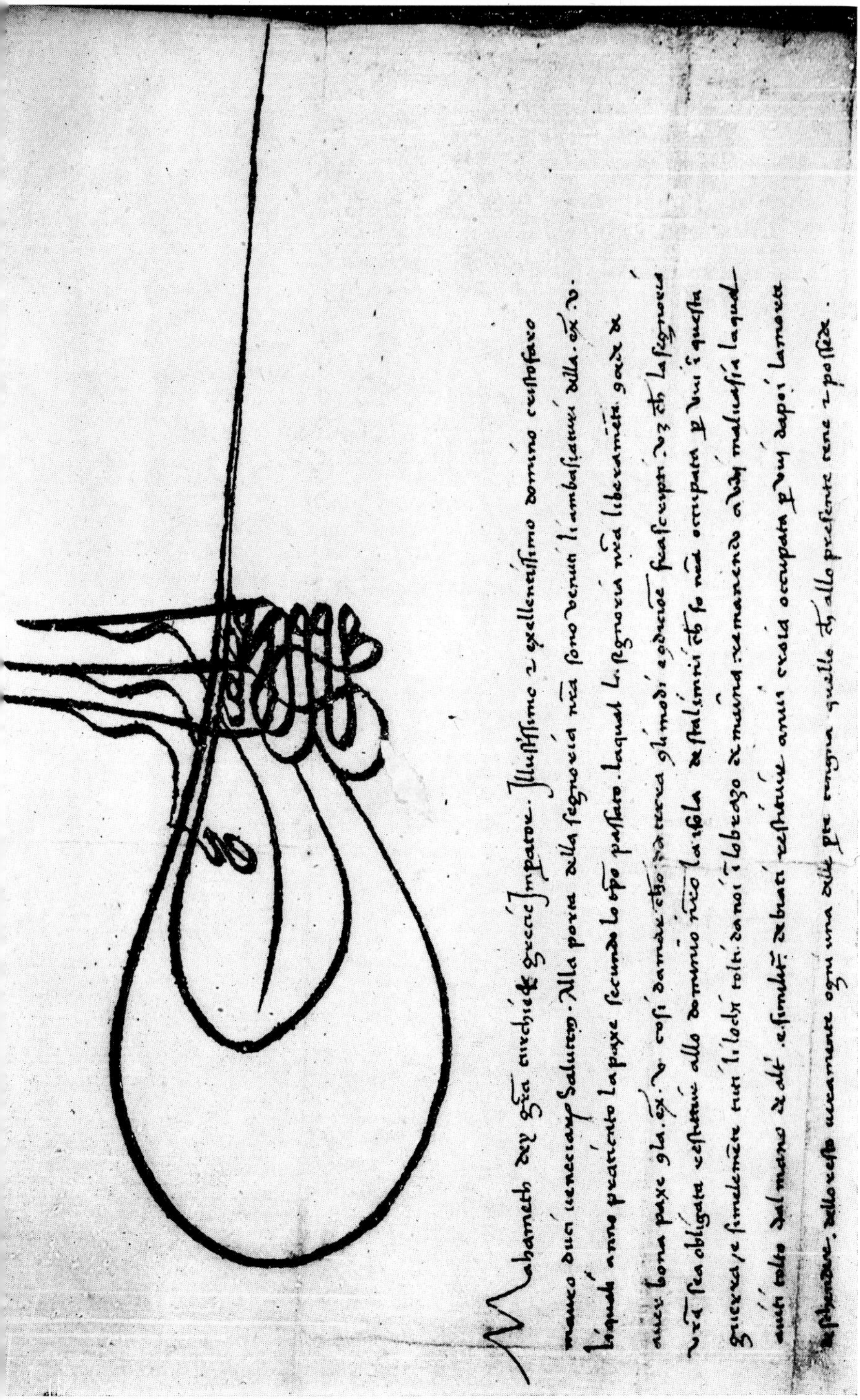

XXX

NO. 1: LETTER IN ITALIAN FROM MEHEMMED II TO THE DOGE CRISTOFERO MORO

lines 1–8

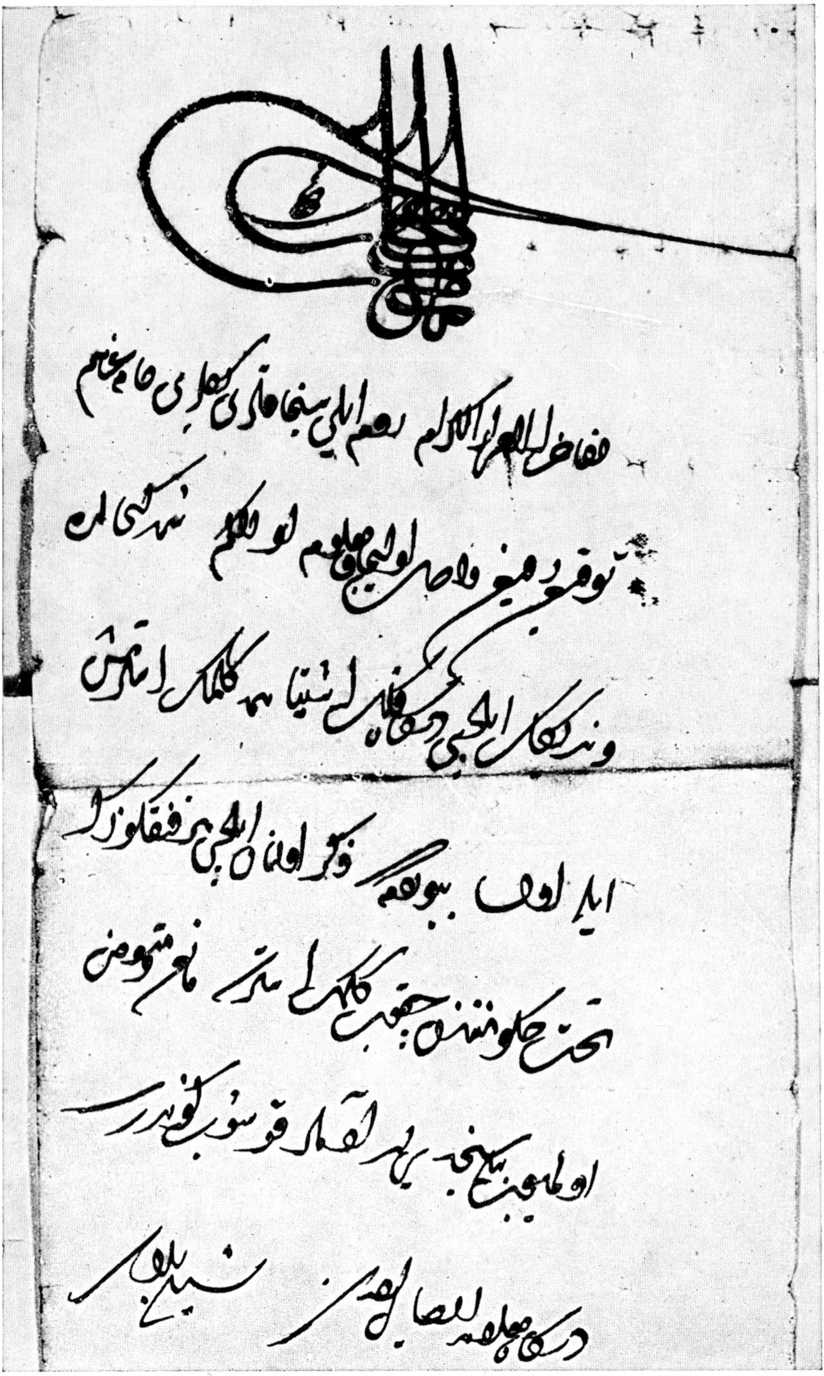

XXXI

NO. 2: FIRMĀN FOR THE SANJAK-BEYS OF RUMELI

lines 1–7

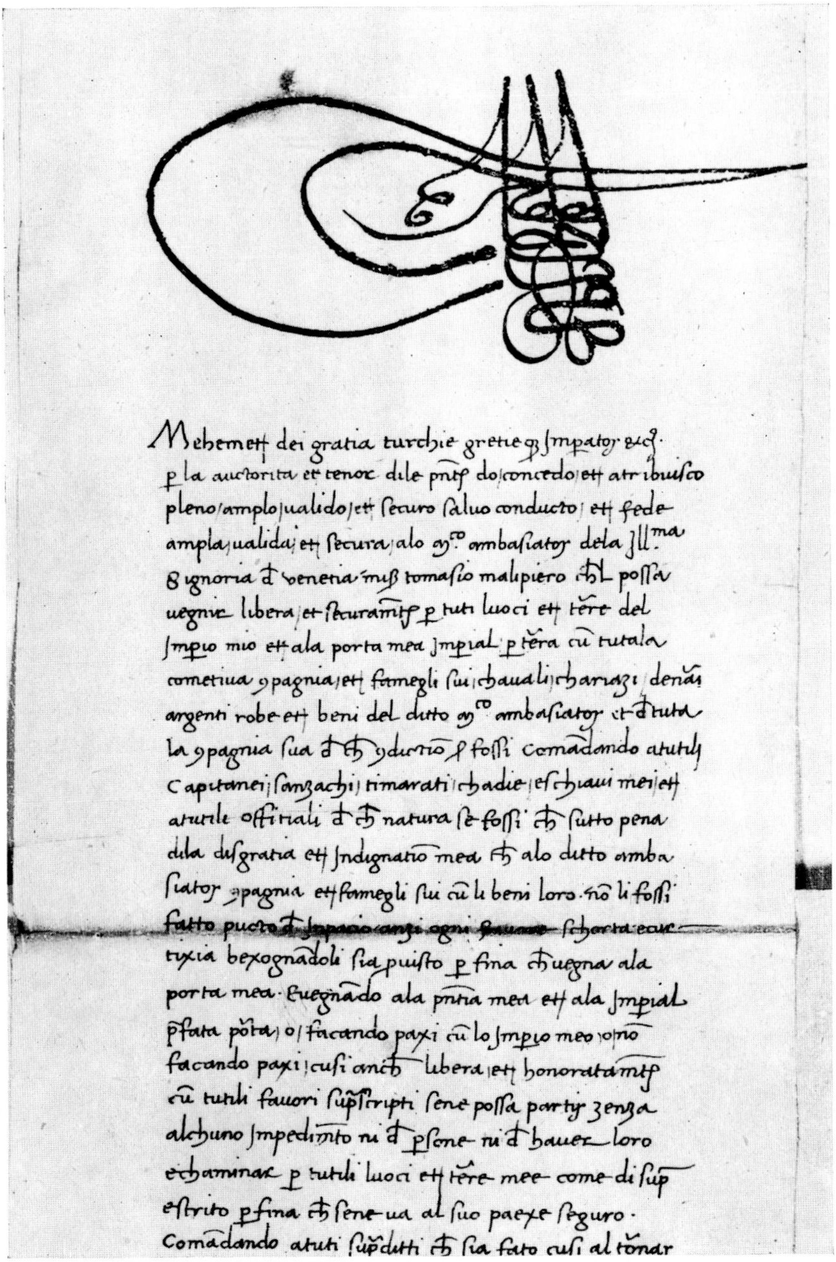
Mehemett dei gratia turchie gretie ez Imperator ecc·
p la auctorita et tenor dile pntj do/concedo/ett atribuisco
pleno/amplo/ualido/ett securo saluo conducto/ ett fede
ampla/ualida/ett secura/alo mco ambasiator dela Illma
Signoria d venetia miss tomasio malipiero chl possa
uegnir libera et securamte p tuti luoci ett tere del
Impio mio ett ala porta mea Impial p tera cu tuta la
cometiua cōpagnia/ett famegli sui/chauali/charazi/ denari
argenti robe ett beni del ditto mco ambasiator et d tuta
la cōpagnia sua d ch cōditio se fossi comadando atutili
Capitanei/sanzachi/timarati/chadie/eschiaui mei/ett
atutili offitiali d ch natura se fossi ch sutto pena
dila disgratia ett Indignatio mea ch alo ditto amba
siator cōpagnia ett famegli sui cu li beni loro no li fossi
fatto pucro d Impacio anzi ogni fauore schorta ecur
tixia bexognadoli sia puisto p fina chuegna ala
porta mea · Euegnado ala pntia mea ett ala Impial
pfata pota/o/facando paxi cu lo Impio meo/o no
facando paxi/cusi anch libera/ett honoratamte
cu tutili fauori supscripti sene possa partir zenza
alchuno Impedimto ni d psone ni d hauer loro
echaminar p tutili luoci ett tere mee come di sup
escrito p fina ch sene ua al suo paexe seguro·
Comadando atuti supditti ch sia fato cusi al tonar

XXXII

NO. 3: SAFE-CONDUCT IN ITALIAN ISSUED BY MEḤEMMED II

lines 1–24

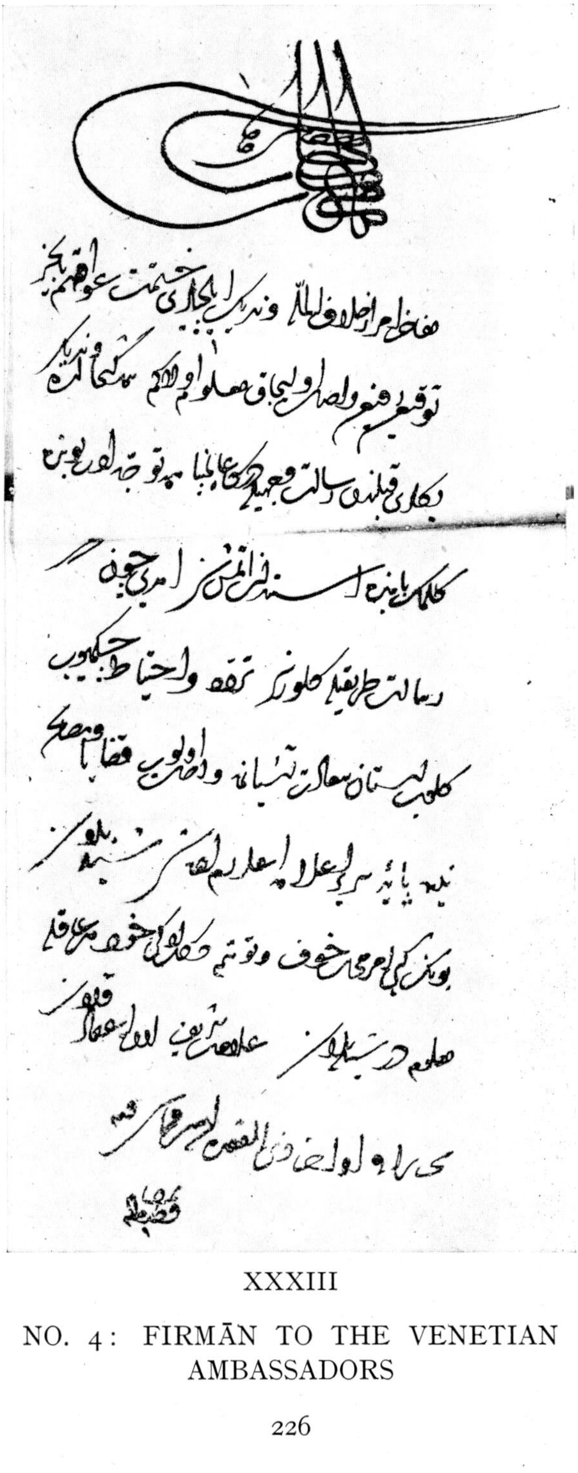

XXXIII

NO. 4: FIRMĀN TO THE VENETIAN AMBASSADORS

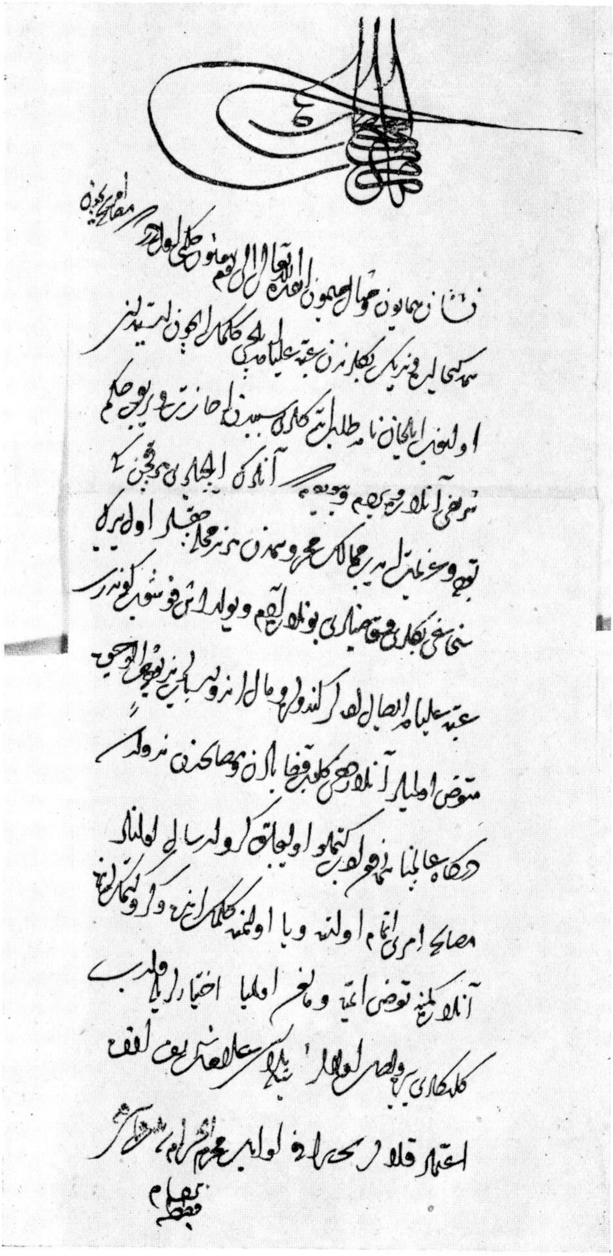

XXXIV

NO. 5: *NISHĀN* TO THE KADIS AND SANJAK-BEYS

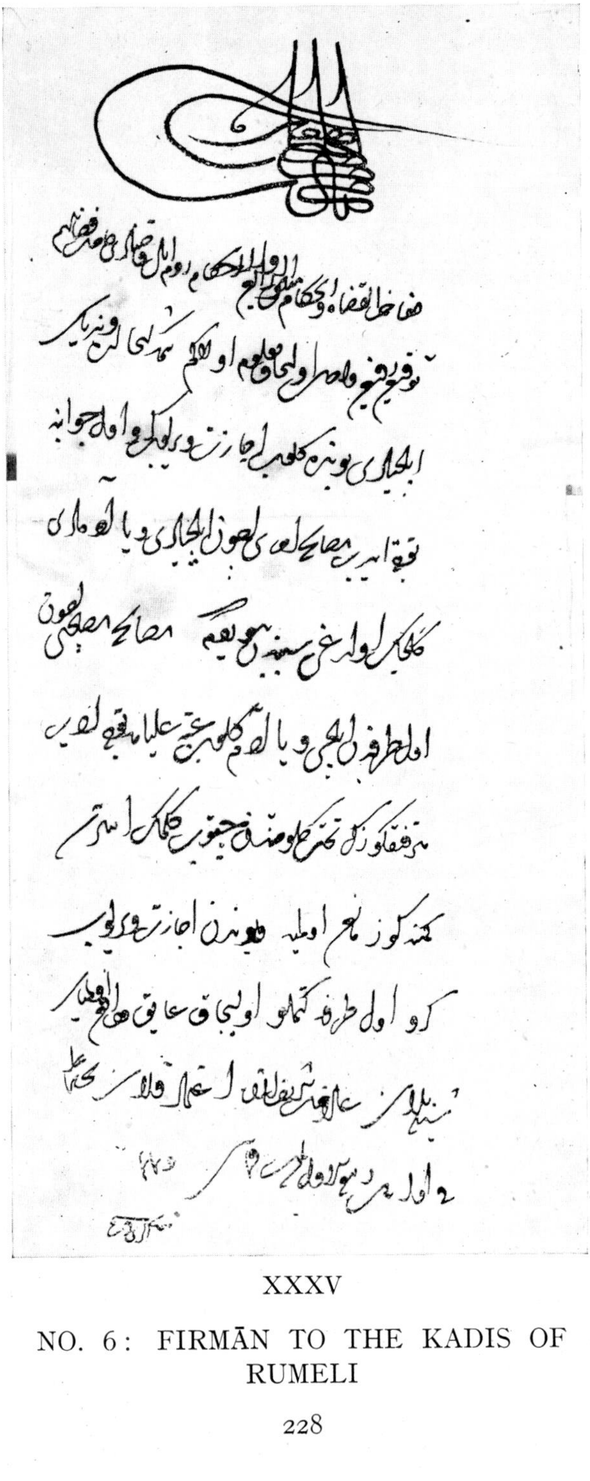

XXXV

NO. 6: FIRMĀN TO THE KADIS OF RUMELI

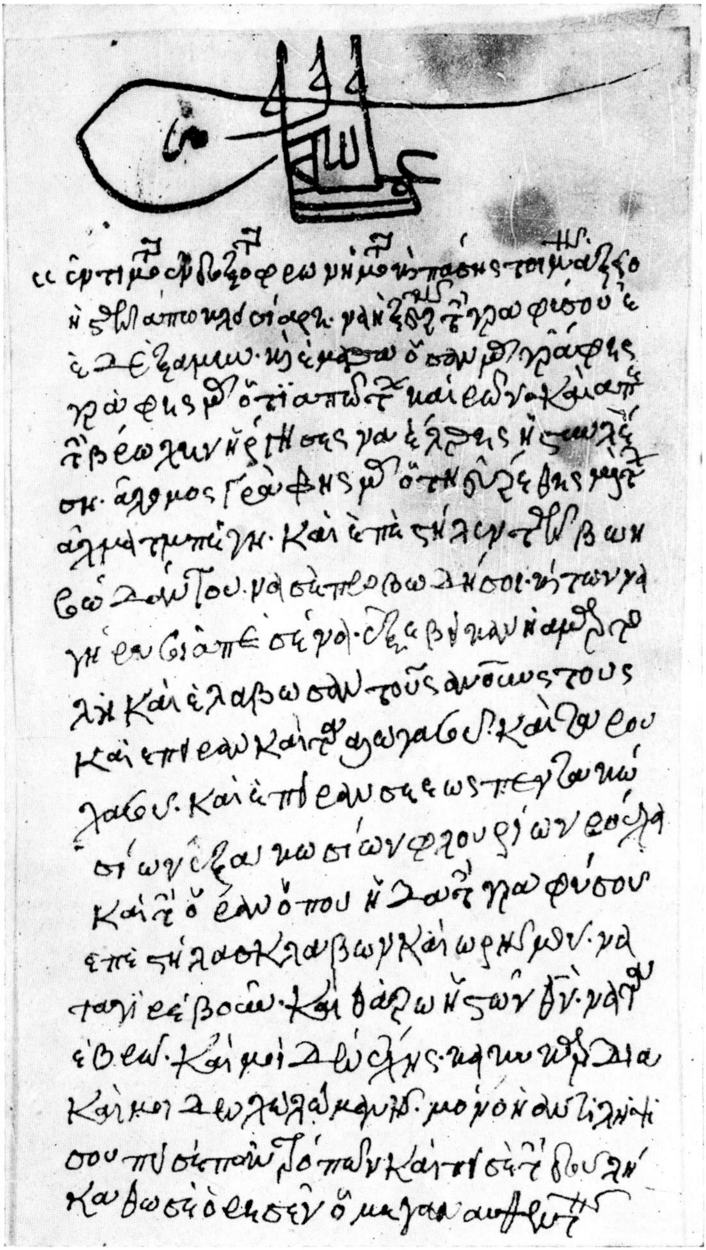

XXXVI

NO. 7: LETTER IN GREEK FROM AN OTTOMAN OFFICER TO A VENETIAN AMBASSADOR

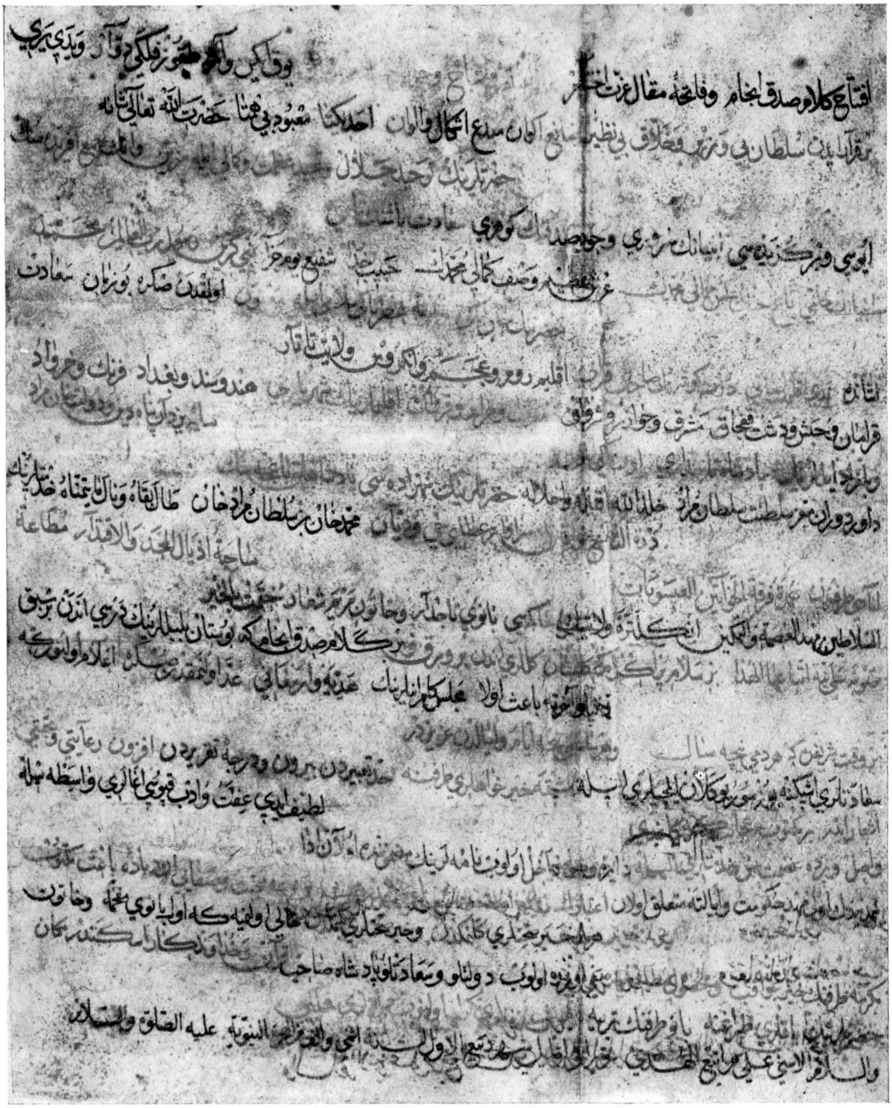

XXXVII

Document I

ṢĀFIYE TO ELIZABETH I

25 NOVEMBER–4 DECEMBER, 1593

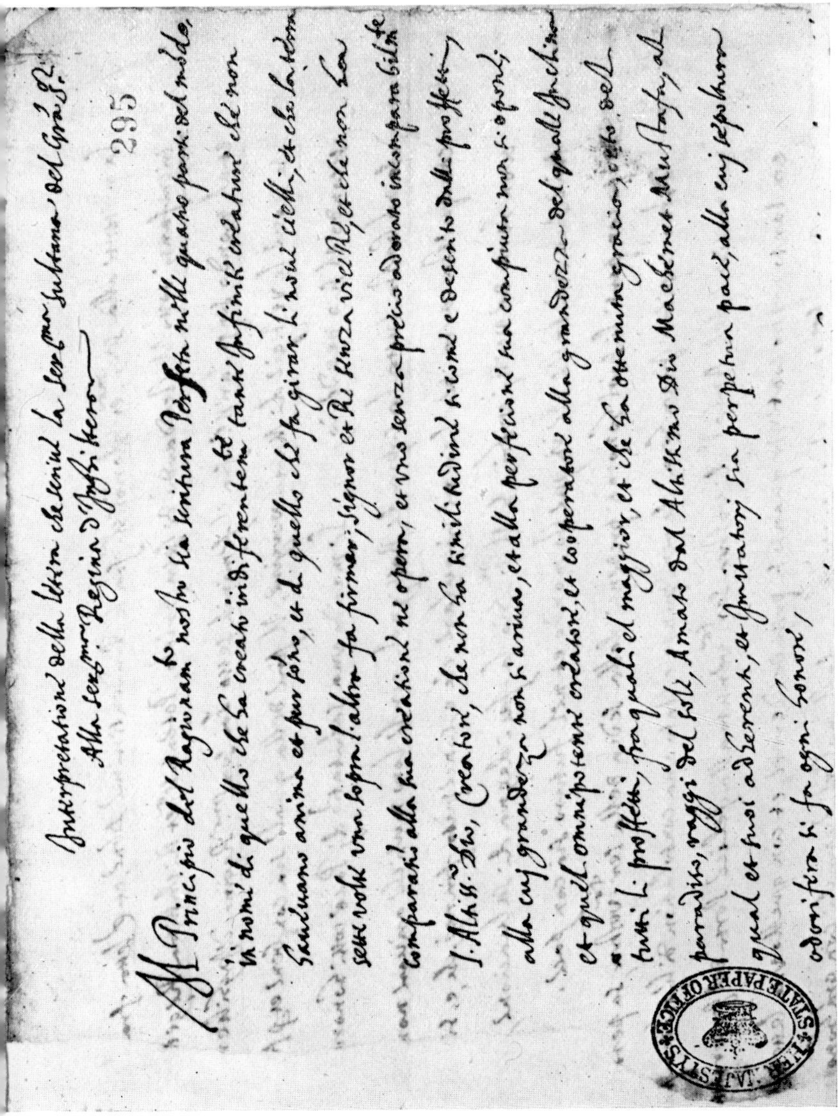

XXXVIII

Document I

FIRST PARAGRAPH OF THE ITALIAN TRANSLATION

افتخار الامراء الفخام الملة المسيحية اختيار
الكبراء الفخام في الملة المسيحية مصلح مصالح
ساحب الذه لايل والوقار صاحب الاذيال
والافتخار انكلتره قراليجه سي ختمت عواقبه
بالخير تحيات صافيات وتسليمات وفيات
وردنيته الفواحات كه محض موالات وفرط
مصافاتدن صادر اولور اتحاف واهدي اولندق
دن صكره انها واعلام اولنان بودركه مكتوبكز
كلوب دكدي هر نه كم دمش سز معلومز اولدي
انشا الله ديديكوكز اوزره عمل اولونور بو خصوصه
دن اوتوري كوكلي كوزي خوش طوته سز اوغلو
مز پادشاه حضرتلرینه دایما تربیه ایدوب
اهد نامه لري موجبنجه عمل ایده سز دیو
سویلمکدن خالي دكلوز انشا الله بو خصوصدن
الم چکمیه سز سزده دایما دوستلق اوزه رینه
باقي الدعا

XXXIX

Document II

ṢĀFIYE TO ELIZABETH I

NOVEMBER 1599

افتخار الامرا العظام الملة المسيحية اختيار
الكبراء الفخام في الملة المسيحية مصلح مصالح
ساحب الذلايل والوقار صاحب الاذيال
والافتخار انكلتره قرالچه سي ختمت عوا
قبه بالخير تحيات صافيات وتسليمات
وافيات ورديته الغوالحات كه محض موالات
وفرط مصافاتدن صادر اولور اتحاف واهدي
اولندقدن صكره انها وعلام اولنان بودركه مكتو
بكز كلوب دكدي هر نه كه ديمش سز معلومز
اولدي انشاالله مرادكيز اوزره عمل اولنو
نور اوغلومز پادشاه حضرتلرينه دايما سو
بينه ايليوب الهدي نامه موجبنجه عمل
ايده سز ديو سويلمكدن خالي دكلوز بو
خصوصدن كوكلكزي خوش طوته سز
وسزده دوستلغكز اوزره ثابت اولاسز
باقي الدعا

XL

Document III

ṢĀFIYE TO ELIZABETH I

NOVEMBER 1599

والده سلطان

جناب عزتمآب رفعت نصاب وندیك وزیری و بكلری كه منبع سعادتلو پادشاه
عالمپناه حضرتلرینك آستانهٔ سعادتلریله اولان دوستلقلری بكزه
لایق اولان سلام تحیت صکره انها اعلام اولنان اولدر که
حالا جلوس همایون تهنیتی ایچون ارسال ایلدوککز بیوك ایلچیکز بو جانبه نامه کوزیده
و بعض دوستلق یادکارلرین کوندروب اظهار ایتمکین اشبو مکتوبمز
جنابکزه تحریر اولنوب ارسال اولنمشدر ان شاء الله تعالی مادامکه سعادتلو
پادشاه عالمپناه حضرتلریله کمال دوستلق ثابت قدم اولاسز سعادتلو
و عزتلو پادشاه حضرتلرینك جانب همایونلرنده دخی هر وجهله ایلچیکزه
و بایلوسلریکزه انعام و احسانلر ایله رعایت ایتمك مقرردر حالا دخی
بیوك ایلچیکزه هر وجهله معزز و محترم اولوب اول جانبه متوجه و روانه اولمشدر
سعادتلو پادشاه حضرتلرینك حضور شریفلرنده دوستنکزه مصالحکزده دوستلقه لایق
اولدوغنی اوزره حسن معاونتمز بزه اولنمق مقرردر شویله معلوم اوله باقی والسلام

XLI

Appendix, Document A

THE WĀLIDE SULṬĀN TO THE DOGE AND SIGNORIA

UNDATED

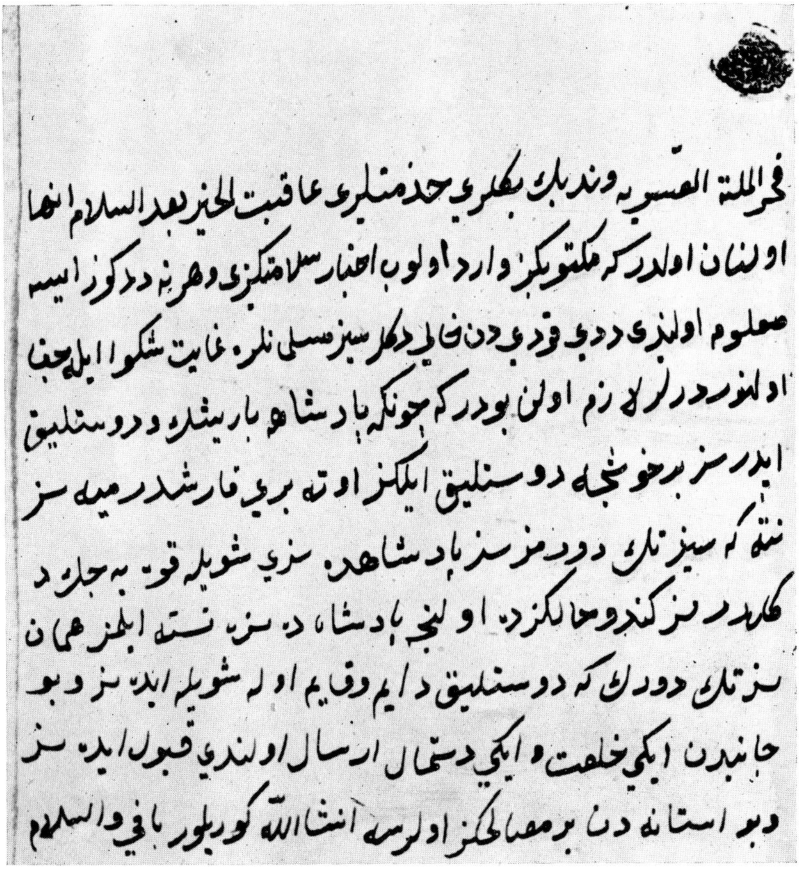

فخر الملة المسيحية وندك بكلري حذمتلري عاقبت الخير بعد السلام انها
اولنان اولدر كه مكتوبكز وارد اولوب اخبار سلامتكز وهر بر دكوز ايسه
معلوم اولندي دديكز قدردن ناشي دكلو سيز مسلي نلر غايت شكوا ايله حفا
اولنور دركلي رزم اولن بودركه چونكه پادشاهم باريشك ودوستليق
ايدرسز بر خوشجه دوستليق ايلكز اوته بري فارشدرميه سز
نته كه سيزنك دودمز سز پادشاهم سزي شويله قوت بجلك د
كلدرسز كندو حالكزده اولنجه پادشاهده سزه نسته ايلمز همان
سزتك دودك كه دوستليق دايم وقايم اوله شويله ايده سز دبو
جانبدن ايكي خلعت وايكي دستمال ارسال اولندي قبول ايده سز
دبو استانه دن بر مصالحكز اولورسه انشا الله كوريلور باقي والسلام

XLII

Appendix, Document B

ṢĀFIYE TO THE DOGE OF VENICE

1589

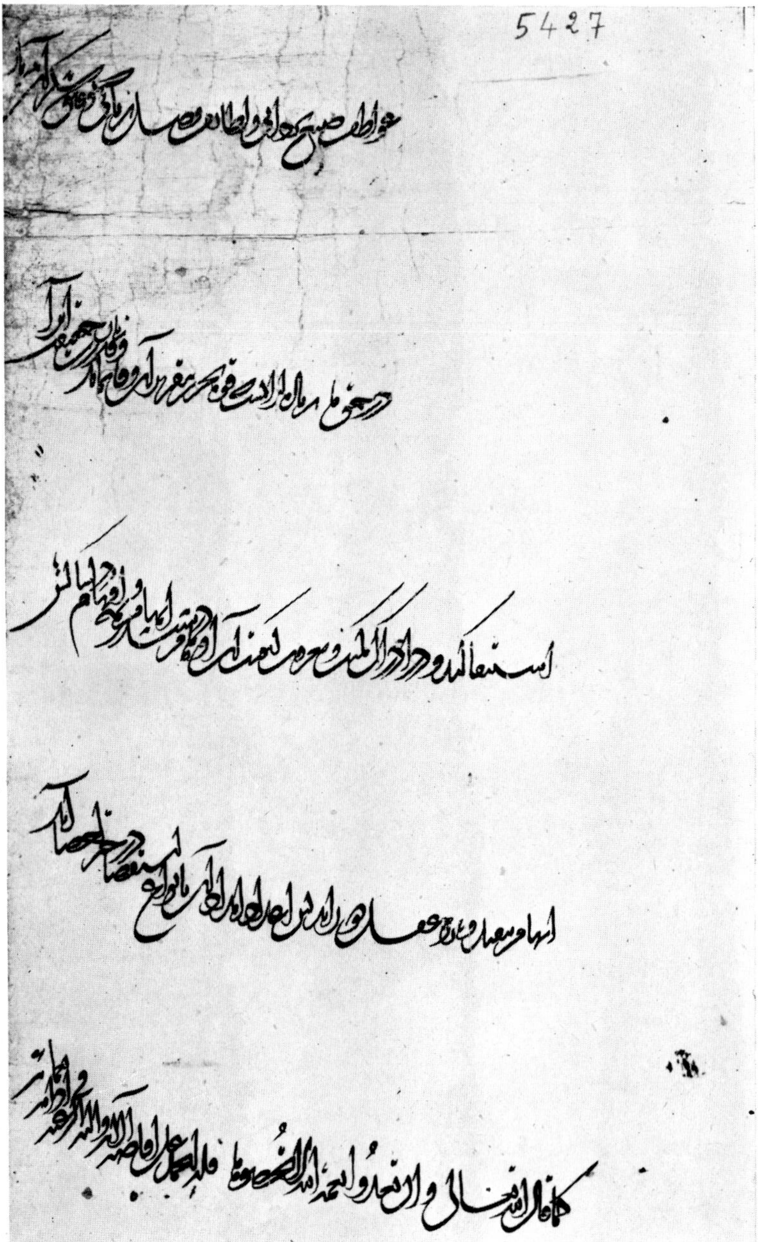
5427

XLIII

SOYURGHAL OF JAHĀN-SHĀH

lines 1–5

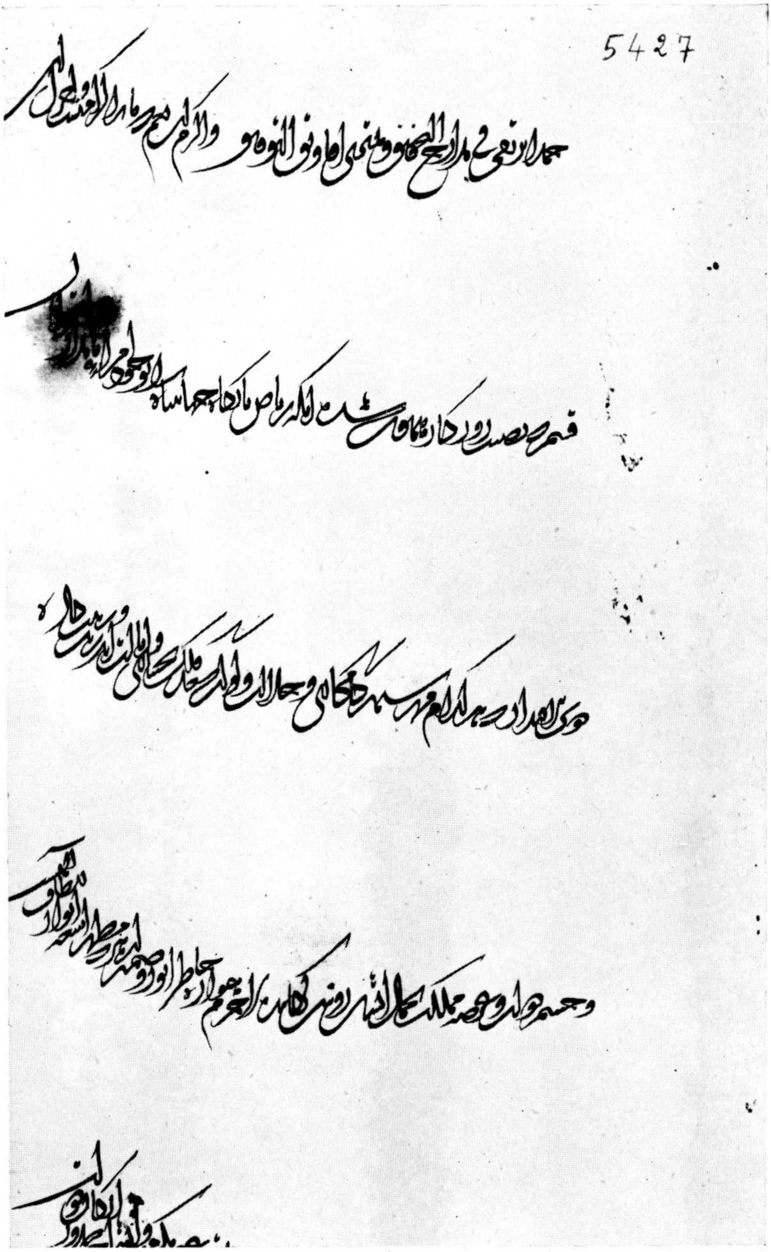

XLIV

SOYURGHAL OF JAHĀN-SHĀH

lines 6–9

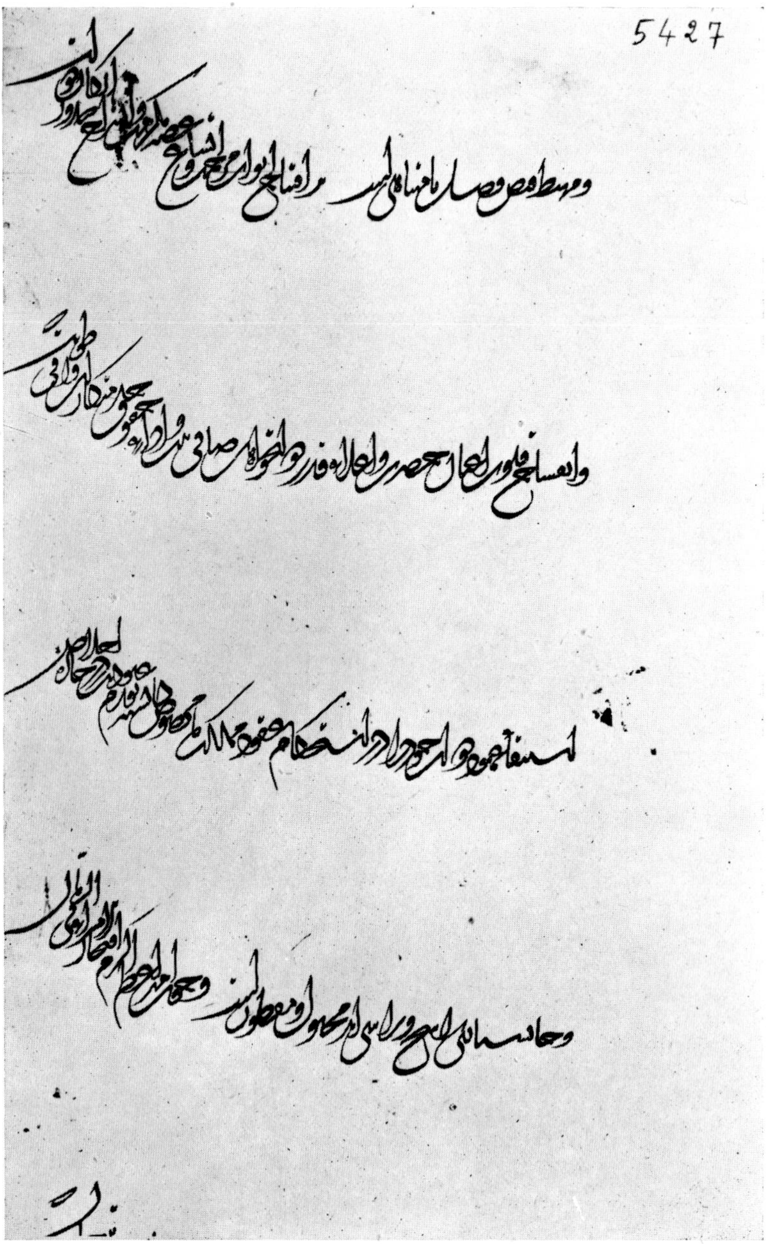

XLV

SOYURGHAL OF JAHĀN-SHĀH

lines 10–13

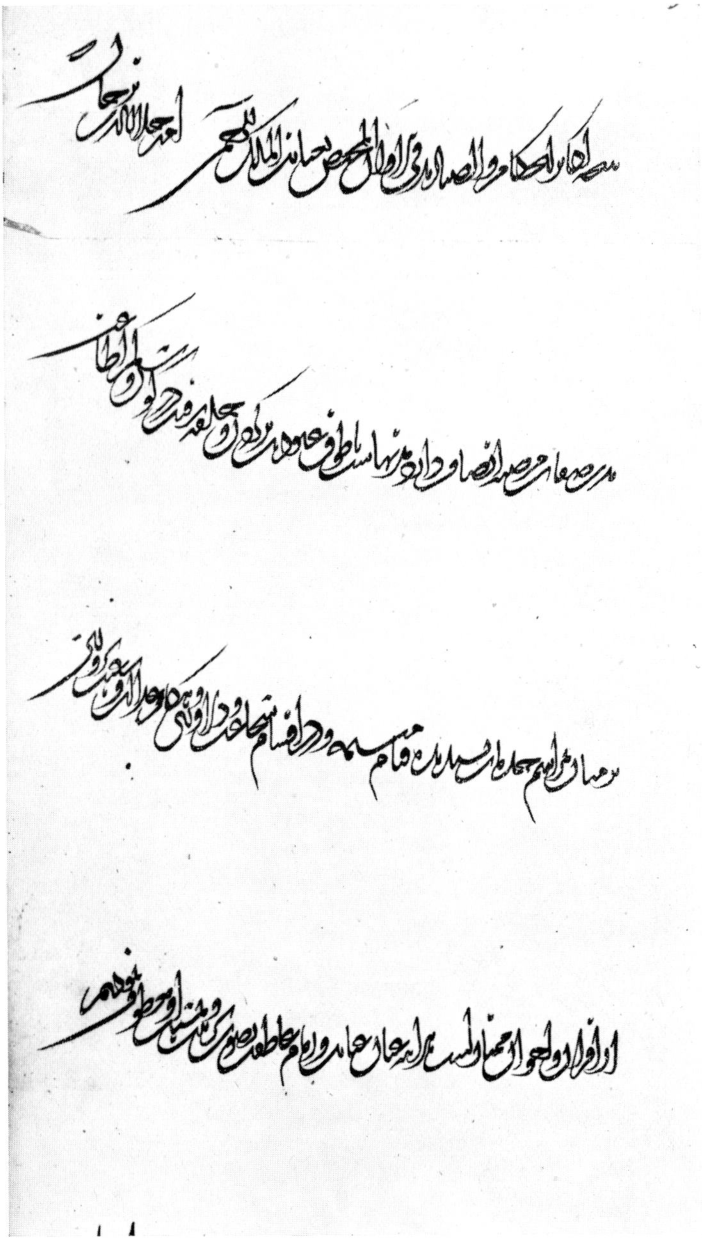

XLVI

SOYURGHAL OF JAHĀN-SHĀH

lines 14–17

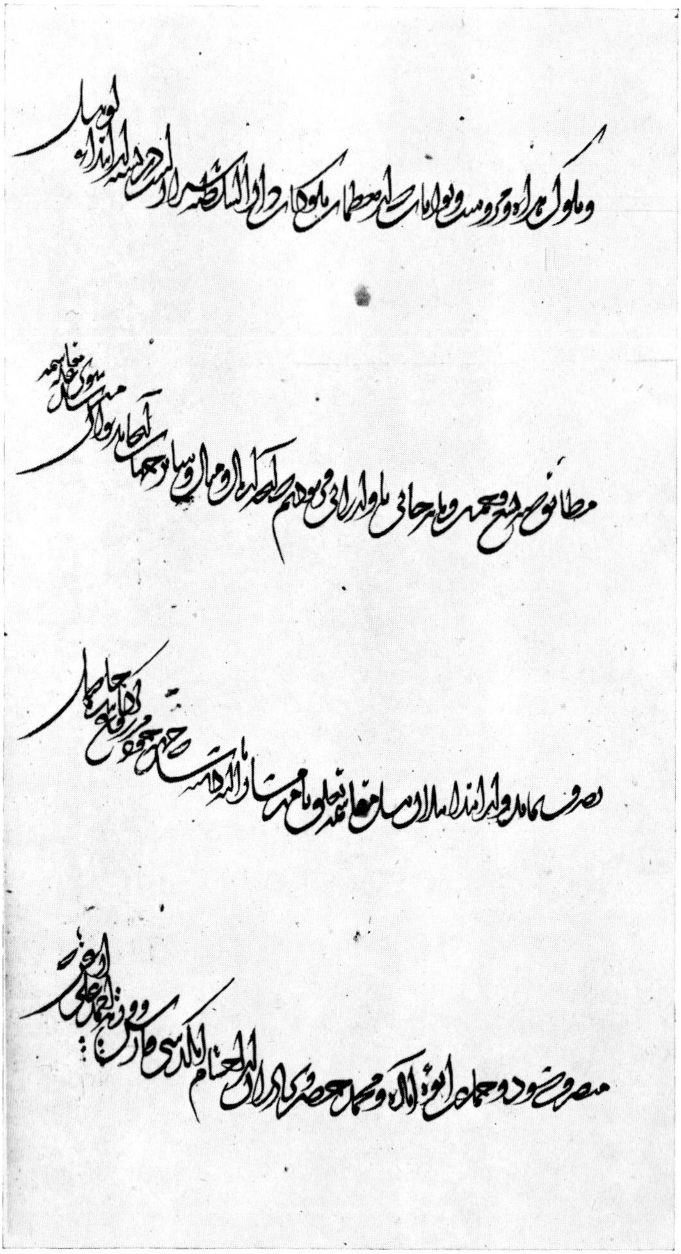

XLVII

SOYURGHAL OF JAHĀN-SHĀH

lines 18–21

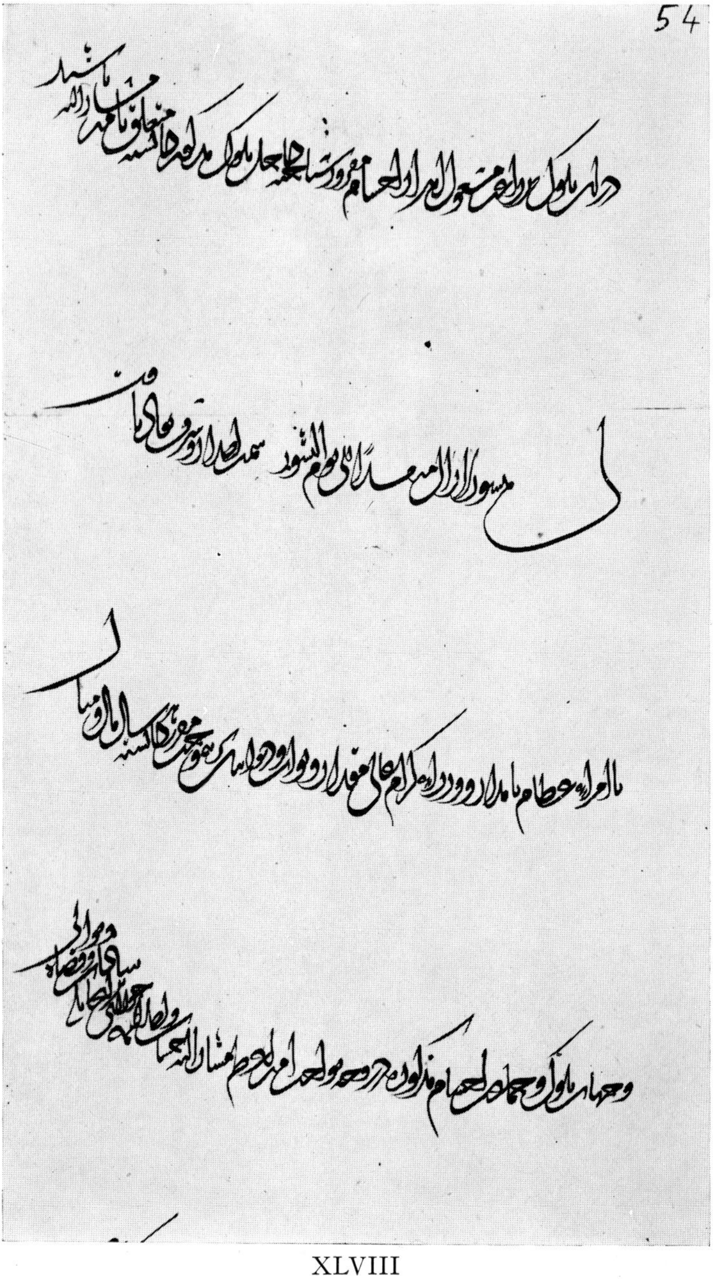

XLVIII

SOYURGHAL OF JAHĀN-SHĀH

lines 22–25

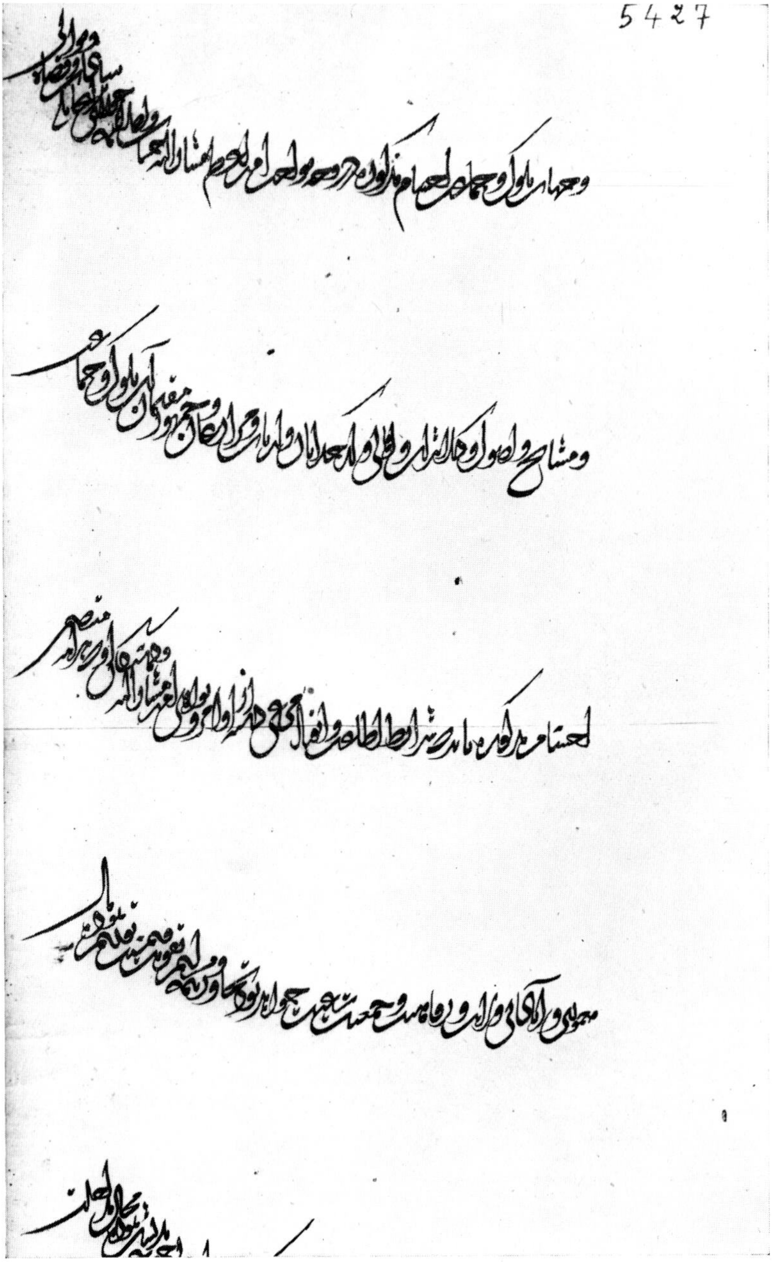

XLIX

SOYURGHAL OF JAHĀN-SHĀH

lines 25–28

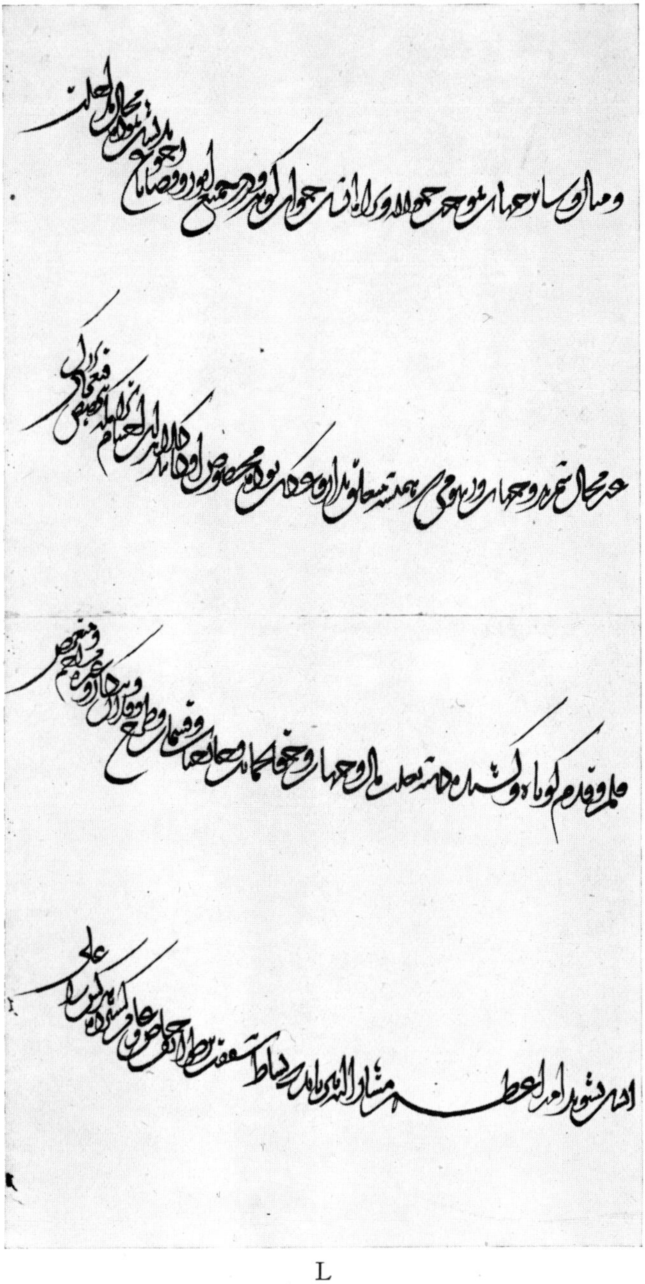

L

SOYURGHAL OF JAHĀN-SHĀH

lines 29–32

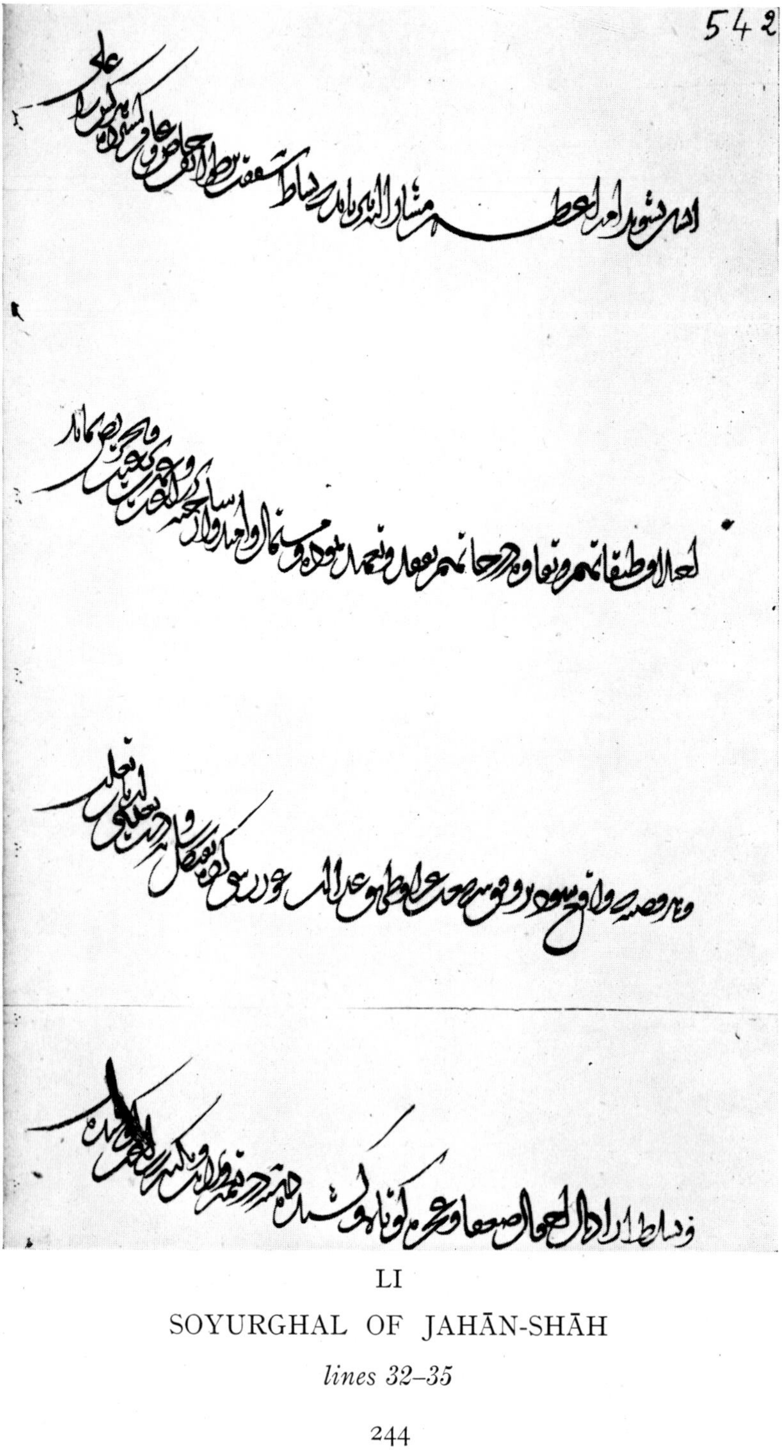

LI

SOYURGHAL OF JAHĀN-SHĀH

lines 32–35

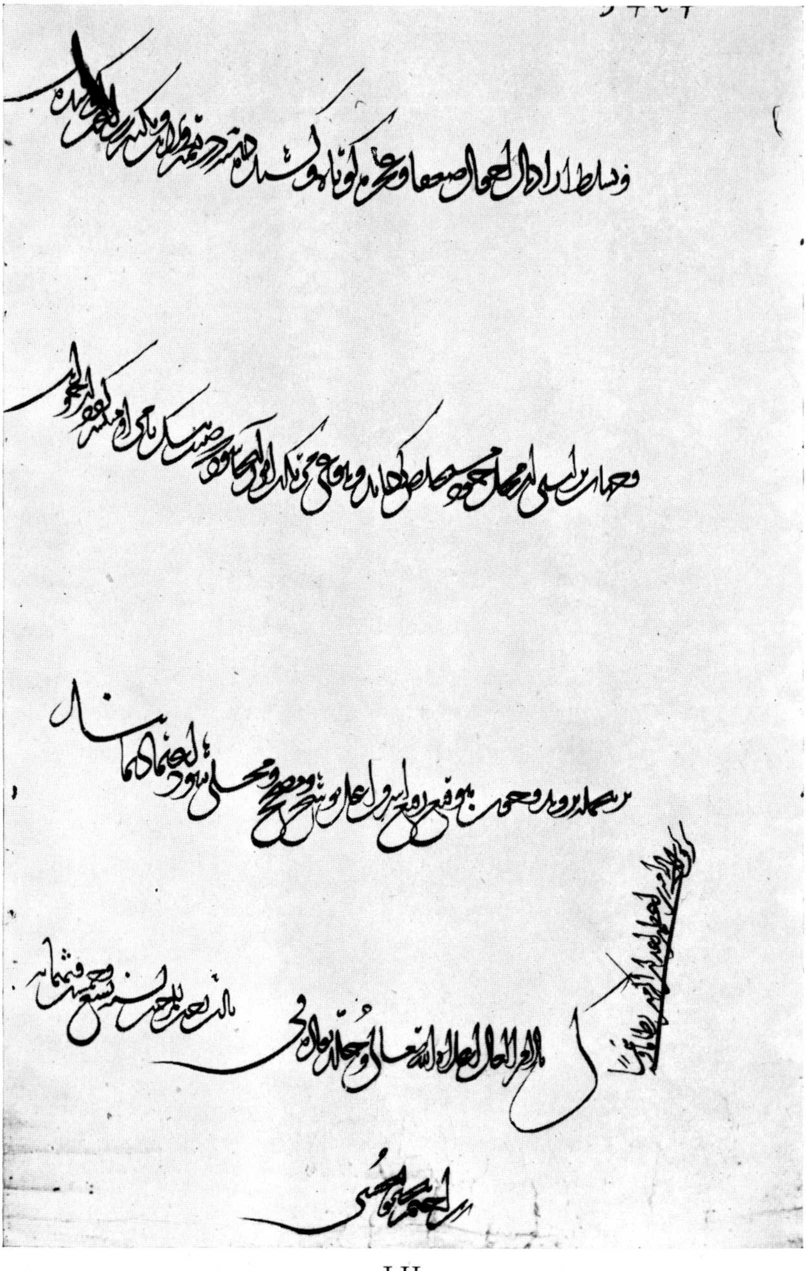

LII

SOYURGHAL OF JAHĀN-SHĀH

lines 35–39

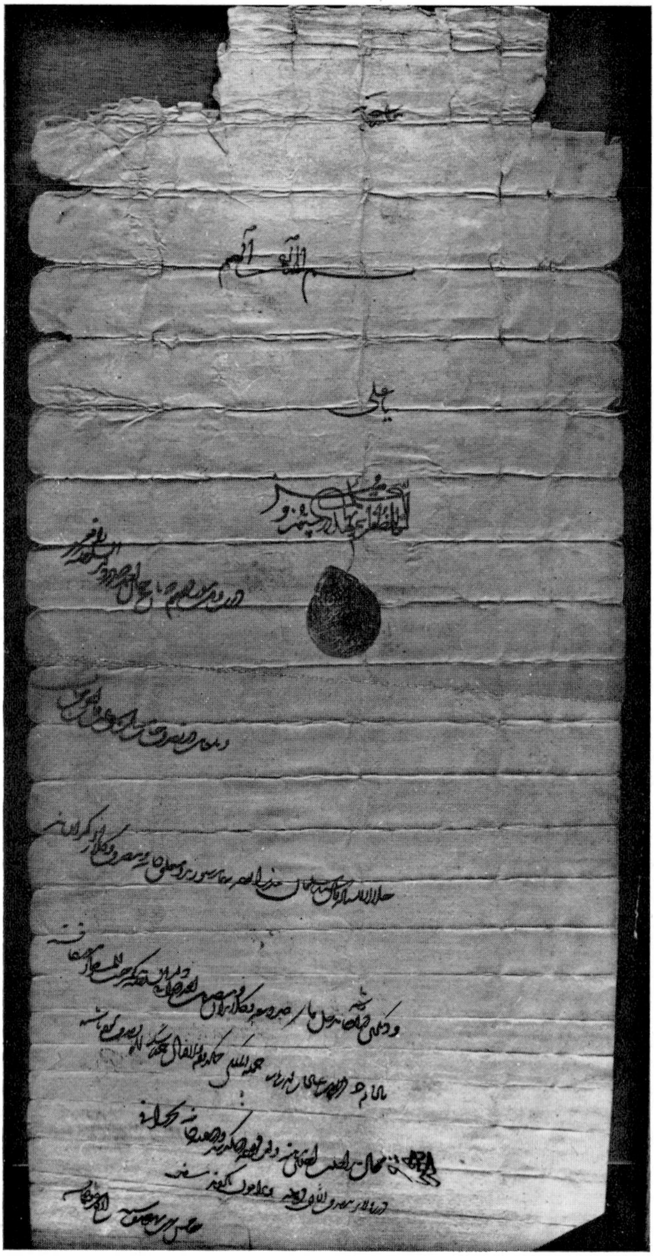

LIII

Document I

FIRMĀN OF SHĀH ISMĀʿĪL I

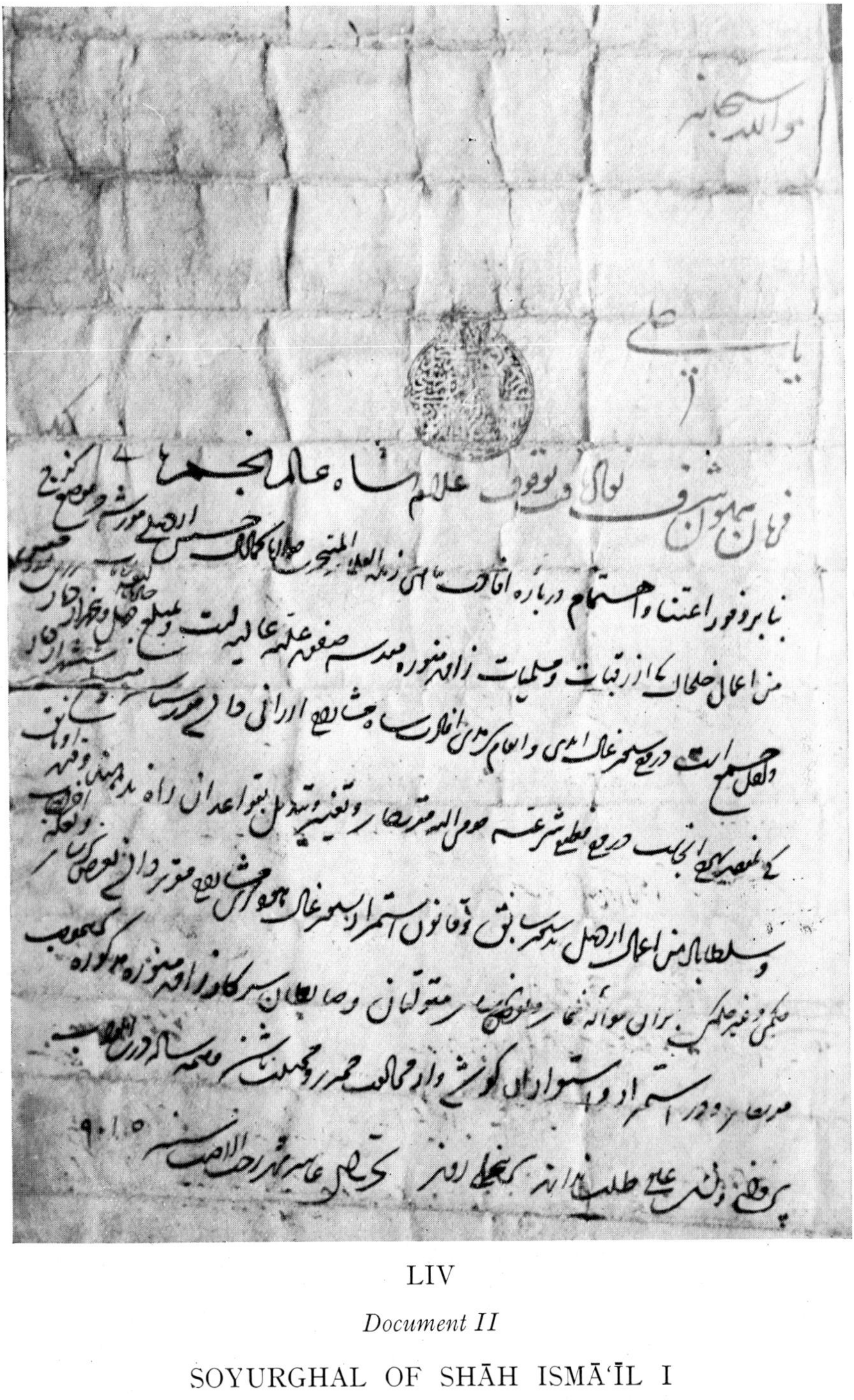

LIV

Document II

SOYURGHAL OF SHĀH ISMĀʿĪL I

LV

Document III

FIRMĀN OF SHĀH ṬAHMĀSP I

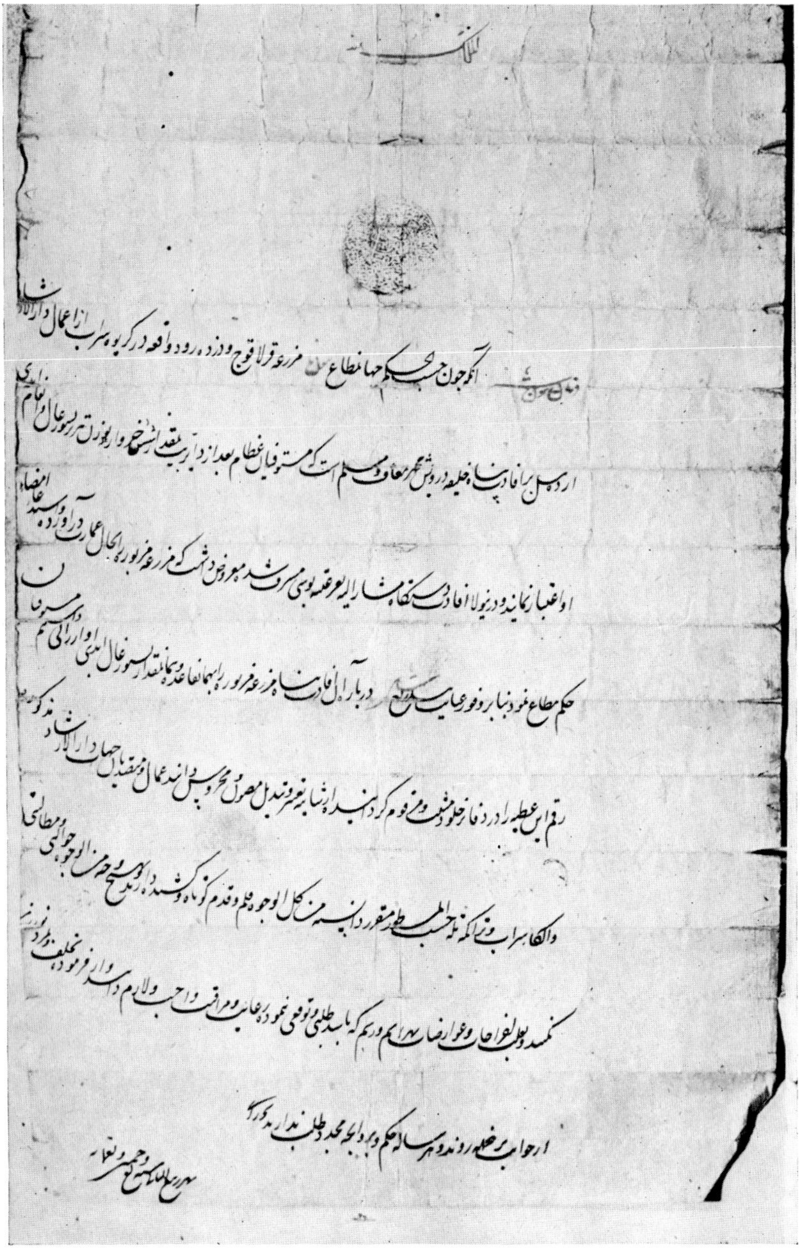

LVI

Document IV

SOYURGHAL OF SHĀH ṬAHMĀSP I

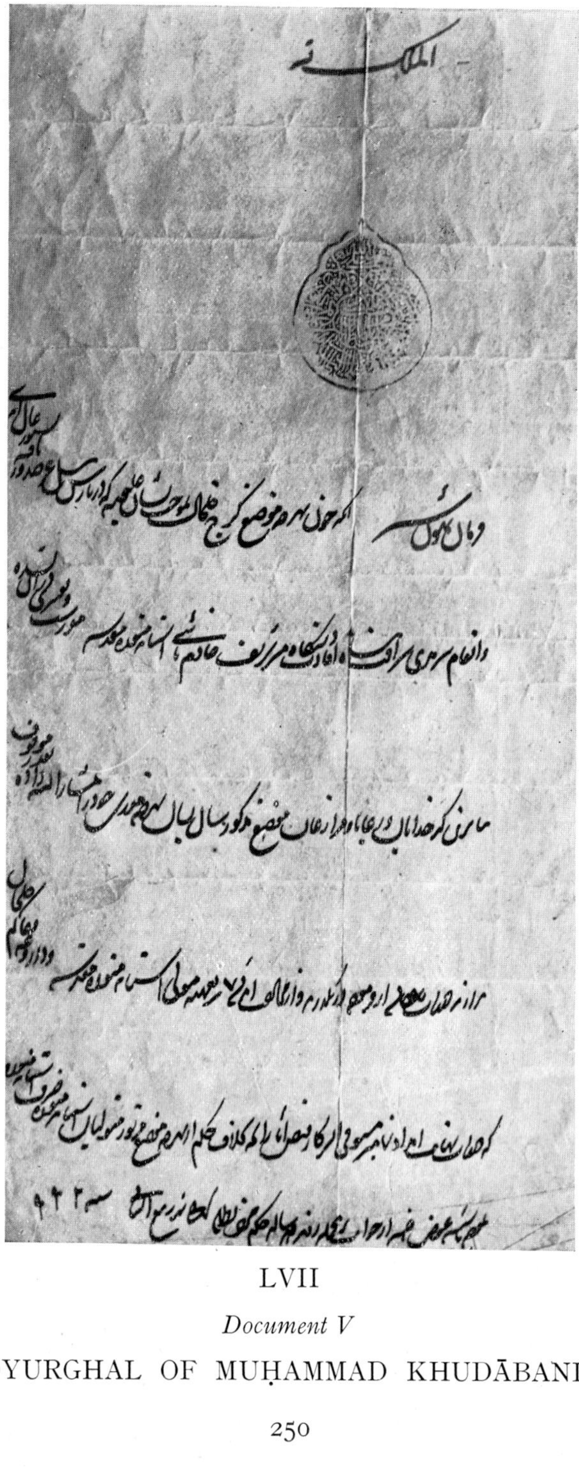

LVII

Document V

SOYURGHAL OF MUḤAMMAD KHUDĀBANDE

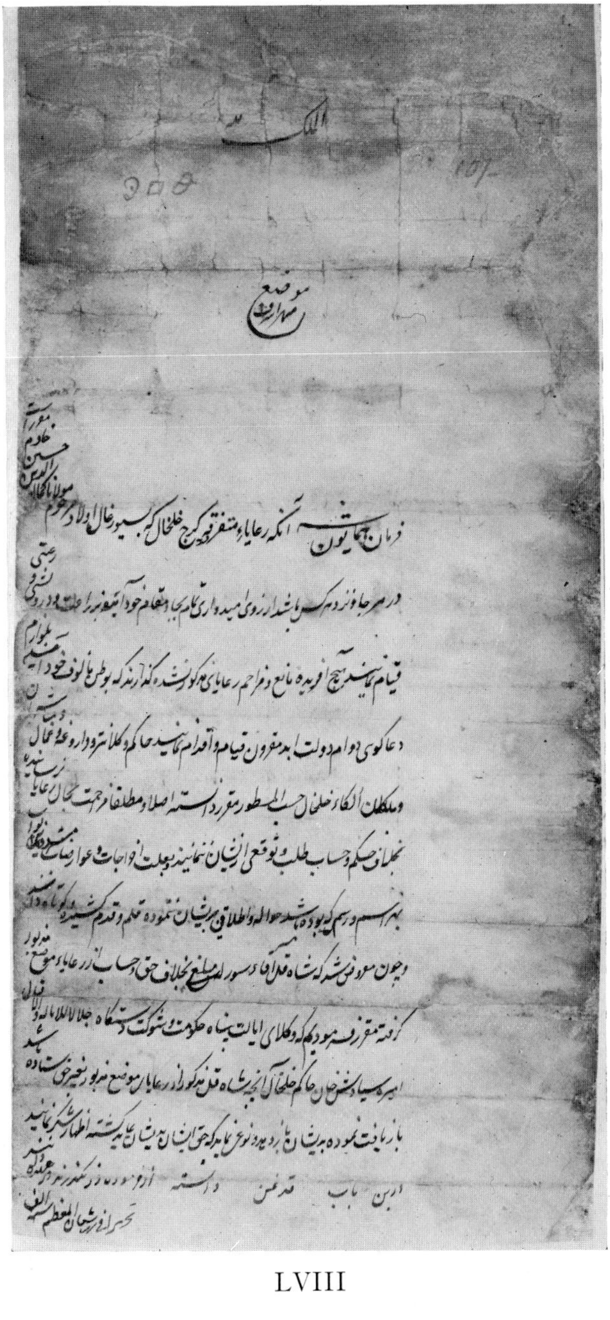

LVIII

Document VI

COPY OF SOYURGHAL OF SHĀH 'ABBĀS I

Document VII

LIX

SOYURGHAL OF SHĀH ʿABBĀS I

lines 1–4

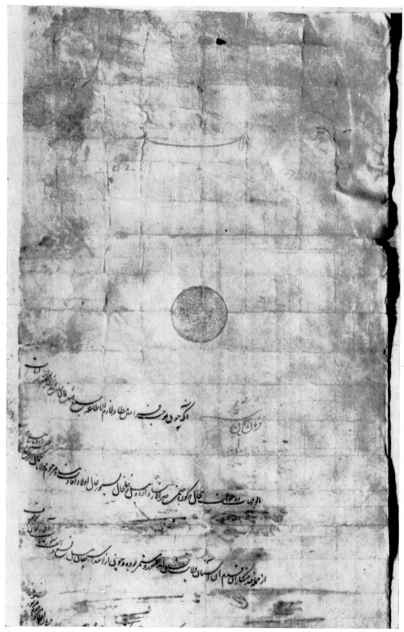

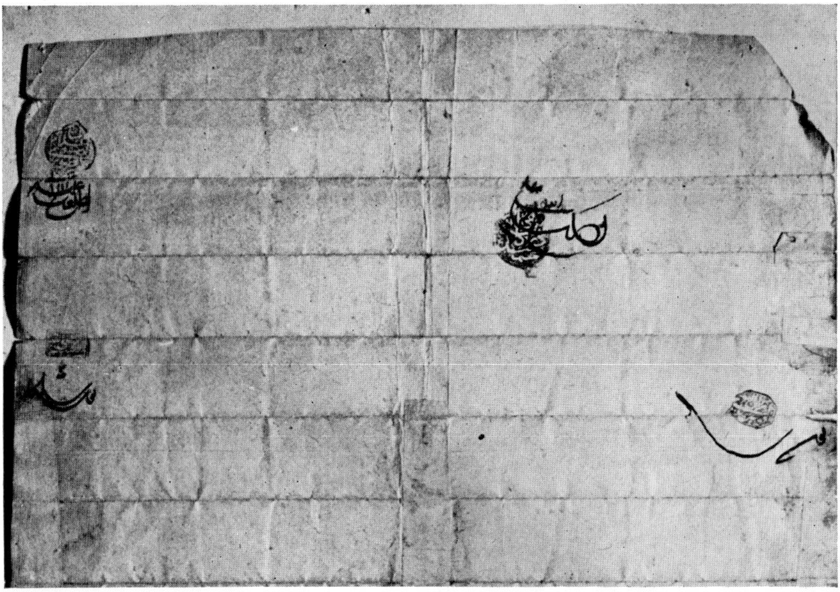

LX

Back of Document IV

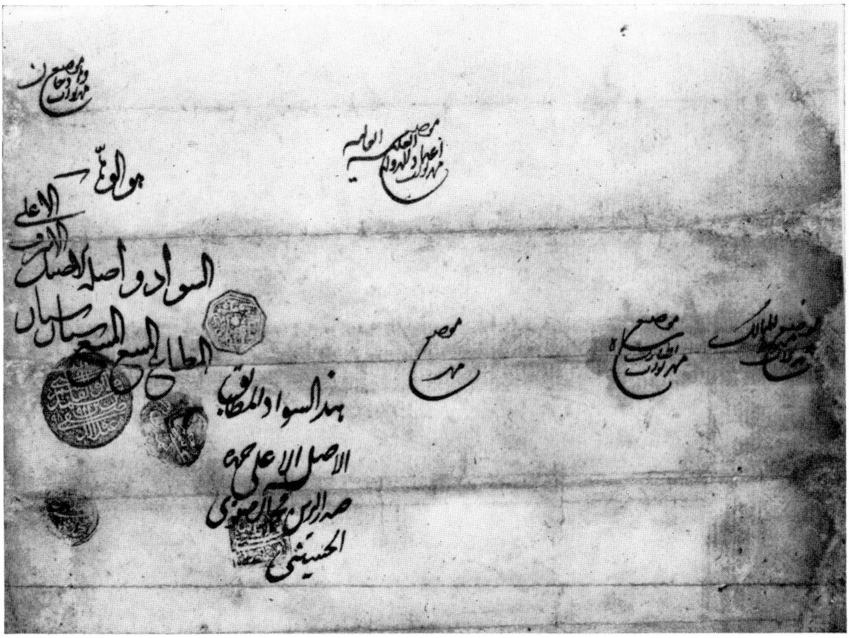

LXI

Back of Document VI

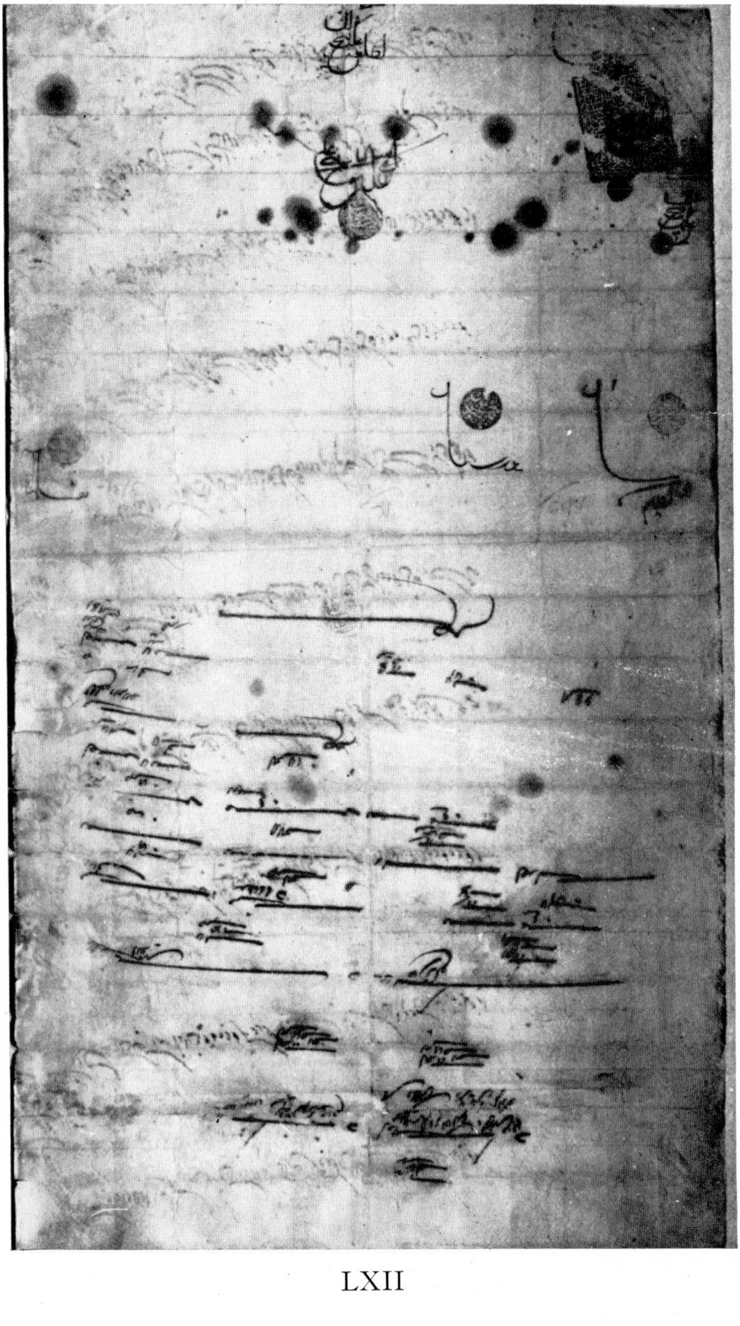

LXII

Back of Document VII